The Ultimate
NSAA Collection

UniAdmissions

Published by *RAR Medical Services Limited, trading as* **Infinity Books**
www.uniadmissions.co.uk
info@uniadmissions.co.uk
0208 068 0438

The Ultimate NSAA Collection

Three Books in One

Dr. Wiraaj Agnihotri
Linh Pham
Dr. Weichao Rachel
Dr. Rohan Agarwal

UniAdmissions

About the Authors

Linh studied graduated from **Natural Sciences at St John's College, Cambridge** in 2015. A keen Physicist, Linh scored in the top 16 students nationwide in the British Physics Olympiad 2012. As a tutor, Linh specialises in helping students with science admissions tests, especially the NSAA.

After winning innovation awards from Facebook, Uber and Google, Linh is now CEO of the venture-funded LOGIVAN Technologies Pte. - a Singapore based company tackling freight transportation problems in Vietnam. Away from work, Linh relaxes by practicing yoga, swimming and badminton.

Weichao Rachel is a research fellow at University of Leeds, Faculty of Medicine and Health. She obtained her Ph.D. in Biophysics at Cambridge University after completing a B.Sc. in Physics at Stanford University where she was awarded the President's Award for Academic Excellence.

Rachel is passionate about tutoring students and has taught Physics and Engineering summer classes at Cambridge University. She has worked with UniAdmissions since 2017 – helping budding natural sciences applicants with their Oxbridge applications. She supervises physics undergraduates at Cambridge and in her free time enjoys travelling and reading detective fictions.

Wiraaj graduated in 2012 with an honours degree in Natural Sciences from Pembroke College, Cambridge where he was selected to receive annual scholarship funding from the Cambridge Trusts. In his final year at Cambridge he specialised in the rigorous Mechanisms of Disease option during which he wrote an independent research dissertation on autoimmune thyroid disease.

Wiraaj subsequently completed graduate medical studies (MBBS) at the University of Sydney in 2016. He is currently a resident medical officer in Sydney where he plans to pursue further clinical specialisation as an internal medicine physician.

With a longstanding passion for teaching, Wiraaj has been heavily involved in tutoring students at various stages of their education. Over the years Wiraaj has successfully coached a great number of students into Oxbridge. Outside of medicine and education, Wiraaj enjoys playing jazz guitar and football.

Rohan is the **Director of Operations** at *UniAdmissions* and is responsible for its technical and commercial arms. He graduated from Gonville and Caius College, Cambridge in natural sciences and is a fully qualified doctor. Over the last five years, he has tutored hundreds of successful Oxbridge and Medical applicants. He has also authored ten books on admissions tests and interviews.

Rohan has taught physiology to undergraduates and interviewed medical school applicants for Cambridge. He has published research on bone physiology and writes education articles for the Independent and Huffington Post. In his spare time, Rohan enjoys playing the piano and table tennis.

How to use this Book

Congratulations on taking the first step to your NSAA preparation! First used in 2016, the NSAA is a difficult exam and you'll need to prepare thoroughly in order to make sure you get that dream university place.

The *Ultimate NSAA Collection* is the most comprehensive NSAA book available – it's the culmination of three top-selling NSAA books:

➢ *The Ultimate NSAA Guide*
➢ *NSAA Past Paper Solutions*
➢ *NSAA Practice Papers*

Whilst it might be tempting to dive straight in with mock papers, this is not a sound strategy. Instead, you should approach the NSAA in the three steps shown below. Firstly, start off by understanding the structure, syllabus and theory behind the test. Once you're satisfied with this, move onto doing the 300 practice questions found in *The Ultimate NSAA Guide* (not timed!). Then, once you feel ready for a challenge, do each past paper under timed conditions. Start with the 2016 paper and work chronologically; check your solutions against the model answers given in *NSAA Past Paper Worked Solutions*. Finally, once you've exhausted these, go through the two NSAA Mock Papers found in *NSAA Practice Papers* – these are a final boost to your preparation.

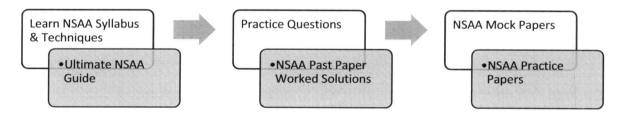

As you've probably realised by now, there are well over 500 questions to tackle meaning that this isn't a test that you can prepare for in a single week. From our experience, the best students will prepare anywhere between four to eight weeks (although there are some notable exceptions!).

Remember that the route to a high score is your approach and practice. Don't fall into the trap that "you can't prepare for the NSAA"– this could not be further from the truth. With knowledge of the test, some useful time-saving techniques and plenty of practice you can dramatically boost your score.

Work hard, never give up and do yourself justice. Good luck!

The Ultimate NSAA Guide

The Basics

What is the NSAA?

The Natural Sciences Admissions Assessment (NSAA) is a 2-hour written exam for prospective Cambridge natural sciences and veterinary sciences applicants.

What does the NSAA consist of?

Section	Timing	Topics Tested	Questions	Mandatory	Calculator
ONE	80 Minutes	1A: Maths 1B: Physics 1C: Chemistry 1D: Biology 1E: Advanced Maths + Physics	18 MCQs per section	Must complete Section 1A AND two from 1B, 1C, 1D or 1E	Not Allowed
TWO	40 Minutes	Advanced Biology, Chemistry & Physics	6 Long Questions	Must Complete 2 Questions from a choice of 6	Allowed

Why is the NSAA used?

Cambridge applicants tend to be a bright bunch and therefore usually have excellent grades. For example, in 2016 over 65% of students who applied to Cambridge for Natural Sciences had UMS greater than 90% in all of their A level subjects. This means that competition is fierce – meaning that the universities must use the NSAA to help differentiate between applicants.

When do I sit NSAA?

The NSAA takes place in the first week of November every year, normally on a Wednesday morning.

Can I resit the NSAA?

No, you can only sit the NSAA once per admissions cycle. If you apply again, you must sit the test again.

Where do I sit the NSAA?

You can usually sit the NSAA at your school or college (ask your exams officer for more information). Alternatively, if your school isn't a registered test centre or you're not attending a school or college, you can sit the NSAA at an authorised test centre.

How is the NSAA scored?

In section 1, each question carries one mark and there is no negative marking. In section 2, marks for each question are indicated alongside it. Unless stated otherwise, you will only score marks for correct answers if you show your working.

How is the NSAA used?

Different Cambridge colleges will place different weightings on different components so it is important you find out as much information about how your marks will be used by emailing the college admissions office.

In general, the university will interview a high proportion of realistic applicants so the NSAA score isn't vital for making the interview shortlist. However, it can play a huge role in the final decision after your interview.

General Advice

Start Early

It is much easier to prepare if you practice little and often. Start your preparation well in advance; ideally by mid September but at the latest by early October. This way you will have plenty of time to complete as many papers as you wish to feel comfortable and won't have to panic and cram just before the test, which is a much less effective and more stressful way to learn. In general, an early start will give you the opportunity to identify the complex issues and work at your own pace.

Prioritise

Some questions can be long and complex – and given the intense time pressure you need to know your limits. It is essential that you don't get stuck with very difficult questions. If a question looks particularly long or complex, mark it for review and move on. You don't want to be caught 5 questions short at the end just because you took more than 3 minutes in answering a challenging multi-step maths question.

If a question is taking too long, choose a sensible answer and move on. Remember that each question carries equal weighting and therefore, you should adjust your timing accordingly. With practice and discipline, you can get very good at this and learn to maximise your efficiency.

Positive Marking

There are no penalties for incorrect answers in the NSAA; you will gain one for each right answer and will not get one for each wrong or unanswered one. This provides you with the luxury that you can always guess should you absolutely be not able to figure out the right answer for a question or run behind time. Since each question provides you with 4 to 6 possible answers, you have a 16-25% chance of guessing correctly. Therefore, if you aren't sure (and are running short of time), then make an educated guess and move on. Before 'guessing' you should try to eliminate a couple of answers to increase your chances of getting the question correct. For example, if a question has 5 options and you manage to eliminate 2 options- your chances of getting the question increase from 20% to 33%!

Avoid losing easy marks on other questions because of poor exam technique. Similarly, if you have failed to finish the exam, take the last 10 seconds to guess the remaining questions to at least give yourself a chance of getting them right.

Practice

This is the best way of familiarising yourself with the style of questions and the timing for this section. You are unlikely to be familiar with the style of questions in both sections when you first encounter them. Therefore, you want to be comfortable at using this before you sit the test.

Practising questions will put you at ease and make you more comfortable with the exam. The more comfortable you are, the less you will panic on the test day and the more likely you are to score highly. Initially, work through the questions at your own pace, and spend time carefully reading the questions and looking at any additional data. When it becomes closer to the test, **make sure you practice the questions under exam conditions**.

Past Papers

The NSAA is a very new exam so there aren't many sample papers available. Specimen papers are freely available online at www.uniadmissions.co.uk/NSAA. Once you've worked your way through the questions in this book, you are highly advised to attempt them.

Repeat Questions

When checking through answers, pay particular attention to questions you have got wrong. Study the worked solution carefully until you feel confident that you understand the reasoning, and then repeat the question without help to check that you can do it. This is the best way to learn from your mistakes, and means you are less likely to make similar mistakes when it comes to the test. The same applies for questions which you were unsure of and made an educated guess which was correct (even if you got it right). When working through this book, **make sure you highlight any questions you are unsure of**, this means you know to spend more time looking over them once marked.

Calculators

You aren't permitted to use calculators in section 1 – thus, it is essential that you have strong numerical skills. For instance, you should be able to rapidly convert between percentages, decimals and fractions. You will seldom get questions that would require calculators but you would be expected to be able to arrive at a sensible estimate. Consider for example:

Estimate 3.962 x 2.322:

3.962 is approximately 4 and 2.323 is approximately $2.33 = \frac{7}{3}$.

Thus, $3.962 \times 2.322 \approx 4 \times \frac{7}{3} = \frac{28}{3} = 9.33$

Since you will rarely be asked to perform difficult calculations, you can use this as a signpost of if you are tackling a question correctly. For example, when solving a section 1 question, you end up having to divide 8,079 by 357- this should raise alarm bells as calculations in section 1 are rarely this difficult.

It goes without saying that you should take time to familiarise yourself with your calculator's functions including the memory functions.

Top tip! Don't leave things too late – do small bits early and often rather than a mad cram in the last w
October. Some of the principles tested in NSAA require a great degree of understanding and you do
yourself justice by trying to cram them into a few hours!

A word on timing...

"If you had all day to do your NSAA, you would get 100%. But you don't."

Whilst this isn't completely true, it illustrates a very important point. Once you've practiced and know how to answer the questions, the clock is your biggest enemy. This seemingly obvious statement has one very important consequence. **The way to improve your NSAA score is to improve your speed.** There is no magic bullet. But there are a great number of techniques that, with practice, will give you significant time gains, allowing you to answer more questions and score more marks.

Timing is tight throughout the NSAA – **mastering timing is the first key to success.** Some candidates choose to work as quickly as possible to save up time at the end to check back, but this is generally not the best way to do it. NSAA questions can have a lot of information in them – each time you start answering a question it takes time to get familiar with the instructions and information. By splitting the question into two sessions (the first run-through and the return-to-check) you double the amount of time you spend on familiarising yourself with the data, as you have to do it twice instead of only once. This costs valuable time. In addition, candidates who do check back may spend 2–3 minutes doing so and yet not make any actual changes. Whilst this can be reassuring, it is a false reassurance as it is unlikely to have a significant effect on your actual score. Therefore it is usually best to pace yourself very steadily, aiming to spend the same amount of time on each question and finish the final question in a section just as time runs out. This reduces the time spent on re-familiarising with questions and maximises the time spent on the first attempt, gaining more marks.

It is essential that you don't get stuck with the hardest questions – no doubt there will be some. In the time spent answering only one of these you may miss out on answering three easier questions. If a question is taking too long, choose a sensible answer and move on. Never see this as giving up or in any way failing, rather it is the smart way to approach a test with a tight time limit. With practice and discipline, you can get very good at this and learn to maximise your efficiency. It is not about being a hero and aiming for full marks – this is almost impossible and very much unnecessary (even Cambridge doesn't expect you to get full marks!). It is about maximising your efficiency and gaining the maximum possible number of marks within the time you have.

Top tip! Ensure that you take a watch that can show you the time in seconds into the exam. This will you have a much more accurate idea of the time you're spending on a question. In general, if you've spe seconds on a section 1 question – move on regardless of how close you think you are to solving it.

Use the Options:

Some questions may try to overload you with information. When presented with large tables and data, it's essential you look at the answer options so you can focus your mind. This can allow you to reach the correct answer a lot more quickly. Consider the example below:

The table below shows the results of a study investigating antibiotic resistance in staphylococcus populations. A single staphylococcus bacterium is chosen at random from a similar population. Resistance to any one antibiotic is independent of resistance to others.

Calculate the probability that the bacterium selected will be resistant to all four drugs.

A   1 in 10^6
B   1 in 10^{12}
C   1 in 10^{20}
D   1 in 10^{25}
E   1 in 10^{30}
F   1 in 10^{35}

Antibiotic	Number of Bacteria tested	Number of Resistant Bacteria
Benzyl-penicillin	10^{11}	98
Chloramphenicol	10^9	1200
Metronidazole	10^8	256
Erythromycin	10^5	2

Looking at the options first makes it obvious that there is **no need to calculate exact values**- only in powers of 10. This makes your life a lot easier. If you hadn't noticed this, you might have spent well over 90 seconds trying to calculate the exact value when it wasn't even being asked for.

In other cases, you may actually be able to use the options to arrive at the solution quicker than if you had tried to solve the question as you normally would. Consider the example below:

A region is defined by the two inequalities: $x - y^2 > 1 \ and \ xy > 1$. Which of the following points is in the defined region?
A.   (10,3)
B.   (10,2)
C.   (-10,3)
D.   (-10,2)
E.   (-10,-3)

Whilst it's possible to solve this question both algebraically or graphically by manipulating the identities, by far **the quickest way is to actually use the options**. Note that options C, D and E violate the second inequality, narrowing down to answer to either A or B. For A: $10 - 3^2 = 1$ and thus this point is on the boundary of the defined region and not actually in the region. Thus the answer is B (as 10-4 = 6 > 1.)

In general, it pays dividends to look at the options briefly and see if they can be help you arrive at the question more quickly. Get into this habit early – it may feel unnatural at first but it's guaranteed to save you time in the long run.

Keywords

If you're stuck on a question; pay particular attention to the options that contain key modifiers like "**always**", "**only**", "**all**" as examiners like using them to test if there are any gaps in your knowledge. E.g. the statement "arteries carry oxygenated blood" would normally be true; "All arteries carry oxygenated blood" would be false because the pulmonary artery carries deoxygenated blood.

SECTION 1

Section 1 is the most time-pressured section of the NSAA. This section tests GCSE biology, chemistry, physics and maths. You have to answer 54 questions in 80 minutes. The questions can be quite difficult and it's easy to get bogged down. However, it's possible to rapidly improve if you prepare correctly so it's well worth spending time on it.

Choosing a Section

As part of section 1, you have to pick two sections from biology, chemistry, physics or advanced maths/physics. In most cases it will be immediately obvious to you which section will suit you best. Generally, applicants for physical natural sciences will choose physics/maths whilst those for biological sciences will choose the biology and chemistry. However, like the natural sciences tripos, this is by no means a hard and fast rule – it is extremely important that you choose the section you want to do ahead of time so that you can focus your preparation accordingly.

If you're unsure, take the time to review the content of each section and try out some questions so you can get a better idea of the style and difficulty of the questions. In general, the biology and chemistry questions in the NSAA require the least amount of time per question whilst the maths and physics are more time-draining as they usually consist of multi-step calculations.

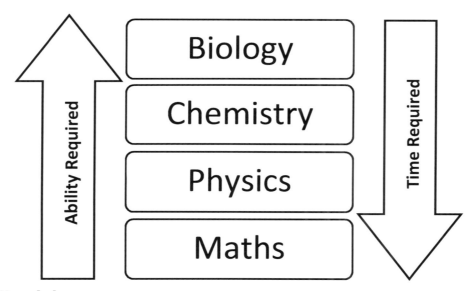

Gaps in Knowledge

The vast majority of applicants for natural sciences will be taking at least 3 science subjects. You are highly advised to go through the NSAA Specification and ensure that you have covered all examinable topics. An electronic copy of this can be obtained from **www.uniadmissions.co.uk/nsaa**.

The questions in this book will help highlight any particular areas of weakness or gaps in your knowledge that you may have. Upon discovering these, make sure you take some time to revise these topics before carrying on – there is little to be gained by attempting questions with huge gaps in your knowledge.

Maths

Being confident with maths is extremely important for the NSAA. Many students find that improving their numerical and algebraic skills usually results in big improvements in both their section 1 and 2 scores. Remember that maths in section 1 not only comes up in the maths questions but also in physics (manipulating equations and standard form) and chemistry (mass calculations). Thus, if you find yourself consistently running out of time in section 1, spending a few hours on brushing up your basic maths skills may do wonders for you.

SECTION 1A: Maths

NSAA maths questions are designed to be time draining- if you find yourself consistently not finishing, it might be worth leaving the maths (and probably physics) questions until the very end.

Good students sometimes have a habit of making easy questions difficult; remember that section 1A is pitched at GCSE level so you are not expected to know or use calculus or advanced trigonometry in it.

Formulas you **MUST** know:

2D Shapes		3D Shapes		
Area			**Surface Area**	**Volume**
Circle	πr^2	**Cuboid**	Sum of all 6 faces	Length x width x height
Parallelogram	Base x Vertical height	**Cylinder**	$2\pi r^2 + 2\pi rl$	πr^2 x l
Trapezium	0.5 x h x (a+b)	**Cone**	$\pi r^2 + \pi rl$	πr^2 x (h/3)
Triangle	0.5 x base x height	**Sphere**	$4\pi r^2$	$(4/3)\pi r^3$

Even good students who are studying maths at A2 can struggle with certain NSAA maths topics because they're usually glossed over at school. These include:

Quadratic Formula

The solutions for a quadratic equation in the form $ax^2 + bx + c = 0$ are given by: $x = \frac{-b \pm \sqrt{b^2 - 4ac}}{2a}$

Remember that you can also use the discriminant to quickly see if a quadratic equation has any solutions:

$$If\ b^2 - 4ac < 0: No\ solutions$$
$$If\ b^2 - 4ac = 0: One\ solution$$
$$If\ b^2 - 4ac > 2: Two\ solutions$$

Completing the Square

If a quadratic equation cannot be factorised easily and is in the format $ax^2 + bx + c = 0$ then you can rearrange it into the form $a\left(x + \frac{b}{2a}\right)^2 + [c - \frac{b^2}{4a}] = 0$

This looks more complicated than it is – remember that in the NSAA, you're extremely unlikely to get quadratic equations where $a > 1$ and the equation doesn't have any easy factors. This gives you an easier equation:

$\left(x + \frac{b}{2}\right)^2 + \left[c - \frac{b^2}{4}\right] = 0$ and is best understood with an example.

Consider: $x^2 + 6x + 10 = 0$

This equation cannot be factorised easily but note that: $x^2 + 6x - 10 = (x + 3)^2 - 19 = 0$

Therefore, $x = -3 \pm \sqrt{19}$. Completing the square is an important skill – make sure you're comfortable with it.

Difference between 2 Squares

If you are asked to simplify expressions and find that there are no common factors but it involves square numbers – you might be able to factorise by using the 'difference between two squares'.

For example, $x^2 - 25$ can also be expressed as $(x + 5)(x - 5)$.

Maths Questions

Question 1:

Robert has a box of building blocks. The box contains 8 yellow blocks and 12 red blocks. He picks three blocks from the box and stacks them up high. Calculate the probability that he stacks two red building blocks and one yellow building block, in **any** order.

A. $\frac{8}{20}$ B. $\frac{44}{95}$ C. $\frac{11}{18}$ D. $\frac{8}{19}$ E. $\frac{12}{20}$ F. $\frac{35}{60}$

Question 2:

Solve $\frac{3x+5}{5} + \frac{2x-2}{3} = 18$

A. 12.11   B. 13.49   C. 13.95   D. 14.2   E. 19   F. 265

Question 3:

Solve $3x^2 + 11x - 20 = 0$

A. 0.75 and $-\frac{4}{3}$ C. 5 and $\frac{4}{3}$ F. -12 only

B. -0.75 and $\frac{4}{3}$ D. 5 and $\frac{4}{3}$

E. 12 only

Question 4:

Express $\frac{5}{x+2} + \frac{3}{x-4}$ as a single fraction.

A. $\frac{15x-120}{(x+2)(x-4)}$ C. $\frac{8x-14}{(x+2)(x-4)}$ F. $\frac{8x-14}{x^2-8}$

B. $\frac{8x-26}{(x+2)(x-4)}$ D. $\frac{15}{8x}$

E. 24

Question 5:

The value of p is directly proportional to the cube root of q. When p = 12, q = 27. Find the value of q when p = 24.

A. 32   B. 64   C. 124   D. 128   E. 216   F. 1728

Question 6:

Write 72^2 as a product of its prime factors.

A. $2^6 \times 3^4$ C. $2^4 \times 3^4$ E. $2^6 \times 3$

B. $2^6 \times 3^5$ D. 2×3^3 F. $2^3 \times 3^2$

Question 7:

Calculate: $\dfrac{2.302 \times 10^5 + 2.302 \times 10^2}{1.151 \times 10^{10}}$

A. 0.0000202

B. 0.00020002

C. 0.00002002

D. 0.00000002

E. 0.000002002

F. 0.000002002

Question 8:

Given that $y^2 + \mathbf{a}y + \mathbf{b} = (y + 2)^2 - 5$, find the values of **a** and **b**.

	a	b
A	-1	4
B	1	9
C	-1	-9
D	-9	1
E	4	-1
F	4	1

Question 9:

Express $\dfrac{4}{5} + \dfrac{m-2n}{m+4n}$ as a single fraction in its simplest form:

A. $\dfrac{6m+6n}{5(m+4n)}$

B. $\dfrac{9m+26n}{5(m+4n)}$

C. $\dfrac{20m+6n}{5(m+4n)}$

D. $\dfrac{3m+9n}{5(m+4n)}$

E. $\dfrac{3(3m+2n)}{5(m+4n)}$

F. $\dfrac{6m+6n}{3(m+4n)}$

Question 10:

A is inversely proportional to the square root of B. When A = 4, B = 25.

Calculate the value of A when B = 16.

A. 0.8   B. 4   C. 5   D. 6   E. 10   F. 20

Question 11:

S, T, U and V are points on the circumference of a circle, and O is the centre of the circle.

Given that angle SVU = 89°, calculate the size of the smaller angle SOU.

A. 89°   B. 91°   C. 102°   D. 178°   E. 182°   F. 212°

Question 12:

Open cylinder A has a surface area of 8π cm² and a volume of 2π cm³. Open cylinder B is an enlargement of A and has a surface area of 32π cm². Calculate the volume of cylinder B.

A. 2π cm³

B. 8π cm³

C. 10π cm³

D. 14π cm³

E. 16π cm³

F. 32π cm³

Question 13:

Express $\frac{8}{x(3-x)} - \frac{6}{x}$ in its simplest form.

A. $\frac{3x-10}{x(3-x)}$

B. $\frac{3x+10}{x(3-x)}$

C. $\frac{6x-10}{x(3-2x)}$

D. $\frac{6x-10}{x(3+2x)}$

E. $\frac{6x-10}{x(3-x)}$

F. $\frac{6x+10}{x(3-x)}$

Question 14:

A bag contains 10 balls. 9 of those are white and 1 is black. What is the probability that the black ball is drawn in the tenth and final draw if the drawn balls are not replaced?

A. 0

B. $\frac{1}{10}$

C. $\frac{1}{100}$

D. $\frac{1}{10^{10}}$

E. $\frac{1}{362,880}$

Question 15:

Gambit has an ordinary deck of 52 cards. What is the probability of Gambit drawing 2 Kings (without replacement)?

A. 0

B. $\frac{1}{169}$

C. $\frac{1}{221}$

D. $\frac{4}{663}$

E. None of the above

Question 16:

I have two identical unfair dice, where the probability that the dice get a 6 is twice as high as the probability of any other outcome, which are all equally likely. What is the probability that when I roll both dice the total will be 12?

A. 0

B. $\frac{4}{49}$

C. $\frac{1}{9}$

D. $\frac{2}{7}$

E. None of the above

Question 17:

A roulette wheel consists of 36 numbered spots and 1 zero spot (i.e. 37 spots in total).

What is the probability that the ball will stop in a spot either divisible by 3 or 2?

A. 0

B. $\frac{25}{37}$

C. $\frac{25}{36}$

D. $\frac{18}{37}$

E. $\frac{24}{37}$

Question 18:

I have a fair coin that I flip 4 times. What is the probability I get 2 heads and 2 tails?

A. $\frac{1}{16}$

B. $\frac{3}{16}$

C. $\frac{3}{8}$

D. $\frac{9}{16}$

E. None of the above

Question 19:

Shivun rolls two fair dice. What is the probability that he gets a total of 5, 6 or 7?

A. $\frac{9}{36}$

B. $\frac{7}{12}$

C. $\frac{1}{6}$

 D. $\frac{5}{12}$

E. None of the above

Question 20:

Dr Savary has a bag that contains x red balls, y blue balls and z green balls (and no others). He pulls out a ball, replaces it, and then pulls out another. What is the probability that he picks one red ball and one green ball?

A. $\frac{2(x+y)}{x+y+z}$

B. $\frac{xz}{(x+y+z)^2}$

C. $\frac{2xz}{(x+y+z)^2}$

D. $\frac{(x+z)}{(x+y+z)^2}$

E. $\frac{4xz}{(x+y+z)^4}$

F. More information necessary

Question 21:

Mr Kilbane has a bag that contains x red balls, y blue balls and z green balls (and no others). He pulls out a ball, does **NOT** replace it, and then pulls out another. What is the probability that he picks one red ball and one blue ball?

A. $\frac{2xy}{(x+y+z)^2}$

B. $\frac{2xy}{(x+y+z)(x+y+z-1)}$

C. $\frac{2xy}{(x+y+z)^2}$

D. $\frac{xy}{(x+y+z)(x+y+z-1)}$

E. $\frac{4xy}{(x+y+z-1)^2}$

F. More information needed

Question 22:

There are two tennis players. The first player wins the point with probability p, and the second player wins the point with probability 1-p. The rules of tennis say that the first player to score four points wins the game, unless the score is 4-3. At this point the first player to get two points ahead wins.

What is the probability that the first player wins in exactly 5 rounds?

A. $4p^4(1-p)$

B. $p^4(1-p)$

C. $4p(1-p)$

D. $4p(1-p)^4$

E. $4p^5(1-p)$

F. More information needed.

Question 23:

Solve the equation $\frac{4x+7}{2} + 9x + 10 = 7$

A. $\frac{22}{13}$

B. $-\frac{22}{13}$

C. $\frac{10}{13}$

D. $-\frac{10}{13}$

E. $\frac{13}{22}$

F. $-\frac{13}{22}$

Question 24:

The volume of a sphere is $V = \frac{4}{3}\pi r^3$, and the surface area of a sphere is $S = 4\pi r^2$. Express S in terms of V

A. $S = (4\pi)^{2/3}(3V)^{2/3}$

B. $S = (8\pi)^{1/3}(3V)^{2/3}$

C. $S = (4\pi)^{1/3}(9V)^{2/3}$

D. $S = (4\pi)^{1/3}(3V)^{2/3}$

E. $S = (16\pi)^{1/3}(9V)^{2/3}$

Question 25:

Express the volume of a cube, V, in terms of its surface area, S.

A. $V = (S/6)^{3/2}$

B. $V = S^{3/2}$

C. $V = (6/S)^{3/2}$

D. $V = (S/6)^{1/2}$

E. $V = (S/36)^{1/2}$

F. $V = (S/36)^{3/2}$

Question 26:

Solve the equations $4x + 3y = 7$ and $2x + 8y = 12$

A. $(x, y) = \left(\frac{17}{13}, \frac{10}{13}\right)$

B. $(x, y) = (\frac{10}{13}, \frac{17}{13})$

C. $(x, y) = (1, 2)$

D. $(x, y) = (2, 1)$

E. $(x, y) = (6, 3)$

F. $(x, y) = (3, 6)$

G. No solutions possible.

Question 27:

Rearrange $\frac{(7x+10)}{(9x+5)} = 3y^2 + 2$, to make x the subject.

A. $\frac{15\,y^2}{7 - 9(3y^2+2)}$

B. $\frac{15\,y^2}{7 + 9(3y^2+2)}$

C. $-\frac{15\,y^2}{7 - 9(3y^2+2)}$

D. $-\frac{15\,y^2}{7 + 9(3y^2+2)}$

E. $-\frac{5\,y^2}{7 + 9(3y^2+2)}$

F. $\frac{5\,y^2}{7 + 9(3y^2+2)}$

Question 28:

Simplify $3x \left(\frac{3x^7}{x^{\frac{1}{3}}}\right)^3$

A. $9x^{20}$ B. $27x^{20}$ C. $87x^{20}$ D. $9x^{21}$ E. $27x^{21}$ F. $81x^{21}$

Question 29:

Simplify $2x[(2x)^7]^{\frac{1}{14}}$

A. $2x\sqrt{2}\,x^4$

B. $2x\sqrt{2x^3}$

C. $2\sqrt{2}\,x^4$

D. $2\sqrt{2x^3}$

E. $8x^3$

F. $8x$

Question 30:

What is the circumference of a circle with an area of 10π?

A. $2\pi\sqrt{10}$

B. $\pi\sqrt{10}$

C. 10π

D. 20π

E. $\sqrt{10}$

F. More information needed.

Question 31:

If $a.b = (ab) + (a + b)$, then calculate the value of $(3.4).5$

A. 19

B. 54

C. 100

D. 119

E. 132

Question 32:

If $a.b = \frac{a^b}{a}$, calculate $(2.3).2$

A. $\frac{16}{3}$

B. 1

C. 2

D. 4

E. 8

Question 33:

Solve $x^2 + 3x - 5 = 0$

A. $x = -\frac{3}{2} \pm \frac{\sqrt{11}}{2}$

B. $x = \frac{3}{2} \pm \frac{\sqrt{11}}{2}$

C. $x = -\frac{3}{2} \pm \frac{\sqrt{11}}{4}$

D. $x = \frac{3}{2} \pm \frac{\sqrt{11}}{4}$

E. $x = \frac{3}{2} \pm \frac{\sqrt{29}}{2}$

F. $x = -\frac{3}{2} \pm \frac{\sqrt{29}}{2}$

Question 34:

How many times do the curves $y = x^3$ and $y = x^2 + 4x + 14$ intersect?

A. 0

B. 1

C. 2

D. 3

E. 4

Question 35:

Which of the following graphs **do not** intersect?

1. $y = x$

2. $y = x^2$

3. $y = 1-x^2$

4. $y = 2$

A. 1 and 2

B. 2 and 3

C. 3 and 4

D. 1 and 3

E. 1 and 4

F. 2 and 4

Question 36:

Calculate the product of 897,653 and 0.009764.

A. 87646.8

B. 8764.68

C. 876.468

D. 87.6468

E. 8.76468

F. 0.876468

Question 37:

Solve for x: $\frac{7x+3}{10} + \frac{3x+1}{7} = 14$

A. $\frac{929}{51}$

B. $\frac{949}{47}$

C. $\frac{949}{79}$

D. $\frac{980}{79}$

Question 38:

What is the area of an equilateral triangle with side length x.

 A. $\frac{x^2\sqrt{3}}{4}$

B. $\frac{x\sqrt{3}}{4}$

 C. $\frac{x^2}{2}$

D. $\frac{x}{2}$

E. x^2

F. x

Question 39:

Simplify $3 - \frac{7x(25x^2 - 1)}{49x^2(5x+1)}$

 A. $3 - \frac{5x-1}{7x}$

B. $3 - \frac{5x+1}{7x}$

C. $3 + \frac{5x-1}{7x}$

D. $3 + \frac{5x+1}{7x}$

E. $3 - \frac{5x^2}{49}$

F. $3 + \frac{5x^2}{49}$

Question 40:

Solve the equation $x^2 - 10x - 100 = 0$

A. $-5 \pm 5\sqrt{5}$

B. $-5 \pm \sqrt{5}$

C. $5 \pm 5\sqrt{5}$

D. $5 \pm \sqrt{5}$

E. $5 \pm 5\sqrt{125}$

F. $-5 \pm \sqrt{125}$

Question 41:

Rearrange $x^2 - 4x + 7 = y^3 + 2$ to make x the subject.

A. $x = 2 \pm \sqrt{y^3 + 1}$

B. $x = 2 \pm \sqrt{y^3 - 1}$

C. $x = -2 \pm \sqrt{y^3 - 1}$

D. $x = -2 \pm \sqrt{y^3 + 1}$

E. x cannot be made the subject for this equation.

Question 42:

Rearrange $3x + 2 = \sqrt{7x^2 + 2x + y}$ to make y the subject.

A. $y = 4x^2 + 8x + 2$

B. $y = 4x^2 + 8x + 4$

C. $y = 2x^2 + 10x + 2$

D. $y = 2x^2 + 10x + 4$

E. $y = x^2 + 10x + 2$

F. $y = x^2 + 10x + 4$

Question 43:

Rearrange $y^4 - 4y^3 + 6y^2 - 4y + 2 = x^5 + 7$ to make y the subject.

A. $y = 1 + (x^5 + 7)^{1/4}$

B. $y = -1 + (x^5 + 7)^{1/4}$

 C. $y = 1 + (x^5 + 6)^{1/4}$

D. $y = -1 + (x^5 + 6)^{1/4}$

Question 44:

The aspect ratio of my television screen is 4:3 and the diagonal is 50 inches. What is the area of my television screen?

A. 1,200 inches²

B. 1,000 inches²

C. 120 inches²

D. 100 inches²

E. More information needed.

Question 45:

Rearrange the equation $\sqrt{1 + 3x^{-2}} = y^5 + 1$ to make x the subject.

A. $x = \dfrac{(y^{10} + 2y^5)}{3}$

B. $x = \dfrac{3}{(y^{10} + 2y^5)}$

C. $x = \sqrt{\dfrac{3}{y^{10} + 2y^5}}$

D. $x = \sqrt{\dfrac{y^{10} + 2y^5}{3}}$

E. $x = \sqrt{\dfrac{y^{10} + 2y^5 + 2}{3}}$

F. $x = \sqrt{\dfrac{3}{y^{10} + 2y^5 + 2}}$

Question 46:

Solve $3x - 5y = 10 \ and \ 2x + 2y = 13$.

A. $(x, y) = \left(\dfrac{19}{16}, \dfrac{85}{16}\right)$

B. $(x, y) = \left(\dfrac{85}{16}, -\dfrac{19}{16}\right)$

C. $(x, y) = \left(\dfrac{85}{16}, \dfrac{19}{16}\right)$

D. $(x, y) = \left(-\dfrac{85}{16}, -\dfrac{19}{16}\right)$

E. No solutions possible.

Question 47:

The two inequalities $x + y \leq 3 \ and \ x^3 - y^2 < 3$ define a region on a plane. Which of the following points is inside the region?

A. (2, 1)

B. (2.5, 1)

C. (1, 2)

D. (3, 5)

E. (1, 2.5)

F. None of the above.

Question 48:

How many times do $y = x + 4 \ and \ y = 4x^2 + 5x + 5$ intersect?

A. 0

B. 1

C. 2

D. 3

E. 4

Question 49:

How many times do $y = x^3$ and $y = x$ intersect?

A. 0   B. 1   C. 2   D. 3   E. 4

Question 50:

A cube has unit length sides. What is the length of a line joining a vertex to the midpoint of the opposite side?

A. $\sqrt{2}$

B. $\sqrt{\frac{3}{2}}$

C. $\sqrt{3}$

D. $\sqrt{5}$

E. $\frac{\sqrt{5}}{2}$

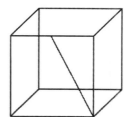

Question 51:

Solve for x, y, and z.

1. $x + y - z = -1$
2. $2x - 2y + 3z = 8$
3. $2x - y + 2z = 9$

	x	y	z
A	2	-15	-14
B	15	2	14
C	14	15	-2
D	-2	15	14
E	2	-15	14
F	No solutions possible		

Question 52:

Fully factorise: $3a^3 - 30a^2 + 75a$

A. $3a(a-3)^3$

B. $a(3a-5)^2$

C. $3a(a^2 - 10a + 25)$

D. $3a(a-5)^2$

E. $3a(a+5)^2$

Question 53:

Solve for x and y:

$$4x + 3y = 48$$
$$3x + 2y = 34$$

	x	y
A	8	6
B	6	8
C	3	4
D	4	3
E	30	12
F	12	30
G	No solutions possible	

Question 54:

Evaluate: $\dfrac{-\left(5^2 - 4 \times 7\right)^2}{-6^2 + 2 \times 7}$

A. $-\dfrac{3}{50}$ 　　 B. $\dfrac{11}{22}$ 　　 C. $-\dfrac{3}{22}$ 　　 D. $\dfrac{9}{50}$ 　　 E. $\dfrac{9}{22}$ 　　 F. 0

Question 55:

All license plates are 6 characters long. The first 3 characters consist of letters and the next 3 characters of numbers.

How many unique license plates are possible?

A. 676,000 　　　　 C. 67,600,000 　　　　 E. 17,576,000

B. 6,760,000 　　　　 D. 1,757,600 　　　　 F. 175,760,000

Question 56:

How many solutions are there for: $2(2(x^2 - 3x)) = -9$

A. 0 　　　　　　　　　　　　 D. 3

B. 1 　　　　　　　　　　　　 E. Infinite solutions.

C. 2

Question 57:

Evaluate: $\left(x^{\frac{1}{2}} y^{-3}\right)^{\frac{1}{2}}$

A. $\dfrac{x^{\frac{1}{2}}}{y}$ 　　　　 C. $\dfrac{x^{\frac{1}{4}}}{y^{\frac{3}{2}}}$ 　　　　 D. $\dfrac{y^{\frac{1}{4}}}{x^{\frac{3}{2}}}$

B. $\dfrac{x}{y^{\frac{3}{2}}}$

Question 58:

Bryan earned a total of £ 1,240 last week from renting out three flats. From this, he had to pay 10% of the rent from the 1-bedroom flat for repairs, 20% of the rent from the 2-bedroom flat for repairs, and 30% from the 3-bedroom flat for repairs. The 3-bedroom flat costs twice as much as the 1-bedroom flat. Given that the total repair bill was £ 276 calculate the rent for each apartment.

	1 Bedroom	2 Bedrooms	3 Bedrooms
A	280	400	560
B	140	200	280
C	420	600	840
D	250	300	500
E	500	600	1,000

Question 59:

Evaluate: $5 [5(6^2 - 5 \times 3) + 400^{\frac{1}{2}}]^{1/3} + 7$

A. 0   B. 25   C. 32   D. 49   E. 56   F. 200

Question 60:

What is the area of a regular hexagon with side length 1?

A. $3\sqrt{3}$ C. $\sqrt{3}$ E. 6

 B. $\frac{3\sqrt{3}}{2}$ D. $\frac{\sqrt{3}}{2}$ F. More information needed

Question 61:

Dexter moves into a new rectangular room that is 19 metres longer than it is wide, and its total area is 780 square metres. What are the room's dimensions?

A. Width = 20 m; Length = -39 m   D. Width = -39 m; Length = 20 m
B. Width = 20 m; Length = 39 m   E. Width = -20 m; Length = 39 m
C. Width = 39 m; Length = 20 m

Question 62:

Tom uses 34 meters of fencing to enclose his rectangular lot. He measured the diagonals to 13 metres long. What is the length and width of the lot?

A. 3 m by 4 m   C. 6 m by 12 m   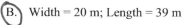 E. 9 m by 15 m
B. 5 m by 12 m   D. 8 m by 15 m   F. 10 m by 10 m

Question 63:

Solve $\frac{3x-5}{2} + \frac{x+5}{4} = x + 1$

A. 1

B. 1.5

C. 3

D. 3.5

E. 4.5

F. None of the above

Question 64:

Calculate: $\frac{5.226 \times 10^6 + 5.226 \times 10^5}{1.742 \times 10^{10}}$

A. 0.033

B. 0.0033

C. 0.00033

D. 0.000033

E. 0.0000033

Question 65:

Calculate the area of the triangle shown to the right:

A. $3 + \sqrt{2}$

B. $\frac{2 + 2\sqrt{2}}{2}$

C. $2 + 5\sqrt{2}$

D. $3 - \sqrt{2}$

E. 3

F. 6

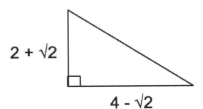

$2 + \sqrt{2}$

$4 - \sqrt{2}$

Question 66:

Rearrange $\sqrt{\frac{4}{x}} + 9 = y - 2$ to make x the subject.

A. $x = \frac{11}{(y-2)^2}$

B. $x = \frac{9}{(y-2)^2}$

C. $x = \frac{4}{(y+1)(y-5)}$

D. $x = \frac{4}{(y-1)(y+5)}$

E. $x = \frac{4}{(y+1)(y+5)}$

F. $x = \frac{4}{(y-1)(y-5)}$

Question 67:

When 5 is subtracted from 5x the result is half the sum of 2 and 6x. What is the value of x?

A. 0   B. 1   C. 2   D. 3   E. 4   F. 6

Question 68:

Estimate $\frac{54.98 + 2.25^2}{\sqrt{905}}$

A. 0   B. 1   C. 2   D. 3   E. 4   F. 5

Question 69:

At a Pizza Parlour, you can order single, double or triple cheese in the crust. You also have the option to include ham, olives, pepperoni, bell pepper, meat balls, tomato slices, and pineapples. How many different types of pizza are available at the Pizza Parlour?

A. 10

B. 96

C. 192

D. 384

E. 768

F. None of the above

Question 70:

Solve the simultaneous equations $x^2 + y^2 = 1$ and $x + y = \sqrt{2}$, for x, y > 0

A. $(x,y) = (\frac{\sqrt{2}}{2}, \frac{\sqrt{2}}{2})$

B. $(x,y) = (\frac{1}{2}, \frac{\sqrt{3}}{2})$

C. $(x,y) = (\sqrt{2} - 1, 1)$

D. $(x,y) = (\sqrt{2}, \frac{1}{2})$

Question 71:

Which of the following statements is **FALSE**?

A. Congruent objects always have the same dimensions and shape.

B. Congruent objects can be mirror images of each other.

C. Congruent objects do not always have the same angles.

D. Congruent objects can be rotations of each other.

E. Two triangles are congruent if they have two sides and one angle of the same magnitude.

Question 72:

Solve the inequality $x^2 \geq 6 - x$

A. $x \leq -3$ and $x \leq 2$

B. $x \leq -3$ and $x \geq 2$

C. $x \geq -3$ and $x \leq 2$

D. $x \geq -3$ and $x \geq 2$

E. $x \geq 2$ only

F. $x \geq -3$ only

Question 73:

The hypotenuse of an isosceles right-angled triangle is x cm. What is the area of the triangle in terms of x?

A. $\frac{\sqrt{x}}{2}$

B. $\frac{x^2}{4}$

C. $\frac{x}{4}$

D. $\frac{3x^2}{4}$

E. $\frac{x^2}{10}$

Question 74:

Mr Heard derives a formula: $Q = \frac{(X+Y)^2 A}{3B}$. He doubles the values of X and Y, halves the value of A and triples the value of B. What happens to value of Q?

 A. Decreases by $\frac{1}{3}$

B. Increases by $\frac{1}{3}$

C. Decreases by $\frac{2}{3}$

D. Increases by $\frac{2}{3}$

E. Increases by $\frac{4}{3}$

F. Decreases by $\frac{4}{3}$

Question 75:

Consider the graphs $y = x^2 - 2x + 3$, and $y = x^2 - 6x - 10$. Which of the following is true?

A. Both equations intersect the x-axis.

B. Neither equation intersects the x-axis.

C. The first equation does not intersect the x-axis; the second equation intersects the x-axis.

D. The first equation intersects the x-axis; the second equation does not intersect the x-axis.

SECTION 1B: Physics

Physics Questions in the NSAA are challenging as they frequently require you to make leaps in logic and calculations. Thus, before you go any further, ensure you have a firm understanding of the major principles and are confident with commonly examined topics like Newtonian mechanics, electrical circuits and radioactive decay as you may not have covered these at school depending on the specification you did.

The first step to improving in this section is to memorise by rote all the equations listed on the next page.

The majority of the physics questions involve a fair bit of maths – this means you need to be comfortable with converting between units and also powers of 10. **Most questions require two step calculations**. Consider the example:

A metal ball is released from the roof a 20 metre building. Assuming air resistance equals is negligible; calculate the velocity at which the ball hits the ground. [g = 10ms⁻²]

A. 5 ms^{-1}
B. 10 ms^{-1}
C. 15 ms^{-1}
D. 20 ms^{-1}
E. 25 ms^{-1}

Solution: When the ball hits the ground, all of its gravitational potential energy has been converted to kinetic energy. Thus, $E_p = E_k$:

$$mg\Delta h = \frac{mv^2}{2}$$

Thus, $v = \sqrt{2gh} = \sqrt{2 \times 10 \times 20}$

$v = \sqrt{400} = 20ms^{-1}$

Here, you were required to not only recall two equations but apply and rearrange them very quickly to get the answer; all in under 60 seconds. Thus, it is easy to understand why the physics questions are generally much harder than the biology and chemistry ones.

NB: A stronger applicant would also spot that this can be solved by using a single suvat equation:

$$v^2 = u^2 + 2as$$

$v = \sqrt{2 \times 10 \times 20} = 20ms^{-1}$

SI Units

Remember that in order to get the correct answer you must always work in SI units i.e. do your calculations in terms of metres (not centimetres) and kilograms (not grams), etc.

ip! Knowing SI units is extremely useful because they allow you to **'work out' equations** if you ever
t them e.g. The units for density are kg/m^3. Since Kg is the SI unit for mass, and m^3 is represented by volume –the equation for density must be = Mass/Volume.

can also work the other way, for example we know that the unit for Pressure is Pascal (Pa). But based on
ıct that Pressure = Force/Area, a Pascal must be equivalent to N/m^2. Some physics questions will test your
y to manipulate units like this so it's important you are comfortable converting between them.

Formulas you MUST know:

Equations of Motion:

- $s = ut + 0.5at^2$
- $v = u + at$
- $a = (v-u)/t$
- $v^2 = u^2 + 2as$

Equations relating to Force:

For objects in equilibrium:

- Sum of Clockwise moments = Sum of Anti-clockwise moments
- Sum of all resultant forces = 0

Equations relating to Energy:

- Kinetic Energy = $0.5 \, mv^2$
- Δ in Gravitational Potential Energy = $mg\Delta h$
- Energy Efficiency = (Useful energy/ Total energy) x 100%

Equations relating to Power:

- Power = Work done / time
- Power = Energy transferred / time
- Power = Force x velocity

Electrical Equations:

- $Q = It$
- $V = IR$
- $P = IV = I^2R = V^2/R$
- V = Potential difference (V, Volts)

- Force = mass x acceleration
- Force = Momentum/Time
- Pressure = Force / Area
- Moment of a Force = Force x Distance
- Work done = Force x Displacement

- R = Resistance (Ohms)
- P = Power (W, Watts)
- Q = Charge (C, Coulombs)
- t = Time (s, seconds)

For Transformers: $\dfrac{V_p}{V_s} = \dfrac{n_p}{n_s}$ where:

- V: Potential difference
- n: Number of turns
- p: Primary
- s: Secondary

Other:

- Weight = mass x g
- Density = Mass / Volume
- Momentum = Mass x Velocity
- $g = 9.81 \text{ ms}^{-2}$ (unless otherwise stated)

Factor	Text	Symbol
10^{12}	Tera	T
10^{9}	Giga	G
10^{6}	Mega	M
10^{3}	Kilo	k
10^{2}	Hecto	h
10^{-1}	Deci	d
10^{-2}	Centi	c
10^{-3}	Milli	m
10^{-6}	Micro	μ
10^{-9}	Nano	n
10^{-12}	Pico	p

Physics Questions

Question 76:

Which of the following statements are **FALSE**?

A. Electromagnetic waves cause things to heat up.
B. X-rays and gamma rays can knock electrons out of their orbits.
C. Loud sounds can make objects vibrate.
D. Wave power can be used to generate electricity.
E. Since waves carry energy away, the source of a wave loses energy.
F. The amplitude of a wave determines its mass.

Question 77:

A spacecraft is analysing a newly discovered exoplanet. A rock of unknown mass falls on the planet from a height of 30 m. Given that $g = 5.4$ ms^{-2} on the planet, calculate the speed of the rock when it hits the ground and the time it took to fall.

	Speed (ms^{-1})	Time (s)
A	18	3.3
B	18	3.1
C	12	3.3
D	10	3.7
E	9	2.3
F	1	0.3

Question 78:

A canoe floating on the sea rises and falls 7 times in 49 seconds. The waves pass it at a speed of 5 ms^{-1}. How long are the waves?

A. 12 m   B. 22 m   C. 25 m   D. 35 m   E. 57 m   F. 75 m

Question 79:

Miss Orrell lifts her 37.5 kg bike for a distance of 1.3 m in 5 s. The acceleration of free fall is 10 ms^{-2}. What is the average power that she develops?

A. 9.8 W   C. 57.9 W   E. 97.5W
B. 12.9 W   D. 79.5 W   F. 98.0 W

Question 80:

A truck accelerates at 5.6 ms^{-2} from rest for 8 seconds. Calculate the final speed and the distance travelled in 8 seconds.

	Final Speed (ms^{-1})	Distance (m)
A	40.8	119.2
B	40.8	129.6
C	42.8	179.2
D	44.1	139.2
E	44.1	179.7
F	44.2	129.2
G	44.8	179.2
H	44.8	179.7

Question 81:
Which of the following statements is true when a sky diver jumps out of a plane?

A. The sky diver leaves the plane and will accelerate until the air resistance is greater than their weight.
B. The sky diver leaves the plane and will accelerate until the air resistance is less than their weight.
C. The sky diver leaves the plane and will accelerate until the air resistance equals their weight.
D. The sky diver leaves the plane and will accelerate until the air resistance equals their weight squared.
E. The sky diver will travel at a constant velocity after leaving the plane.

Question 82:
A 100 g apple falls on Isaac's head from a height of 20 m. Calculate the apple's momentum before the point of impact. Take $g = 10$ ms^{-2}

A. 0.1 kgms^{-1}
B. 0.2 kgms^{-1}
C. 1 kgms^{-1}
D. 2 kgms^{-1}
E. 10 kgms^{-1}
F. 20 kgms^{-1}

Question 83:
Which of the following do all electromagnetic waves all have in common?

1. They can travel through a vacuum.
2. They can be reflected.
3. They are the same length.
4. They have the same amount of energy.
5. They can be polarised.

A. 1, 2 and 3 only
B. 1, 2, 3 and 4 only
C. 4 and 5 only
D. 3 and 4 only
E. 1, 2 and 5 only
F. 1 and 5 only

Question 84:
A battery with an internal resistance of 0.8 Ω and e.m.f of 36 V is used to power a drill with resistance 1 Ω. What is the current in the circuit when the drill is connected to the power supply?

A. 5 A   B. 10 A   C. 15 A   D. 20 A   E. 25 A   F. 30 A

Question 85:
Officer Bailey throws a 20 g dart at a speed of 100 ms^{-1}. It strikes the dartboard and is brought to rest in 10 milliseconds. Calculate the average force exerted on the dart by the dartboard.

A. 0.2 N
B. 2 N
C. 20 N
D. 200 N
E. 2,000 N
F. 20,000 N

Question 86:
Professor Huang lifts a 50 kg bag through a distance of 0.7 m in 3 s. What average power does she develop to 3 significant figures? Take $g = 10$ms^{-2}

A. 112 W
B. 113 W
C. 114 W
D. 115 W
E. 116 W
F. 117 W

Question 87:
An electric scooter is travelling at a speed of 30 ms^{-1} and is kept going against a 50 N frictional force by a driving force of 300 N in the direction of motion. Given that the engine runs at 200 V, calculate the current in the scooter.

A. 4.5 A
B. 45 A
C. 450 A
D. 4,500 A
E. 45,000 A
F. More information needed.

Question 88:

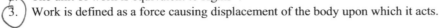

Which of the following statements about the physical definition of work are correct?

1. $Work\ done = \frac{Force}{distance}$
2. The unit of work is equivalent to Kgms^{-2}.
3. Work is defined as a force causing displacement of the body upon which it acts.

A. Only 1
B. Only 2
C. Only 3
D. 1 and 2
E. 2 and 3
F. 1 and 3

Question 89:
Which of the following statements about kinetic energy are correct?

1. It is defined as $E_k = \frac{mv^2}{2}$
2. The unit of kinetic energy is equivalent to Pa x m^3.
3. Kinetic energy is equal to the amount of energy needed to decelerate the body in question from its current speed.

A. Only 1
B. Only 2
C. Only 3
D. 1 and 2
E. 2 and 3
F. 1 and 3
G. 1, 2 and 3

Question 90:
In relation to radiation, which of the following statements is **FALSE**?

A. Radiation is the emission of energy in the form of waves or particles.
B. Radiation can be either ionizing or non-ionizing.
C. Gamma radiation has very high energy.
D. Alpha radiation is of higher energy than beta radiation.
E. X-rays are an example of wave radiation.

Question 91:
In relation to the physical definition of half-life, which of the following statements are correct?

1. In radioactive decay, the half-life is independent of atom type and isotope.
2. Half-life is defined as the time required for exactly half of the entities to decay.
3. Half-life applies to situations of both exponential and non-exponential decay.

A. Only 1
B. Only 2
C. Only 3
D. 1 and 2
E. 2 and 3
F. 1 and 3

Question 92:
In relation to nuclear fusion, which of the following statements is **FALSE**?

A. Nuclear fusion is initiated by the absorption of neutrons.
B. Nuclear fusion describes the fusion of hydrogen atoms to form helium atoms.
C. Nuclear fusion releases great amounts of energy.
D. Nuclear fusion requires high activation temperatures.
E. All of the statements above are false.

Question 93:
In relation to nuclear fission, which of the following statements is correct?

A. Nuclear fission is the basis of many nuclear weapons.
B. Nuclear fission is triggered by the shooting of neutrons at unstable atoms.
C. Nuclear fission can trigger chain reactions.
D. Nuclear fission commonly results in the emission of ionizing radiation.
E. All of the above.

Question 94:

Two identical resistors (R_a and R_b) are connected in a series circuit. Which of the following statements are true?

1. The current through both resistors is the same.
2. The voltage through both resistors is the same.
3. The voltage across the two resistors is given by Ohm's Law.

A. Only 1
B. Only 2
C. Only 3
D. 1 and 2

E. 2 and 3
F. 1 and 3
G. 1, 2 and 3
H. None of the statements are true.

Question 95:

The Sun is 8 light-minutes away from the Earth. Estimate the circumference of the Earth's orbit around the Sun. Assume that the Earth is in a circular orbit around the Sun. Speed of light = 3×10^8 ms^{-1}

A. 10^{24} m
B. 10^{21} m

C. 10^{18} m
D. 10^{15} m

E. 10^{12} m
F. 10^9 m

Question 96:

Which of the following statements about the physical definition of speed are true?

1. Speed is the same as velocity.
2. The internationally standardised unit for speed is ms^{-2}.
3. Velocity = distance/time.

A. Only 1
B. Only 2
C. Only 3
D. 1 and 2

E. 2 and 3
F. 1 and 3
G. 1, 2 and 3
H. None of the statements are true.

Question 97:

Which of the following statements best defines Ohm's Law?

A. The current through an insulator between two points is indirectly proportional to the potential difference across the two points.
B. The current through an insulator between two points is directly proportional to the potential difference across the two points.
C. The current through a conductor between two points is inversely proportional to the potential difference across the two points.
D. The current through a conductor between two points is proportional to the square of the potential difference across the two points.
E. The current through a conductor between two points is directly proportional to the potential difference across the two points.

Question 98:

Which of the following statements regarding Newton's Second Law are correct?

1. For objects at rest, Resultant Force must be 0 Newtons
2. Force = Mass x Acceleration
3. Force = Rate of change of Momentum

A. Only 1
B. Only 2
C. Only 3
D. 1 and 2

E. 2 and 3
F. 1 and 3
G. 1, 2 and 3

Question 99:

Which of the following equations concerning electrical circuits are correct?

1. $Charge = \dfrac{Voltage \times time}{Resistance}$

2. $Charge = \dfrac{Power \times time}{Voltage}$

3. $Charge = \dfrac{Current \times time}{Resistance}$

A. Only 1
B. Only 2
C. Only 3
D. 1 and 2

E. 2 and 3
F. 1 and 3
G. 1, 2 and 3
H. None of the equations are correct.

Question 100:

An elevator has a mass of 1,600 kg and is carrying passengers that have a combined mass of 200 kg. A constant frictional force of 4,000 N retards its motion upward. What force must the motor provide for the elevator to move with an upward acceleration of 1 ms^{-2}? Assume: $g = 10$ ms^{-2}

A. 1,190 N
B. 11,900 N
C. 18,000 N

D. 22,000 N
E. 23,800 N

Question 101:

A 1,000 kg car accelerates from rest at 5 ms^{-2} for 10 s. Then, a braking force is applied to bring it to rest within 20 seconds. What distance has the car travelled?

A. 125 m
B. 250 m

C. 650 m
D. 750 m

E. 1,200 m
F. More information needed

Question 102:

An electric heater is connected to 120 V mains by a copper wire that has a resistance of 8 ohms. What is the power of the heater?

A. 90 W
B. 180 W
C. 900 W
D. 1800 W

E. 9,000W
F. 18,000 W
G. More information needed

Question 103:

In a particle accelerator electrons are accelerated through a potential difference of 40 MV and emerge with an energy of 40MeV (1 MeV = 1.60 x 10^{-13} J). Each pulse contains 5,000 electrons. The current is zero between pulses. Assuming that the electrons have zero energy prior to being accelerated what is the power delivered by the electron beam?

A. 1 kW
B. 10 kW

C. 100 kW
D. 1,000 kW

E. 10,000 kW
F. More information needed

Question 104:

Which of the following statements is true?

A. When an object is in equilibrium with its surroundings, there is no energy transferred to or from the object and so its temperature remains constant.
B. When an object is in equilibrium with its surroundings, it radiates and absorbs energy at the same rate and so its temperature remains constant.
C. Radiation is faster than convection but slower than conduction.
D. Radiation is faster than conduction but slower than convection.
E. None of the above.

Question 105:

A 6kg block is pulled from rest along a horizontal frictionless surface by a constant horizontal force of 12 N. Calculate the speed of the block after it has moved 300 cm.

A. $2\sqrt{3}\ ms^{-1}$
B. $4\sqrt{3}\ ms^{-1}$
C. $4\sqrt{3}\ ms^{-1}$
D. $12\ ms^{-1}$

E. $\sqrt{\frac{3}{2}}\ ms^{-1}$

Question 106:

A 100 V heater heats 1.5 litres of pure water from 10°C to 50°C in 50 minutes. Given that 1 kg of pure water requires 4,000 J to raise its temperature by 1°C, calculate the resistance of the heater.

A. 12.5 ohms
B. 25 ohms
C. 125 ohms
D. 250 ohms
E. 500 ohms
F. 850 ohms

Question 107:

Which of the following statements are true?

1. Nuclear fission is the basis of nuclear energy.
2. Following fission, the resulting atoms are a different element to the original one.
3. Nuclear fission often results in the production of free neutrons and photons.

A. Only 1
B. Only 2
C. Only 3
D. 1 and 2
E. 2 and 3
F. 1 and 3
G. 1, 2 and 3
H. None of the statements are true

Question 108:

Which of the following statements are true? Assume $g = 10$ ms^{-2}.

1. Gravitational potential energy is defined as $\Delta E_p = m \times g \times \Delta h$.
2. Gravitational potential energy is a measure of the work done against gravity.
3. A reservoir situated 1 km above ground level with 10^6 litres of water has a potential energy of 1 Giga Joule.

A. Only 1
B. Only 2
C. Only 3
D. 1 and 2
E. 2 and 3
F. 1 and 3
G. 1, 2 and 3
H. None of the statements are true

Question 109:

Which of the following statements are correct in relation to Newton's 3rd law?

1. For every action there is an equal and opposite reaction.
2. According to Newton's 3rd law, there are no isolated forces.
3. Rockets cannot accelerate in deep space because there is nothing to generate an equal and opposite force.

A. Only 1
B. Only 2
C. Only 3
D. 1 and 2
E. 2 and 3
F. 1 and 3

Question 110:

Which of the following statements are correct?

1. Positively charged objects have gained electrons.
2. Electrical charge in a circuit over a period of time can be calculated if the voltage and resistance are known.
3. Objects can be charged by friction.

A. Only 1
B. Only 2
C. Only 3
D. 1 and 2

E. 2 and 3
F. 1 and 3
G. 1, 2 and 3

Question 111:

Which of the following statements is true?

A. The gravitational force between two objects is independent of their mass.
B. Each planet in the solar system exerts a gravitational force on the Earth.
C. For satellites in a geostationary orbit, acceleration due to gravity is equal and opposite to the lift from engines.
D. Two objects that are dropped from the Eiffel tower will always land on the ground at the same time if they have the same mass.
E. All of the above.
F. None of the above.

Question 112:

Which of the following best defines an electrical conductor?

A. Conductors are usually made from metals and they conduct electrical charge in multiple directions.
B. Conductors are usually made from non-metals and they conduct electrical charge in multiple directions.
C. Conductors are usually made from metals and they conduct electrical charge in one fixed direction.
D. Conductors are usually made from non-metals and they conduct electrical charge in one fixed direction.
E. Conductors allow the passage of electrical charge with zero resistance because they contain freely mobile charged particles.
F. Conductors allow the passage of electrical charge with maximal resistance because they contain charged particles that are fixed and static.

Question 113:

An 800 kg compact car delivers 20% of its power output to its wheels. If the car has a mileage of 30 miles/gallon and travels at a speed of 60 miles/hour, how much power is delivered to the wheels? 1 gallon of petrol contains 9 x 10^8 J.

A. 10 kW   B. 20 kW   C. 40 kW   D. 50 kW   E. 100 kW

Question 114:

Which of the following statements about beta radiation are true?

1. After a beta particle is emitted, the atomic mass number is unchanged.
2. Beta radiation can penetrate paper but not aluminium foil.
3. A beta particle is emitted from the nucleus of the atom when an electron changes into a neutron.

A. 1 only
B. 2 only

C. 1 and 3
D. 1 and 2

E. 2 and 3
F. 1, 2 and 3

Question 115:
A car with a weight of 15,000 N is travelling at a speed of 15 ms^{-1} when it crashes into a wall and is brought to rest in 10 milliseconds. Calculate the average braking force exerted on the car by the wall. Take $g = 10$ ms^{-2}

A. $1.25 \times 10^4 N$
B. $1.25 \times 10^5 N$

C. $1.25 \times 10^6 N$
D. $2.25 \times 10^4 N$

E. $2.25 \times 10^5 N$
F. $2.25 \times 10^6 N$

Question 116:
Which of the following statements are correct?

1.   Electrical insulators are usually metals e.g. copper.
2.   The flow of charge through electrical insulators is extremely low.
3.   Electrical insulators can be charged by rubbing them together.

A.   Only 1
B.   Only 2
C.   Only 3
D.   1 and 2

 E.   2 and 3
F.   1 and 3
G.   1, 2 and 3

The following information is needed for Questions 117 and 118:

The graph below represents a car's movement. At t=0 the car's displacement was 0 m.

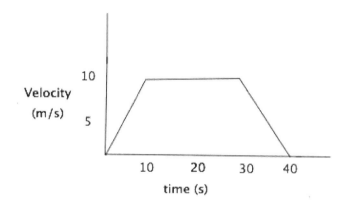

Question 117:
Which of the following statements are **NOT true**?

1.   The car is reversing after t = 30.
2.   The car moves with constant acceleration from t = 0 to t = 10.
3.   The car moves with constant speed from t = 10 to t = 30.

 A.   1 only
B.   2 only
C.   3 only
D.   1 and 3

E.   1 and 2
F.   2 and 3
G.   1, 2 and 3

Question 118:
Calculate the distance travelled by the car.

 A.   200 m
B.   300 m

C.   350 m
D.   400 m

E.   500 m
F.   More information needed

Question 119:
A 1,000 kg rocket is launched during a thunderstorm and reaches a constant velocity 30 seconds after launch. Suddenly, a strong gust of wind acts on it for 5 seconds with a force of 10,000 N in the direction of movement. What is the resulting change in velocity?

A. 0.5 ms^{-1} C. 50 ms^{-1} E. 5000 ms^{-1}

B. 5 ms^{-1} D. 500 ms^{-1} F. More information needed

Question 120:
A 0.5 tonne crane lifts a 0.01 tonne wardrobe by 100 cm in 5,000 milliseconds.
Calculate the average power developed by the crane. Take $g = 10$ ms^{-2}.

A. 0.2 W   C. 5 W   E. 50 W

B. 2 W   D. 20 W   F. More information needed

Question 121:
A 20 V battery is connected to a circuit consisting of a 1 Ω and 2 Ω resistor in parallel. Calculate the overall current of the circuit.

A. 6.67 A   B. 8 A   C. 10 A   D. 12 A   E. 20 A   F. 30 A

Question 122:
Which of the following statements is correct?

A. The speed of light changes when it enters water.
B. The speed of light changes when it leaves water.
C. The direction of light changes when it enters water.
D. The direction of light changes when it leaves water.
E. All of the above.
F. None of the above.

Question 123:
In a parallel circuit, a 60 V battery is connected to two branches. Branch A contains 6 identical 5 Ω resistors and branch B contains 2 identical 10 Ω resistors.

Calculate the current in branches A and B.

	I_A (A)	I_B (A)
A	0	6
B	6	0
C	2	3
D	3	2
E	3	3
F	1	5
G	5	1

Question 124:

Calculate the voltage of an electrical circuit that has a power output of 50,000,000,000 nW and a current of 0.000000004 GA.

A. 0.0125 GV

B. 0.0125 MV

C. 0.0125 kV

D. 0.0125 V

E. 0.0125 mV

F. 0.0125 μV

G. 0.0125 nV

Question 125:

Which of the following statements about radioactive decay is correct?

A. Radioactive decay is highly predictable.

B. An unstable element will continue to decay until it reaches a stable nuclear configuration.

C. All forms of radioactive decay release gamma rays.

D. All forms of radioactive decay release X-rays.

E. An atom's nuclear charge is unchanged after it undergoes alpha decay.

F. None of the above.

Question 126:

A circuit contains three identical resistors of unknown resistance connected in series with a 15 V battery. The power output of the circuit is 60 W.

Calculate the overall resistance of the circuit when two further identical resistors are added to it.

A. 0.125 Ω

B. 1.25 Ω

C. 3.75 Ω

D. 6.25 Ω

E. 18.75 Ω

F. More information needed.

Question 127:

A 5,000 kg tractor's engine uses 1 litre of fuel to move 0.1 km. 1 ml of the fuel contains 20 kJ of energy. Calculate the engine's efficiency. Take $g = 10$ ms^{-2}

A. 2.5 %

B. 25 %

C. 38 %

D. 50 %

E. 75 %

F. More information needed.

Question 128:

Which of the following statements are correct?

1. Electromagnetic induction occurs when a wire moves relative to a magnet.
2. Electromagnetic induction occurs when a magnetic field changes.
3. An electrical current is generated when a coil rotates in a magnetic field.

A. Only 1

B. Only 2

C. Only 3

D. 1 and 2

E. 2 and 3

F. 1 and 3

G. 1, 2 and 3

Question 129:

Which of the following statements are correct regarding parallel circuits?

1.   The current flowing through a branch is dependent on the branch's resistance.
2.   The total current flowing into the branches is equal to the total current flowing out of the branches.
3.   An ammeter will always give the same reading regardless of its location in the circuit.

A.   Only 1
B.   Only 2
C.   Only 3
D.   1 and 2

E.   2 and 3
F.   1 and 3
G.   All of the above

Question 130:

Which of the following statements regarding series circuits are true?

1.   The overall resistance of a circuit is given by the sum of all resistors in the circuit.
2.   Electrical current moves from the positive terminal to the negative terminal.
3.   Electrons move from the positive terminal to the negative terminal.

A.   Only 1
B.   Only 2

C.   Only 3
D.   1 and 2

E.   2 and 3
F.   1 and 3

Question 131:

The graphs below show current vs. voltage plots for 4 different electrical components.

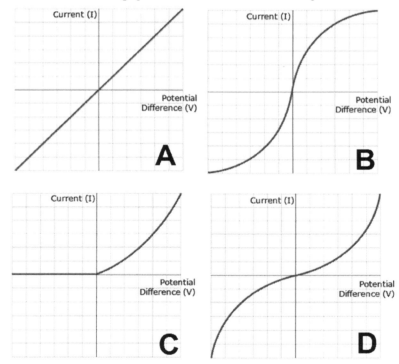

Which of the following graphs represents a resistor at constant temperature, and which a filament lamp?

	Fixed Resistor	Filament Lamp
A	A	B
B	A	C
C	A	D
D	C	A
E	C	C
F	C	D

Question 132:

Which of the following statements are true about vectors?

A. Vectors can be added or subtracted.
B. All vector quantities have a defined magnitude.
C. All vector quantities have a defined direction.
D. Displacement is an example of a vector quantity.
E. All of the above.
F. None of the above.

Question 133:

The acceleration due to gravity on the Earth is six times greater than that on the moon. Dr Tyson records the weight of a rock as 250 N on the moon.

Calculate the rock's density given that it has a volume of 250 cm³. Take g_{Earth} = 10 ms^{-2}

A. 0.2 kg/cm³   C. 0.6 kg/cm³   E. 0.8 kg/cm³
B. 0.5 kg/cm³   D. 0.7 kg/cm³   F. More information needed.

Question 134:

A radioactive element X_{78}^{225} undergoes alpha decay. What is the atomic mass and atomic number after 5 alpha particles have been released?

	Mass Number	Atomic Number
A	200	56
B	200	58
C	205	64
D	205	68
E	215	58
F	215	73
G	225	78
H	225	83

Question 135:

A 20 A current passes through a circuit with resistance of 10 Ω. The circuit is connected to a transformer that contains a primary coil with 5 turns and a secondary coil with 10 turns. Calculate the potential difference exiting the transformer.

A. 100 V   E. 2,000 V
B. 200 V   F. 4,000 V
C. 400 V   G. 5,000 V
D. 500 V

Question 136:

A metal sphere of unknown mass is dropped from an altitude of 1 km and reaches terminal velocity 300 m before it hits the ground. Given that resistive forces do a total of 10 kJ of work for the last 100 m before the ball hits the ground, calculate the mass of the ball. Take g = 10ms^{-2}.

A. 1 kg   C. 5 kg   E. 20 kg
B. 2 kg   D. 10 kg   F. More information needed.

Question 137:
Which of the following statements is true about the electromagnetic spectrum?

A. The wavelength of ultraviolet waves is shorter than that of x-rays.
B. For waves in the electromagnetic spectrum, wavelength is directly proportional to frequency.
C. Most electromagnetic waves can be stopped with a thin layer of aluminium.
D. Waves in the electromagnetic spectrum travel at the speed of sound.
E. Humans are able to visualise the majority of the electromagnetic spectrum.
F. None of the above.

Question 138:
In relation to the Doppler Effect, which of the following statements are true?

1. If an object emitting a wave moves towards the sensor, the wavelength increases and frequency decreases.
2. An object that originally emitted a wave of a wavelength of 20 mm followed by a second reading delivering a wavelength of 15 mm is moving towards the sensor.
3. The faster the object is moving away from the sensor, the greater the increase in frequency.

A. Only 1
B. Only 2
C. Only 3
D. 1 and 2

E. 1 and 3
F. 2 and 3
G. 1, 2 and 3
H. None of the above statements are true.

Question 139:
A 5 g bullet is travels at 1 km/s and hits a brick wall. It penetrates 50 cm before being brought to rest 100 ms after impact. Calculate the average braking force exerted by the wall on the bullet.

A. 50 N
B. 500 N

C. 5,000 N
D. 50,000 N

E. 500,000 N
F. More information needed.

Question 140:
Polonium (Po) is a highly radioactive element that has no known stable isotope. Po^{210} undergoes radioactive decay to Pb^{206} and Y. Calculate the number of protons in 10 moles of Y. [Avogadro's Constant = 6×10^{23}]

A. 0
B. 1.2×10^{24}

C. 1.2×10^{25}
D. 2.4×10^{24}

E. 2.4×10^{25}
F. More information needed

Question 141:
Dr Sale measures the background radiation in a nuclear wasteland to be 1,000 Bq. He then detects a spike of 16,000 Bq from a nuclear rod made up of an unknown material. 300 days later, he visits and can no longer detect a reading higher than 1,000 Bq from the rod, even though it hasn't been disturbed.
What is the longest possible half-life of the nuclear rod?

A. 25 days
B. 50 days

C. 75 days
D. 100 days

E. 150 days
F. More information needed

Question 142:

A radioactive element Y_{89}^{200} undergoes a series of beta (β^-) and gamma decays. What are the number of protons and neutrons in the element after the emission of 5 beta particles and 2 gamma waves?

	Protons	Neutrons
A	79	101
B	84	111
C	84	116
D	89	111
E	89	106
F	94	111
G	94	106
H	109	111

Question 143:

Most symphony orchestras tune to 'standard pitch' (frequency = 440 Hz). When they are tuning, sound directly from the orchestra reaches audience members that are 500 m away in 1.5 seconds.
Estimate the wavelength of 'standard pitch'.

  0.05 m
B. 0.5 m

  0.75 m
D. 1.5 m

E. 15 m
F. More information needed

Question 144:

A 1 kg cylindrical artillery shell with a radius of 50 mm is fired at a speed of 200 ms^{-1}. It strikes an armour plated wall and is brought to rest in 500 μs.

Calculate the average pressure exerted on the entire shell by the wall at the time of impact.

A. 5×10^6 Pa
B. 5×10^7 Pa

C. 5×10^8 Pa
D. 5×10^9 Pa

E. 5×10^{10} Pa
F. More information needed

Question 145:

A 1,000 W display fountain launches 120 litres of water straight up every minute. Given that the fountain is 10% efficient, calculate the maximum possible height that the stream of water could reach.
Assume that there is negligible air resistance and $g = 10$ ms^{-2}.

A. 1 m
B. 5 m

C. 10 m
D. 20 m

E. 50m
F. More information needed

Question 146:

In relation to transformers, which of the following is true?
1. Step up transformers increase the voltage leaving the transformer.
2. In step down transformers, the number of turns in the primary coil is smaller than in the secondary coil.
3. For transformers that are 100% efficient: $I_p V_p = I_s V_s$

A. Only 1
B. Only 2
C. Only 3
D. 1 and 2

E. 1 and 3
F. 2 and 3
G. 1, 2 and 3
H. None of the above.

Question 147:

The half-life of Carbon-14 is 5,730 years. A bone is found that contains 6.25% of the amount of C^{14} that would be found in a modern one. How old is the bone?

A. 11,460 years
B. 17,190 years
C. 22,920 years
D. 28,650 years
E. 34,380 years
F. 40,110 years

Question 148:

A wave has a velocity of 2,000 mm/s and a wavelength of 250 cm. What is its frequency in MHz?

A. 8×10^{-3} MHz
B. 8×10^{-4} MHz
C. 8×10^{-5} MHz
D. 8×10^{-6} MHz
E. 8×10^{-7} MHz
F. 8×10^{-8} MHz

Question 149:

A radioactive element has a half-life of 25 days. After 350 days it has a count rate of 50. What was its original count rate?

A. 102,400
B. 162,240
C. 204,800
D. 409,600
E. 819,200
F. 1,638,400
G. 3,276,800

Question 150:

Which of the following units is **NOT** equivalent to a Volt (V)?

A. $A\Omega$
B. WA^{-1}
C. $Nms^{-1}A^{-1}$
D. NmC
E. JC^{-1}
F. $JA^{-1}s^{-1}$

SECTION 1C: Chemistry

Most students don't struggle with NSAA chemistry - however, there are certain questions that even good students tend to struggle with under time pressure e.g. balancing equations and mass calculations. It is essential that you're able to do these quickly as they take up by far the most time in the chemistry questions.

Balancing Equations

For some reason, most students are rarely shown how to formally balance equations – including those studying it at A-level. Balancing equations intuitively or via trial and error will only get you so far in the NSAA as the equations you'll have to work with will be fairly complex. To avoid wasting valuable time, it is essential you learn a method that will allow you to solve these in less than 60 seconds on a consistent basis. The method shown below is the simplest way and requires you to be able to do quick mental arithmetic (which is something you should be aiming for anyway). The easiest way to do learn it is through an example:

The following equation shows the reaction between Iodic acid, hydrochloric acid and copper Iodide:

$$\textbf{a } HIO_3 + \textbf{b } CuI_2 + \textbf{c } HCl \rightarrow \textbf{d } CuCl_3 + \textbf{e } ICl + \textbf{f } H_2O$$

What values of **a**, **b**, **c**, **d**, **e** and **f** are needed in order to balance the equation?

	a	b	c	d	e	f
A	5	4	25	4	13	15
B	5	4	20	4	8	15
C	5	6	20	6	8	15
D	2	8	10	8	8	15
E	6	8	24	10	16	15
F	6	10	22	10	16	15

Step 1: Pick an element and see how many atoms there are on the left and right sides.

Step 2: Form an equation to represent this. For Cu: b = d

Step 3: See if any of the answer options don't satisfy b=d. In this case, for option **E**, b is 8 and d is 10. This allows us to eliminate option E.

Once you've eliminated as many options as possible, go back to step 1 and pick another element.
For Hydrogen (H): a + c = 2f

Then see if any of the answer options don't satisfy a + c = 2f.

➢ Option **A**: 5 + 25 is equal to 2 x 15
➢ Option **B**: 5 + 20 is not equal to 2 x 15
➢ Option **C**: 5 + 20 is not equal to 2 x 15
➢ Option **D**: 2 + 10 is not equal to 2 x 15
This allows us to eliminate option **B, C & D**. Since **E** was eliminated earlier, **A** is the only possible solution. This method works best when you get given a table above as this allows you to quickly eliminate options. However, it is still a viable method even if you don't get this information.

Chemistry Calculations

Equations you **MUST** know:

- Number of moles $n = \frac{m}{M_r}$

- Amount (mol) = Concentration (mol/dm³) x Volume (dm³)

- Gas law $pV = NRT$

- Enthalpy of formation $\Delta H_f^{\ominus} = \Delta H_{products}^{\ominus} - \Delta H_{reactants}^{\ominus}$

- Enthalpy of combustion $\Delta H_c^{\ominus} = \Delta H_{reactants}^{\ominus} - \Delta H_{products}^{\ominus}$

- pH formula $pH = -log_{10}([H^+])$

- Equilibrium $[A] + [B] = [C] + [D]$

- Equilibrium constant $10^{-pK} = \frac{[A][B]}{[C][D]}$

Essential constants

- Atomic mass constant u = 1.66×10^{-27} kg
- Atomic mass of Hydrogen = 1u
- Atomic mass of Carbon = 12u
- Avogadro's constant $R_a = 6.023 \times 10^{23}$

Avogadro's Constant:

One mole of anything contains 6 x 10^{23} of it e.g. 5 Moles of water contain 5 x 6 x 10^{23} number of water molecules.

Abundances:

The average atomic mass takes the abundances of all isotopes into account. Thus:

A_r = (Abundance of Isotope 1) x (Mass of Isotope 1) + (Abundance of Isotope 2) x (Mass of Isotope 2) +…

Chemistry Questions

Question 151:

Which of the following most accurately defines an isotope?

A. An isotope is an atom of an element that has the same number of protons in the nucleus but a different number of neutrons orbiting the nucleus.
B. An isotope is an atom of an element that has the same number of neutrons in the nucleus but a different number of protons orbiting the nucleus.
C. An isotope is any atom of an element that can be split to produce nuclear energy.
D. An isotope is an atom of an element that has the same number of protons in the nucleus but a different number of neutrons in the nucleus.
E. An isotope is an atom of an element that has the same number of protons in the nucleus but a different number of electrons orbiting it.

Question 152:

Which of the following is an example of a displacement reaction?

1. $Fe + SnSO4 \rightarrow FeSO_4 + Sn$
2. $Cl_2 + 2KBr \rightarrow Br_2 + 2KCl$
3. $H_2SO_4 + Mg \rightarrow MgSO_4 + H_2$
4. $Pb(NO_3)_2 + 2NaCl \rightarrow PbCl_2 + 2NaNO_3$

A. 1 only
B. 1 and 2 only
C. 2 and 3 only
D. 3 and 4 only
E. 1, 2 and 3 only
F. 1,2, 3 and 4 only

Question 153:

What values of **a**, **b** and **c** are needed to balance the equation below?

$$aCa(OH)_2 + bH_3PO_4 \rightarrow Ca_3(PO_4)_2 + cH_2O$$

A. $a = 3\ b = 2\ c = 6$
B. $a = 2\ b = 2\ c = 4$
C. $a = 3\ b = 2\ c = 1$
D. $a = 1\ b = 2\ c = 3$
E. $a = 4\ b = 2\ c = 6$
F. $a = 3\ b = 2\ c = 4$

Question 154:

What values of **s**, **t** and **u** are needed to balance the equation below?

$$sAgNO_3 + tK_3PO_4 \rightarrow 3Ag_3PO_4 + uKNO_3$$

A. $s = 9\ t = 3\ u = 9$
B. $s = 6\ t = 3\ u = 9$
C. $s = 9\ t = 3\ u = 6$
D. $s = 9\ t = 6\ u = 9$
E. $s = 3\ t = 3\ u = 9$
F. $s = 9\ t = 3\ u = 3$

Question 155:
Which of the following statements are true with regard to displacement?

1. A less reactive halogen can displace a more reactive halogen.
2. Chlorine cannot displace bromine or iodine from an aqueous solution of its salts.
3. Bromine can displace iodine because of the trend of reactivity.
4. Fluorine can displace chlorine as it is higher up the group.
5. Lithium can displace francium as it is higher up the group.

A. 3 only
B. 5 only
C. 1 and 2 only

D. 3 and 4 only
E. 2 , 3 and 5 only
F. 3, 4 and 5 only

Question 156:
What mass of magnesium oxide is produced when 75g of magnesium is burned in excess oxygen?
Relative Atomic Masses: Mg = 24, O = 16

A. 80g   B. 100g   C. 125g   D. 145g   E. 175g   F. 225g

Question 157:
Hydrogen can combine with hydroxide ions to produce water. Which process is involved in this?

A. Hydration
B. Oxidation

C. Reduction
D. Dehydration

E. Evaporation
F. Precipitation

Question 158:
Which of the following statements about Ammonia are correct?

1. It has a formula of NH_3.
2. Nitrogen contributes 82% to its mass.
3. It can be broken down again into nitrogen and hydrogen.
4. It is covalently bonded.
5. It is used to make fertilisers.

A. 1 and 2 only
B. 1 and 4 only
C. 1, 2 and 3 only

D. 1, 2 and 5 only
E. 3, 4 and 5 only
F. 1, 2, 3, 4 and 5

Question 159:
What colour will a universal indicator change to in a solution of milk and lipase?

A. From green to orange.
B. From red to green.
C. From purple to green.

D. From purple to orange.
E. From yellow to purple.
F. From purple to red.

Question 160:
Vitamin C [$C_6H_8O_6$] can be artificially synthesised from glucose [$C_6H_{12}O_6$]. What type of reaction is this likely to be?

A. Dehydration
B. Hydration

C. Oxidation
D. Reduction

E. Displacement
F. Evaporation

Question 161:

Which of the following statements are true?

1. Cu^{64} will undergo oxidation faster than Cu^{65}.
2. Cu^{65} will undergo reduction faster than Cu^{64}.
3. Cu^{65} and Cu^{64} have the same number of electrons.

A. 1 only	C. 3 only	E. 1 and 3 only
B. 2 only	D. 2 and 3 only	F. 1, 2 and 3

Question 162:

6g of Mg^{24} is added to a solution containing 30g of dissolved sulphuric acid (H_2SO_4). Which of the following statements are true?
Relative Atomic Masses: S = 32, Mg = 24, O = 16, H = 1

1. In this reaction, the magnesium is the limiting reagent
2. In this reaction, sulphuric acid is the limiting reagent
3. The mass of salt produced equals the original mass of sulphuric acid

A. 1 only	C. 3 only	E. 1 and 3 only
B. 2 only	D. 1 and 2 only	F. 2 and 3 only

Question 163:

In which of the following mixtures will a displacement reaction occur?

1. $Cu + 2AgNO_3$
2. $Cu + Fe(NO_3)_2$
3. $Ca + 2H_2O$
4. $Fe + Ca(OH)_2$

A. 1 only	C. 3 only	E. 1 and 2 only	G. 1, 2 and 3
B. 2 only	D. 4 only	F. 1 and 3 only	H. 1, 2, 3 and 4

Question 164:

Which of the following statements is true about the following chain of metals?

$$Na \rightarrow Ca \rightarrow Mg \rightarrow Al \rightarrow Zn$$

Moving from left to right:

1. The reactivity of the metals increases.
2. The likelihood of corrosion of the metals increases.
3. More energy is required to separate these metals from their ores.
4. The metals lose electrons more readily to form positive ions.

A.   1 and 2 only
B.   1and 3 only
C.   2 and 3 only
D.   1 and 4 only
E.   2, 3 and 4 only
F.   1, 2, 3 and 4
G.   None of the statements is correct.

Question 165:
In which of the following mixtures will a displacement reaction occur?

1. $I_2 + 2KBr$
2. $Cl_2 + 2NaBr$
3. $Br_2 + 2KI$

A. 1 only
B. 2 only
C. 3 only
D. 1 and 2 only
E. 1 and 3 only
F. 2 and 3 only
G. 1, 2 and 3

Question 166:
Which of the following statements about Al and Cu are true?

1. Al is used to build aircraft because it is lightweight and resists corrosion.
2. Cu is used to build electrical wires because it is a good insulator.
3. Both Al and Cu are good conductors of heat.
4. Al is commonly alloyed with other metals to make coins.
5. Al is resistant to corrosion because of a thin layer of aluminium hydroxide on its surface.

A. 1 and 3 only
B. 1 and 4 only
C. 1, 3 and 5 only
D. 1, 3, 4, 5 only
E. 2, 4 and 5 only
F. 2, 3, 4, 5 only

Question 167:
21g of Li^7 reacts completely with excess water. Given that the molar gas volume is 24 dm^3 under the conditions, what is the volume of hydrogen produced?

A. 12 dm^3
B. 24 dm^3
C. 36 dm^3
D. 48 dm^3
E. 72 dm^3
F. 120 dm^3

Question 168:
Which of the following statements regarding bonding are true?

1. NaCl has stronger ionic bonds than $MgCl_2$.
2. Transition metals are able to lose varying numbers of electrons to form multiple stable positive ions.
3. All covalently bonded structures have lower melting points than ionically bonded compounds.
4. All covalently bonded structures do not conduct electricity.

A. 1 only
B. 2 only
C. 3 only
D. 4 only
E. 1 and 2 only
F. 2 and 3 only
G. 3 and 4 only
H. 1, 2 and 4 only

Question 169:

Consider the following two equations:

A.	$C + O_2 \rightarrow CO_2$	$\Delta H = -394$ kJ per mole
B.	$CaCO_3 \rightarrow CaO + CO_2$	$\Delta H = +178$ kJ per mole

Which of the following statements are true?

1. Reaction **A** is exothermic and Reaction **B** is endothermic.
2. CO_2 has less energy than C and O_2.
3. CaO is more stable than $CaCO_3$.

A. 1 only
B. 2 only
C. 3 only
D. 1 and 2
E. 1 and 3
F. 2 and 3
G. 1, 2 and 3

Question 170:

Which of the following are true of regarding the oxides formed by Na, Mg and Al?

1. All of the metals and their solid oxides conduct electricity.
2. MgO has stronger bonds than Na_2O.
3. Metals are extracted from their molten ores by fractional distillation.

A. 1 only
B. 2 only
C. 3 only
D. 1 and 2 only
E. 2 and 3 only
F. 1, 2 and 3

Question 171:

Which of the following pairs have the same electronic configuration?

1. Li^+ and Na^+
2. Mg^{2+} and Ne
3. Na^{2+} and Ne
4. O^{2+} and a Carbon atom

A. 1 only
B. 1 and 2 only
C. 1 and 3 only
D. 2 and 3 only
E. 2 and 4 only
F. 1, 2, 3 and 4

Question 172:

In relation to reactivity of elements in group 1 and 2, which of the following statements is correct?

1. Reactivity decreases as you go down group 1.
2. Reactivity increases as you go down group 2.
3. Group 1 metals are generally less reactive than group 2 metals.

A. Only 1
B. Only 2
C. Only 3
D. 1 and 2
E. 2 and 3
F. 1 and 3

Question 173:
What role do catalysts fulfil in an endothermic reaction?

A. They increase the temperature, causing the reaction to occur at a faster rate.
B. They decrease the temperature, causing the reaction to occur at a faster rate.
C. They reduce the energy of the reactants in order to trigger the reaction.
D. They reduce the activation energy of the reaction.
E. They increase the activation energy of the reaction.

Question 174:
Tritium H^3 is an isotope of Hydrogen. Why is tritium commonly referred to as 'heavy hydrogen'.

A. Because H^3 contains 3 protons making it heavier than H^1 that contains 1 proton.
B. Because H^3 contains 3 neutrons making it heavier than H^1 that contains 1 neutron.
C. Because H^3 contains 1 neutron and 2 protons making it heavier than H^1 that contains 1 neutron and 1 proton.
D. Because H^3 contains 1 proton and 2 neutrons making it heavier than H^1 that contains 1 proton.
E. Because H^3 contains 3 electrons making it heavier than H^1 that contains 1 electron.

Question 175:
In relation to redox reactions, which of the following statements are correct?

1. Oxidation describes the loss of electrons.
2. Reduction increases the electron density of an ion, atom or molecule.
3. Halogens are powerful reducing agents.

A. Only 1   C. Only 3   E. 2 and 3
B. Only 2   D. 1 and 2   F. 1 and 3

Question 176:
Which of the following statements is correct?

A. At higher temperatures, gas molecules move at angles that cause them to collide with each other more frequently.
B. Gas molecules have lower energy after colliding with each other.
C. At higher temperatures, gas molecules attract each other resulting in more collisions.
D. The average kinetic energy of gas molecules is the same for all gases at the same temperature.
E. The momentum of gas molecules decreases as pressure increases.

Question 177:
Which of the following are exothermic reactions?

1. Burning Magnesium in pure oxygen
2. The combustion of hydrogen
3. Aerobic respiration
4. Evaporation of water in the oceans
5. Reaction between a strong acid and a strong base

A. 1, 2 and 4   C. 1, 3 and 5   E. 1, 2, 3 and 5
B. 1, 2 and 5   D. 2, 3 and 4   F. 1, 2, 3, 4 and 5

Question 178:
Ethene reacts with oxygen to produce water and carbon dioxide. Which elements are oxidised/reduced?

A. Carbon is reduced and oxygen is oxidised.
B. Hydrogen is reduced and oxygen is oxidised.
C. Carbon is oxidised and hydrogen is reduced.
D. Hydrogen is oxidised and carbon is reduced.
E. Carbon is oxidised and oxygen is reduced.
F. None of the above.

Question 179:
In the reaction between Zinc and Copper (II) sulphate which elements act as oxidising + reducing agents?

A. Zinc is the reducing agent while sulfur is the oxidizing agent.
B. Zinc is the reducing agent while copper in $CuSO_4$ is the oxidizing agent.
C. Copper is the reducing agent while zinc is the oxidizing agent.
D. Oxygen is the reducing agent while copper in $CuSO_4$ is the oxidizing agent.
E. Sulfur is the reducing agent while oxygen is the oxidizing agent.
F. None of the above.

Question 180:
Which of the following statements is true?

A. Acids are compounds that act as proton acceptors in aqueous solution.
B. Acids only exist in a liquid state.
C. Strong acids are partially ionized in a solution.
D. Weak acids generally have a pH or 6 - 7.
E. The reaction between a weak and strong acid produces water and salt.

Question 181:
An unknown element, Z, has 3 isotopes: Z^5, Z^6 and Z^8. Given that the atomic mass of Z is 7, and the relative abundance of Z^5 is 20%, which of the following statements are correct?

1. Z^5 and Z^6 are present in the same abundance.
2. Z^8 is the most abundant of the isotopes.
3. Z^8 is more abundant than Z^5 and Z^6 combined.

A. 1 only
B. 2 only
C. 3 only
D. 1 and 2 only

E. 2 and 3 only
F. 1 and 3 only
G. 1, 2 and 3
H. None of the statements are correct.

Question 182:
Which of following best describes the products when an acid reacts with a metal that is more reactive than hydrogen?

A. Salt and hydrogen
B. Salt and ammonia
C. Salt and water
D. A weak acid and a weak base
E. A strong acid and a strong base
F. No reaction would occur.

Question 183:

Choose the option which balances the following equation:

$$\textbf{a } FeSO_4 + \textbf{b } K_2Cr_2O_7 + \textbf{c } H_2SO_4 \rightarrow \textbf{d } (Fe)_2(SO_4)_3 + \textbf{e } Cr_2(SO_4)_3 + \textbf{f } K_2SO_4 + \textbf{g } H_2O$$

	a	b	c	d	e	f	g
A	6	1	8	3	1	1	7
B	6	1	7	3	1	1	7
C	2	1	6	2	1	1	6
D	12	1	14	4	1	1	14
E	4	1	12	4	1	1	12
F	8	1	8	4	2	1	8

Question 184:

Which of the following statements is correct?

A. Matter consists of atoms that have a net electrical charge.
B. Atoms and ions of the same element have different numbers of protons and electrons but the same number of neutrons.
C. Over 80% of an atom's mass is provided by protons.
D. Atoms of the same element that have different numbers of neutrons react at significantly different rates.
E. Protons in the nucleus of atoms repel each other as they are positively charged.
F. None of the above.

Question 185:

Which of the following statements is correct?

A. The noble gasses are chemically inert and therefore useless to man.
B. All the noble gasses have a full outer electron shell.
C. The majority of noble gasses are brightly coloured.
D. The boiling point of the noble gasses decreases as you progress down the group.
E. Neon is the most abundant noble gas.

Question 186:

In relation to alkenes, which of the following statements is correct?

1. They all contain double bonds.
2. They can all be reduced to alkanes.
3. Aromatic compounds are also alkenes as they contain double bonds.

A. Only 1
B. Only 2
C. Only 3
D. 1 and 2

E. 2 and 3
F. 1 and 3
G. All of the above.
H. None of the above.

Question 187:

Chlorine is made up of two isotopes, Cl^{35} (atomic mass 34.969) and Cl^{37} (atomic mass 36.966). Given that the atomic mass of chlorine is 35.453, which of the following statements is correct?

A. Cl^{35} is about 3 times more abundant than Cl^{37}.
B. Cl^{35} is about 10 times more abundant than Cl^{37}.
C. Cl^{37} is about 3 times more abundant than Cl^{35}.
D. Cl^{37} is about 10 times more abundant than Cl^{35}.
E. Both isotopes are equally abundant.

Question 188:
Which of the following statements regarding transition metals is correct?

A. Transition metals form ions that have multiple colours.
B. Transition metals usually form covalent bonds.
C. Transition metals cannot be used as catalysts as they are too reactive.
D. Transition metals are poor conductors of electricity.
E. Transition metals are frequently referred to as f-block elements.

Question 189:
20 g of impure Na^{23} reacts completely with excess water to produce 8,000 cm^3 of hydrogen gas under standard conditions. What is the percentage purity of sodium?
[Under standard conditions 1 mole of gas occupies 24 dm^3]

A. 88.0%   B. 76.5%   C. 66.0%   D. 38.0%   E. 15.3%

Question 190:
An organic molecule contains 70.6% Carbon, 5.9% Hydrogen and 23.5% Oxygen. It has a molecular mass of 136. What is its chemical formula?

A. C_4H_4O B. C_5H_4O C. $C_8H_8O_2$ D. $C_{10}H_8O_2$ E. C_2H_2O

Question 191:
Choose the option which balances the following reaction:

$$aS + bHNO_3 \rightarrow cH_2SO_4 + dNO_2 + eH_2O$$

	a	b	c	d	e
A	3	5	3	5	1
B	1	6	1	6	2
C	6	14	6	14	2
D	2	4	2	4	4
E	2	3	2	3	2
F	4	4	4	4	2

Question 192:
Which of the following statements is true?
1. Ethane and ethene can both dissolve in organic solvents.
2. Ethane and ethene can both be hydrogenated in the presence of Nickel.
3. Breaking C=C requires double the energy needed to break C-C.

A. 1 only
B. 2 only
C. 3 only
D. 1 and 2 only
E. 2 and 3 only
F. 1 and 3 only
G. 1, 2 and 3

Question 193:

Diamond, Graphite, Methane and Ammonia all exhibit covalent bonding. Which row adequately describes the properties associated with each?

	Compound	Melting Point	Able to conduct electricity	Soluble in water
1.	Diamond	High	Yes	No
2.	Graphite	High	Yes	No
3.	$CH_{4 (g)}$	Low	No	No
4.	$NH_{3 (g)}$	Low	No	Yes

A. 1 and 2 only
B. 2 and 3 only
C. 1 and 3 only
D. 1 and 4 only

E. 1, 2 and 3
F. 2, 3 and 4
G. 1,2 and 4
H. 1, 2, 3 and 4

Question 194:

Which of the following statements about catalysts are true?

1. Catalysts reduce the energy required for a reaction to take place.
2. Catalysts are used up in reactions.
3. Catalysed reactions are almost always exothermic.

A. 1 only   B. 2 only   C. 1 and 2   D. 2 and 3   E. 1, 2 and

Question 195:

What is the name of the molecule below?

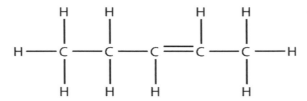

A. But-1-ene
B. But-2-ene
C. Pent-3-ene
D. Pent-1-ene
E. Pent-2-ene
F. Pentane
G. Pentanoic acid

Question 196:

Which of the following statements is correct regarding Group 1 elements? [Excluding Hydrogen]

A. The oxidation number of Group 1 elements usually decreases in most reactions.
B. Reactivity decreases as you progress down Group 1.
C. Group 1 elements do not react with water.
D. All Group 1 elements react instantaneously with oxygen.
E. All of the above.
F. None of the above.

Question 197:
Which of the following statements about electrolysis are correct?

1. The cathode attracts negatively charged ions.
2. Atoms are reduced at the anode.
3. Electrolysis can be used to separate mixtures.

A. Only 1
B. Only 2
C. Only 3
D. 1 and 2
E. 2 and 3
F. 1 and 3
G. 1, 2 and 3
H. None of the statement are correct.

Question 198:
Which of the following is **NOT** an isomer of pentane?

A. $CH_3CH_2CH_2CH_2CH_3$
B. $CH_3C(CH_3)CH_3CH_3$

C. $CH_3(CH_2)_3CH_3$
D. $CH_3C(CH_3)_2CH_3$

Question 199:
Choose the option which balances the following reaction:

$Cu + HNO_3 \rightarrow Cu(NO_3)_2 + NO + H_2O$

A. $8\ Cu + 3\ HNO_3 \rightarrow 8\ Cu(NO_3)_2 + 4\ NO + 2\ H_2O$
B. $3\ Cu + 8\ HNO_3 \rightarrow 2\ Cu(NO_3)_2 + 3\ NO + 4\ H_2O$
C. $5\ Cu + 7\ HNO_3 \rightarrow 5\ Cu(NO_3)_2 + 4\ NO + 8\ H_2O$
D. $6\ Cu + 10\ HNO_3 \rightarrow 6\ Cu(NO_3)_2 + 3\ NO + 7\ H_2O$
E. $3\ Cu + 8\ HNO_3 \rightarrow 3\ Cu(NO_3)_2 + 2\ NO + 4\ H_2O$

Question 200:
What of the following statements regarding alkenes is correct?

A. Alkenes are an inorganic homologous series.
B. Alkenes always have three times as many hydrogen atoms as they do carbon atoms.
C. Bromine water changes from clear to brown in the presence of an alkene.
D. Alkenes are more reactive than alkanes because they are unsaturated.
E. Alkenes frequently take part in subtraction reactions.
F. All of the above.

Question 201:
Which of the following statements is correct regarding Group 17?

A. All Group 17 elements are electrophilic and therefore form negatively charged ions.
B. All Group 17 elements are gasses a room temperature.
C. The reaction between Sodium and Fluorine is less vigorous than Sodium and Iodine.
D. All Group 17 elements are non-coloured.
E. Some Group 17 elements are found naturally as unbonded atoms.
F. All of the above.
G. None of the above.

Question 202:

Why does the electrolysis of NaCl solution (brine) require the strict separation of the products of anode and cathode?

A. To prevent the preferential discharge of ions.
B. In order to prevent spontaneous combustion.
C. In order to prevent production of H_2.
D. In order to prevent the formation of HCl.
E. In order to avoid CO poisoning.
F. All of the above.

Question 203:

In relation to the electrolysis of brine (NaCl), which of the following statements are correct?

1. Electrolysis results in the production of hydrogen and chlorine gas.
2. Electrolysis results in the production of sodium hydroxide.
3. Hydrogen gas is released at the anode and chlorine gas is released at the cathode.

A. Only 1
B. Only 2
C. Only 3
D. 1 and 2

E. 1 and 3
F. 2 and 3
G. All of the above

Question 204:

Which of the following statements is correct?

A. Alkanes consist of multiple C-H bonds that are very weak.
B. An alkane with 14 hydrogen atoms is called Heptane.
C. All alkanes consist purely of hydrogen and carbon atoms.
D. Alkanes burn in excess oxygen to produce carbon monoxide and water.
E. Bromine water is decolourised in the presence of an alkane.
F. None of the above.

Question 205:

Which of the following statements are correct?

1. All alcohols contain a hydroxyl functional group.
2. Alcohols are highly soluble in water.
3. Alcohols are sometimes used a biofuels.

A. Only 1
B. Only 2
C. Only 3
D. 1 and 2
E. 2 and 3
F. 1 and 3
G. 1, 2 and 3

Question 206:

Which row of the table below is correct?

	Non-Reducible Hydrocarbon			Reducible Hydrocarbon		
A	C_nH_{2n}	$Br_{2(aq)}$ remains brown	Saturated	C_nH_{2n+2}	Turns $Br_{2(aq)}$ colourless	Unsaturated
B	C_nH_{2n+2}	Turns $Br_{2(aq)}$ colourless	Unsaturated	C_nH_{2n}	$Br_{2(aq)}$ remains brown	Saturated
C	C_nH_{2n}	$Br_{2(aq)}$ remains brown	Unsaturated	C_nH_{2n+2}	Turns $Br_{2(aq)}$ colourless	Saturated
D	C_nH_{2n+2}	Turns $Br_{2(aq)}$ colourless	Saturated	C_nH_{2n}	$Br_{2(aq)}$ remains brown	Unsaturated
E	C_nH_{2n+2}	$Br_{2(aq)}$ remains brown	Saturated	C_nH_{2n}	Turns $Br_{2(aq)}$ colourless	Unsaturated

Question 207:

How many grams of magnesium chloride are formed when 10 grams of magnesium oxide are dissolved in excess hydrochloric acid? Relative atomic masses: $Mg = 24$, $O = 16$, $H = 1$, $Cl = 35.5$

A.   10.00
B.   14.95

C.   20.00
D.   23.75

E.   47.55
F.   More information needed

Question 208:

Pentadecane has the molecular formula $C_{15}H_{32}$. Which of the following statements is true?

A.   Pentadecane has a lower boiling point than pentane.
B.   Pentadecane is more flammable than pentane.
C.   Pentadecane is more volatile than pentane.
D.   Pentadecane is more viscous than pentane.
E.   All of the above.
F.   None of the above.

Question 209:

The rate of reaction is normally dependent upon:
1.   The temperature.
2.   The concentration of reactants.
3.   The concentration of the catalyst.
4.   The surface area of the catalyst.

A.   1 and 2
B.   2 and 3

C.   2, 3 and 4
D.   1, 3 and 4

E.   1, 2 and 3
F.   1, 2, 3 and 4

Question 210:

The equation below shows the complete combustion of a sample of unknown hydrocarbon in excess oxygen.

$$C_aH_b + O_2 \rightarrow cCO_2 + dH_2O$$

The product yielded 176 grams of CO_2 and 108 grams of H_2O. What is the most likely formula of the unknown hydrocarbon? Relative atomic masses: $H = 1$, $C = 12$, $O = 16$.

A. CH_4
B. CH_3

C. C_2H_6
D. C_3H_9

E. C_2H_4
F. C_4H_{10}

Question 211:
What type of reaction must ethanol undergo in order to be converted to ethylene oxide (C_2H_4O)?

A. Oxidation
B. Reduction
C. Dehydration
D. Hydration
E. Redox
F. All of the above

Question 212:
What values of a, b and c balance the equation below?

$$a\ Ba_3N_2 + 6H_2O \rightarrow b\ Ba(OH)_2 + c\ NH_3$$

	a	b	c
A	1	2	3
B	1	3	2
C	2	1	3
D	2	3	1
E	3	1	2
F	3	2	1

Question 213:
What values of a, b and c balance the equation below?

$$a\ FeS + 7O_2 \rightarrow b\ Fe_2O_3 + c\ SO_2$$

	a	b	c
A	3	2	2
B	2	4	1
C	3	1	5
D	4	1	3
E	4	2	4

Question 214:
Magnesium consists of 3 isotopes: Mg^{23}, Mg^{25}, and Mg^{26} which are found naturally in a ratio of 80:10:10. Calculate the relative atomic mass of magnesium.

A. 23.3   B. 23.4   C. 23.5   D. 23.6   E. 24.6   F. 25.2   G. 25.5

Question 215:
Consider the three reactions:
1. $Cl_2 + 2Br^- \rightarrow 2Cl^- + Br_2$
2. $Cu^{2+} + Mg \rightarrow Cu + Mg^{2+}$
3. $Fe_2O_3 + 3CO \rightarrow 2Fe + 3CO_2$

Which of the following statements are correct?

A. Cl_2 and Fe_2O_3 are reducing agents.
B. CO and Cu^{2+} are oxidising agents.
C. Br_2 is a stronger oxidising agent than Cl_2.
D. Mg is a stronger reducing agent than Cu.
E. All of the above.
F. None of the above.

Question 216:

Which row best describes the properties of NaCl?

	Melting Point	Solubility in Water	Conducts electricity?	
			As solid	In solution
A	High	Yes	Yes	Yes
B	High	No	Yes	No
C	High	Yes	No	Yes
D	High	No	No	No
E	Low	Yes	Yes	Yes
F	Low	No	Yes	No
G	Low	Yes	No	Yes
H	Low	No	No	No

Question 217:

80g of Sodium hydroxide reacts with excess zinc nitrate to produce zinc hydroxide. Calculate the mass of zinc hydroxide produced. Relative atomic mass: N = 14, Zn = 65, O = 16, Na = 23.

A. 49g

B. 95g

C. 99g

D. 100g

E. 198g

F. More information needed.

Question 218:

Which of the following statements is correct?

A. The reaction between all Group 1 metals and water is exothermic.

B. All Group 1 metals react with water to produce a metal hydroxide.

C. All Group 1 metals react with water to produce elemental hydrogen.

D. Sodium reacts less vigorously with water than Potassium.

E. All of the above.

F. None of the above.

Question 219:

Which of the following statements is correct?

A. NaCl can be separated using sieves.

B. CO_2 can be separated using electrolysis.

C. Dyes in a sample of ink can be separated using chromatography.

D. Oil and water can be separated using fractional distillation.

E. Methane and diesel can be separated using a separating funnel.

F. None of the above.

Question 220:
Which of the following statements about the reaction between caesium and fluoride are correct?

1. It is an exothermic reaction and therefore requires catalysts.
2. It results in the formation of a salt.
3. The addition of water will make the reaction safer.

A. Only 1
B. Only 2
C. Only 3
D. 1 and 2

E. 2 and 3
F. 1 and 3
G. All of the above.
H. None of the above.

Question 221:
Which of the following statements is generally true about stable isotopes?
1. The nucleus contains an equal number of neutrons and protons.
2. The nuclear charge is equal and opposite to the peripheral charge due to the orbiting electrons.
3. They can all undergo radioactive decay into more stable isotopes.

A. Only 1
B. Only 2
C. Only 3
D. 1 and 2

E. 2 and 3
F. 1 and 3
G. All of the above.
H. None of the above.

Question 222:
Why do most salts have very high melting temperatures?
A. Their surface is able to radiate away a significant portion of heat to their environment.
B. The ionic bonds holding them together are very strong.
C. The covalent bonds holding them together are very strong.
D. They tend to form large macromolecules as each salt molecule bonds with multiple other molecules.
E. All of the above.

Question 223:
A bottle of water contains 306ml of pure deionised water. How many protons are in the bottle from the water? Avogadro Constant = 6×10^{23}.

A. 1×10^{22} B. 1×10^{23} C. 1×10^{24} D. 1×10^{25} E. 1×10^{26}

Question 224:
On analysis, an organic substance is found to contain 41.4% Carbon, 55.2% Oxygen and 3.45% Hydrogen by mass. Which of the following could be the empirical formula of this substance?
A. $C_3O_3H_6$
B. $C_3O_3H_{12}$

C. $C_4O_2H_4$
D. $C_4O_4H_4$

E. $C_4O_2H_8$
F. More information needed.

Question 225:
A is a Group 2 element and B is a Group 17 element. Which row best describes what happens when A reacts with B?

	B is	Formula
A	Reduced	AB
B	Reduced	A_2B
C	Reduced	AB_2
D	Oxidised	AB
E	Oxidised	A_2B
F	Oxidised	AB_2

SECTION 1D: Biology

Thankfully, the biology questions tend to be fairly straightforward and require the least amount of time. You should be able to do the majority of these within the time limit (often far less). This means that you should be aiming to make up time in these questions. In the majority of cases – you'll either know the answer or not i.e. they test advanced recall so the trick is to ensure that there are no obvious gaps in your knowledge.

Before going onto to do the practice questions in this book, ensure you are comfortable with the following commonly tested topics:

- Structure of animal, plant and bacterial cells
- Osmosis, Diffusion and Active Transport
- Cell Division (mitosis + meiosis)
- Family pedigrees and Inheritance
- DNA structure and replication
- Gene Technology & Stem Cells
- Enzymes – Function, mechanism and examples of digestive enzymes
- Aerobic and Anaerobic Respiration

- The central vs. peripheral nervous system
- The respiratory cycle including movement of ribs and diaphragm
- The Cardiac Cycle
- Hormones
- Basic immunology
- Food chains and food webs
- The carbon and nitrogen cycles

tip! If you find yourself getting less than 50% of biology questions correct in this book, make sure you t the syllabus before attempting more questions as this is the best way to maximise your efficiency. In l there is no reason why you shouldn't be able to get the vast majority of biology questions correct (and in well under 60 seconds) with sufficient practice.

Biology Questions

Question 226:

In relation to the human genome, which of the following are correct?

1. The DNA genome is coded by 4 different bases.
2. The sugar backbone of the DNA strand is formed of glucose.
3. DNA is found in the nucleus of bacteria.

A. 1 only
B. 2 only
C. 3 only
D. 1 and 2
E. 1 and 3
F. 2 and 3
G. 1, 2 and 3

Question 227:

Animal cells contain organelles that take part in vital processes. Which of the following is true?

1. The majority of energy production by animal cells occurs in the mitochondria.
2. The cell wall protects the animal cell membrane from outside pressure differences.
3. The endoplasmic reticulum plays a role in protein synthesis.

A. 1 only
B. 2 only
C. 3 only
D. 1 and 2
E. 2 and 3
F. 1 and 3
G. 1, 2 and 3

Question 228:

With regards to animal mitochondria, which of the following is correct?

A. Mitochondria are not necessary for aerobic respiration.
B. Mitochondria are the sole cause of sperm cell movement.
C. The majority of DNA replication happens inside mitochondria.
D. Mitochondria are more abundant in fat cells than in skeletal muscle.
E. The majority of protein synthesis occurs in mitochondria.
F. Mitochondria are enveloped by a double membrane.

Question 229:

In relation to bacteria, which of the following is **FALSE**?

A. Bacteria always lead to disease.
B. Bacteria contain plasmid DNA.
C. Bacteria do not contain mitochondria.
D. Bacteria have a cell wall and a plasma membrane.
E. Some bacteria are susceptible to antibiotics.

Question 230:
In relation to bacterial replication, which of the following is correct?

A. Bacteria undergo sexual reproduction.
B. Bacteria have a nucleus.
C. Bacteria carry genetic information on circular plasmids.
D. Bacterial genomes are formed of RNA instead of DNA.
E. Bacteria require gametes to replicate.

Question 231:
Which of the following are correct regarding active transport?

A. ATP is necessary and sufficient for active transport.
B. ATP is not necessary but sufficient for active transport.
C. The relative concentrations of the material being transported have little impact on the rate of active transport.
D. Transport proteins are necessary and sufficient for active transport.
E. Active transport relies on transport proteins that are powered by an electrochemical gradient.

Question 232:
Concerning mammalian reproduction, which of the following is **FALSE**?

A. Fertilisation involves the fusion of two gametes.
B. Reproduction is sexual and the offspring display genetic variation.
C. Reproduction relies upon the exchange of genetic material.
D. Mammalian gametes are diploid cells produced via meiosis.
E. Embryonic growth requires carefully controlled mitosis.

Question 233:
Which of the following apply to Mendelian inheritance?

1. It only applies to plants.
2. It treats different traits as either dominant or recessive.
3. Heterozygotes have a 25% chance of expressing a recessive trait.

A. 1 only
B. 2 only
C. 3 only
D. 1 and 2
E. 1 and 3
F. 2 and 3
G. All of the above.

Question 234:
Which of the following statements are correct?

A. Hormones are secreted into the blood stream and act over long distances at specific target organs.
B. Hormones are substances that almost always cause muscles to contract.
C. Hormones have no impact on the nervous or enteric systems.
D. Hormones are always derived from food and never synthesised.
E. Hormones act rapidly to restore homeostasis.

Question 235:
With regard to neuronal signalling in the body, which of the following are true?

1. Neuronal transmission can be caused by both electrical and chemical stimulation.
2. Synapses ultimately result in the production of an electrical current for signal transduction.
3. All synapses in humans are electrical and unidirectional.

A. 1 only
B. 2 only
C. 3 only
D. 1 and 2
E. 1 and 3
F. 2 and 3
G. 1, 2 and 3

Question 236:
What is the **primary** reason that pH is controlled so tightly in humans?

A. To allow rapid protein synthesis.
B. To allow for effective digestion throughout the GI tract.
C. To ensure ions can function properly in neural signalling.
D. To prevent changes in electrical charge in polypeptide chains.
E. To prevent changes in core body temperature.

Question 237:
Which of the following statements are correct regarding cell walls?

1. The cell wall confers protection against external environmental stimuli.
2. The cell wall is an evolutionary remnant and now has little functional significance in most bacteria.
3. The cell wall is made up primarily of glucose.

A. Only 1
B. Only 2
C. Only 3
D. 1 and 2
E. 2 and 3
F. 1 and 3
G. 1, 2 and 3

Question 238:
Which of the following statements are correct regarding mitosis?

1. It is important in sexual reproduction.
2. A single round of mitosis results in the formation of 2 genetically distinct daughter cells.
3. Mitosis is vital for tissue growth, as it is the basis for cell multiplication.

A. Only 1
B. Only 2
C. Only 3
D. 1 and 2
E. 2 and 3
F. 1 and 3
G. 1, 2 and 3

Question 239:
Which of the following is the best definition of a mutation?

A. A mutation is a permanent change in DNA.
B. A mutation is a permanent change in DNA that is harmful to an organism.
C. A mutation is a permanent change in the structure of intra-cellular organelles caused by changes in DNA/RNA.
D. A mutation is a permanent change in chromosomal structure caused by DNA/RNA changes.

Question 340:
In relation to mutations, which of the following are correct?

1. Mutations always lead to discernible changes in the phenotype of an organism.
2. Mutations are central to natural processes such as evolution.
3. Mutations play a role in cancer.

A. Only 1
B. Only 2
C. Only 3
D. 1 and 2
E. 2 and 3
F. 1 and 3
G. 1, 2 and 3

Question 241:
Which of the following is the most accurate definition of an antibody?

A. An antibody is a molecule that protects red blood cells from changes in pH.
B. An antibody is a molecule produced only by humans and has a pivotal role in the immune system.
C. An antibody is a toxin produced by a pathogen to damage the host organism.
D. An antibody is a molecule that is used by the immune system to identify and neutralize foreign objects and molecules.
E. Antibodies are small proteins found in red blood cells that help increase oxygen carriage.

Question 242:
Which of the following statements about the kidney are correct?

1. The kidneys filter the blood and remove waste products from the body.
2. The kidneys are involved in the digestion of food.
3. In a healthy individual, the kidneys produce urine that contains high levels of glucose.

A. Only 1
B. Only 2
C. Only 3
D. 1 and 2
E. 2 and 3
F. 1 and 3
G. 1, 2 and 3

Question 243:
Which of the following statements are correct?

1. Hormones are slower acting than nerves.
2. Hormones act for a very short time.
3. Hormones act more generally than nerves.
4. Hormones are released when you get a scare.

A. 1 only
B. 1 and 3 only
C. 2 and 4 only
D. 1, 3 and 4 only
E. 1, 2, 3 and 4

Question 244:
Which statements about homeostasis are correct?

1. Homeostasis is about ensuring the inputs within your body exceed the outputs to maintain a constant internal environment.
2. Homeostasis is about ensuring the inputs within your body are less than the outputs to maintain a constant internal environment.
3. Homeostasis is about balancing the inputs within your body with the outputs to ensure your body fluctuates with the needs of the external environment.
4. Homeostasis is about balancing the inputs within your body with the outputs to maintain a constant internal environment.

A. 1 only
B. 2 only
C. 3 only
D. 4 only
E. 1 and 3 only
F. 2 and 4 only
G. 2 and 3 only

Question 245:
Which of the following statement is true?

A. There is more energy and biomass each time you move up a trophic level.
B. There is less energy and biomass each time you move up a trophic level.
C. There is more energy but less biomass each time you move up a trophic level.
D. There is less energy but more biomass each time you move up a trophic level.
E. There is no difference in the energy or biomass when you move up a trophic level.

Question 246:
Which of the following statements are true about asexual reproduction?

1. There is no fusion of gametes.
2. There are two parents.
3. There is no mixing of chromosomes.
4. There is genetic variation.

A. 1 and 3 only   C. 2 and 3 only   E. 2 and 4 only
B. 1 and 4 only   D. 3 and 4 only   F. 1, 2, 3 and 4

Question 247:
Put the following in the order which they occur when Jonas sees a bowl of chicken and moves towards it.

1. Retina
2. Motor neuron
3. Sensory neuron
4. Brain
5. Muscle

A. 1 - 3 - 4 - 5 - 2   D. 1 - 3 - 2 - 4 - 5
B. 1 - 2 - 3 - 4 - 5   E. 1 - 3 - 4 - 2 - 5
C. 5 - 1 - 3 - 2 - 4   F. 4 - 1 - 3 - 2 - 5

Question 248:
What path does blood take from the kidney to the liver?

1. Pulmonary artery
2. Inferior vena cava
3. Hepatic artery
4. Aorta
5. Pulmonary vein
6. Renal vein

A. 2 - 1 - 4 - 3 - 5 - 6   D. 6 - 2 - 1 - 5 - 4 - 3
B. 1 - 2 - 3 - 4 - 5 - 6   E. 3 - 2 - 1 - 4 - 6 - 5
C. 6 - 2 - 5 - 1 - 4 - 3   F. 3 - 6 - 2 - 4 - 1 – 5

Question 249:
Which of the following statements are true about animal cloning?

1. Animals cloned from embryo transplants are genetically identical.
2. The genetic material is removed from an unfertilised egg during adult cell cloning.
3. Cloning can cause a reduced gene pool.
4. Cloning is only possible with mammals.

A. 1 only
B. 2 only
C. 3 only
D. 4 only
E. 1 and 2 only
F. 1, 2 and 3 only
G. 1, 2, 3 and 4

Question 250:
Which of the following statements are true with regard to evolution?

1. Individuals within a species show variation because of differences in their genes.
2. Beneficial mutations will accumulate within a population.
3. Gene differences are caused by sexual reproduction and mutations.
4. Species with similar characteristics never have similar genes.

A. 1 only   C. 2 and 3 only   E. 3 and 4 only
B. 1 and 4 only   D. 2 and 4 only   F. 1, 2 and 3 only

Question 251:
Which of the following genetic statements are correct?

1. Alleles are a similar version of different cells.
2. If you are homozygous for a trait, you have three alleles the same for that particular gene.
3. If you are heterozygous for a trait, you have two different alleles for that particular gene.
4. To show the characteristic that is caused by a recessive allele, both carried alleles for the gene have to be recessive.

A. 1 only
B. 2 only
C. 3 only
D. 4 only
E. 1 and 2 only
F. 3 and 4 only
G. 1, 2, and 3 only

Question 252:
Which of the following statements are correct about meiosis?

1. The DNA content of a gamete is half that of a human red blood cell.
2. Meiosis requires ATP.
3. Meiosis only takes place in reproductive tissue.
4. In meiosis, a diploid cell divides in such a way so as to produce two haploid cells.

A. 1 only
B. 3 only
C. 1 and 2 only
D. 2 and 3 only
E. 2 and 4 only
F. 1, 2, 3 and 4

Question 253:
Put the following statements in the correct order of events for when there is too little water in the blood.

1. Urine is more concentrated
2. Pituary gland releases ADH
3. Blood water level returns to normal
4. Hypothalamus detects too little water in blood
5. Kidney affects water level

A. 1 - 2 - 3 - 4 - 5
B. 5 - 4 - 3 - 2 - 1
C. 4 - 2 - 5 - 1 - 3
D. 3 - 2 - 4 - 1 - 5
E. 5 - 2 - 3 - 4 - 1
F. 4 - 2 – 1- 5 - 3

Question 254:
The pH of venous blood is 7.35. Which of the following is the likely pH of arterial blood?

A. 4.4
B. 5.2
C. 6.5
D. 7.0
E. 7.4
F. 7.95

Question 255:

Which of the following are true of the cytoplasm?

1. The vast majority of the cytoplasm is made up of water.
2. All contents of animal cells are contained in the cytoplasm.
3. The cytoplasm contains electrolytes and proteins.

A. 1 only   C. 3 only   E. 1 and 3 only
B. 2 only   D. 1 and 2 only   F. 1, 2 and 3

Question 256:

ATP is produced in which of the following organelles?

1. The golgi apparatus
2. The rough endoplasmic reticulum
3. The mitochondria
4. The nucleus

A. 1 only
B. 2 only
C. 3 only
D. 4 only
E. 1 and 2
F. 2 and 3 only
G. 3 and 4 only
H. 1, 2, 3 and 4

Question 257:

The cell membrane:
A. Is made up of a phospholipid bilayer which only allows active transport across it.
B. Is not found in bacteria.
C. Is a semi-permeable barrier to ions and organic molecules.
D. Consists purely of enzymes.

Question 258:

Cells of the *Polyommatus atlantica* butterfly of the Lycaenidae family have 446 chromosomes. Which of the following statements about a *P. atlantica* butterfly are correct?

1. Mitosis will produce 2 daughter cells each with 223 pairs of chromosomes
2. Meiosis will produce 4 daughter cells each with 223 chromosomes
3. Mitosis will produce 4 daughter cells each with 446 chromosomes
4. Meiosis will produce 2 daughter cells each with 223 pairs of chromosomes

A. 1 and 2 only
B. 1 and 3 only
C. 2 and 3 only
D. 3 and 4 only
E. 1, 2 and 3 only
F. 1, 2, 3 and 4

Questions 259-261 are based on the following information:

Assume that hair colour is determined by a single allele. The R allele is dominant and results in black hair. The r allele is recessive for red hair. Mary (red hair) and Bob (black hair) are having a baby girl.

Question 259:

What is the probability that she will have red hair?

A. 0% only
B. 25% only
C. 50% only
D. 0% or 25%
E. 0% or 50%
F. 25% or 50%

Question 260:

Mary and Bob have a second child, Tim, who is born with red hair. What does this confirm about Bob?

A. Bob is heterozygous for the hair allele.
B. Bob is homozygous dominant for the hair allele.
C. Bob is homozygous recessive for the hair allele.
D. Bob does not have the hair allele.

Question 261:

Mary and Bob go on to have a third child. What are the chances that this child will be born homozygous for black hair?

A. 0%
B. 25%
C. 50%
D. 75%
E. 100%

Question 262:

Why does air flow into the chest on inspiration?

1. Atmospheric pressure is smaller than intra-thoracic pressure during inspiration.
2. Atmospheric pressure is greater than intra-thoracic pressure during inspiration.
3. Anterior and lateral chest expansion decreases absolute intra-thoracic pressure.
4. Anterior and lateral chest expansion increases absolute intra-thoracic pressure.

A. 1 only
B. 2 only
C. 2 and 3
D. 1 and 4
E. 1 and 3
F. 2 and 4

Question 263:
Which of the following components of a food chain represent the largest biomass?

A. Producers
B. Decomposers
C. Primary consumers
D. Secondary consumers
E. Tertiary consumers

Question 264:
Concerning the nitrogen cycle, which of the following are true?

1. The majority of the Earth's atmosphere is nitrogen.
2. Most of the nitrogen in the Earth's atmosphere is inert.
3. Bacteria are essential for nitrogen fixation.
4. Nitrogen fixation occurs during lightning strikes.

A. 1 and 2
B. 1 and 3
C. 2 and 3
D. 2 and 4
E. 3 and 4
F. 1, 2, 3 and 4

Question 265:
Which of the following statement are correct regarding mutations?

1. Mutations always cause proteins to lose their function.
2. Mutations always change the structure of the protein encoded by the affected gene.
3. Mutations always result in cancer.

A. Only 1
B. Only 2
C. Only 3
D. 1 and 2
E. 2 and 3
F. 1 and 3
G. 1, 2 and 3
H. None of the statements are correct.

Question 266:
Which of the following is not a function of the central nervous system?

A. Coordination of movement
B. Decision making and executive functions
C. Control of heart rate
D. Cognition
E. Memory

Question 267:
Which of the following control mechanisms are involved in modulating cardiac output?

1. Voluntary control.
2. Sympathetic control to decrease heart rate.
3. Parasympathetic control to increase heart rate.

A. Only 1
B. Only 2
C. Only 3
D. 1 and 2
E. 2 and 3
F. 1 and 3
G. 1, 2 and 3
H. None of the statements are correct.

Question 268:
Vijay goes to see his GP with fatty, smelly stools that float on water. Which of the following enzymes is most likely to be malfunctioning?

A. Amylase
B. Lipase
C. Protease
D. Sucrase
E. Lactase

Question 269:
Which of the following statements concerning the cardiovascular system is correct?

A. Oxygenated blood from the lungs flows to the heart via the pulmonary artery.
B. All arteries carry oxygenated blood.
C. All animals have a double circulatory system.
D. The superior vena cava contains oxygenated blood
E. All veins have valves.
F. None of the above.

Question 270:
Which part of the GI tract has the least amount of enzymatic digestion occurring?

A. Mouth
B. Stomach
C. Small intestine
D. Large intestine
E. Rectum

Question 271:

Oge touches a hot stove and immediately moves her hand away. Which of the following components are **NOT** involved in this reaction?

1. Thermo-receptor
2. Brain
3. Spinal Cord
4. Sensory nerve
5. Motor nerve
6. Muscle

A. 1 only
B. 2 only
C. 3 only
D. 1 and 2 only
E. 1, 2 and 3 only
F. 3, 4, 5 and 6

Question 272:

Which of the following represents a scenario with an appropriate description of the mode of transport?

1. Water moving from a hypotonic solution outside of a potato cell, across the cell wall and cell membrane and into the hypertonic cytoplasm of the potato cell→ Osmosis.
2. Carbon dioxide moving across a respiring cell's membrane and dissolving in blood plasma →Active transport.
3. Reabsorption of amino acids against a concentration gradient in the glomeruluar apparatus → Diffusion.

A. 1 only
B. 2 only
C. 3 only
D. 1 and 2 only
E. 2 and 3 only
F. 1 and 3 only
G. 1, 2 and 3

Question 273:

Which of the following equations represents anaerobic respiration?

1. Carbohydrate + Oxygen → Energy + Carbon Dioxide + Water
2. Carbohydrate → Energy + Lactic Acid + Carbon dioxide
3. Carbohydrate → Energy + Lactic Acid
4. Carbohydrate → Energy + Ethanol + Carbon dioxide

A. 1 only
B. 2 only
C. 3 only
D. 4 only
E. 1 and 2
F. 1 and 3
G. 1 and 4
H. 2 and 4 only
I. 3 and 4 only

Question 274:

Which of the following statements regarding respiration are correct?

1. The mitochondria are the centres for both aerobic and anaerobic respiration.
2. The cytoplasm is the main site of anaerobic respiration.
3. For every two moles of glucose that is respired aerobically, 12 moles of CO_2 are liberated.
4. Anaerobic respiration is more efficient than aerobic respiration.

A. 1 and 2
B. 1 and 4
C. 2 and 3
D. 2 and 4
E. 3 and 4

Question 275:

Which of the following statements are true?

1. The nucleus contains the cell's chromosomes.
2. The cytoplasm consists purely of water.
3. The plasma membrane is a single phospholipid layer.
4. The cell wall prevents plants cells from lysing due to osmotic pressure.

A. 1 and 2
B. 1 and 4
C. 1, 3 and 4
D. 1, 2 and 3
E. 1, 2 and 4
F. 2, 3 and 4

Question 276:

Which of the following statements are true about osmosis?

1. If a medium is hypertonic relative to the cell cytoplasm, the cell will gain water through osmosis.
2. If a medium is hypotonic relative to the cell cytoplasm, the cell will gain water through osmosis.
3. If a medium is hypotonic relative to the cell cytoplasm, the cell will lose water through osmosis.
4. If a medium is hypertonic relative to the cell cytoplasm, the cell will lose water through osmosis.
5. The medium's tonicity has no impact on the movement of water.

A. 1 only
B. 2 only
C. 1 and 3
D. 2 and 4
E. 5 only

Question 277:

Which of the following statements are true about stem cells?

1. Stem cells have the ability to differentiate into other mature types of cells.
2. Stem cells are unable to maintain their undifferentiated state.
3. Stem cells can be classified as embryonic stem cells or adult stem cells.
4. Stem cells are only found in embryos.

A. 1 and 3
B. 3 and 4
C. 2 and 3
D. 1 and 2
E. 2 and 4

Question 278:

Which of the following are **NOT** examples of natural selection?

1. Giraffes growing longer necks to eat taller plants.
2. Antibiotic resistance developed by certain strains of bacteria.
3. Pesticide resistance among locusts in farms.
4. Breeding of horses to make them run faster.

A. 1 only
B. 4 only
C. 1 and 3
D. 1 and 4
E. 2 and 4

Question 279:

Which of the following statements are true?

1. Enzymes stabilise the transition state and therefore lower the activation energy.
2. Enzymes distort substrates in order to lower activation energy.
3. Enzymes decrease temperature to slow down reactions and lower the activation energy.
4. Enzymes provide alternative pathways for reactions to occur.

A. 1 only
B. 1 and 2
C. 1 and 4
D. 2 and 4
E. 3 and 4

Question 280:

Which of the following are examples of negative feedback?

1. Salivating whilst waiting for a meal.
2. Throwing a dart.
3. The regulation of blood pH.
4. The regulation of blood pressure.

A. 1 only
B. 1 and 2
C. 3 and 4
D. 2, 3, and 4
E. 1, 2, 3 and 4

Question 281:

Which of the following statements about the immune system are true?

1. White blood cells defend against bacterial and fungal infections.
2. White blood cells can temporarily disable but not kill pathogens.
3. White blood cells use antibodies to fight pathogens.
4. Antibodies are produced by bone marrow stem cells.

A. 1 and 3
B. 1 and 4
C. 2 and 3
D. 2 and 4
E. 1, 2, and 3
F. 1, 3, and 4

Question 282:

The cardiovascular system does **NOT**:

A. Deliver vital nutrients to peripheral cells.
B. Oxygenate blood and transports it to peripheral cells.
C. Act as a mode of transportation for hormones to reach their target organ.
D. Facilitate thermoregulation.
E. Respond to exercise by increasing cardiac output to exercising muscles.

Question 283:

Which of the following statements is correct?

A. Adrenaline can sometimes decrease heart rate.
B. Adrenaline is rarely released during flight or fight responses.
C. Adrenaline causes peripheral vasoconstriction.
D. Adrenaline only affects the cardiovascular system.
E. Adrenaline travels primarily in lymphatic vessels.
F. None of the above.

Question 284:
Which of the following statements is true?

A. Protein synthesis occurs solely in the nucleus.
B. Each amino acid is coded for by three DNA bases.
C. Each protein is coded for by three amino acids.
D. Red blood cells can create new proteins to prolong their lifespan.
E. Protein synthesis isn't necessary for mitosis to take place.
F. None of the above.

Question 285:
A solution of amylase and carbohydrate is present in a beaker, where the pH of the contents is 6.3. Assuming amylase is saturated, which of the following will increase the rate of production of the product?

1. Add sodium bicarbonate
2. Add carbohydrate
3. Add amylase
4. Increase the temperature to 100° C

A. 1 only   C. 3 only   E. 1 and 2   G. 1, 2 and 3
B. 2 only   D. 4 only   F. 1 and 3   H. 1, 3 and 4

Question 286:
Celestial Necrosis is a newly discovered autosomal recessive disorder. A female carrier and a male with the disease produce two boys. What is the probability that neither boy's genotype contains the celestial necrosis allele?

A. 100%   B. 75%   C. 50%   D. 25%   E. 0%

Question 287:
Which among the following has no endocrine function?

A. The thyroid   C. The pancreas   E. The testes
B. The ovary   D. The adrenal gland   F. None of the above.

Question 288:
Which of the following statements are true?

1. Increasing levels of insulin cause a decrease in blood glucose levels.
2. Increasing levels of glycogen cause an increase in blood glucose levels.
3. Increasing levels of adrenaline decrease the heart rate.

A. 1 only
B. 2 only
C. 3 only
D. 1 and 2
E. 2 and 3
F. 1 and 3
G. 1, 2 and 3

Question 289:

Which of the following rows is correct?

	Oxygenated Blood		Deoxygenated Blood	
A.	Left atrium	Left ventricle	Right atrium	Right ventricle
B.	Left atrium	Right atrium	Left ventricle	Right ventricle
C.	Left atrium	Right ventricle	Right atrium	Right ventricle
D.	Right atrium	Right ventricle	Left atrium	Left ventricle
E.	Left ventricle	Right atrium	Left atrium	Right ventricle

Questions 290-292 are based on the following information:

The pedigree below shows the inheritance of a newly discovered disease that affects connective tissue called Nafram syndrome. Individual 1 is a normal homozygote.

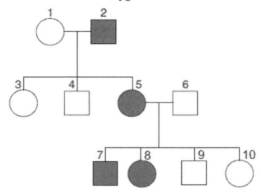

Question 290:

What is the inheritance of Nafram syndrome?

A. Autosomal dominant
B. Autosomal recessive
C. X-linked dominant

D. X-linked recessive
E. Co-dominant

Question 291:

Which individuals must be heterozygous for Nafram syndrome?

A. 1 and 2
B. 8 and 9

C. 2 and 5
D. 5 and 6

E. 6 and 8
F. 6 and 10

Question 292:

Taking N to denote a diseased allele and n to denote a normal allele, which of the following are **NOT** possible genotypes for 6's parents?

1. NN x NN
2. NN x Nn
3. Nn x nn
4. Nn x Nn
5. nn x nn

A. 1 and 2
B. 1 and 3

C. 2 and 3
D. 2 and 5

E. 3 and 4
F. 4 and 5

Question 293:

Which of the following correctly describes the passage of urine through the body?

	1st	2nd	3rd	4th
A	Kidney	Ureter	Bladder	Urethra
B	Kidney	Urethra	Bladder	Ureter
C	Urethra	Bladder	Ureter	Kidney
D	Ureter	Kidney	Bladder	Urethra

Question 294:

Which of the following best describes the passage of blood from the body, through the heart, back to the body?

A. Aorta → Left Ventricle → Left Atrium → Inferior Vena Cava → Right Atrium → Right Ventricle → Lungs → Aorta

B. Inferior vena cava → Left Atrium → Left Ventricle → Lungs → Right Atrium → Right Ventricle → Aorta

C. Inferior vena cava → Right Ventricle → Right Atrium → Lungs → Left Atrium → Left Ventricle → Aorta

D. Aorta → Left Atrium → Left Ventricle → Lungs → Right Atrium → Right Ventricle → Inferior Vena Cava

E. Right Atrium → Left Atrium → Inferior vena cava → Lungs → Left Atrium → Right Ventricle → Aorta

F. None of the above.

Question 295:

Which of the following best describes the events during inspiration?

	Intrathoracic Pressure	Intercostal Muscles	Diaphragm
A	Increases	Contract	Contracts
B	Increases	Relax	Contracts
C	Increases	Contract	Relaxes
D	Increases	Relax	Relaxes
E	Decreases	Contract	Contracts
F	Decreases	Relax	Contracts
G	Decreases	Contract	Relaxes
H	Decreases	Relax	Relaxes

Questions 296-297 are based on the following information:

DNA is made up of the four nucleotide bases: adenine, cytosine, guanine and thymine. A triplet repeat or codon is a sequence of three nucleotides which code for an amino acid. While there are only 20 amino acids there are 64 different combinations of the four DNA nucleotide bases. This means that more than one combination of 3 DNA nucleotides sequences code for the same amino acid.

Question 296:
Which property of the DNA code is described above?

A. The code is unambiguous.
B. The code is universal.
C. The code is non-overlapping.
D. The code is degenerate.
E. The code is preserved.
F. The code has no punctuation.

Question 297:
Which type of mutation does the described property protect against the most?
A. An insertion - where a single nucleotide is inserted.
B. A point mutation - where a single nucleotide is replaced for another.
C. A deletion - where a single nucleotide is deleted.
D. A repeat expansion - where a repeated trinucleotide sequence is added.
E. A duplication - where a piece of DNA is abnormally copied.

Question 298:
Which row of the table below describes what happens when external temperature decreases?

	Temperature Change Detected by	Sweat Gland Secretion	Cutaneous Blood Flow
A	Hypothalamus	Increases	Increases
B	Hypothalamus	Increases	Decreases
C	Hypothalamus	Decreases	Increases
D	Hypothalamus	Decreases	Decreases
E	Cerebral Cortex	Increases	Increases
F	Cerebral Cortex	Increases	Decreases
G	Cerebral Cortex	Decreases	Increases
H	Cerebral Cortex	Decreases	Decreases

Question 299:

Which of the following processes involve active transport?

1. Reabsorption of glucose in the kidney.
2. Movement of carbon dioxide into the alveoli in the lungs.
3. Movement of chemicals in a neural synapse.

A. 1 only
B. 2 only
C. 3 only
D. 1 and 2
E. 1 and 3
F. 2 and 3
G. 1, 2 and 3

Question 300:

Which of the following statements is correct about enzymes?

A. All enzymes are made up of amino acids only.
B. Enzymes can sometimes slow the rate of reactions.
C. Enzymes have no impact on reaction temperatures.
D. Enzymes are heat sensitive but resistant to changes in pH.
E. Enzymes are unspecific in their substrate use.
F. None of the above.

SECTION 1E: Advanced Maths

Section 1E requires a much broader knowledge of the A level Maths curriculum and you're highly advised to revise the topics below before proceeding further with the practice questions in this book.

Algebra:

- Laws of Indices
- Manipulation of Surds
- Quadratic Functions: Graphs, use of discrimant, completing the square
- Solving Simulatenous Equations via Substitution
- Solving Linear and Quadratic Inequalities
- Manipulation of polynomials e.g. expanding brackets, factorising
- Use of Factor Theorem + Remainder Theorem

Graphing Functions:

- Sketching of common functions including lines, quadratics, cubics, trigonometric functions, logarithmic functions and exponential functions
- Manipulation of functions using simple transformations
- Graph of $y = a^x$ series

Law of Lograithms

- $a^b = c \leftrightarrow b = log_a c$
- $log_a x + log_a y = log_a(xy)$
- $log_a x - log_a y = log_a(\frac{x}{y})$
- $k \, log_a x = log_a(x^k)$
- $log_a \frac{1}{x} = - log_a x$
- $log_a a = 1$

Differentiation:

- First order and second order derivatives
- Familiarity with notation: $\frac{dy}{dx}, \frac{d^2y}{dx^2}, f'(x), f''(x)$
- Differentiation of functions like $y = x^n$

Integration:

- Definite and indefinite integrals for $y = x^n$
- Solving Differential Equations in the form: $\frac{dy}{dx} = f(x)$
- Understanding of the Fundamental Theorem of Calculus and its application:
   - $\int_a^b f(x)dx = F(b) - F(a), where \, F'(x) = f(x)$
   - $\frac{d}{dx}\int_a^x f(t)dt = f(x)$

Logic Arguments:

- Terminology: True, flase, and, or not, necessary, sufficient, for all, for some, there exists.
- Arguments in the format:
   - If A then B
   - A if B
   - A only if B
   - A if and only if B

Geometry:

➤ Equations for a circle:
  ○ $(x - a)^2 + (y - b)^2 = r^2$
  ○ $x^2 + y^2 + cx + dy + e = 0$
➤ Equations for a straight line: $y - y_1 = m(x - x_1)$ & $Ax + by + c = 0$
➤ Circle Properties:
  ○ The angle subtended by an arc at the centre of a circle is double the size of the angle subtended by the arc on the circumference
  ○ The opposite angles in a cyclic quadrilateral summate to 180 degrees
  ○ The angle between the tanent and chord at the point of contact is equal to the angle in the alternate segment
  ○ The tangent at any point on a circle is perpendicular to the radius at that point
  ○ Triangles formed using the full diameter are right-angled triangles
  ○ Angles in the same segment are equal
  ○ The Perpendicular from the centre to a chord bisects the chord

Series:

➤ Arithmetic series and Geometric Series
➤ Summing to a finite and infinite geometric series
➤ Binomial Expansions
➤ Factorials

Trignometry:

➤ Solution of trigonometric identities
➤ Values of sin, cost, tan for 0, 30, 45, 60 and 90 degrees
➤ Sine, Cosine, Tangent graphs, symmetries, perioditicties
➤ Sin Rule: $\frac{a}{SinA} = \frac{b}{Sin\,B} = \frac{c}{Sin\,C}$
➤ Cosine Rule: $c^2 = a^2 + b^2 - 2ab\,cosC$
➤ $Area\ of\ Triangle = \frac{1}{2}ab \sin C$
➤ $\sin^2 \theta + \cos^2 \theta = 1$
➤ $tan\theta = \frac{sin\theta}{\cos \theta}$

Advanced Maths Questions

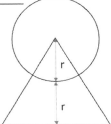

Question 301:
The vertex of an equilateral triangle is covered by a circle whose radius is half the height of the triangle. What percentage of the triangle is covered by the circle?

A. 12%   C. 23%   E. 41%

B. 16%   D. 33%   F. 50%

Question 302:
Three equal circles fit into a quadrilateral as shown, what is the height of the quadrilateral?

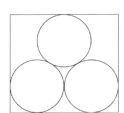

A. $2\sqrt{3}r$

B. $(2 + \sqrt{3})r$ D. $3r$

C. $(4 - \sqrt{3})r$ E. $4r$

                                   F. Information Needed

Question 303:
Two pyramids have equal volume and height, one with a square of side length *a* and one with a hexagonal base of side length *b*. What is the ratio of the side length of the bases?

A. $\sqrt{\dfrac{3\sqrt{3}}{2}}$ B. $\sqrt{\dfrac{2\sqrt{3}}{3}}$ C. $\sqrt{\dfrac{3}{2}}$ D. $\dfrac{2\sqrt{3}}{3}$ E. $\dfrac{3\sqrt{3}}{2}$

Question 304:
One 9 cm cube is cut into 3 cm cubes. The total surface area increases by a factor of:

A. $\dfrac{1}{3}$ B. $\sqrt{3}$ C. 3   E. 27

                                                        D. 9

Question 305:
A cone has height twice its base width (four times the circle radius). What is the cone angle (half the angle at the vertex)?

A. 30°   B. $\sin^{-1}\left(\dfrac{r}{2}\right)$ C. $\sin^{-1}\left(\dfrac{1}{\sqrt{17}}\right)$ D. $\cos^{-1}(\sqrt{17})$

Question 306:
A hemispherical speedometer has a maximum speed of 200 mph. What is the angle travelled by the needle at a speed of 70 mph?

A. 28°   B. 49°   C. 63°   D. 88°   E. 92°

Question 307:
Two rhombuses, A and B, are similar. The area of A is 10 times that of B. What is the ratio of the smallest angles over the ratio of the shortest sides? $\dfrac{angle\ A / angle\ B}{length\ A / length\ B}$

A. 0   C. $\dfrac{1}{\sqrt{10}}$ D. $\sqrt{10}$

B. $\dfrac{1}{10}$ E. ∞

Question 308:
If $f^{-1}(-x) = \ln(2x^2)$ what is $f(x)$

A. $\sqrt{\dfrac{e^y}{2}}$ B. $\sqrt{\dfrac{e^{-y}}{2}}$ C. $\dfrac{e^y}{2}$ D. $\dfrac{-e^y}{2}$ E. $\sqrt{\dfrac{e^y}{2}}$

Question 309:
Which of the following is largest for $0 < x < 1$
A. $\log_8(x)$ B. $\log_{10}(x)$ C. e^x D. x^2 E. $\sin(x)$

Question 310:
x is proportional to y cubed, y is proportional to the square root of z. $x \propto y^3, y \propto \sqrt{z}$.
If z doubles, x changes by a factor of:
A. $\sqrt{2}$ B. 2 C. $2\sqrt{2}$ D. $\sqrt[3]{4}$ E. 4

Question 311:
The area between two concentric circles (shaded) is three times that of the inner circle.
What's the size of the gap?
A. r C. $\sqrt{3}r$ E. $3r$
B. $\sqrt{2}r$ D. $2r$ F. $4r$

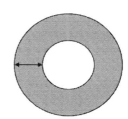

Question 312:
Solve $-x^2 \leq 3x - 4$
A. $x \geq \frac{4}{3}$
B. $1 \leq x \leq 4$
C. $x \leq 2$
D. $x \geq 1$ or $x \geq -4$
E. $-1 \leq x \leq \frac{3}{4}$

Question 313:
The volume of a sphere is numerically equal to its projected area. What is its radius?
A. $\frac{1}{2}$ B. $\frac{2}{3}$ C. $\frac{3}{4}$ D. $\frac{4}{3}$ E. $\frac{3}{2}$

Question 314:
What is the range where $x^2 < \frac{1}{x}$?
A. $x < 0$ C. $x > 0$ E. None
B. $0 < x < 1$ D. $x \geq 1$

Question 315:
Solve $\begin{pmatrix} -1 & 2 & -1 \\ 2 & 1 & 3 \\ 2 & -1 & 4 \end{pmatrix} \begin{pmatrix} x \\ y \\ z \end{pmatrix} = \begin{pmatrix} 1 \\ 7 \\ 9 \end{pmatrix}$

A. $\begin{pmatrix} -3 \\ 0 \\ 2 \end{pmatrix}$ B. $\begin{pmatrix} 1 \\ 3 \\ 4 \end{pmatrix}$ C. $\begin{pmatrix} -2 \\ 1 \\ 3 \end{pmatrix}$ D. $\begin{pmatrix} -3 \\ 1 \\ 4 \end{pmatrix}$ E. $\begin{pmatrix} 4 \\ 2 \\ 0 \end{pmatrix}$

Question 316:
Find the value of k such that the vectors $a = -i + 6j$ and $b = 2i + kj$ are perpendicular.
A. -2 B. $-\frac{1}{3}$ C. $\frac{1}{3}$ D. 2

Question 317:
What is the perpendicular distance between point p with position vector $4i + 5j$ and the line L given by vector
equation $r = -3i + j + \lambda(i + 2j)$
A. $2\sqrt{7}$ B. $5\sqrt{2}$ C. $2\sqrt{5}$ D. $7\sqrt{2}$

Question 318:
Find k such that point $\begin{pmatrix} 2 \\ k \\ -7 \end{pmatrix}$ lies within the plane $r = \begin{pmatrix} 2 \\ 3 \\ -1 \end{pmatrix} + \lambda \begin{pmatrix} 4 \\ 1 \\ 0 \end{pmatrix} + \mu \begin{pmatrix} 2 \\ 1 \\ 3 \end{pmatrix}$
A. -2 B. -1 C. 0 D. 1 E. 2

Question 319:

What is the largest solution to $\sin(-2\theta) = 0.5$ for $\frac{\pi}{2} \le x \le 2\pi$?

A. $\frac{5\pi}{3}$ B. $\frac{4\pi}{3}$ C. $\frac{5\pi}{6}$ D. $\frac{7\pi}{6}$ E. $\frac{11\pi}{6}$

Question 320:

$\cos^4(x) - \sin^4(x) \equiv$

A. $\cos(2x)$ B. $2\cos(x)$ C. $\sin(2x)$ D. $\sin(x)\cos(x)$ E. $\tan(x)$

Question 321:

How many real roots does $y = 2x^5 - 3x^4 + x^3 - 4x^2 - 6x + 4$ have?

A. 1   B. 2   C. 3   D. 4   E. 5

Question 322:

What is the sum of 8 terms, $\sum_1^8 u_n$, of an arithmetic progression with $u_1 = 2$ and $d = 3$.

A. 15   B. 82   C. 100   D. 184   E. 282

Question 323:

What is the coefficient of the x^2 term in the binomial expansion of $(2 - x)^5$?

A. -80   B. -48   C. 40   D. 48   E. 80

Question 324:

Given you have already thrown a 6, what is the probability of throwing three consecutive 6s using a fair die?

A. $\frac{1}{216}$ B. $\frac{1}{36}$ C. $\frac{1}{6}$ D. $\frac{1}{2}$ E. 1

Question 325:

Three people, A, B and C play darts. The probability that they hit a bullseye are respectively $\frac{1}{5}, \frac{1}{4}, \frac{1}{3}$. What is the probability that at least two shots hit the bullseye?

A. $\frac{1}{60}$ B. $\frac{1}{30}$ C. $\frac{1}{12}$ D. $\frac{1}{6}$ E. $\frac{3}{20}$

Question 326:

If probability of having blonde hair is 1 in 4, the probability of having brown eyes is 1 in 2 and the probability of having both is 1 in 8, what is the probability of having neither blonde hair nor brown eyes?

A. $\frac{1}{2}$ B. $\frac{3}{4}$ C. $\frac{3}{8}$ D. $\frac{5}{8}$ E. $\frac{7}{8}$

Question 327:

Differentiate and simplify $y = x(x + 3)^4$

A. $(x + 3)^3$ C. $x(x + 3)^3$
B. $(x + 3)^4$ D. $(x + 3)^3(5x + 3)$

Question 328:

Evaluate $\int_1^2 \frac{2}{x^2} dx$

A. -1 B. $\frac{1}{3}$ C. 1   D. $\frac{21}{4}$ E. 2

Question 329:

Express $\frac{5i}{1+2i}$ in the form $a + bi$

A. $1 + 2i$ B. $4i$ C. $1 - 2i$ D. $2 + i$ E. $5 - i$

Question 330:

Simplify $7\log_a(2) - 3\log_a(12) + 5\log_a(3)$

A. $log_{2a}(18)$ B. $log_a(18)$ C. $log_a(7)$ D. $9log_a(17)$ E. $-log_a(7)$

Question 331:

What is the equation of the asymptote of the function $y = \frac{2x^2 - x + 3}{x^2 + x - 2}$

A. $x = 0$ B. $x = 2$ C. $y = 0.5$ D. $y = 0$ E. $y = 2$

Question 332:

Find the intersection(s) of the functions $y = e^x - 3$ and $y = 1 - 3e^{-x}$

A. 0 *and* $ln(3)$ B. 1 C. $In(4)$ *and* 1 D. $In(3)$

Question 333:

Find the radius of the circle $x^2 + y^2 - 6x + 8y - 12 = 0$

A. 3 B. $\sqrt{13}$ C. 5 D. $\sqrt{37}$ E. 12

Question 334:

What value of **a** minimises $\int_0^a 2\sin(-x)\,dx$?

A. 0.5π B. π C. 2π D. 3π E. 4π

Question 335:

When $\frac{2x+3}{(x-2)(x-3)^2}$ is expressed as partial fractions, what is the numerator in the $\frac{A}{(x-2)}$ term:

A. -7   B. -1   C. 3   D. 6   E. 7

SECTION 1E: Advanced Physics

Physics Syllabus

➤ Calculate, manipulate and resolve Vectors and their components & resultants
➤ Calculate the moment of a force
➤ Difference between normal and frictional components of contact forces
➤ Concept of 'Limiting Equilibrium'
➤ Understand how to use the coefficient of Friction including $F = \mu R$ and $F \leq \mu R$
➤ Use of the equations of Motion
➤ Graphical interpretations of vectors + scalars
➤ Derivation + Integration of physical values e.g. Velocity from an acceleration-time graph
➤ Principle of conservation of momentum (including coalescence)+ Linear Momenum
➤ Principle of conservation of energy and its application to kinetic/gravitational potential energy
➤ Application of Newton's laws e.g.
   o Linear Motion of point masses
   o Modelling of objects moving vertically or on a plante
   o Objects connected by a rod or pulleys

Essential Equations

Mechanics & Motion

➤ Conservation of momentum $\Delta mv = 0$
➤ Force $F = \frac{\Delta mv}{t}$
➤ Angular velocity $\omega = \frac{v}{r} = 2\pi f$

Simple Harmonic Motion & Oscillations

➤ Displacement $x = A Cos(2\pi f t)$
➤ $a = -(2\pi f)^2 x = -(2\pi f)^2 A Cos(2\pi f t)$
➤ Speed $v = \pm 2\pi f \sqrt{A^2 - x^2}$

Gravitational forces

➤ Force $F = \frac{Gm_1 m_2}{r^2} = \frac{GMm}{r^2}$
➤ Potential $V = \frac{Gm}{r}$
➤ Acceleration $a = \frac{GM}{r^2} = \frac{\partial V}{\partial r}$

Magnetic fields

➤ Magnetic flux $\emptyset = BA$
➤ Magnetic flux linkage $\emptyset N = BAN$
➤ Magnitude of induced emf $\varepsilon = N \frac{\Delta \emptyset}{\Delta t}$

Radioactivity

➤ Decay $N = N_0 e^{-\lambda t}$
➤ Half life $T_{1/2} = \frac{ln2}{\lambda}$
➤ Activity $A = \lambda N$
➤ Energy $E = mc^2$

Current & electricity

➤ emf $\varepsilon = \frac{E}{Q} = I(R + r)$
➤ Resistivity $\rho = \frac{RA}{l}$
➤ Resistors in series $R = \sum_{i=1}^{n} R_i$
➤ Resistors in parallel s $R = \sum_{i=1}^{n} \frac{1}{R_i}$

Waves

➤ Speed $c = f \lambda$
➤ Period $T = \frac{1}{f}$
➤ Snell's law $n_1 sin\theta_1 = n_2 sin\theta_2$

: advanced physics questions will require multi-step calculations and you simply won't have time to recall
ions in the real exam. Thus, its important to rote learn these so you can be as quick as possible in the exam.

Advanced Physics Questions

Question 336:
A ball is swung in a vertical circle from a string (of negligible mass). What is the minimum speed at the top of the arc for it to continue in a circular path?

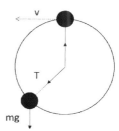

A. 0

B. mgr

C. $2r^2$

D. mg

E. $\sqrt{gr}$

Question 337:
A person pulls on a rope at 60° to the horizontal to exert a force on a mass m as shown. What is the power needed to move the mass up the 30° incline at a constant velocity, v, given a friction force F?

A. $\left(mg + \frac{F}{2}\right)v$

B. $\frac{mg}{\sqrt{2}} - F$

C. $\left(\frac{mg}{2}\right)v$

D. $\sqrt{2}Fv$

E. $\left(\frac{mg}{2} + F\right)v$

Question 338:
What is the maximum speed of a point mass, m, suspended from a string of length l, (a pendulum) if it is released from an angle θ where the string is taught?

A. $2gl(1 - \cos(\theta))$

B. $2gl(1 - \sin(\theta))$

C. $\sqrt{2gl(1 - \cos(\theta))}$

D. $\sqrt{2gl(1 - \sin(\theta))}$

E. $\sqrt{2gl(1 - \cos^2(\theta))}$

Question 339:
Two spheres of equal mass, m, one at rest and one moving at velocity u1 towards the other as shown. After the collision, they move at angles φ and θ from the initial velocity u1 at respective velocities v_1 and v_2 where $v_2 = 2v_1$. What is the angle θ?

A. 0°

B. sin(50)

C. 30°

D. 45°

E. 90°

$15°$ $V_1 = 2V_2$

Question 340:
The first ball is three times the mass of the others. If this is an elastic collision, how many of the other ball move and at what velocity after the collision?

	Number of Balls	Velocity
A	1	3v
B	1	v/3
C	3	v/3
D	3	v
E	3	$\sqrt{v}$

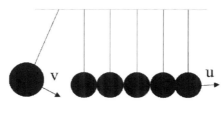

Question 341:
A ball is kicked over a 3 m fence from 6 m away with an initial height of zero. It does not strike the fence and lands 6m behind it. Assuming no air resistance, what is the minimum angle the ball must leave the ground at to make it over the fence?

A. $\arctan(1)$

B. $\arctan\left(\frac{1}{2}\right)$

C. $\arcsin\left(\frac{1}{2}\right)$

D. $30°$

E. $\arccos\left(\frac{-1}{2}\right)$

Question 342:
A mass on a spring of spring constant k is in simple harmonic motion at frequency f. If the mass is halved and the spring constant is double, by what factor will the frequency of oscillation change?

A. Stay the same

B. 2

C. 4

D. $\frac{1}{2}$

E. $\sqrt{2}$

Question 343:
A ball is dropped from 3 m above the ground and rebounds to a maximum height of 1 m. How much kinetic energy does it have just before hitting the ground and at the top of its bounce, and what is the maximum speed the ball reaches in any direction?

	E_k at Bottom	E_k at Top	Max speed
A	0	30m	$2\sqrt{15}$
B	0	30m	30
C	30m	0	$2\sqrt{15}$
D	30m	0	60
E	60m	0	60

Question 344:
An object approaches a stationary observer at a 10% of the speed of light, c. If the observer is 2 m tall, how tall will it look to the object?

A. $0.9l$ B. $1.1l$ C. l D. $l\sqrt{0.99}$ E. $l\sqrt{1.01}$

Question 345:
What is the stopping distance of a car moving at v m/s if its breaking force is half its weight?

A. v^2 B. $\frac{v^2}{g}$ C. $2mv$ D. $\frac{v^2}{2}$ E. $\sqrt{mg}$

Question 346:
The amplitude of a wave is damped from an initial amplitude of 200 to 25 over 12 seconds. How many seconds did it take to reach half its original amplitude?

A. 1   B. 2   C. 3   D. 4   E. 6

Question 347:
Two frequencies, f and $\frac{7}{8}f$, interfere to produce beats of 10 Hz. What is the original frequency f?

A. 11 Hz

B. 60 Hz

C. 80 Hz

D. 160 Hz

E. 200 Hz

Question 348:
Study the diagram opposite. The two waves represent:

A. A standing wave with both ends fixed
B. The 4th harmonic
C. Destructive interference
D. A reflection from a plane surface
E. All of the above

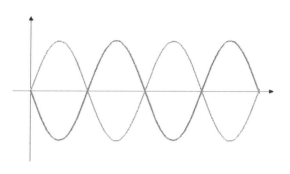

Question 349:
Radioactive element $_b^a X$ undergoes beta decay, and the product of this decay emits an alpha particle to become $_d^c Y$. What are the atomic number and atomic mass?

	c	d
A	a-4	b+1
B	a-3	b-2
C	a-4	b-1
D	a-5	b
E	a-1	b-4

Question 350:
A gas is heated to twice its temperature (in Kelvin) and allowed to increase in volume by 10%. What is the change in pressure?

A. 82% increase
B. 90% increase
C. 110% increase
D. 18% decrease
E. 40% decrease
F. 82% decrease

Question 351:
A beam of alpha particles enters perpendicular to the magnetic field, B, shown below coming out of the page and is deflected to follow path T. What path would a beam of electrons follow?

A. P
B. Q
C. R
D. S

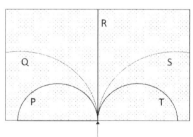

Question 352:
If all light bulbs and power supplies are identical and the joining wires have negligible resistance, which of the following light bulbs will shine brightest?

A. 1,2,3
B. 6
C. 7,8,9
D. 1,2,3,6
E. 4,5

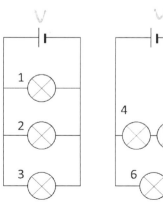
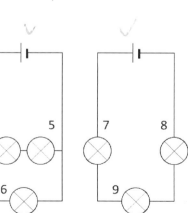

Question 353:

A convex lens with focal length f is used to create an image of object O. Where is the image formed?

A. V
B. W
C. X
D. Y
E. Z

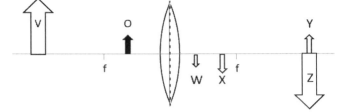

Question 354:

A flower pot hangs on the end of a rod protruding at right angles from a wall, held up by string attached two thirds of the way along. What must the tension in the string be if the rod is weightless and the system is at equilibrium?

A. $mg \sin \theta$

B. $\frac{3mg}{2 \sin \theta}$

C. $\frac{3mg}{2 \cos \theta}$

D. $\frac{2mg}{3 \sin \theta}$

E. $\frac{2mg}{3 \cos \theta}$

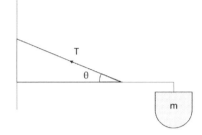

Question 355:

When a clean, negatively charged metal surface is irradiated with electromagnetic radiation of sufficient frequency, electrons are emitted. This observation describes what phenomenon and what property does the intercept on the experimental plot below represent?

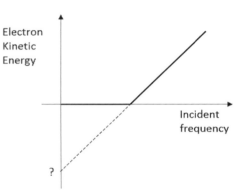

A	Photoelectric effect	Stopping potential
B	Evaporation	Stopping potential
C	Wave particle duality	Work function
D	Thermionic emission	Work function
E	Photoabsorbtion	Stopping potential

Question 356:

Which of these wave phenomena can be explained by Huygen's principle of wave propagation?

1. Diffraction   2. Refraction   3. Reflection   4. Interference   5. Damping

A. None   B. 1,2,3   C. 1,4   D. 1,2,3,4   E. All

Question 357:

What is the maximum efficiency of an engine where the isothermal expansion of a gas takes place at $T_1 = 420$ K and the reversible isothermal compression of the gas occurs at temperature $T_2 = 280$ K?

A. 43%   B. 57%   C. 75%   D. 92%   E. 100%

Question 358:
Which of the following statements is true?

A. A capacitor works based on the principle of electromagnetic induction.
B. A motor requires a AC input
C. Transformers produce DC current
D. The magnetic field produced by a current carrying wire is parallel to the direction of flow of charge.
E. A generator must have a moving wire.

Question 359:
For the logic gate below, if inputs are all set to 1, what would the value of X, Y and Z be?

	X	Y	Z
A	0	0	0
B	0	0	1
C	0	1	0
D	1	0	0
E	1	1	1

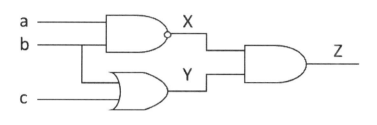

Question 360:
What material property is given by each point P, Q and R on a stress-strain curve?

	P	Q	R
A	Elastic Modulus	Yield stress	Fracture toughness
B	Tensile Modulus	Plastic onset	Yield stress
C	Hardness	Stiffness	Ductile failure
D	Ductility	Elastic limit	Brittle fracture
E	Young's Modulus	Yield stress	Fracture stress

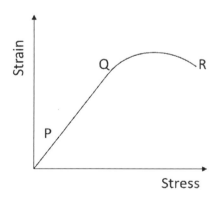

SECTION 2

Section 2 questions are designed to stretch you by putting you out of your comfort zone. In addition to the core knowledge required for section 1, you will need to apply core scientific principles in unfamiliar contexts.

All section 2 questions require you to have the knowledge from section 1A maths as well as the corresponding subject knowledge from section 1. For example biology section 2 questions require 1A maths and 1D Biology. Similarly, physics Section 2 questions require 1A maths, 1B physics and 1E advanced maths/physics. Each question is out of 25 marks.

Specialise
The very nature of the exam allows you to tailor your answers to your preferences and your abilities with regards to the different topic areas. This applies for both sections of the exam. You are expected to answer the maths questions (part 1), but other than that, you can choose freely which parts you want to answer. In section 2 you are even freer being able to choose any 2 questions of 6 covering Biology, chemistry and Physics. With regards to preparation, this means you should prepare to be able to apply your math skills, but the other parts should be easier to prepare for. It may for this reason pay of to "specialise" on specific topic areas. In general, it is best to focus on the same topics for both sections.

Thrive on Adversity
The NSAA is specifically designed to be challenging and to take you out of your comfort zone. This is done in order to separate different tiers of students depending on their academic ability. The reason for this type of exam is that Cambridge attracts excellent students that will almost invariable score well in exams. If, for this reason, during your preparation, you come across questions that you find very difficult, use this as motivation to try and further your knowledge beyond the simple school syllabus. This is where the option for specialisation ties in.

Be Efficient
You have 40 minutes to answer 2 questions that may be text based and include graphs. This leaves you with roughly 20 minutes per question. It is vital that you manage your time well. The best way to deal with this is to shorten the time you give yourself during your preparation progressively until you are able to finish your Section 2 question within roughly 30 minutes. This will give you the confidence for the exam. Another way to improve your performance in section 2 is to get familiar with different types of graphs and how to represent scientific information efficiently. This will help you to be as efficient as possible.

Practice Calculus
Section 2 does allow you to use calculators. For this reason, practicing calculus might seem unnecessary. But it will give you a big advantage to be confident with it as you will be significantly more efficient and faster. As the math part is core knowledge for all section 2 questions, you can be certain that to some degree or other you will be required to apply your calculus. The better you prepare for your section 1 maths part, the better you will fare in section 2.

Don't be afraid to show off!
Examiners in the NSAA are not only looking for someone who has the correct answers to the questions being asked, but also for someone who has that extra spark. There may be some open-ended questions in the NSAA, which leave room for the student to input any extra knowledge on the subject they may have. Do not be afraid to use any extra knowledge that you have!

Section 2: Physics

Think in Applied Formulas

Trying to answer section 2 physics questions without first learning all the core formulas is like trying to run before you can walk – ensure you're completely confident with all the formulas given in sections 1B + 1E before starting the practice questions.

Graphs

Graph sketching is usually a tricky area for many students. When tackling a graph sketching problem, there are many approaches however it is useful to start with the basics:

➤ What is the value of y when x is zero?
➤ What is the value of x when y is zero?
➤ Are there any special values of x and y?
➤ If there is a fraction involved, at what values of x is the numerator or denominator equal to zero?

If you asked to draw a function that is the sum, product or division of two (sub) functions, start by drawing out all of the sub functions. Which function is the dominant function when x > 0 and x < 0.

Answering these basic questions will tell you where the asymptotes and intercepts etc. are, which will help with drawing the function.

Remember the Basics

A surprisingly large number of students do not know what the properties of basic shapes etc. are. For example, the area of a circle is πr^2, the surface area of a sphere is $4\pi r^2$ and the volume of a sphere is $\frac{4}{3}\pi r^3$. To 'go up' a dimension (i.e. to go from an area to a volume) you need to integrate and to 'go down' a dimension you need to differentiate. Learning this will make it easy to remember formulas for the areas and volumes of basic shapes. It is also important to remember important formulas even though they may be included in formula booklets. The reason for this is that although you may have access to formula booklets during exams, this will not be the case in interviews which will follow the NSAA. In addition, flicking through formula booklets takes up time during an exam and can be avoided if you are able to memorise important formulas.

Variety

Physics is a very varied subject, and the questions you may be asked in an exam will reflect this variety. Many students have a preferred area within physics, e.g. electronics, astrophysics or mechanics. However, it is important to remember not to neglect any subject area in its entirety on the basis that you will answer questions on another subject. It is entirely possible that of the two physics questions in the NSAA, both will be on subjects outside of you comfort zone. As it is common for students who study physics not to study biology, this would be a bad situation as you would have a very limited number of questions left to choose from.

Show Working

It is very important to show all working clearly, and not just write the final answer. If you compare a physics question to an English or history essay, most people would agree that an essay would not simply consist of the writer's final opinion and conclusions. For the same reasons, when answering any physics problem you must show all working clearly so that examiner can see how you arrived at an answer, even if the answer is incorrect. When calculating an answer, it is strongly advisable to write out everything algebraically as this is the clearest way in which working can be written.

For example, the examiner will not know what $\frac{(6.67\times10^{-11})\times3.14^2\times28.6581}{12.9/0.0036}$ means, but they will understand what $\frac{G\pi^2\rho}{\sigma/\alpha}$ means (if the numbers correspond to the symbols). Furthermore, if you are to make a silly mistake (e.g. you mistype something into you calculator at the end etc.), the examiner will be able to give you credit for writing the correct method, which may amount to most of the marks available in a question even if your final answer is incorrect. This is not possible if you write everything out numerically, as the examiner will not have the time or inclination to spend a long time over deciphering your working to see where you went wrong.

Similarly, it's very important that you clearly state any assumptions that you're making e.g. when calculating the gravitational force between two masses do you assume the masses are point masses?

Physics Question 1

The Earth receives radiation from the Sun which is both absorbed and reflected from the Earth's surface and atmosphere. The solar flux has a value of Ω.

a) Draw a diagram showing the distribution of solar flux across the Earth's surface. Use this to calculate the proportion of solar flux incident on the Earth's surface.

[7 marks]

b) The solar flux incident on the Earth's surface is absorbed and converted to infrared radiation which is emitted away from the surface. Objects that are maximally efficient absorbers are called blackbodies. The relationship between the temperature of blackbodies and their rate of radiation is given by the Stefan-Boltzmann law,

$$F = \sigma T_0^4$$

Where F is the total emitted thermal radiation, σ = Stefan-Boltzmann constant = 5.67×10^{-8} Jm^{-2}K^{-4} and T_0 is the absolute temperature of the blackbody.

Solar energy is also reflected by the atmosphere. The ratio of solar radiation reflected by the atmosphere to total incoming solar radiation is called the albedo, a.

Write expressions for the total radiation that is reflected by the Earth's atmosphere and the radiation emitted as infrared radiation from the Earth's surface.

[2 marks]

c) Using you answers to parts a and b, calculate the surface temperature of the Earth in terms of the solar flux, Ω.

[3 marks]

d) Solar flux, Ω, of the Sun's unimpeded rays at a distance equal to the distance between Sun and the Earth is 1372 Wm^{-2}, and the albedo of the Earth is 0.3. Use these values to calculate the blackbody temperature of the Earth.

[1 mark]

e) Is the value of T_0 greater or lower than what you would expect? What factors have not been considered during your calculations?

[5 marks]

f) This distance between the Sun and the Earth is 1.5×10^{11} m and the radius of the Sun is 6.96×10^8 m. Use these values and the value of Ω given above to calculate the blackbody temperature of the Sun.

[5 marks]

g) What assumptions have you made in the calculation above?

[2 marks]

[Total: 25 Marks]

Physics Question 2

a) Sketch the graph $y = \dfrac{\sqrt{x^2+1}-\sqrt{x^2-1}}{\sqrt{x^4-1}}$

[8 marks]

b) Evaluate the integral $\int \dfrac{\sqrt{x^2+1}-\sqrt{x^2-1}}{\sqrt{x^4-1}}\, dx$

[10 marks]

c) If the velocity of a train, $v(t)$ is given by:

$$v(t) = \begin{cases} 5t & 0 < t < 1.5 \\[2mm] \dfrac{\sqrt{t^2+1}-\sqrt{t^2-1}}{\sqrt{t^4-1}} & 1.5 < t < 2.0 \\[2mm] 2t^2 - 5t & 2.0 < t < 2.5 \end{cases}$$

Where t = time in hours and v = velocity in km s^{-1}.
Sketch a graph showing velocity as a function of time, t.

[4 marks]

d) Calculate the distance travelled by the train between $t = 0$ and $t = 2.5$ hours.

[3 marks]

[Total: 25 Marks]

Physics Question 3

Radioactive decay of any radiogenic atom is a random process that is independent of neighbouring atoms, physical conditions and the temperature state of the atom. The probability of a radiogenic isotope undergoing radioactive decay is called the decay constant, λ, and is different for every isotope.

a) If at time T there are t atoms of a radioactive isotope, and at time $T + \partial t$ there are ∂N atoms have decayed, derive an equation that relates the number of atoms N at time t to the decay constant, λ.

[5 marks]

b) The rate of decay is also called the activity, A. Use your answer from part a to express the activity as a function of time, t.

[1 mark]

c) At time $t = t_{1/2}$, half of the original atoms of a radioactive isotope will be present and the half will have undergone radioactive decay. At this time, $A = \frac{1}{2}A_0$, and time $t_{1/2}$ is known as the radioactive half-life. Use your answer to part a to express $t_{1/2}$ as a function of λ.

[3 marks]

d) (i) Complete the empty column in the table below:

[4 marks]

Parent Isotope	Daughter Isotope	Decay Products	λ (a⁻¹)
^{238}U	^{206}Pb		1.55×10^{-10}
^{235}U	^{207}Pb		9.85×10^{-10}
^{232}Th	^{208}Pb		4.95×10^{-11}
^{87}Rb	^{87}Sr		1.42×10^{-11}
^{147}Sm	^{143}Nd		6.54×10^{-12}
^{40}K	^{40}Ca & ^{40}Ar		4.95×10^{-10} & 5.81×10^{-11}
^{39}Ar	^{39}Ar		2.57×10^{-3}
^{176}Lu	^{176}Hf		1.94×10^{-11}
^{187}Re	^{187}Os		1.52×10^{-11}
^{14}C	^{15}N		1.21×10^{-4}

(ii) If the total number of daughter isotope atoms present at time t is D, write an expression that expresses t as a function of D and N.

[3 marks]

(iii) State and explain which of the parent isotopes listed in the table would be best suited to date:

→ Age of the Earth　　　　　　　　　　　　　　　　　　　　**[2 marks]**
→Ancient artefacts　　　　　　　　　　　　　　　　　　　　**[2 marks]**

(e) An igneous rock contains 11.7×10^{-5}g of ^{238}U and 3.58×10^{-5}g of ^{206}Pb and a negligible amount of ^{208}Pb. Stating your assumptions, determine the approximate age at which the rock formed.

[5 marks]

[Total: 25 Marks]

Physics Question 4

a) For two point masses m_1 and m_2 at a distance r apart, the gravitational force of attraction between the two masses is given by: $F = \frac{Gm_1m_2}{r^2}$

Whereby $G = 6.67 \times 10^{-11} \, \text{m}^3 \, \text{kg}^{-1} \, \text{s}^{-1}$. The gravitational potential, V due to mass m_1 is defined as $V = -\frac{Gm_1}{r}$

(i) What is the gravitational potential energy of a mass m_2 at distance r from mass m_1?

[1 mark]

(ii) What is the relationship between gravitational potential, V, and gravitational acceleration, a, of mass m_2 towards m_1?

[2 marks]

b) (i) For a spherical shell of radius b, calculate the area of a circular strip (hint: if θ is the angle between the centre of the shell and the surface, and $d\theta$ is the difference in angle between two nearby points on the outside of the shell, then $d\theta \ll \theta$)

[3 marks]

(ii) Assume the shell has a thickness t and uniform density ρ. Given that for a distribution of masses, the gravitational potential is given by: $V = -G \int_m \frac{dm}{r}$

Calculate the gravitational potential due to the shell at an arbitrary point P at distance D away from the shell, for cases when P is inside and outside of the shell.

[15 Marks]

(iii) Is the gravitational potential of position P for a point inside the shell dependent or independent of position?

[1 mark]

(iv) What is the gravitational acceleration of a point P inside the spherical shell?

[1 Mark]

(v) What is the gravitational acceleration at a point which is at a distance r from the centre of a sphere of radius b (where $\ll r$) and of density ρ?

[2 marks]

[Total: 25 Marks]

Physics Question 5

a) (i) What is meant by the term electromagnetic induction?

[2 marks]

(ii) Using diagrams, state and explain Lenz's law in relation to electromagnetic induction

[5 marks]

(iii) State Faraday's law, and write down equations that show its relation to Lenz's law and the voltage of the generated current

[5 marks]

(iv) Calculate the voltage generated when a rectangular coil of length 5 cm, width 10 cm and 35 turns is rotated at a rate of 50 rotations per minute through a magnetic field of strength 0.4T

[3 marks]

b) (i) Describe the dynamo theory as an explanation to the presence of the Earth's magnetic field

[3 marks]

(ii) Planets such as Mars have very weak magnetic fields. What would the effect of losing the Earth's magnetic field be on the planet? What would this mean with regards to the internal structure of the Earth? Why has Earth lasted longer than Mars?

[5 marks]

(iii) Many planetary bodies which are not thought to have an internally-generated magnetic dynamo still have magnetic fields. Give an example of such a planetary body and explain how its dynamo is generated.

[2 marks]

[Total: 25 Marks]

Section 2: Chemistry

Keep things Simple

Chemistry is a science of simplification. The more flexible you are with the application of your knowledge, the better you will be able to apply it to the changing environment of the questions. This will allow you to use principles and apply them for various questions helping with time conservation.

Remember Applications

Chemistry is dominated by applications in the real world and you can expect the questions to reflect this. If you design your revision round this idea, it will help you not only prepare better as you are more likely to retain the information, but it will also make sure that you are not thrown off by challenging application questions.

Analyse the Questions

There are two main types of chemistry questions: organic and inorganic. Organic chemistry questions often involve drawing and naming molecules, whilst inorganic chemistry questions can be more mathematical. It is paramount that you analyse each question in advance to ensure that you are aware of what is coming up. You do not want to be halfway through a question and realise that you would rather have answered another question!

Focus on Clarity

Chemistry often involves drawing things like molecules and writing out sometimes long chemical reactions. It is very important that your writing is clear and legible - a wayward dash or heavy smudge may be taken by an examiner to be a minus sign etc. It is worth buying a mechanical pencil and rubber ahead of an exam and having spare leads.

Memorise Formulas

It goes without mentioning the importance of basic formulas, such as the gas law ($pV = nRT$), molar amount ($n = M/M_r$) etc. Although these formulas are provided in formula books, many students waste time during an exam looking these up. Such basic equations should become second-nature to you as your revision progresses, and with practice you should be able to apply the correct formulas to problems automatically.

Practice makes Perfect

Perhaps the one of the trickiest questions possible in a chemistry exam is being asked to draw a complex molecule. There is an almost unlimited amount of material on the internet which can be used to prepare from. What can also be helpful to do is to slightly alter examples from books/the internet (e.g. move a methyl group to another carbon atom etc.) and re-draw a molecule. This way, you ensure that you fully understand how nomenclature in chemistry works. It is also a good idea to memorise other standard chemical processes/reactions, such as the free radical breakdown of ozone etc. which is available freely online.

Chemistry Question 1

Compounds added to pure water react, and undergo changes in concentration until the products reach equilibrium. If two reactants, **A** and **B** are added to pure water, the reaction that takes place is: $A + B \leftrightarrow C + D$

a) When the products and reactants are at chemical equilibrium, describe the rates of the forward and backward reactions and concentration of the reactants and products.

[2 marks]

b) Write three balanced equations describing the reactions that occur when CO_2 is dissolved in water.

[3 marks]

c) When the reaction between the reactants and products of the above reaction has reach chemical equilibrium, the following relationship describes the concentration of the products and reactants: $\frac{[A][B]}{[C][D]} = 10^{-pK}$

Whereby pK is the dissociation constant that characterises this relationship for a specific reaction, and is determined through experimental research. The table below lists the values for the Henry's constant, pK, for the reactants and products of the reaction of part b:

Reaction	10^{-pk}
$H_2CO_3 \leftrightarrow H^+ + HCO_3^-$	$10^{-6.35}$
$HCO_3^- \leftrightarrow H^+ + CO_3^{2-}$	$10^{-10.33}$
$H^+ + OH^- \leftrightarrow H_2O$	10^{-14}

At the equator, atmospheric CO_2 has a partial pressure, $p[CO_2]$, of 340 ppm(v). The concentration of atmospheric CO_2 is given by the following relationship: $\frac{[H_2CO_3]}{p[CO_2]} = 10^{1.47}$ molecules/litre

Use the values from the table to calculate the concentration of H_2CO_3.

[1 mark]

d) In order to calculate the pH of pristine precipitation, use the relationship: $[H^+] = [HCO_3^-] + 2[CO_3^{2-}] + [OH^-]$ to write down equations that express $[H^+]$ in terms of the products of the above reaction.

[8 marks]

e) For $[H^+]^n = 10^X$, $[H^+] = 10^{X/n}$. Using an appropriate approximation, calculate the concentration of H^+ of CO_2 in equilibrium with the Earth's oceans.

[2 marks]

f) What is the relationship between pH and the concentration of H^+?

[1 mark]

g) Use your answers to calculate the pH of rain water in equilibrium with atmospheric CO_2.

[1 mark]

h) CO_2 is not the only gas that contributes to the acidification of precipitation. Sulphur dioxide, both naturally and anthropogenically produced also contributes to acid rain.

Reaction	10^{-pk}
$H_2SO_3 \leftrightarrow H^+ + HSO_3^-$	$10^{-1.77}$
$HSO_3^- \leftrightarrow H^+ + SO_3^{2-}$	$10^{-7.21}$

The concentration of atmospheric SO_2 is 0.2 ppb(v), and $\frac{[H_2SO_3]}{p[SO_2]} = 10^{0.096}$ molecules/litre. The charge-balance equation for the combined $CO_2 + SO_2$ systems is: $[H^+] = [HCO_3^-] + 2[CO_3^{2-}] + [HSO_3^-] + 2[SO_3^{2-}] + [OH^-]$

Using the values above and the approximation equation from part e, calculate a new value for the pH of rainwater that is in equilibrium with the atmosphere.

[5 marks]

i) What are the main sources of atmospheric SO_2?

[2 marks]

[Total: 25 marks]

Chemistry Question 2

a) Draw shapes representing the distribution of electron density in p-orbitals around atom X.

[3 marks]

b) (i) Species XH_4 can carry a zero, positive or negative charge. Write formulas for reactions between XH_3 and H^+ ions, and draw dot and cross diagrams representing the products, stating their charge.

[6 marks]

(ii) What shape is the molecule XH_4, and what are the bond angles?

[2 marks]

(iii) State which atoms X can be

[3 marks]

c) An aqueous solution of 2,2 di-methyl butanoic acid with a concentration of 0.05 mol dm^{-1} has a pH of 3.2.
(i) Draw the structure of the acid and write its chemical formula

[3 marks]

(ii) Calculate the pK_a of the acid, showing your working

[3 marks]

(iii) Phenol has a pK_a of 7.5. Draw the molecule phenol (C_6H_5OH) and calculate the pH of a solution containing phenol and 2,2 di-methyl butanoic acid in 3:1 proportion.

[5 marks]

[Total: 25 Marks]

Chemistry Question 3

a) Draw full diagrams showing every atom and bond for the following molecules:

(i) 3-methyl butane
(ii) Heptanal
(iii) Methyl propanoate
(iv) Ethano nitrile
(v) 2-bromo,3-methyl butane

[10 marks]

b) (i) What process is used in the oil industry to break down long-chain hydrocarbon molecules into shorter-chain hydrocarbon molecules?

[1 mark]

(ii) Write down an equation and draw the structures of the broken down products of decane, $C_{10}H_{22}$.

[3 marks]

(iii) In what order will the following products be produced during the breakdown of long-chain hydrocarbons?

Gasoline, diesel oil, bitumen, lubricants, petroleum gases and kerosene

[2 marks]

(iv) In industry, catalysts are used to speed up the thermal decomposition of long-chain hydrocarbons. What are these catalysts called?

[1 mark]

(v) Write out equations outlining all of the reaction phases of the breakdown of ethane using free radicals.

[6 marks]

(vi) What impurities are commonly found in naturally produced hydrocarbons, and what are the main risks involved in the process of breaking down long-chain to short-chain hydrocarbons?

[2 marks]

[Total: 25 Marks]

Chemistry Question 4

a) (i) What is isomerism?

[2 marks]

(ii) Draw all of the isomers of the molecule C_4H_8

[12 marks]

(iii) Which of the molecules you have drawn above are structural isomers and stereoisomers and why?

[2 marks]

b) Write out the mechanisms for the following reactions:
(i) Ethene and HBr
(ii) Cyclohexane and HBr

[8 marks]

(iii) What is this process called?

[1 mark]

[Total: 25 Marks]

Chemistry Question 5

a) Organic compounds can react with the compound H–X (where X = halogen), however the rate of reaction varies. Why does the rate of reaction vary depending on X and how does this relate to bond strength? Write the different H–X molecules in order of reactivity, with the most reactive molecule first.

[4 marks]

b) Elimination reactions are a type of organic reaction in which two substituents are removed from a molecule in either a one step or two step reaction.

(i) Write the one-step reaction mechanism between isobutyl bromide with potassium ethanoxide, dissolved in ethanol.

[5 marks]

(ii) Write out the two-step reaction between C_4H_9Br and potassium ethanoxide, dissolved in ethanol. Label clearly all hydrogen bonds present in the transitional stage.

[6 Marks]

c) (i) Write an expression between pK_a and ethanoic acid, CH_3COOH

[2 marks]

(ii) Calculate the pH of 0.017 M of aqueous ethanoic acid, where $pK_a = 4.76$.

[4 marks]

(iii) Explain why the pK_a of ethanoic acid is different to the pK_a of ethanol, where $pK_a = 16.0$ for ethanol.

[4 marks]

[Total: 25 Marks]

Section 2: Biology

Preparation

Biology questions are heavily knowledge based and require you to apply a principle in order to get to the correct answer. Thus, it essential you're familiar with concepts like genetics, natural selection, cells, organs systems and species interaction. It will make your life a lot easier if you feel comfortable with all the different aspects of biology. Specialisation here can go a long way. Chances are that if you prepare well for as many of the different topics as possible you will not be caught off guard and you will not have to waste time on trying to recall them.

Think in Principles

Tying in with the previous point, thinking in principles in biology will help you select relevant information and separate it from irrelevant information. This will allow you to work efficiently and you will be able to produce high quality answers. Try and figure out why a certain system makes sense from an efficiency perspective.

Remember, biology is about producing the maximum result with a minimum of energy expenditure. It can sometimes also help to use case studies for revision. This will allow you to study an entire variety of biological topics under one common headline that will make it easier to think through the context. For example diabetes lets you revise hormones associated with digestion and energy control as well response mechanisms to cellular stimulation and metabolism.

Language

Get used to using scientific language. The more precise you can be with your answers, the less time it will take you to convey your information meaning you will be that much more likely to answer all the questions. Technical terms are a great tool as they are so precise and make you look a lot more professional. In this context however you MUST ensure that you are using the technical terms correctly! Using technical terms incorrectly is a very quick way to getting the question completely wrong, even if you might be in the right path.

Logic is Key

The very nature of the exam is designed to throw you off guard and force you to use your knowledge to come to conclusions you might not have been taught at school. This is what separates good and great students. Applying the principles you have learned securely and efficiently will allow you to answer most questions correctly, even if you have never addressed them before.

Biology is a very logical science that is largely based on the idea that the goal is always to reach the maximum mount of effect with a minimum of energy expenditure. Thus, it is obvious that you need to have a sound scientific basis in order to recognise the different connections between topics.

Time = Marks

Due to the large amount of information that can be examined in the biology questions, it is essential to keep an eye on your time. You have about 20 minutes per question which means that it is easy to run out of time, especially if you are required to make a drawing or if there are large amounts of text resource to read. One catch to be aware of is that there can be some degree of interconnection between different sub-questions making it necessary to think through one first part before progressing to the next.

Biology Question 1:

In healthy humans, the blood sugar levels are controlled by the secretion of insulin from the pancreas. During episodes of high blood sugar levels, the beta cells in the pancreas secrete the insulin, a protein hormone, which allows cells to take up sugar from the blood.

A.   The following DNA sequence is part of the human insulin gene:

3' … GAC ACG CCG AGT … 5'

5' … CTG TGC GGC TCA … 3'

Using the decoding wheel, what amino acid sequence does this encode?

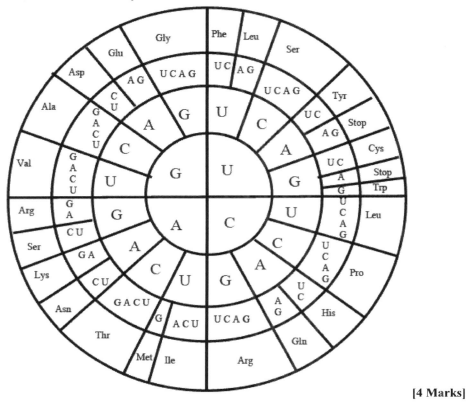

[4 Marks]

B.   Would a point mutation on the first space of the first base triplet be possible without changing the original amino acid sequence?

[2 Marks]

C.   In the past, insulin was derived from slaughtered animals such as pigs and beef. Introducing this foreign protein to the human body resulted in a variety of hypersensitivity reactions. After isolating the insulin gene in the human genome, mass production in bacteria was possible.

How would you produce human insulin in bacteria?

[6 Marks]

D. Hyperinsulinemia is a disorder commonly associated with individuals using insulin for therapeutic means in the context of diabetes mellitus. It can also occur in the context of a genetic disease affecting the natural control mechanisms of insulin release.

Understanding that insulin release is controlled through the binding of glucose to a beta cell surface receptor which causes the release of insulin by triggering vesicle release through an amplification protein, where would you expect the mutation to be located?

[4 Marks]

E. Insulin acts by allowing sugar to enter cells. Explain what happens in type 2 diabetes using the drawing below:

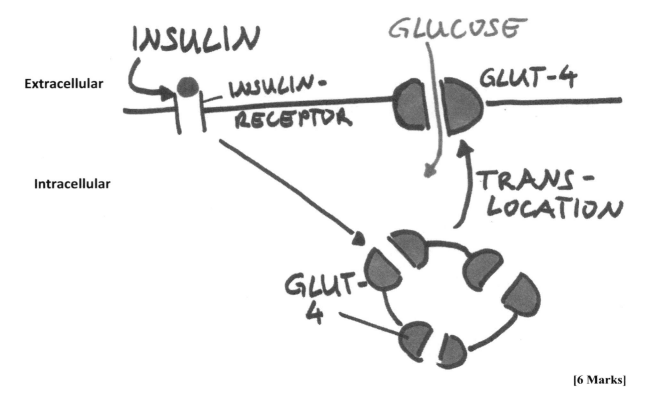

[6 Marks]

F. Glucagon is another hormone produced by the pancreas. What action does glucagon have on liver cells?

[3 Marks]

[Total: 25 Marks]

Biology Question 2:

Many insects possess a stinger for personal defence against predators. This includes insects such as bees and wasps. In nature, it often happens that frogs, especially if not confronted with stingered insects in the past, attempt to eat these insects.

The hunting behaviour of frogs involves them sitting motionless, waiting for their prey to move past them. Hunting happens through rapid extension of the tongue, grabbing of the prey and swallowing in one fluent and extremely rapid motion. Attempting to eat a stinger armed insects leads to the frog immediately spitting out the prey followed by retching and attempts to remove the insect from the mouth, despite it being gone already.

A. Compare the frogs, as a representative of vertebrates, and the insects nerve fibres with regards to speed of information transmission.

[4 Marks]

B. Draw a schematic representation of a reflex arc.

[4 Marks]

C. The perception of pain is due to pain receptors in the skin. The perception of pain is relayed to the spinal cord as well as to the brain. In the spinal cord, the pain impulse produces a specific reflex. Describe the purpose of relaying the pain impulse both to the spine and the brain.

[4 Marks]

D. Describe the evolutionary basis for mimicry amongst poisonous and non-poisonous species.

[3 Marks]

E. Pain impulses is transmitted along the nerve fibre through action potentials which are maintained by ion channels. Describe how action potentials are generated.

[6 Marks]

F. Lidocaine is a local anaesthetic used to control pain in many medical environments. It acts by blocking sodium channels. Explain how lidocaine blocks transmission of pain signals along nerve fibres.

[4 Marks]

[Total: 25 Marks]

Biology Question 3:

Chimpanzees live in large, hierarchical groups of up to 100 individuals. They are omnivores and eat plant materials as well as insects. They also hunt for small mammals. The large groups of chimps, often split up into smaller groups for food gathering and hunting and it has been observed that the hunting success rate increases proportionally with the size of the subgroups - in groups, larger than 6 individuals, success rate approaches roughly 90%.

A. Describe how large units like this group of chimpanzees are organized.

[4 Marks]

B. What are the evolutionary advantages of organisation of individuals in large groups?

[4 Marks]

C. Many animals living in groups have developed forms of communication. What is the purpose of being able to communicate and do you think there is any limitation on the type of species developing communication mechanisms?

[4 Marks]

D. In some animals, such as certain mountain goat species, reproduction is limited to a few weeks each year. This increases reproductive pressure on both males and females in the population. What reasons can you see for this behaviour?

[3 Marks]

E. What role does genetic diversity play in the survival of populations?

[3 Marks]

F. Provide a hypothesis why most animal groups are organized in a male dominance pattern and female dominance is rarer.

[7 Marks]

[Total: 25 Marks]

Biology Question 4:

Palicourea marcgravii is a plant occurring in South America. Ingestion of this plant causes sudden death in ruminants such as cows but not in monogastriers such as horses where it causes a more slowly progressing disease. The symptoms of the sudden death variant include muscle cramps, shortness of breath and abnormal movements of extremities followed by death within roughly 10 minutes.

A. Formulate a hypothesis why the sudden death variant of the reaction is exclusive to ruminants.

[4 Marks]

B. What action does Adrenaline have on organs such as the heart, the gut, the lungs and the blood vessels?

[3 Marks]

C. Recently the toxic ingredients of the plant have been isolated. One of them, fluoroacetate, directly interferes with the production of ATP in the citric acid cycle. The third chemical component, N-Methyltyramine, is not by itself toxic but accelerates the toxic action of fluoroacetate by acting as a competitive substrate to Monoamine oxidase A (MAO-A) and thereby increasing adrenalin concentration in the body. Explain how this causes death.

[5 Marks]

D. How does enzyme inhibition via competitive agonist work?

[3 Marks]

E. Suggest a possible treatment ingestion of Palicourea marcgravii.

[3 Marks]

F. Describe the purpose of the fight or flight with regards to the physiologic changes associated with it.

[7 Marks]

[Total: 25 Marks]

Biology Question 5:

In E. Coli, the expression of different enzymes can be controlled by operons that rapid to the presence of specific substrates in the environment. One example of this, is the response to arabinose. In absence of arabinose, the digesting enzymes are not being synthesized as the RNA polymerase cannot bind to a promotor triggering expression of the required gene. In the presence of arabinose in the environment, it binds to a regulator protein which in turn binds to the promotor causing activation of the enzyme gene.

A. Draw a schematic representation of the expression control in presence of arabinose.

[3 Marks]

B. Using the information provided above, formulate a hypothesis of how E coli controls the expression of lactase.

[2 Marks]

C. How would a gain of function mutation in the operon affect enzyme expression and what consequences would this have for the bacterium?

[3 Marks]

D. Why do bacteria have mechanisms to control enzyme production based on environmental substrates?

[5 Marks]

E. Operon mediated enzyme expression also plays a role in facultative antibiotic resistance in certain bacteria. What do you think this means?

[5 Marks]

F. Why is operon controlled expression mechanisms less common in humans?

[7 Marks]

[Total: 25 Marks]

ANSWERS

Question	Answer	Question	Answer	Question	Answer	Question	Answer
1	B	51	D	101	D	151	D
2	C	52	D	102	G	152	F
3	C	53	B	103	F	153	A
4	C	54	E	104	B	154	A
5	E	55	E	105	A	155	D
6	A	56	B	106	C	156	C
7	C	57	C	107	G	157	B
8	E	58	A	108	D	158	F
9	E	59	C	109	D	159	A
10	C	60	B	110	E	160	C
11	E	61	B	111	B	161	C
12	E	62	B	112	A	162	E
13	E	63	C	113	E	163	F
14	B	64	C	114	D	164	G
15	C	65	A	115	F	165	F
16	B	66	C	116	E	166	A
17	B	67	D	117	A	167	C
18	C	68	C	118	B	168	B
19	D	69	D	119	C	169	D
20	C	70	A	120	D	170	B
21	B	71	C	121	F	171	E
22	A	72	B	122	E	172	B
23	F	73	B	123	C	173	D
24	D	74	A	124	C	174	D
25	A	75	C	125	B	175	D
26	B	76	F	126	D	176	D
27	A	77	A	127	F	177	E
28	F	78	D	128	G	178	E
29	D	79	E	129	D	179	B
30	A	80	G	130	D	180	G
31	D	81	C	131	A	181	A
32	D	82	D	132	E	182	A
33	F	83	E	133	C	183	B
34	B	84	D	134	D	184	E
35	C	85	D	135	C	185	B
36	B	86	F	136	D	186	D
37	C	87	B	137	F	187	A
38	A	88	C	138	B	188	A
39	A	89	G	139	A	189	B
40	C	90	D	140	C	190	C
41	B	91	E	141	C	191	B
42	D	92	A	142	G	192	A
43	C	93	E	143	C	193	F
44	A	94	G	144	B	194	A
45	C	95	E	145	B	195	E
46	C	96	H	146	E	196	F
47	C	97	E	147	C	197	H
48	B	98	G	148	E	198	B
49	D	99	D	149	E	199	E
50	E	100	E	150	D	200	D

Question	Answer	Question	Answer	Question	Answer	Question	Answer
	A	251	F	301	C	351	E
	D	252	D	302	B	352	D
	D	253	C	303	A	353	A
	C	254	E	304	C	354	B
	G	255	E	305	C	355	C
	E	256	C	306	C	356	D
207	D	257	C	307	A	357	A
208	D	258	A	308	E	358	B
209	F	259	E	309	C	359	C
210	C	260	A	310	C	360	E
211	A	261	A	311	A		
212	B	262	C	312	D		
213	E	263	A	313	C		
214	C	264	F	314	B		
215	D	265	H	315	D		
216	C	266	C	316	C		
217	C	267	H	317	C		
218	E	268	B	318	E		
219	C	269	F	319	E		
220	B	270	E	320	A		
221	B	271	B	321	C		
222	B	272	A	322	C		
223	E	273	I	323	E		
224	D	274	C	324	A		
225	C	275	B	325	D		
226	A	276	D	326	C		
227	F	277	A	327	D		
228	F	278	B	328	C		
229	A	279	C	329	D		
230	C	280	C	330	B		
231	C	281	A	331	E		
232	D	282	B	332	A		
233	B	283	C	333	D		
234	A	284	B	334	C		
235	D	285	F	335	E		
236	D	286	E	336	E		
237	A	287	F	337	E		
238	C	288	A	338	C		
239	A	289	A	339	E		
240	E	290	A	340	D		
241	D	291	C	341	A		
242	A	292	A	342	B		
243	D	293	A	343	C		
244	D	294	F	344	D		
245	B	295	E	345	B		
246	A	296	D	346	D		
247	E	297	B	347	C		
248	D	298	D	348	E		
249	F	299	A	349	C		
250	F	300	F	350	A		

Section 1: Worked Answers

Question 1: B

Each three-block combination is mutually exclusive to any other combination, so the probabilities are added. Each block pick is independent of all other picks, so the probabilities can be multiplied. For this scenario there are three possible combinations:

P(2 red blocks and 1 yellow block) = P(red then red then yellow) + P(red then yellow then red) + P(yellow then red then red) =

$(\frac{12}{20} \times \frac{11}{19} \times \frac{8}{18}) + (\frac{12}{20} \times \frac{8}{19} \times \frac{11}{18}) + (\frac{8}{20} \times \frac{12}{19} \times \frac{11}{18}) =$

$\frac{3 \times 12 \times 11 \times 8}{20 \times 19 \times 18} = \frac{44}{95}$

Question 2: C

Multiply through by 15: $3(3x + 5) + 5(2x - 2) = 18 \times 15$

Thus: $9x + 15 + 10x - 10 = 270$

$9x + 10x = 270 - 15 + 10$

$19x = 265$

$x = 13.95$

Question 3: C

This is a rare case where you need to factorise a complex polynomial:

(3x   )(x   ) = 0, possible pairs: 2 x 10, 10 x 2, 4 x 5, 5 x 4

(3x - 4)(x + 5) = 0

3x - 4 = 0, so x = $\frac{4}{3}$

x + 5 = 0, so x = -5

Question 4: C

$\frac{5(x-4)}{(x+2)(x-4)} + \frac{3(x+2)}{(x+2)(x-4)}$

$= \frac{5x-20+3x+6}{(x+2)(x-4)}$

$= \frac{8x-14}{(x+2)(x-4)}$

Question 5: E

$p \propto \sqrt[3]{q}$, so $p = k\sqrt[3]{q}$

$p = 12$ when $q = 27$ gives $12 = k\sqrt[3]{27}$, so $12 = 3k$ and $k = 4$

so $p = 4\sqrt[3]{q}$

Now $p = 24$:

$24 = 4\sqrt[3]{q}$, so $6 = \sqrt[3]{q}$ and $q = 6^3 = 216$

Question 6: A

8 x 9 = 72

8 = (4 x 2) = 2 x 2 x 2

9 = 3 x 3

$(2 x 2 x 2 x 3 x 3)^2 = 2 x 2 x 2 x 2 x 2 x 2 x 3 x 3 x 3 x 3 = 2^6 x 3^4$

Question 7: C

Note that 1.151 x 2 = 2.302.

Thus: $\frac{2 \times 10^5 + 2 \times 10^2}{10^{10}} = 2 \times 10^{-5} + 2 \times 10^{-8}$

$= 0.00002 + 0.00000002 = 0.00002002$

Question 8: E

$y^2 + ay + b$

$= (y +2)^2 - 5 = y^2 + 4y + 4 - 5$

$= y^2 + 4y + 4 - 5 = y^2 + 4y - 1$

So a = 4 and y = -1

Question 9: E

Take $5(m + 4n)$ as a common factor to give: $\frac{4(m+4n)}{5(m+4n)} + \frac{5(m-2n)}{5(m+4n)}$

Simplify to give: $\frac{4m+16n+5m-10n}{5(m+4n)} = \frac{9m+6n}{5(m+4n)} = \frac{3(3m+2n)}{5(m+4n)}$

Question 10: C

$A \propto \frac{1}{\sqrt{B}}$. Thus, $= \frac{k}{\sqrt{B}}$.

Substitute the values in to give: $4 = \frac{k}{\sqrt{25}}$.

Thus, $k = 20$.

Therefore, $A = \frac{20}{\sqrt{B}}$.

When B = 16, $A = \frac{20}{\sqrt{16}} = \frac{20}{4} = 5$

Question 11: E

Angles SVU and STU are opposites and add up to 180°, so STU = 91°

The angle of the centre of a circle is twice the angle at the circumference so SOU

$= 2 \times 91° = 182°$

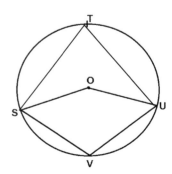

Question 12: E

The surface area of an open cylinder $A = 2\pi rh$. Cylinder B is an enlargement of A, so the increases in radius (r) and height (h) will be proportional: $\frac{r_A}{r_B} = \frac{h_A}{h_B}$. Let us call the proportion coefficient n, where $n = \frac{r_A}{r_B} = \frac{h_A}{h_B}$.

So $\frac{Area\ A}{Area\ B} = \frac{2\pi r_A h_A}{2\pi r_B h_B} = n\ x\ n = n^2$. $\frac{Area\ A}{Area\ B} = \frac{32\pi}{8\pi} = 4$, so $n = 2$.

The proportion coefficient $n = 2$ also applies to their volumes, where the third dimension (also radius, i.e. the r^2 in $V = \pi r^2 h$) is equally subject to this constant of proportionality. The cylinder's volumes are related by $n^3 = 8$.

If the smaller cylinder has volume 2π cm^3, then the larger will have volume $2\pi\ x\ n^3 = 2\pi\ x\ 8 = 16\pi$ cm^3.

Question 13: E

$$= \frac{8}{x(3-x)} - \frac{6(3-x)}{x(3-x)}$$

$$= \frac{8 - 18 + 6x}{x(3-x)}$$

$$= \frac{6x - 10}{x(3-x)}$$

Question 14: B

For the black ball to be drawn in the last round, white balls must be drawn every round. Thus the probability is given by $P = \frac{9}{10}\ x\ \frac{8}{9}\ x\ \frac{7}{8}\ x\ \frac{6}{7}\ x\ \frac{5}{6}\ x\ \frac{4}{5}\ x\ \frac{3}{4}\ x\ \frac{2}{3}\ x\ \frac{1}{2}$

$$= \frac{9\ x\ 8\ x\ 7\ x\ 6\ x\ 5\ x\ 4\ x\ 3\ x\ 2\ x\ 1}{10\ x\ 9\ x\ 8\ x\ 7\ x\ 6\ x\ 5\ x\ 4\ x\ 3\ x\ 2\ x\ 1} = \frac{1}{10}$$

Question 15: C

The probability of getting a king the first time is $\frac{4}{52} = \frac{1}{13}$, and the probability of getting a king the second time is $\frac{3}{51}$. These are independent events, thus, the probability of drawing two kings is $\frac{1}{13}\ x\ \frac{3}{51} = \frac{3}{663} = \frac{1}{221}$

Question 16: B

The probabilities of all outcomes must sum to one, so if the probability of rolling a 1 is x, then: $x + x + x + x + 2x = 1$. Therefore, $x = \frac{1}{7}$.

The probability of obtaining two sixes $P_{12} = \frac{2}{7}\ x\ \frac{2}{7} = \frac{4}{49}$

Question 17: B

There are plenty of ways of counting, however the easiest is as follows: 0 is divisible by both 2 and 3. Half of the numbers from 1 to 36 are even (i.e. 18 of them). 3, 9, 15, 21, 27, 33 are the only numbers divisible by 3 that we've missed. There are 25 outcomes divisible by 2 or 3, out of 37.

Question 18: C

List the six ways of achieving this outcome: HHTT, HTHT, HTTH, TTHH, THTH, and THHT. There are 2^4 possible outcomes for 4 consecutive coin flips, so the probability of two heads and two tails is: $6\ x\ \frac{1}{2^4} = \frac{6}{16} = \frac{3}{8}$

Question 19: D

Count the number of ways to get a 5, 6 or 7 (draw the square if helpful). The ways to get a 5 are: 1, 4; 2, 3; 3, 2; 4, 1. The ways to get a 6 are: 1, 5; 2, 4; 3, 3; 4, 2; 5, 1. The ways to get a 7 are: 1, 6; 2, 5; 3, 4; 4, 3; 5, 2; 6, 1. That is 15 out of 36 possible outcomes.

	1	2	3	4	5	6
1	2	3	4	5	6	7
2	3	4	5	6	7	8
3	4	5	6	7	8	9
4	5	6	7	8	9	10
5	6	7	8	9	10	11
6	7	8	9	10	11	12

Question 20: C

There are x+y+z balls in the bag, and the probability of picking a red ball is $\frac{x}{(x+y+z)}$ and the probability of picking a green ball is $\frac{z}{(x+y+z)}$. These are independent events, so the probability of picking red then green is $\frac{xz}{(x+y+z)^2}$ and the probability of picking green then red is the same. These outcomes are mutually exclusive, so are added.

Question 21: B

There are two ways of doing it, pulling out a red ball then a blue ball, or pulling out a blue ball and then a red ball. Let us work out the probability of the first: $\frac{x}{(x+y+z)} \times \frac{y}{x+y+z-1}$, and the probability of the second option will be the same. These are mutually exclusive options, so the probabilities may be summed.

Question 22: A

[x: Player 1 wins point, y: Player 2 wins point]

Player 1 wins in five rounds if we get: yxxxx, xyxxx, xxyxx, xxxyx.

(Note the case of xxxxy would lead to player 1 winning in 4 rounds, which the question forbids.)

Each of these have a probability of $p^4(1-p)$. Thus, the solution is $4p^4(1-p)$.

Question 23: F

$4x + 7 + 18x + 20 = 14$

$22x + 27 = 14$

Thus, $22x = -13$

Giving $x = -\frac{13}{22}$

Question 24: D

$r^3 = \frac{3V}{4\pi}$

Thus, $r = \left(\frac{3V}{4\pi}\right)^{1/3}$

Therefore, $S = 4\pi \left[\left(\frac{3V}{4\pi}\right)^{\frac{1}{3}}\right]^2 = 4\pi \left(\frac{3V}{4\pi}\right)^{\frac{2}{3}}$

$= \frac{4\pi(3V)^{\frac{2}{3}}}{(4\pi)^{\frac{2}{3}}} = (3V)^{\frac{2}{3}} \times \frac{(4\pi)^1}{(4\pi)^{\frac{2}{3}}}$

$= (3V)^{\frac{2}{3}} (4\pi)^{1-\frac{2}{3}} = (4\pi)^{\frac{1}{3}}(3V)^{\frac{2}{3}}$

Question 25: A

Let each unit length be x.

Thus, $S = 6x^2$. Therefore, $x = \left(\frac{S}{6}\right)^{\frac{1}{2}}$

$V = x^3$. Thus, $V = [\left(\frac{S}{6}\right)^{\frac{1}{2}}]^3$ so $V = \left(\frac{S}{6}\right)^{\frac{3}{2}}$

Question 26: B

Multiplying the second equation by 2 we get $4x + 16y = 24$. Subtracting the first equation from this we get $13y = 17$, so $y = \frac{17}{13}$. Then solving for x we get $x = \frac{10}{13}$. You could also try substituting possible solutions one by one, although given that the equations are both linear and contain easy numbers, it is quicker to solve them algebraically.

Question 27: A

Multiply by the denominator to give: $(7x + 10) = (3y^2 + 2)(9x + 5)$

Partially expand brackets on right side: $(7x + 10) = 9x(3y^2 + 2) + 5(3y^2 + 2)$

Take x terms across to left side: $7x - 9x(3y^2 + 2) = 5(3y^2 + 2) - 10$

Take x outside the brackets: $x[7 - 9(3y^2 + 2)] = 5(3y^2 + 2) - 10$

Thus: $x = \frac{5(3y^2 + 2) - 10}{7 - 9(3y^2 + 2)}$

Simplify to give: $x = \frac{(15y^2)}{(7 - 9(3y^2 + 2))}$

Question 28: F

$$3x\left(\frac{3x^7}{x^{\frac{1}{3}}}\right)^3 = 3x\left(\frac{3^3 x^{21}}{x^{\frac{3}{3}}}\right)$$

$$= 3x \frac{27x^{21}}{x} = 81x^{21}$$

Question 29: D

$$2x[2^{\frac{7}{14}} x^{\frac{7}{14}}] = 2x[2^{\frac{1}{2}} x^{\frac{1}{2}}]$$

$$= 2x(\sqrt{2}\sqrt{x}) = 2\left[\sqrt{x}\sqrt{x}\right][\sqrt{2}\sqrt{x}]$$

$$= 2\sqrt{2x^3}$$

Question 30: A

$A = \pi r^2$, therefore $10\pi = \pi r^2$

Thus, $r = \sqrt{10}$

Therefore, the circumference is $2\pi\sqrt{10}$

Question 31: D

$3.4 = 12 + (3 + 4) = 19$

$19.5 = 95 + (19 + 5) = 119$

Question 32: D

$$2.3 = \frac{2^3}{2} = 4$$

$$4.2 = \frac{4^2}{4} = 4$$

Question 33: F

This is a tricky question that requires you to know how to 'complete the square':

$(x + 1.5)(x + 1.5) = x^2 + 3x + 2.25$

Thus, $(x + 1.5)^2 - 7.25 = x^2 + 3x - 5 = 0$

Therefore, $(x + 1.5)^2 = 7.25 = \frac{29}{4}$

Thus, $x + 1.5 = \sqrt{\frac{29}{4}}$

Thus $x = -\frac{3}{2} \pm \sqrt{\frac{29}{4}} = -\frac{3}{2} \pm \frac{\sqrt{29}}{2}$

Question 34: B

Whilst you definitely need to solve this graphically, it is necessary to complete the square for the first equation to allow you to draw it more easily:

$(x + 2)^2 = x^2 + 4x + 4$

Thus, $y = (x + 2)^2 + 10 = x^2 + 4x + 14$

This is now an easy curve to draw ($y = x^2$ that has moved 2 units left and 10 units up). The turning point of this quadratic is to the left and well above anything in x^3, so the only solution is the first intersection of the two curves in the upper right quadrant around (3.4, 39).

Question 35: C

By far the easiest way to solve this is to sketch them (don't waste time solving them algebraically). As soon as you've done this, it'll be very obvious that $y = 2$ and $y = 1-x^2$ don't intersect, since the latter has its turning point at (0, 1) and zero points at $x = -1$ and 1. $y = x$ and $y = x^2$ intersect at the origin and (1, 1), and $y = 2$ runs through both.

Question 36: B

Notice that you're not required to get the actual values – just the number's magnitude. Thus, 897653 can be approximated to 900,000 and 0.009764 to 0.01. Therefore, 900,000 x 0.01 = 9,000

Question 37: C

Multiply through by 70: $7(7x + 3) + 10(3x + 1) = 14 \times 70$

Simplify: $49x + 21 + 30x + 10 = 980$

$79x + 31 = 980$

$x = \frac{949}{79}$

Question 38: A

Split the equilateral triangle into 2 right-angled triangles and apply Pythagoras' theorem:

$x^2 = \left(\frac{x}{2}\right)^2 + h^2$. Thus $h^2 = \frac{3}{4}x^2$

$h = \sqrt{\frac{3x^2}{4}} = \frac{\sqrt{3x^2}}{2}$

The area of a triangle $= \frac{1}{2}$ x base x height $= \frac{1}{2}x\frac{\sqrt{3x^2}}{2}$

Simplifying gives: $x\frac{\sqrt{3x^2}}{4} = x\frac{\sqrt{3}\sqrt{x^2}}{4} = \frac{x^2\sqrt{3}}{4}$

Question 39: A

This is a question testing your ability to spot 'the difference between two squares'.

Factorise to give: $3 - \frac{7x(5x-1)(5x+1)}{(7x)^2(5x+1)}$

Cancel out: $3 - \frac{(5x-1)}{7x}$

Question 40: C

The easiest way to do this is to 'complete the square':

$(x-5)^2 = x^2 - 10x + 25$

Thus, $(x-5)^2 - 125 = x^2 - 10x - 100 = 0$

Therefore, $(x-5)^2 = 125$

$x - 5 = \pm\sqrt{125} = \pm\sqrt{25}\sqrt{5} = \pm5\sqrt{5}$

$x = 5 \pm 5\sqrt{5}$

Question 41: B

Factorise by completing the square:

$x^2 - 4x + 7 = (x-2)^2 + 3$

Simplify: $(x-2)^2 = y^3 + 2 - 3$

$x - 2 = \pm\sqrt{y^3 - 1}$

$x = 2 \pm \sqrt{y^3 - 1}$

Question 42: D

Square both sides to give: $(3x+2)^2 = 7x^2 + 2x + y$

Thus: $y = (3x+2)^2 - 7x^2 - 2x = (9x^2 + 12x + 4) - 7x^2 - 2x$

$y = 2x^2 + 10x + 4$

Question 43: C

This is a fourth order polynomial, which you aren't expected to be able to factorise at GCSE. This is where looking at the options makes your life a lot easier. In all of them, opening the bracket on the right side involves making $(y \pm 1)^4$ on the left side, i.e. the answers are hinting that $(y \pm 1)^4$ is the solution to the fourth order polynomial. Since there are negative terms in the equations (e.g. $-4y^3$), the solution has to be:

$(y-1)^4 = y^4 - 4y^3 + 6y^2 - 4y + 1$

Therefore, $(y-1)^4 + 1 = x^5 + 7$

Thus, $y - 1 = (x^5 + 6)^{\frac{1}{4}}$

$y = 1 + (x^5 + 6)^{1/4}$

Question 44: A

Let the width of the television be 4x and the height of the television be 3x.

Then by Pythagoras: $(4x)^2 + (3x)^2 = 50^2$

Simplify: $25x^2 = 2500$

Thus: $x = 10$. Therefore: the screen is 30 inches by 40 inches, i.e. the area is 1,200 inches^2.

Question 45: C

Square both sides to give: $1 + \frac{3}{x^2} = (y^5 + 1)^2$

Multiply out: $\frac{3}{x^2} = (y^{10} + 2y^5 + 1) - 1$

Thus: $x^2 = \frac{3}{y^{10}+2y^5}$

Therefore: $x = \sqrt{\frac{3}{y^{10} + 2y^5}}$

Question 46: C

The easiest way is to double the first equation and triple the second to get:

$6x - 10y = 20 \; and \; 6x + 6y = 39$.

Subtract the first from the second to give: $16y = 19$,

Therefore, $y = \frac{19}{16}$.

Substitute back into the first equation to give $x = \frac{85}{16}$.

Question 47: C

This is fairly straightforward; the first inequality is the easier one to work with: B and D and E violate it, so we just need to check A and C in the second inequality.

C: $1^3 - 2^2 < 3$, but A: $2^3 - 1^2 > 3$

Question 48: B

Whilst this can be done graphically, it's quicker to do algebraically (because the second equation is not as easy to sketch). Intersections occur where the curves have the same coordinates.

Thus: $x + 4 = 4x^2 + 5x + 5$

Simplify: $4x^2 + 4x + 1 = 0$

Factorise: $(2x + 1)(2x + 1) = 0$

Thus, the two graphs only intersect once at $x = -\frac{1}{2}$

Question 49: D

It's better to do this algebraically as the equations are easy to work with and you would need to sketch very accurately to get the answer. Intersections occur where the curves have the same coordinates. Thus: $x^3 = x$

$x^3 - x = 0$

Thus: $x(x^2 - 1) = 0$

Spot the 'difference between two squares': $x(x + 1)(x - 1) = 0$

Thus there are 3 intersections: at $x = 0, 1 \ and - 1$

Question 50: E

Note that the line is the hypotenuse of a right angled triangle with one side unit length and one side of length ½.

By Pythagoras, $\left(\frac{1}{2}\right)^2 + 1^2 = x^2$

Thus, $x^2 = \frac{1}{4} + 1 = \frac{5}{4}$

$$x = \sqrt{\frac{5}{4}} = \frac{\sqrt{5}}{\sqrt{4}} = \frac{\sqrt{5}}{2}$$

Question 51: D

We can eliminate z from equation (1) and (2) by multiplying equation (1) by 3 and adding it to equation (2):

3x + 3y – 3z = -3	Equation (1) multiplied by 3
2x – 2y +3z = 8	Equation (2) then add both equations
5x + y = 5	We label this as equation (4)

Now we must eliminate the same variable z from another pair of equations by using equation (1) and (3):

2x + 2y – 2z = -2	Equation (1) multiplied by 2
2x – y + 2z = 9	Equation (3) then add both equations
4x + y = 7	We label this as equation (5)

We now use both equations (4) and (5) to obtain the value of x:

5x + y = 5	Equation (4)
- 4x - y = -7	Equation (5) multiplied by -1
x = -2	

Substitute x back in to calculate y:

4x + y = 7

4(-2) + y = 7

- 8 + y = 7

y = 15

Substitute x and y back in to calculate z:

x + y – z = -1

-2 + 15 – z = -1

13 – z = -1

-z = -14

z = 14

Thus: x = -2, y = 15, z = 14

Question 52: D

This is one of the easier maths questions. Take 3a as a factor to give:

$3a(a^2 - 10a + 25) = 3a(a - 5)(a - 5) = 3a(a - 5)^2$

Question 53: B

Note that 12 is the Lowest Common Multiple of 3 and 4. Thus:

-3 (4x + 3y) = -3 (48)   Multiply each side by -3

4 (3x + 2y) = 4 (34)   Multiply each side by 4

-12x – 9y = -144

$\underline{12x + 8y = 136}$ Add together

-y = -8

y = 8

Substitute y back in: 4x + 3y = 48

4x + 3(8) = 48

4x + 24 = 48

4x = 24

x = 6

Question 54: E

Don't be fooled, this is an easy question, just obey BODMAS and don't skip steps.

$\frac{-(25-28)^2}{-36+14} = \frac{-(-3)^2}{-22}$

This gives: $\frac{-(9)}{-22} = \frac{9}{22}$

Question 55: E

Since there are 26 possible letters for each of the 3 letters in the license plate, and there are 10 possible numbers (0-9) for each of the 3 numbers in the same plate, then the number of license plates would be:

(26) x (26) x (26) x (10) x (10) x (10) = 17,576,000

Question 56: B

Expand the brackets to give: $4x^2 - 12x + 9 = 0$.

Factorise: $(2x - 3)(2x - 3) = 0$.

Thus, only one solution exists, x = 1.5.

Note that you could also use the fact that the discriminant, $b^2 - 4ac = 0$ to get the answer.

Question 57: C

$= \left(x^{\frac{1}{2}}\right)^{\frac{1}{2}} (y^{-3})^{\frac{1}{2}}$

$= x^{\frac{1}{4}} y^{-\frac{3}{2}} = \frac{x^{\frac{1}{4}}}{y^{\frac{3}{2}}}$

Question 58: A

Let x, y, and z represent the rent for the 1-bedroom, 2-bedroom, and 3-bedroom flats, respectively. We can write 3 different equations: 1 for the rent, 1 for the repairs, and the last one for the statement that the 3-bedroom unit costs twice as much as the 1-bedroom unit.

(1) x + y + z = 1240

(2) 0.1x + 0.2y + 0.3z = 276

(3) z = 2x

Substitute z = 2x in both of the two other equations to eliminate z:

(4) x + y + 2x = 3x + y = 1240

(5) 0.1x + 0.2y + 0.3(2x) = 0.7x + 0.2y = 276

-2(3x + y) = -2(1240)   Multiply each side of (4) by -2

10(0.7x + 0.2y) = 10(276)   Multiply each side of (5) by 10

(6) -6x -2y = -2480   Add these 2 equations

<u>**(7)** 7x + 2y = 2760</u>

x = 280

z = 2(280) = 560   Because z = 2x

280 + y + 560 = 1240   Because x + y + z = 1240

y = 400

Thus the units rent for £ 280, £ 400, £ 560 per week respectively.

Question 59: C

Following BODMAS:

$$= 5 \left[5(6^2 - 5 \times 3) + 400^{\frac{1}{2}} \right]^{1/3} + 7$$

$$= 5 \left[5(36 - 15) + 20 \right]^{\frac{1}{3}} + 7$$

$$= 5 \left[5(21) + 20 \right]^{\frac{1}{3}} + 7$$

$$= 5 \left(105 + 20 \right)^{\frac{1}{3}} + 7$$

$$= 5 \left(125 \right)^{\frac{1}{3}} + 7$$

$$= 5 (5) + 7$$

$$= 25 + 7 = 32$$

Question 60: B

Consider a triangle formed by joining the centre to two adjacent vertices. Six similar triangles can be made around the centre – thus, the central angle is 60 degrees. Since the two lines forming the triangle are of equal length, we have 6 identical equilateral triangles in the hexagon.

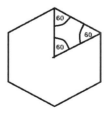

Now split the triangle in half and apply Pythagoras' theorem:

$$1^2 = 0.5^2 + h^2$$

Thus, $h = \sqrt{\frac{3}{4}} = \frac{\sqrt{3}}{2}$

Thus, the area of the triangle is: $\frac{1}{2} bh = \frac{1}{2} \times 1 \times \frac{\sqrt{3}}{2} = \frac{\sqrt{3}}{4}$

Therefore, the area of the hexagon is: $\frac{\sqrt{3}}{4} \times 6 = \frac{3\sqrt{3}}{2}$

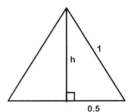

Question 61: B

Let x be the width and x+19 be the length.

Thus, the area of a rectangle is x(x + 19) = 780.

Therefore:

$x^2 + 19x - 780 = 0$

$(x - 20)(x + 39) = 0$

$x - 20 = 0$ or $x + 39 = 0$

$x = 20$ or $x = -39$

Since length can never be a negative number, we disregard x = -39 and use x = 20 instead.

Thus, the width is 20 metres and the length is 39 metres.

Question 62: B

The quickest way to solve is by trial and error, substituting the provided options. However, if you're keen to do this algebraically, you can do the following:

Start by setting up the equations: Perimeter = 2L + 2W = 34

Thus: L + W = 17

Using Pythagoras: $L^2 + W^2 = 13^2$

Since L + W = 17, W = 17 - L

Therefore: $L^2 + (17 - L)^2 = 169$

$L^2 + 289 - 34L + L^2 = 169$

$2L^2 - 34L + 120 = 0$

$L^2 - 17L + 60 = 0$

$(L - 5)(L - 12) = 0$

Thus: L = 5 and L = 12

And: W = 12 and W = 5

Question 63: C

Multiply both sides by 8:	$4(3x - 5) + 2(x + 5) = 8(x + 1)$
Remove brackets:	$12x - 20 + 2x + 10 = 8x + 8$
Simplify:	$14x - 10 = 8x + 8$
Add 10:	$14x = 8x + 18$
Subtract 8x:	$6x = 18$
Therefore:	$x = 3$

Question 64: C

Recognise that 1.742 x 3 is 5.226. Now, the original equation simplifies to: $= \frac{3 \times 10^6 + 3 \times 10^5}{10^{10}}$

$= 3 \times 10^{-4} + 3 \times 10^{-5} = 3.3 \times 10^{-4}$

Question 65: A

$Area = \frac{(2 + \sqrt{2})(4 - \sqrt{2})}{2}$

$= \frac{8 - 2\sqrt{2} + 4\sqrt{2} - 2}{2}$

$= \frac{6 + 2\sqrt{2}}{2}$

$= 3 + \sqrt{2}$

Question 66: C

Square both sides: $\frac{4}{x} + 9 = (y - 2)^2$

$\frac{4}{x} = (y - 2)^2 - 9$

Cross Multiply: $\frac{x}{4} = \frac{1}{(y-2)^2 - 9}$

$x = \frac{4}{y^2 - 4y + 4 - 9}$

Factorise: $x = \frac{4}{y^2 - 4y - 5}$

$x = \frac{4}{(y+1)(y-5)}$

Question 67: D

Set up the equation: $5x - 5 = 0.5(6x + 2)$

$10x - 10 = 6x + 2$

$4x = 12$

$x = 3$

Question 68: C

Round numbers appropriately: $\frac{55 + (\frac{9}{4})^2}{\sqrt{900}} = \frac{55 + \frac{81}{16}}{30}$

81 rounds to 80 to give: $\frac{55 + 5}{30} = \frac{60}{30} = 2$

Question 69: D

There are three outcomes from choosing the type of cheese in the crust. For each of the additional toppings to possibly add, there are 2 outcomes: 1 to include and another not to include a certain topping, for each of the 7 toppings

Thus, the number of different kinds of pizza is: $3 \times 2 \times 2 \times 2 \times 2 \times 2 \times 2 \times 2 = 3 \times 2^7$

$= 3 \times 128 = 384$

Question 70: A

Although it is possible to do this algebraically, by far the easiest way is via trial and error. The clue that you shouldn't attempt it algebraically is the fact that rearranging the first equation to make x or y the subject leaves you with a difficult equation to work with (e.g. $x = \sqrt{1 - y^2}$) when you try to substitute in the second.

An exceptionally good student might notice that the equations are symmetric in x and y, i.e. the solution is when x = y. Thus $2x^2 = 1$ and $2x = \sqrt{2}$ which gives $\frac{\sqrt{2}}{2}$ as the answer.

Question 71: C

If two shapes are congruent, then they are the same size and shape. Thus, congruent objects can be rotations and mirror images of each other. The two triangles in E are indeed congruent (SAS). Congruent objects must, by definition, have the same angles.

Question 72: B

Rearrange the equation: $x^2 + x - 6 \geq 0$

Factorise: $(x + 3)(x - 2) \geq 0$

Remember that this is a quadratic inequality so requires a quick sketch to ensure you don't make a silly mistake with which way the sign is.

Thus, $y = 0$ when $x = 2$ and $x = -3$. $y > 0$ when $x > 2$ or $x < -3$.

Thus, the solution is: $x \leq -3 \ and \ x \geq 2$.

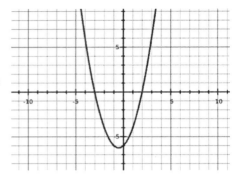

Question 73: B

Using Pythagoras: $a^2 + b^2 = x^2$

Since the triangle is isosceles: $a = b, \ so \ 2a^2 = x^2$

Area $= \frac{1}{2} base \ x \ height = \frac{1}{2}a^2$. From above, $a^2 = \frac{x^2}{2}$

Thus the area $= \frac{1}{2}x\frac{x^2}{2} = \frac{x^2}{4}$

Question 74: A

If X and Y are doubled, the value of Q increases by 4. Halving the value of A reduces this to 2. Finally, tripling the value of B reduces this to ⅔, i.e. the value decreases by ⅓.

Question 75: C

The quickest way to do this is to sketch the curves. This requires you to factorise both equations by completing the square:

$x^2 - 2x + 3 = (x - 1)^2 + 2$

$x^2 - 6x - 10 = (x - 3)^2 - 19$ Thus, the first equation has a turning point at (1, 2) and doesn't cross the x-axis. The second equation has a turning point at (3, -19) and crosses the x-axis twice.

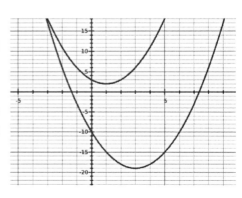

Question 76: F
That the amplitude of a wave determines its mass is false. Waves are not objects and do not have mass.

Question 77: A
We know that displacement s = 30 m, initial speed u = 0 ms^{-1}, acceleration a = 5.4 ms^{-2}, final speed v = ?, time t = ?
And that $v^2 = u^2 + 2as$
$v^2 = 0 + 2$ x 5.4 x 30
$v^2 = 324$ so v = 18 ms^{-1}
and s = ut + 1/2 at^2 so 30 = 1/2 x 5.4 x t^2
$t^2 = 30/2.7$ so t = 3.3 s

Question 78: D
The wavelength is given by: velocity v = λf and frequency f = 1/T so v = λ/T giving wavelength λ = vT
The period T = 49 s/7 so λ = 5 ms^{-1} x 7 s = 35 m

Question 79: E
This is a straightforward question as you only have to put the numbers into the equation (made harder by the numbers being hard to work with).
$Power = \frac{Force \; x \; Distance}{Time} = \frac{375 \; N \; x \; 1.3 \; m}{5 \; s}$
$= 75 \; x \; 1.3 = 97.5 \; W$

Question 80: G
v = u + at
v = 0 + 5.6 x 8 = 44.8 ms^{-1}
And $s = ut + \frac{at^2}{2} = 0 + 5.6 \; x \frac{8^2}{2} = 179.2$

Question 81: C
The sky diver leaves the plane and will accelerate until the air resistance equals their weight – this is their terminal velocity. The sky diver will accelerate under the force of gravity. If the air resistance force exceeded the force of gravity the sky diver would accelerate away from the ground, and if it was less than the force of gravity they would continue to accelerate toward the ground.

Question 82: D
 s = 20 m, u = 0 ms^{-1}, a = 10 ms^{-2}
and $v^2 = u^2 + 2as$
$v^2 = 0 + 2$ x 10 x 20
$v^2 = 400$;   v = 20 ms^{-1}
Momentum = Mass x velocity = 20 x 0.1 = 2 kgms^{-1}

Question 83: E
Electromagnetic waves have varying wavelengths and frequencies and their energy is proportional to their frequency.

Question 84: D
The total resistance = R + r = 0.8 + 1 = 1.8 Ω
and $I = \frac{e.m.f}{total \; resistance} = \frac{36}{1.8} = 20 \; A$

Question 85: C
Use Newton's second law and remember to work in SI units:
So $Force = mass \; x \; accelaration = mass \; x \frac{\Delta velocity}{time}$

$= 20 \; x \; 10^{-3} \; x \; \frac{100 - 0}{10 \; x \; 10^{-3}}$

$= 200 \; N$

Question 86: F

In this case, the work being done is moving the bag 0.7 m

i.e. $Work\ Done\ =\ Bag's\ Weight\ x\ Distance\ =\ 50 \times 10 \times 0.7 = 350\ N$

$Power = \frac{Work}{Time} = \frac{350}{3} = 116.7\ W$

$= 117\ W$ to 3 significant figures

Question 87: B

Firstly, use $P = Fv$ to calculate the power [Ignore the frictional force as we are not concerned with the resultant force here].

So $P = 300 \times 30 = 9000\ W$

Then, use $P = IV$ to calculate the current.

$I = P/V = 9000/200 = 45\ A$

Question 88: C

Work is defined as $W = F \times s$. Work can also be defined as work = force x distance moved in the direction of force. Work is measured in joules and 1 Joule = 1 Newton x 1 Metre, and 1 Newton = 1 Kg x ms^{-2} [F = ma].

Thus, 1 Joule = Kgm^2s^{-2}

Question 89: G

Joules are the unit of energy (and also Work = Force x Distance). Thus, 1 Joule = 1 N x 1 m.

Pa is the unit of Pressure (= Force/Area). Thus, Pa = N x m^{-2}. So J = Nm^{-2} x m^3 = Pa x m^3. Newton's third law describes that every action produces an equal and opposite reaction. For this reason, the energy required to decelerate a body is equal to the amount of energy it possess during movement, i.e. its kinetic energy, which is defined as in statement 1.

Question 90: D

Alpha radiation is of the lower energy, as it represents the movement of a fairly large particle consisting of 2 neutrons and 2 protons. Beta radiation consists of high-energy, high-speed electrons or positrons.

Question 91: E

The half-life does depend on atom type and isotope, as these parameters significantly impact on the physical properties of the atom in general, so statement 1 is false. Statement 2 is the correct definition of half-life. Statement 3 is also correct: half-life in exponential decay will always have the same duration, independent of the quantity of the matter in question; in non-exponential decay, half-life is dependent on the quantity of matter in question.

Question 92: A

In contrast to nuclear fission, where neutrons are shot at unstable atoms, nuclear fusion is based on the high speed, high-temperature collision of molecules, most commonly hydrogen, to form a new, stable atom while releasing energy.

Question 93: E

Nuclear fission releases a significant amount of energy, which is the basis of many nuclear weapons. Shooting neutrons at unstable atoms destabilises the nuclei which in turn leads to a chain reaction and fission. Nuclear fission can lead to the release of ionizing gamma radiation.

Question 94: G

The total resistance of the circuit would be twice the resistance of one resistor and proportional to the voltage, as given by Ohm's Law. Since it is a series circuit, the same current flows through each resistor and since they are identical the potential difference across each resistor will be the same.

Question 95: E

The distance between Earth and Sun = Time x Speed = 60 x 8 seconds x 3×10^8 ms^{-1} = $480 \times 3 \times 10^8$ m

Approximately = 1500×10^8 = 1.5×10^{11} m.

The circumference of Earth's orbit around the sun is given by $2\pi r = 2 \times 3 \times 1.5 \times 10^{11}$

$= 9 \times 10^{11} = 10^{12}$ m

Question 96: H

Speed is a scalar quantity whilst velocity is a vector describing both magnitude and direction. Speed describes the distance a moving object covers over time (i.e. speed = distance/time), whereas velocity describes the rate of change of the displacement of an object (i.e. velocity = displacement/time). The internationally standardised unit for speed is meters per second (ms^{-1}), while ms^{-2} is the unit of acceleration.

Question 97: E

Ohm's Law only applies to conductors and can be mathematically expressed as $V \alpha I$. The easiest way to do this is to write down the equations for statements c, d and e. C: $I \alpha \frac{1}{V}$; D: $I \alpha V^2$; E: $I \alpha V$. Thus, statement E is correct.

Question 98: G

Any object at rest is not accelerating and therefore has no resultant force. Strictly speaking, Newton's second law is actually: Force = rate of change of momentum, which can be mathematically manipulated to give statement 2:

$$Force = \frac{momentum}{time} = \frac{mass \text{ x } velocity}{time} = mass \text{ x } accelaration$$

Question 99: D

Statement 3 is incorrect, as $Charge = Current \text{ } x \text{ } time$. Statement 1 substitutes $I = \frac{V}{R}$ and statement 2 substitutes $I = \frac{P}{V}$.

Question 100: E

Weight of elevator + people = mg = 10 x (1600 + 200) = 18,000 N
Applying Newton's second law of motion on the car gives:
Thus, the resultant force is given by:
F_M = Motor Force – [Frictional Force + Weight]
F_M = M – 4,000 – 18,000
Use Newton's second law to give: F_M = M – 22,000 N = ma
Thus, M – 22,000 N = 1,800a
Since the lift must accelerate at $1ms^{-2}$: M = 1,800 kg x 1 ms^{-2} + 22,000 N
M = 23,800 N

Question 101: D

Total Distance = Distance during acceleration phase + Distance during braking phase
Distance during <u>acceleration phase</u> is given by:
$$s = ut + \frac{at^2}{2} = 0 + \frac{5 \text{ x } 10^2}{2} = 250 \text{ } m$$
$$v = u + at = 0 + 5 \text{ x } 10 = 50 \text{ } ms^{-1}$$
And use $a = \frac{v-u}{t}$ to calculate the deceleration: $a = \frac{0-50}{20} = -2.5 \text{ ms}^{-2}$
Distance during the <u>deceleration phase</u> is given by:
$$s = ut + \frac{at^2}{2} = 50 \text{ x } 20 + \frac{-2.5 \text{ x } 20^2}{2} = 1000 - \frac{2.5 \text{ x } 400}{2}$$
$$s = 1000 - 500 = 500 \text{ } m$$
Thus, $Total \text{ } Distance = 250 + 500 = 750 \text{ } m$

Question 102: G

It is not possible to calculate the power of the heater as we don't know the current that flows through it or its internal resistance. The 8 ohms refers to the external copper wire and not the heater. Whilst it's important that you know how to use equations like P = IV, it's more important that you know when you *can't* use them!

Question 103: F

This question has a lot of numbers but not any information on time, which is necessary to calculate power. You cannot calculate power by using P= IV as you don't know how many electrons are accelerated through the potential difference per unit time. Thus, more information is required to calculate the power.

Question 104: B
When an object is in equilibrium with its surroundings, it radiates and absorbs energy at the same rate and so its temperature remains constant i.e. there is no *net* energy transfer. Radiation is slower than conduction and convection.

Question 105: A
The work done by the force is given by: $Work\ Done = Force\ x\ Distance = 12\ N\ x\ 3\ m = 36\ J$

Since the surface is frictionless, $Work\ Done = Kinetic\ Energy$.
$$E_k = \frac{mv^2}{2} = \frac{6v^2}{2}$$
Thus, $36 = 3v^2$
$v = \sqrt{12} = \sqrt{4}\sqrt{3} = 2\sqrt{3}\ ms^{-1}$

Question 106: C
$Total\ energy\ supplied\ to\ water = Change\ in\ temperature\ x\ Mass\ of\ water\ x\ 4,000\ J$
$= 40\ x\ 1.5\ x\ 4,000 = 240,000\ J$

$Power\ of\ the\ heater = \frac{Work\ Done}{time} = \frac{240,000}{50\ x\ 60} = \frac{240,000}{3,000} = 80\ W$

Using $P = IV = \frac{v^2}{R}$:

$R = \frac{v^2}{P} = \frac{100^2}{80} = \frac{10,000}{80} = 125\ ohms$

Question 107: G
The large amount of energy released during atomic fission is the basis underlying nuclear power plants. Splitting an atom into two or more parts will by definition produce molecules of different sizes than the original atom; therefore it produces two new atoms. The free neutrons and photons produced by the splitting of atoms form the basis of the energy release.

Question 108: D
Gravitational potential energy is just an extension of the equation work done = force x distance (force is the weight of the object, *mg*, and distance is the height, *h*). The reservoir in statement 3 would have a potential energy of 10^{10} Joules i.e. 10 Giga Joules ($E_p = 10^6$ kg x 10 N x 10^3 m).

Question 109: D
Statement 1 is the common formulation of Newton's third law. Statement 2 presents a consequence of the application of Newton's third law.

Statement 3 is false: rockets can still accelerate because the products of burning fuel are ejected in the opposite direction from which the rocket needs to accelerate.

Question 110: E
Positively charged objects have lost electrons. $Charge = Current\ x\ Time = \frac{Voltage}{Resistance}\ x\ Time.$
Objects can become charged by friction as electrons are transferred from one object to the other.

Question 111: B
Each body of mass exerts a gravitational force on another body with mass. This is true for all planets as well. Gravitational force is dependent on the mass of both objects. Satellites stay in orbit due to centripetal force that acts tangentially to gravity (not because of the thrust from their engines). Two objects will only land at the same time if they also have the same shape or they are in a vaccum (as otherwise air resistance would result in different terminal velocities).

Question 112: A
Metals conduct electrical charge easily and provide little resistance to the flow of electrons. Charge can also flow in several directions. However, all conductors have an internal resistance and therefore provide *some* resistance to electrical charge.

Question 113: E

First, calculate the rate of petrol consumption:

$$\frac{Speed}{Consumption} = \frac{60 \ miles/hour}{30 \ miles/gallon} = 2 \ gallons/hour$$

Therefore, the total power is:

$2 \ gallons = 2 \times 9 \times 10^8 = 18 \times 10^8 J$

$1 \ hour = 60 \times 60 = 3600 \ s$

Power $= \frac{Energy}{Time} = \frac{18 \times 10^8}{3600}$

$P = \frac{18}{36} \times 10^6 = 5 \times 10^5 \ W$

Since efficiency is 20%, the power delivered to the wheels $= 5 \times 10^5 \times 0.2 = 10^5 \ W = 100 \ kW$

Question 114: D

Beta radiation is stopped by a few millimetres of aluminium, but not by paper. In β⁻ radiation, a neutron changes into a proton plus an emitted electron. This means the atomic mass number remains unchanged.

Question 115: F

Firstly, calculate the mass of the car $= \frac{Weight}{g} = \frac{15,000}{10} = 1,500 \ kg$

Then using $v = u + at$ where v = 0 ms⁻¹ and u = 15 ms⁻¹ and t = 10 x 10⁻³ s

$a = \frac{0-15}{0.01} = 1500 ms^{-2}$

$F = ma = 1500 \times 1500 = 2\,250\,000 \ N$

Question 116: E

Electrical insulators offer high resistance to the flow of charge. Insulators are usually non-metals; metals conduct charge very easily. Since charge does not flow easily to even out, they can be charged with friction.

Question 117: A

The car accelerates for the first 10 seconds at a constant rate and then decelerates after t=30 seconds. It does not reverse, as the velocity is not negative. Therefore only statement 1 is not true.

Question 118: B

The distance travelled by the car is represented by the area under the curve (integral of velocity) which is given by the area of two triangles and a rectangle:

$Area = \left(\frac{1}{2} \times 10 \times 10\right) + (20 \times 10) + \left(\frac{1}{2} \times 10 \times 10\right)$

$Area = 50 + 200 + 50 = 300 \ m$

Question 119: C

Using the equation force = mass x acceleration, where the unknown acceleration = change in velocity over change in time.

Hence: $\frac{F}{m} = \frac{change \ in \ velocity}{change \ in \ time}$

We know that F = 10,000 N, mass = 1,000 kg and change in time is 5 seconds.

So, $\frac{10,000}{1,000} = \frac{change \ in \ velocity}{5}$

So change in velocity $= 10 \times 5 = 50 \ m/s$

Question 120: D

This question tests both your ability to convert unusual units into SI units and to select the relevant values (e.g. the crane's mass is not important here).

0.01 tonnes = 10 kg; 100 cm = 1 m; 5,000 ms = 5 s

$$Power = \frac{Work\ Done}{Time} = \frac{Force\ x\ Distance}{Time}$$

In this case the force is the weight of the wardrobe = $10 \times g = 10 \times 10 = 100N$

Thus, $Power = \frac{100 \times 1}{5} = 20\ W$

Question 121: F

Remember that the resistance of a parallel circuit (R_T) is given by: $\frac{1}{R_T} = \frac{1}{R_1} + \frac{1}{R_2} + \ldots$

Thus, $\frac{1}{R_T} = \frac{1}{1} + \frac{1}{2} = \frac{3}{2}$ and therefore $R = \frac{2}{3}\ \Omega$

Using Ohm's Law: $I = \frac{20\ V}{\frac{2}{3}\Omega} = 20 \times \frac{3}{2} = 30$ A

Question 122: E

Water is denser than air. Therefore, the speed of light decreases when it enters water and increases when it leaves water. The direction of light also changes when light enters/leaves water. This phenomenon is known as refraction and is governed by Snell's Law.

Question 123: C

The voltage in a parallel circuit is the same across each branch, i.e. branch A Voltage = branch B Voltage.

The resistance of Branch $A = 6 \times 5 = 30\ \Omega$; the resistance of Branch $B = 10 \times 2 = 20\ \Omega$.

Using Ohm's Law: I= V/R. Thus, $I_A = \frac{60}{30} = 2\ A$; $I_B = \frac{60}{20} = 3\ A$

Question 124: C

This is a very straightforward question made harder by the awkward units you have to work with. Ensure you are able to work comfortably with prefixes of 10^9 and 10^{-9} and convert without difficulty.

50,000,000,000 nano Watts = 50 W and 0.000000004 Giga Amperes = 4 A.

Using $P = IV$: $V = \frac{P}{I} = \frac{50}{4} = 12.5\ V = 0.0125\ kV$

Question 125: B

Radioactive decay is highly random and unpredictable. Only gamma decay releases gamma rays and few types of decay release X-rays. The electrical charge of an atom's nucleus decreases after alpha decay as two protons are lost.

Question 126: D

Using $P = IV$: $I = \frac{P}{V} = \frac{60}{15} = 4\ A$

Now using Ohm's Law: $R = \frac{V}{I} = \frac{15}{4} = 3.75\ \Omega$

So each resistor has a resistance of $\frac{3.75}{3} = 1.25\ \Omega$.

If two more resistors are added, the overall resistance = $1.25 \times 5 = 6.25\ \Omega$

Question 127: F

To calculate the useful work done and hence the efficiency, we must know the resistive forces on the tractor, whether it is stationery or moving at the end point and if there is any change in vertical height.

Question 128: G

Electromagnetic induction is defined by statements 1 and 2. An electrical current is generated when a coil moves in a magnetic field.

Question 129: D

An ammeter will always give the same reading in a series circuit, not in a parallel circuit where current splits at each branch in accordance with Ohm's Law.

Question 130: D
Electrons move in the opposite direction to current (i.e. they move from negative to positive).

Question 131: A
For a fixed resistor, the current is directly proportional to the potential difference. For a filament lamp, as current increases, the metal filament becomes hotter. This causes the metal atoms to vibrate and move more, resulting in more collisions with the flow of electrons. This makes it harder for the electrons to move through the lamp and results in increased resistance. Therefore, the graph's gradient decreases as current increases.

Question 132: E
Vector quantities consist of both direction and magnitude, e.g. velocity, displacement, etc., and can be added by taking account of direction in the sum.

Question 133: C
The gravity on the moon is 6 times less than 10 ms^{-2}. Thus, $g_{moon} = \frac{10}{6} = \frac{5}{3}$ ms^{-2}.

Since weight = mass x gravity, the mass of the rock $= \frac{250}{\frac{5}{3}} = \frac{750}{5} = 150 \, kg$

Therefore, the density $= \frac{mass}{volume} = \frac{150}{250} = 0.6 \, kg/cm^3$

Question 134: D
An alpha particle consists of a helium nucleus. Thus, alpha decay causes the mass number to decrease by 4 and the atomic number to decrease by 2. Five iterations of this would decrease the mass number by 20 and the atomic number by 10.

Question 135: C
Using Ohm's Law: The potential difference entering the transformer (V_1) = 10 x 20 = 200 V

Now use $\frac{N1}{N2} = \frac{V1}{V2}$ to give: $\frac{5}{10} = \frac{200}{V2}$

Thus, $V_2 = \frac{2,000}{5} = 400$ V

Question 136: D
For objects in free fall that have reached terminal velocity, acceleration = 0.
Thus, the sphere's weight = resistive forces.
Using Work Done = Force x Distance: Force = 10,000 J/100 m = 100 N.
Therefore, the sphere's weight = 100 N and since $g = 10$ms^{-2}, the sphere's mass = 10 kg

Question 137: F
The wave length of ultraviolet waves is longer than that of x-rays. Wavelength is inversely proportional to frequency. Most electromagnetic waves are not stopped with aluminium (and require thick lead to stop them), and they travel at the speed of light. Humans can only see a very small part of the spectrum.

Question 138: B
If an object moves towards the sensor, the wavelength will appear to decrease and the frequency increase. The faster this happens, the faster the increase in frequency and decrease in wavelength.

Question 139: A
$Acceleration = \frac{Change \; in \; Velocity}{Time} = \frac{1,000}{0.1} = 10,000 \, ms^{-2}$

Using Newton's second law: The Braking Force = Mass x Acceleration.

Thus, Braking Force = 10,000 x 0.005 = 50 N

Question 140: C
Polonium has undergone alpha decay. Thus, Y is a helium nucleus and contains 2 protons and 2 neutrons.
Therefore, 10 moles of Y contain $2 \times 10 \times 6 \times 10^{23}$ protons $= 120 \times 10^{23} = 1.2 \times 10^{25}$ protons.

Question 141: C
The rod's activity is less than 1,000 Bq after 300 days. In order to calculate the longest possible half-life, we must assume that the activity is just below 1,000 Bq after 300 days. Thus, the half-life has decreased activity from 16,000 Bq to 1,000 Bq in 300 days.
After one half-life: Activity = 8,000 Bq
After two half-lives: Activity = 4,000 Bq
After three half-lives: Activity = 2,000 Bq
After four half-lives: Activity = 1,000 Bq
Thus, the rod has halved its activity a minimum of 4 times in 300 days. 300/4 = 75 days

Question 142: G
There is no change in the atomic mass or proton numbers in gamma radiation. In β decay, a neutron is transformed into a proton (and an electron is released). This results in an increase in proton number by 1 but no overall change in atomic mass. Thus, after 5 rounds of beta decay, the proton number will be $89 + 5 = 94$ and the mass number will remain at 200. Therefore, there are 94 protons and $200-94 = 106$ neutrons.
NB: You are not expected to know about β^+ decay.

Question 143: C
Calculate the speed of the sound $= \frac{distance}{time} = \frac{500}{1.5} = 333 \ ms^{-1}$

Thus, the $Wavelength = \frac{Speed}{Frequency} = \frac{333}{440}$

Approximate 333 to 330 to give: $\frac{330}{440} = \frac{3}{4} = 0.75 \ m$

Question 144: B
Firstly, note the all the answer options are a magnitude of 10 apart. Thus, you don't have to worry about getting the correct numbers as long as you get the correct power of 10. You can therefore make your life easier by rounding, e.g. approximate π to 3, etc.
The area of the shell $= \pi r^2$.
$= \pi \times (50 \times 10^{-3})^2 = \pi \times (5 \times 10^{-2})^2$
$= \pi \times 25 \times 10^{-4} = 7.5 \times 10^{-3} \ m^2$
The deceleration of the shell $= \frac{u-v}{t} = \frac{200}{500 \times 10^{-6}} = 0.4 \times 10^6 \ ms^{-2}$
Then, using Newton's Second Law: $Braking \ force = mass \times acceleration = 1 \times 0.4 \times 10^6 = 4 \times 10^5 N$
Finally: $Pressure = \frac{Force}{Area} = \frac{4 \times 10^5}{7.5 \times 10^{-3}} = \frac{8}{15} \times 10^8 \ Pa \approx 5 \times 10^7 Pa$

Question 145: B
The fountain transfers 10% of 1,000 J of energy per second into 120 litres of water per minute. Thus, it transfers 100 J into 2 litres of water per second.
Therefore the Total Gravitational Potential Energy, $E_p = mg\Delta h$
Thus, $100 \ J = 2 \times 10 \times h$
Hence, $h = \frac{100}{20} = 5 \ m$

Question 146: E
In step down transformers, the number of turns of the primary coil is larger than that of the secondary coil to decrease the voltage. If a transformer is 100% efficient, the electrical power input = electrical power output (P=IV).

Question 147: C
The percentage of C^{14} in the bone halves every 5,730 years. Since it has decreased from 100% to 6.25%, it has undergone 4 half-lives. Thus, the bone is $4 \times 5,730$ years old = 22,920 years

Question 148: E
This is a straightforward question in principle, as it just requires you to plug the values into the equation:
$Velocity = Wavelength\ x\ Frequency$ – Just ensure you work in SI units to get the correct answer.
$Frequency = \frac{2\ m/s}{2.5\ m} = 0.8\ Hz = 0.8\ x\ 10^{-6}MHz = 8\ x\ 10^{-7}\ MHz$

Question 149: E
If an element has a half-life of 25 days, its BQ value will be halved every 25 days.
A total of 350/25 = 14 half-lives have elapsed. Thus, the count rate has halved 14 times. Therefore, to calculate the original rate, the final count rate must be doubled 14 times = 50 x 2^{14}.
$2^{14} = 2^5\ x\ 2^5\ x\ 2^4 = 32\ x\ 32\ x\ 16 = 16,384$.
Therefore, the original count rate = 16,384 x 50 = 819,200

Question 150: D

Remember that $V = IR = \frac{P}{I}$ and $Power = \frac{Work\ Done}{Time} = \frac{Force\ x\ Distance}{Time} = Force\ x\ Velocity$;

Thus, A is derived from: $V = IR$,

B is derived from: $= \frac{P}{I}$,

C is derived from: $Voltage = \frac{Power}{Current} = \frac{Force\ x\ Velocity}{Current}$,

Since $Charge = Current\ x\ Time$, E and F are derived from: $Voltage = \frac{Power}{Current} = \frac{Force\ x\ Distance}{Time\ x\ Current} = \frac{J}{As} = \frac{J}{C}$,

D is incorrect as Nm = J. Thus the correct variant would be NmC^{-1}

Question 151: D
Different isotopes are differentiated by the number of neutrons in the core. This gives them different molecular weights and different chemical properties with regards to stability. The number of protons defines each element, and the number of electrons its charge.

Question 152: E
A displacement reaction occurs when a more reactive element displaces a less reactive element in its compound. All 4 reactions are examples of displacement reactions as a less reactive element is being replaced by a more reactive one.

Question 153: A
There needs to be 3Ca, 12H, 14O and 2P on each side. Only option A satisfies this.

Question 154: A
To balance the equation there needs to be 9Ag, 9N, 9O$_3$, 9K, 3P on each side. Only option A satisfies this.

Question 155: D
A more reactive halogen can displace a less reactive halogen. Thus, chlorine can displace bromine and iodine from an aqueous solution of its salts, and fluorine can replace chlorine. The trend is the opposite for alkali metals, where reactivity increases down the group as electrons are further from the core and easier to lose.

Question 156: C
$2Mg + O_2 = 2MgO$
so 2 x 24 = 48 and 2 x (24 + 16) = 80
so 48 g of magnesium produces 80g of magnesium oxide
so 1g of magnesium produces 1g x 80g/48g = 1.666g oxide
so 75g x 1.666 = 125g

Question 157: B
$H_2 + 2OH^- \rightarrow 2H_2O + e^-$
Thus, the hydrogen loses electrons i.e. is oxidised.

Question 158: F

Ammonia is 1 nitrogen and 3 hydrogen atoms bonded covalently. N = 14g and H = 1g per mole, so percentage of N in NH_3 = 14g/17g = 82%. It can be produced from N_2 through fixation or the industrial Haber process for use in fertiliser, and may break down to its components.

Question 159: A

Milk is weakly acidic, pH 6.5-7.0, and contains fat. This is broken down by lipase to form fatty acids - turning the solution slightly more acidic.

Question 160: C

Glucose loses four hydrogen atoms; one definition of an oxidation reaction is a reaction in which there is loss of hydrogen.

Question 161: C

Isotopes have the same number of protons and electrons, but a different number of neutrons. The number of neutrons has no impact on the rate of reactions.

Question 162: E

$Mg + H_2SO_4 \rightarrow MgSO_4 + H_2$

Number of moles of Mg $= \frac{6}{24} = 0.25$ moles.

1 mole of Mg reacts with 1 mole H_2SO_4 to produce 1 mole of magnesium sulphate. Therefore, 0.25 moles H_2SO_4 will react to produce 0.25 moles of $MgSO_4$.

M_r of $H_2SO_4 = 2 + 32 + 64 = 98$g per mole

The mass of H_2SO_4 used = 0.25 moles x 98g per mole = 24.5g.

Since 30g of H_2SO_4 is present, H_2SO_4 is in excess and the magnesium is the limiting reagent.

M_r of $MgSO_4 = 24 + 32 + 64 = 120$g per mole

The mass of $MgSO_4$ produced = 0.25 moles x 120g per mole = 30g which is the same mass as that of sulphuric acid in the original reaction.

Question 163: F

Reactivity series of metals:

Cu is more reactive than Ag and will displace it.

Ca is more reactive than H and will displace it.

2 and 4 are incorrect because Fe is higher in the reactivity series than Cu and Fe is lower in the reactivity series than Ca, so no displacement will occur.

Question 164: G

Moving left to right is the equivalent of moving down the metal reactivity series (i.e. Na is most reactive and Zn is least reactive). Therefore, moving from left to right, the reactivity of the metals decreases, likelihood of corrosion decreases, less energy is required to separate metals from their ores and metals lose electrons less readily to form positive ions.

Question 165: F

Halogens become less reactive as you progress down group 17. Thus in order of increasing reactivity from left to right: I$\rightarrow$ Br$\rightarrow$ Cl. Therefore, I will not displace Br, Cl will displace Br and Br will displace I.

Question 166: A

Wires are made out of copper because it is a good conductor of electricity. Copper is also used in coins (not aluminium). Aluminium is resistant to corrosion but because of a layer of aluminium oxide (not hydroxide).

Question 167: C

$2Li + 2H_2O \rightarrow 2LiOH + H_2$

Therefore, 2 moles of Li react to produce 1 mole of H_2 gas (24 dm^3).

The number of moles of Li $= \frac{21}{7} = 3$ moles.

Thus, 1.5 moles of H_2 gas are produced = 36 dm^3.

Question 168: B

$MgCl_2$ contains stronger bonds than NaCl because Mg ions have a 2+ charge, thus having a stronger electrostatic pull for negative chloride ions. The smaller atomic radius also means that the nucleus has less distance between it and incoming electrons. Transition metals are able to form multiple stable ions e.g. Fe^{2+} and Fe^{3+}.

Covalently bonded structures do tend to have lower MPs than ionically bonded, but the giant covalent structures (diamond and graphite for example) have very high melting points. Graphite is an example of a covalently bonded structure which conducts electricity.

Question 169: D

Energy is released from reaction **A**, as shown by a negative enthalpy. The reaction is therefore exothermic. Since energy is released, the product CO_2 has less energy than the reactants did. Therefore, CO_2 is more stable. Reaction **B** has a positive enthalpy, which means energy must be put into the reaction for it to occur i.e. it's an endothermic reaction. That means that the products (CaO and CO_2) have more energy and are less stable than the reactants ($CaCO_3$).

Question 170: B

Solid oxides are unable to conduct electricity because the ions are immobile. Metals are extracted from their molten ores by electrolysis. Fractional distillation is used to separate miscible liquids with similar boiling points. Mg^{2+} ions have a greater positive charge and a smaller ionic radius than Na^+ ions, and therefore have stronger bonds.

Question 171: E

Li^+ (2) and Na^+ (2, 8)
Mg^{2+} (2, 8) and Ne (2, 8)
Na^{2+} (2, 7) and Ne (2, 8)
O^{2+} (2, 4) and a Carbon atom (2, 4)

Question 172: B

Reactivity of both group 1 and 2 increases as you go down the groups because the valence electrons that react are further away from the positively charged nucleus (which means the electrostatic attraction between them is weaker). Group 1 metals are usually more reactive because they only need to donate one electron, whilst group 2 metals must donate two electrons.

Question 173: D

This is a straightforward question that tests basic understanding of kinetics. Catalysts help overcome energy barriers by reducing the activation energy necessary for a reaction.

Question 174: D

H^1 contains 1 proton and no neutrons. Isotopes have the same numbers of protons, but different numbers of neutrons. Thus, H^3 contains two more neutrons than H^1.

Question 175: D

Oxidation is the loss of electrons and reduction is the gain of electrons (therefore increasing electron density). Halogens tend to act as electron recipients in reactions and are therefore good oxidising agents.

Question 176: D

These statements all come from the Kinetic Theory of Gases, an idealised model of gases that allows for the derivation of the ideal gas law. The angle at which gas molecules move is not related to temperature; movement is random. Gas molecules lose no energy when they collide with each other, collisions are assumed elastic. The average kinetic energy of gas molecules is the same for all gases at the same temperature as they are assumed to be point masses. Momentum = mass x velocity. Therefore, the momentum of gas molecules increases with pressure as a greater force is exerted on each molecule.

Question 177: E

An exothermic reaction is defined as a chemical reaction that releases energy. Thus, aerobic respiration producing life energy, the burning of magnesium, and the reacting of acids/bases are almost always exothermic processes. Similarly, the combustion of most things (including hydrogen) is exothermic. Evaporation of water is a physical process in which no chemical reaction is taking place.

Question 178: E

$2 C_3H_6 + 9 O_2 \rightarrow 6 H_2O + 6 CO_2$

Assign the oxidation numbers for each element:

For C_3H_6: C = -2; H = +1

For O_2: O = 0

For H_2O: H = +1; O = -2

For CO_2: C = +4; O = -2

Look for the changes in the oxidation numbers:

H remained at +1

C changed from -2 to +4. Thus, it was oxidized

O changed from 0 to -2. Thus, it was reduced.

Question 179: B

The equation for the reaction is: $Zn + CuSO_4 \rightarrow ZnSO_4 + Cu$

Assign oxidation numbers for each element:

For Zn: Zn = 0

For $CuSO_4$: Cu = +2; S = +6; O = -2

For $ZnSO_4$: Zn = +2; S = +6; O = -2

For Cu: Cu = 0

With these oxidation numbers, we can see that Zn was oxidized and Cu in $CuSO_4$ was reduced. Thus, Zn acted as the reducing agent and Cu in $CuSO_4$ is the oxidizing agent.

Question 180: B

Acids are proton donors which only exist in aqueous solution, which is a liquid state. Strong acids are fully ionised in solution and the reaction between an acid and a base $\rightarrow$ salt + water.

The pH of weak acids is usually between 4 and 6.

Question 181: G

Let x be the relative abundance of Z^6 and y the relative abundance of Z^8.

The average atomic mass takes the abundances of all 3 isotopes into account.

Thus, (Abundance of Z^5)(Mass Z^5) + (Abundance of Z^6)(Mass Z^6) + (Abundance of Z^8)(Mass Z^8) = 7

Therefore: $(5 \times 0.2) + 6x + 8y = 7$

So: $6x + 8y = 6$

Divide by two to give: $3x + 4y = 3$

The abundances of all isotopes = 100% = 1

This gives: $0.2 + x + y = 1$

Solve the two equations simultaneously:

$y = 0.8 - x$

$3x + 4(0.8 - x) = 3$

$3x + 3.2 - 4x = 3$

Therefore, x = 0.2

$y = 0.8 - 0.2 = 0.6$

Thus, the overall abundances are Z^5 = 20%, Z^6 = 20% and Z^8 = 60%. Therefore, all the statements are correct.

Question 182: A

If a metal is more reactive than hydrogen, a displacement reaction will occur resulting in the formation of a salt with the metal cation and hydrogen.

Question 183: B

$6 \ FeSO_4 + K_2Cr_2O_7 + 7 \ H_2SO_4 \rightarrow 3 \ (Fe)_2(SO_4)_3 + Cr_2(SO_4)_3 + K_2SO_4 + 7 \ H_2O$

In order to save time, you have to quickly eliminate options (rather than try every combination out). The quickest way is to do this is algebraically:

For Potassium:
$2b = 2e = 2f$
Therefore, $b = f$.
Option F does not fulfil $b = e = f$.

For Iron:
$a = 2d$
Options C, D and E don't fulfil $a = 2d$.

For Hydrogen:
$2c = 2g$
Therefore, $c = g$.
Option A does not fulfil $c = g$.
This leaves option B as the answer.

Question 184: E

Atoms are electrically neutral. Ions have different numbers of electrons when compared to atoms of the same element. Protons provide just under 50% of an atom's mass, the other 50% is provided by neutrons. Isotopes don't exhibit significantly different kinetics. Protons do indeed repel each other in the nucleus (which is one reason why neutrons are needed: to reduce the electrical charge density).

Question 185: B

The noble gasses are extremely useful, e.g. helium in blimps, neon signs, argon in bulbs. They are colourless and odourless and have no valence electrons. As with the rest of the periodic table, boiling point increases as you progress down the group (because of increased Van der Waals forces). Helium is the most abundant noble gas (and indeed the 2nd most abundant element in the universe).

Question 186: D

Alkenes can be hydrogenated (i.e. reduced) to alkanes. Aromatic compounds are commonly written as cyclic alkenes, but their properties differ from those of alkenes. Therefore alkenes and aromatic compounds do not belong to the same chemical class.

Question 187: A

The average atomic mass takes the abundances of both isotopes into account:
(Abundance of Cl^{35})(Mass Cl^{35}) + (Abundance of Cl^{37})(Mass Cl^{37}) = 35.453
34.969(Abundance of Cl^{35}) + 36.966(Abundance of Cl^{37}) = 35.453
The abundances of both isotopes = 100% = 1
I.e. abundance of Cl^{35} + abundance of Cl^{37} = 1
Therefore: $x + y = 1$ which can be rearranged to give: $y = 1-x$
Therefore: $x + (1 - x) = 1$.
$34.969x + 36.966(1-x) = 35.453$
$x = 0.758$
$1 - x = 0.242$
Therefore, Cl^{35} is 3 times more abundant than Cl^{37}.
Note that you could approximate the values here to arrive at the solution even quicker, e.g. $34.969 \rightarrow 35$, $36.966 \rightarrow 37$ and $35.453 \rightarrow 35.5$

Question 188: A

Transition metals form multiple stable ions which may have many different colours (e.g. green Fe^{2+} and brown Fe^{3+}). They usually form ionic bonds and are commonly used as catalysts (e.g. iron in the Haber process, Nickel in alkene hydrogenation). They are excellent conductors of electricity and are known as the d-block elements.

Question 189: B

$2Na + 2H_2O \rightarrow 2NaOH + H_2$

$8000 \text{ cm}^3 = 8 \text{ dm}^3 = \frac{1}{3}$ moles of H_2

2 moles of Na react completely to form 1 mole of H_2.

Therefore, $\frac{2}{3}$ moles of Na must have reacted to produce $\frac{1}{3}$ moles of Hydrogen. $\frac{2}{3}$ x 23g per mole = 15.3g.

% Purity of sample $= \frac{15.3}{20}$ x 100 = 76.5%

Question 190: C

Assume total mass of molecule is 100g. Therefore, it contains 70.6g carbon, 5.9g hydrogen and 23.5g oxygen.

Now, calculate the number of moles of each element using $Moles = \frac{Mass}{Molar\ Mass}$

$Moles\ of\ Carbon = \dfrac{70.6}{12} \approx 6$

$Moles\ of\ Hydrogen = \dfrac{5.9}{1} \approx 6$

$Moles\ of\ Oxygen = \dfrac{23.5}{16} \approx 1.5$

Therefore, the molar ratios give an empirical formula of $C_6H_6O_{1.5} = C_4H_4O$.

Molar mass of the empirical formula = (4 x 12) + (4 x 1) + 16 = 68.

Molar mass of chemical formula = 136. Therefore, the chemical formula = $C_8H_8O_2$.

Question 191: B

$S + 6\ HNO_3 \rightarrow H_2SO_4 + 6\ NO_2 + 2\ H_2O$

In order to save time, you have to quickly eliminate options (rather than try every combination out).

The quickest way to do this is algebraically:

For Hydrogen:

b = 2c + 2e

Options A, C, D, E and F don't fulfil b = 2c + 2e.

This leaves options B as the only possible answer.

Note how quickly we were able to get the correct answer here by choosing an element that appears in 3 molecules (as opposed to Sulphur or Nitrogen which only appear in 2).

Question 192: A

Alkenes undergo addition reactions, such as that with hydrogen, when catalysed by nickel, whilst alkanes do not as they are already fully saturated. The C=C bond is stronger than the C-C bond, but it is not exactly twice as strong, so will not require twice the energy to break it. Both molecules are organic and will dissolve in organic solvents.

Question 193: F

Diamond is unable to conduct electricity because all the electrons are involved in covalent bonds. Graphite is insoluble in water + organic solvents. Graphite is also able to conduct electricity because there are free electrons that are not involved in covalent bonds.

Methane and Ammonia both have low melting points. Methane is not a polar molecule, so cannot conduct electricity or dissolve in water. Ammonia is polar and will dissolve in water. It can conduct electricity in aqueous form, but not as a gas.

Question 194: A

Catalysts increase the rate of reaction by providing an alternative reaction path with a lower activation energy, which means that less energy is required and so costs are reduced. The point of equilibrium, the nature of the products, and the overall energy change are unaffected by catalysts.

Question 195: E

The 5 carbon atoms in this hydrocarbon make it a "pent" stem. The C=C bond makes it an alkene, and the location of this bond is the 2nd position, making the molecule pent-2-ene.

Question 196: F

Group 1 elements form positively charged ions in most reactions and therefore lose electrons. Thus, the oxidation number must increase. Their reactivity increases as the valence electrons are further away from the positively charged nucleus down group. Whilst they all react **spontaneously** with oxygen, only the latter half of Group 1 elements react **instataneously**.

Question 197: H

The cathode attracts positively charged ions. The cathode reduces ions and the anode oxidises ions. Electrolysis can be used to separate compounds but not mixtures (i.e. substances that are not chemically joined).

Question 198: B

Pentane, C_5H_{12}, has a total of 3 isomers. A, C and D are correctly configured. However, the 4th Carbon atom in option B has more than 4 bonds which wouldn't be possible. If you're stuck on this – draw them out!

Question 199: E

$3 Cu + 8 HNO_3 \rightarrow 3 Cu(NO_3)_2 + 2 NO + 4 H_2O$

In order to save time, you have to quickly eliminate options (rather than try every combination out).

The quickest way to do this is algebraically, by first assigning coefficients to the equation:

$aCu + bHNO_3 \rightarrow cCu(NO_3)_2 + dNO + eH_2O$

For Nitrogen: $b = 2c + d$.

In this case, only option E satisfies $b = 2c + d$.

Note that using copper wouldn't be as useful, as all the options satisfy $a = c$.

Question 200: D

Alkenes are an organic series and have twice as many hydrogen atoms as carbon atoms. Bromine water is decolourised in their presence and they take part in addition reactions. Alkenes are more reactive than alkanes because they contain a C=C bond.

Question 201: A

Group 17 elements are missing one valence electron, so form negative ions. Bromine is a liquid at room temperature, and is also coloured brown. Reactivity decreases as you progress down Group 17, so fluorine reacts more vigorously than iodine. All Group 17 elements are found bound to each other, e.g. F_2 and Cl_2.

Question 202: D

CO poisoning and spontaneous combustion do not occur in the electrolysis of brine. The products of cathode and anode in the electrolysis of brine are Cl_2 and H_2. If these two gases react with each other they can form HCl, which is extremely corrosive.

Question 203: D

The hydrogen produced is positively charged and therefore needs to be reduced by the addition of an electron before being released. This happens at the cathode. The chlorine produced is negatively charged and therefore needs to lose electrons. This happens at the anode. NaOH is formed in this process.

Question 204: C

Alkanes are made of chains of singly bonded carbon and hydrogen atoms. C-H bonds are very strong and confer alkanes a great deal of stability. An alkane with 14 hydrogen atoms is called Hexane, as it has 6 carbon atoms. Alkanes burn in excess oxygen to produce carbon dioxide and water. Bromine water is decolourised in the presence of alkenes.

Question 205: G

You've probably got a lot of experience of organic chemistry by now, so this should be fairly straightforward. Alcohols by definition contain an R-OH functional group and because of this polar group are highly soluble in water. Ethanol is a common biofuel.

Question 206: E

Alkanes are saturated (and therefore non-reducible), have the general formula C_nH_{2n+2} and have no effect on Bromine solution. Alkenes are unsaturated (and therefore reducible), have the general formula C_nH_{2n} and turn bromine water colourless because they can undergo an addition reaction with bromine.

Question 207: D

The balanced equation for the reaction between magnesium oxide and hydrochloric acid is:

$O + 2HCl \rightarrow MgCl_2 + H_2$

The relative molecular mass of MgO is $24 + 16 = 40g$ per mole.

Therefore 10g of MgO represents $10/40 = 0.25$ moles.

As the ratio of MgO to $MgCl_2$ is 1:1, we know that the amount of $MgCl_2$ produced will also be 0.25 moles. One mole of $MgCl_2$ has a molecular mass of $24 + (2 \times 35.5) = 95g$ per mole.

Therefore the reaction will produce $0.25 \times 95 = 23.75g$ of $MgCl_2$.

Question 208: D

Moving up the alkane series, as size and mass of the molecule increases (and thus the Van der Waals forces increase), the boiling point and viscosity increase and the flammability and volatility decrease. Therefore pentadecane will be more viscous than pentane.

Question 209: F

All of the factors mentioned will affect the rate of a reaction. The temperature affects the movement rate of particles, which if moving faster in higher temperatures will collide more often, thus increasing the rate of reaction. Collision rate is also increased with a higher concentration of reactants, and with a higher concentration of a catalyst or one with larger surface area, which will provide more active sites, thus increasing the rate of reaction.

Question 210: C

The total atomic mass of the end product is $C[12 + (2 \times 16)] + D[(2 \times 1) + 16] = 44C + 18D$

We know that $176 = 44C$. Therefore $C = 4$, and that $108 = 18D$ so $D = 6$.

Thus, the equation becomes: $C_aH_b + O_2 \rightarrow 4CO_2 + 6H_2O$.

This gives a ratio of 4C to 12H, which is a ratio of 1:3 carbon to hydrogen. This means the unknown hydrocarbon must be a multiple of this ratio. By balancing the equation we can see that the unknown hydrocarbon must be ethane, C_2H_6: $2C_2H_6 + 7O_2 \rightarrow 4CO_2 + 6H_2O$.

Question 211: A

$C_2H_5OH \rightarrow C_2H_4O$. Thus, ethanol has lost two hydrogen atoms, i.e. has been oxidised. Note that although another substrate may be reduced (therefore making it a redox reaction), ethanol has only been oxidised.

Question 212: B

This is fairly straightforward but you can save time by doing it algebraically:

For Barium: $3a = b$

For Nitrogen: $2a = c$

Let $a = 1$, thus, $b = 3$ and $c = 2$

Question 213: E

There are 14 oxygen atoms on the left side. Thus: $3b + 2c = 14$.

Note also that for Sulphur: $a = c$, and for Iron: $a = 2b$.

This sets up an easy trio of simultaneous equations:

Substitute a into the first equation to give: $1.5a + 2a = 14$. Thus: $a = 14/3.5 = 4$.

Therefore, $a = c = 4$ and $b = 2$

Question 214: C

The average atomic mass takes the abundances of all isotopes into account:

Mass = (Abundance of Mg^{23})(Mass Mg^{23}) + (Abundance of Mg^{25})(Mass Mg^{25}) + (Abundance of Mg^{26})(Mass Mg^{26})

$Mass = 23 \times 0.80 + 25 \times 0.10 + 26 \times 0.10$

$= 18.4 + 2.5 + 2.6 = 23.5$

Question 215: D

Cl_2 and Fe_2O_3 are reduced in their reactions and are therefore oxidising agents. Similarly, CO and Cu^{2+} are oxidised in their reactions and are therefore reducing agents. Cl is a stronger oxidising agent than Br as it is higher up in the reactivity series, and will displace negative Br ions from its compounds to form the oxidised Br_2. Mg is a stronger reducing agent than Cu, as it is higher up in the reactivity series. Thus, Mg would displace a positive copper ion from its compound to form copper atoms. Therefore Mg reduces Cu.

Question 216: C

NaCl is an ionic compound and therefore has a high melting point. It is highly soluble in water but only conducts electricity in solution/as a liquid.

Question 217: C

The equation for the reaction is: $2NaOH + Zn(NO_3)_2 \rightarrow 2NaNO_3 + Zn(OH)_2$
Therefore, the molar ratio between NaOH and $Zn(OH)_2$ is 2:1.
Molecular Mass of NaOH = 23 + 16 + 1 = 40
Molecular Mass of $Zn(OH)_2$= 65 + 17 x 2 = 99
Thus, the number of moles of NaOH that react = 80/40 = 2 moles.
Therefore, 1 mole of $Zn(OH)_2$ is produced. Mass = 99g per mole x 1 mole = 99g

Question 218: E

Metal + Water $\rightarrow$ Hydroxide + Hydrogen gas; the reaction is always exothermic. Reactivity increases down the group, so potassium reacts more vigorously with water than sodium. Therefore all are correct.

Question 219: C

Electrolysis separates NaCl into sodium and chloride ions but not CO_2 (which is a covalently bound gas). Sieves cannot separate ionically bound compounds like NaCl. Dyes are miscible liquids and can be separated by chromatography. Oil and water are immiscible liquids, so a separating funnel is necessary to separate the mixtures. Methane and diesel are separated from each other during fractional distillation, as they have different boiling points.

Question 220: B

The reaction between water and caesium can cause spontaneous combustion and therefore doesn't make the reaction safer. The reaction between caesium and fluoride is highly exothermic and does not require a catalyst. The reaction produces CsF which is a salt.

Question 221: B

The nucleus of larger elements contain more neutrons than protons to reduce the charge density, e.g. Br^{80} contains 35 protons but 45 neutrons. Stable isotopes very rarely undergo radioactive decay.

Question 222: B

The vast majority of salts contain ionic bonds that require a significant amount of heat energy to break.

Question 223: E

306ml of water is 306g, which is the equivalent of 306g/18g per mole of H_2O = 17 moles. 17 times Avogadro's constant gives the number of molecules present, which is 1.02×10^{25}. There are 10 protons and 10 electrons in each water molecule. Hence there are 1.02×10^{26} protons.

Question 224: D

The number of moles of each element = Mass/Molar Mass. Let the % represent the mass in grams: Hydrogen: 3.45g/1g per mole = 3.45 moles
Oxygen: 55.2g/16g per mole = 3.45 moles
Carbon: 41.4g/12g per mole = 3.45 moles
Thus, the molar ratio is 1:1:1. The only option that satisfies this is option D.

Question 225: C

- Group 17 elements are non-metals, whilst group 2 elements are metals. Thus, the Group 17 element must gain electrons when it reacts with the Group 2 element, i.e. B is reduced. The easy way to calculate the formula is to swap the valences of both elements: A is +2 and B is -1. Thus, the compound is AB_2.

Question 226: A

DNA consists of 4 bases: adenine, guanine, thymine and cysteine. The sugar backbone consists of deoxyribose, hence the name DNA. DNA is found in the cytoplasm of prokaryotes.

Question 227: F

Mitochondria are responsible for energy production by ATP synthesis. Animal cells do not have a cell wall, only a cell membrane. The endoplasmic reticulum is important in protein synthesis, as this is where the proteins are assembled.

Question 228: F

If you aren't studying A-level biology, this question may stretch you. However, it is possible to reach an answer by process of elimination. Mitochondria are the 'powerhouse' of the cell in aerobic respiration, responsible for cell energy production rather than DNA replication or protein synthesis. As energy producers they are required in muscle cells in large numbers, and in sperm cells to drive the tail responsible for movement. They are enveloped by a double membrane, possibly because they started out as independent prokaryotes engulfed by eukaryotic cells.

Question 229: A

The majority of bacteria are commensals and don't lead to disease.

Question 230: C

Bacteria carry genetic information on plasmids and not in nuclei like animal cells. They don't need meiosis for replication, as they do not require gametes. Bacterial genomes consist of DNA, just like animal cells.

Question 231: C

Active transport requires a transport protein and ATP, as work is being done against an electrochemical gradient. Unlike diffusion, the relative concentrations of the materials being transported aren't important.

Question 232: D

Meiosis produces haploid gametes. This allows for fusion of 2 gametes to reach a full diploid set of chromosomes again in the zygote.

Question 233: B

Mendelian inheritance separates traits into dominant or recessive. It applies to all sexually reproducing organisms. Don't get confused by statement C – the offspring of 2 heterozygotes has a 25% chance of expressing a recessive trait, but it will be homozygous recessive.

Question 234: A

Hormones are released into the bloodstream and act on receptors in different organs in order to cause relatively slow changes to the body's physiology. Hormones frequently interact with the nervous system, e.g. Adrenaline and Insulin, however, they don't directly cause muscles to contract. Almost all hormones are synthesised.

Question 235: D

Neuronal signalling can happen via direct electrical stimulation of nerves or via chemical stimulation of synapses which produces a current that travels along the nerves. Electrical synapses are very rare in mammals, the majority of mammalian synapses are chemical.

Question 236: D

Remember that pH changes cause changes in electrical charge on proteins (= polypeptides) that could interfere with protein – protein interactions. Whilst the other statements are all correct to a certain extent, they are the downstream effects of what would happen if enzymes (which are also proteins) didn't work.

Question 237: A

The bacterial cell wall is made up of cellulose and protects the bacterium from the external environment, in particular from osmotic stresses, and is important in most bacteria.

Question 238: C

Sexual reproduction relies on formation of gametes during **meiosis**. Mitosis doesn't produce genetically distinct cells. Mitosis is, however, the basis for tissue growth.

Question 239: A

A mutation is a permanent change in the nucleotide sequence of DNA. Whilst mutations may lead to changes in organelles and chromosomes, or even be harmful, they are strictly defined as permanent changes to the DNA or RNA sequence.

Question 240: E

Mutations are fairly common, but in the vast majority of cases do not have any impact on phenotype due to the redundancy of the genome. Sometimes they can confer selective advantages and allow organisms to survive better (i.e. evolve by natural selection), or they can lead to cancers as cells start dividing uncontrollably.

Question 241: D

Antibodies represent a pivotal molecule of the immune system. They provide very pointed and selective targeting of pathogens and toxins without causing damage to the body's own cells.

Question 242: A

Kidneys are not involved in digestion, but do filter the blood of waste products. Glucose is found in high concentrations in the urine of diabetics, who cannot absorb it without working insulin.

Question 243: D

Hormones are slower acting than nerves and act for a longer time. Hormones also act in a more general way. Adrenaline is also a hormone released into the body causing the fight-or-flight response. Although it is quick acting, it still lasts for a longer time than a nervous response, as you can still feel its effects for a time after the response, e.g. shaking hands.

Question 244: D

Homeostasis is about minimising changes to the internal environment by modulating both input and output.

Question 245: B

There is less energy and biomass each time you move up a trophic level. Only 10% of consumed energy is transferred to the next trophic level, so only one tenth of the previous biomass can be sustained in the next trophic level up.

Question 246: A

In asexual reproduction, there is no fusion of gametes as the single parent cell divides. There is therefore no mixing of chromosomes and, as a result, no genetic variation.

Question 247: E

The image is first formed on the retina which conveys it to the brain via a sensory nerve. The brain then sends an impulse to the muscle via a motor neuron.

Question 248: D

Blood from the kidney returns to the heart via the renal (kidney-related) vein, which drains into the inferior vena cava. The blood then passes through the pulmonary vasculature (veins carry blood to the heart, arteries away from the heart) before going into the aorta and eventually the hepatic (liver-related) artery.

Question 249: F

Clones are genetically identical by definition, and a large number of them could conceivably reduce the gene pool of a population. In adult cell cloning, the genetic material of an egg is replaced with the genetic material of an adult cell. Cloning is possible for all DNA based life forms, including plants and other types of animals.

Question 250: F

Gene varieties cause intraspecies variation, e.g. different eye colours. If mutations confer a selective advantage, those individuals with the mutation will survive to reproduce and grow in numbers. Genetic variation is caused by mixing of parent genomes and mutations. Species with similar characteristics often do have similar genes.

Question 251: F
Alleles are different versions of the same gene. If you are a homozygous for a trait, you have two identical alleles for that particular gene, and if you are heterozygous you have two different alleles of that gene. Recessive traits only appear in the phenotype when there are no dominant alleles for that trait, i.e. two recessive alleles are carried.

Question 252: D
Remember that red blood cells don't have a nucleus and therefore have no DNA. In meiosis, a diploid cell divides in such a way so as to produce four haploid cells. Any type of cell division will require energy.

Question 253: C
The hypothalamus detects too little water in the blood, so the pituary gland releases ADH. The kidney maintains the blood water level, and allows less water to be lost in the urine until the blood water level returns to normal.

Question 254: E
Venous blood has a higher level of carbon dioxide and lower oxygen. Carbon dioxide forms carbonic acid in aqueous solution, thus making the pH of venous blood slightly more acidic than arterial blood. This leaves only E and F as possibilities, but releasing pH levels cannot fluctuate significantly gives pH 7.4.

Question 255: E
The cytoplasm is 80% water, but also contains, among other things, electrolytes and proteins. The cytoplasm doesn't contain everything, e.g. DNA is found in the nucleus.

Question 256: C
ATP is produced in mitochondria in aerobic respiration and in the cytoplasm during anaerobic respiration only.

Question 257: C
The cell membrane allows both active transport and passive transport by diffusion of certain ions and molecules, and is found in eukaryotes and prokaryotes like bacteria. It is a phospholipid bilayer.

Question 258: A
1 and 2 only: 223 PAIRS = 446 chromosomes; meiosis produces 4 daughter cells with half of the original number of chromosomes each, while mitosis produces two daughter cells with the original number of chromosomes each.

Question 259: E
If Bob is homozygous dominant (RR) the probability of having a child with red hair is 0%. However, if Bob is heterozygous (Rr), there is a 50% chance of having a child with red hair, since Mary must be homozygous recessive (rr) to have red hair. As we do not know Bob's genotype, both possibilities must be considered.

Question 260 A
If an offspring is born with red hair, it confirms Bob is heterozygous (Rr). He cannot have a red-haired child if he is homozygous dominant (RR), and would himself have red hair were he homozygous recessive (rr).

Question 261: A
Monohybrid cross rr and Rr results in 50% Rr and 50% rr offspring. 50% of offspring will have black hair, but they will be heterozygous for the hair allele.

Question 262: C
When the chest walls expand, the intra-thoracic pressure decreases. This causes the atmospheric pressure outside the chest to be greater than pressure inside the chest, resulting in a flow of air into the chest.

Question 263: A
Producers are found at the bottom of food chains and always have the largest biomass.

Question 264: F

All the statements are true; the carbon and nitrogen cycles are examinable in Section 2, so make sure you understand them! The atmosphere is 79% inert N_2 gas, which must be 'fixed' to useable forms by high-energy lightning strikes or by bacterial mediation. Humans also manually fix nitrogen for fertilisers with the Haber process.

Question 265: H

None of the above statements are correct. Mutations can be silent, cause a loss of function, or even a gain in function, depending on the exact location in the gene and the base affected. Mutations only cause a change in protein structure if the amino acids expressed by the gene affected are changed. This is normally due to a shift in reading frame. Whilst cancer arises as a result of a series of mutations, very few mutations actually lead to cancer.

Question 266: C

Remember that heart rate is controlled via the autonomic nervous system, which isn't a part of the central nervous system.

Question 267: H

None of the above are correct. There is no voluntary input to the heart in the form of a neuronal connection. Parasympathetic neurones slow the heart and sympathetic nervous input accelerates heart rate.

Question 268: B

If lipase is not working, fat from the diet will not be broken down, and will build up in the stool. Lactase, for instance, is responsible for breaking down lactose, and its malfunctioning causes lactose-intolerance.

Question 269: F

Oxygenated blood flows from the lungs to the heart via the pulmonary vein. The pulmonary artery carries deoxygenated blood from the heart to the lungs. Animals like fish have single circulatory systems. Deoxygenated blood is found in the superior vena cava, returning to the heart from the body. Veins in the arms and hands frequently don't have valves.

Question 270: E

Enzymatic digestion takes place throughout the GI tract, including in the mouth (e.g. amylase), stomach (e.g. pepsin), and small intestine (e.g. trypsin). The large intestine is primarily responsible for water absorption, whilst the rectum acts as a temporary store for faecal matter (i.e. digestion has finished by the rectum).

Question 271: B

This is an example of the monosynaptic stretch reflex; these reflexes are performed at the spinal level and therefore don't involve the brain.

Question 272: A

Statement 2 describes diffusion, as CO_2 is moving with the concentration gradient. Statement 3 describes active transport, as amino acids are moving against the concentration gradient.

Question 273: I

3 is the correct equation for animals, and 4 is correct for plants.

Question 274: C

The mitochondria are only the site for aerobic respiration, as anaerobic respiration occurs in the cytoplasm. Aerobic respiration produces more ATP per substrate than anaerobic respiration, and therefore is also more efficient. The chemical equation for glucose being respired aerobically is: $C_6H_{12}O_6 + 6O_2 \rightarrow 6CO_2 + 6H_2O$. Thus, the molar ratio is 1:6 (i.e. each mole glucose produces 6 moles of CO_2).

Question 275: B

The nucleus contains the DNA and chromosomes of the cell. The cytoplasm contains enzymes, salts and amino acids in addition to water. The plasma membrane is a bilayer. Lastly, the cell wall is indeed responsible for protecting vs. increased osmotic pressures.

Question 276: D
When a medium is hypertonic relative to the cell cytoplasm, it is more concentrated than the cytoplasm, and when it is hypotonic, it is less concentrated. So, when a medium is hypotonic relative to the cell cytoplasm, the cell will gain water through osmosis. When the medium is isotonic, there will be no net movement of water across the cell membrane. Lastly, when the medium is hypertonic relative to the cell cytoplasm, the cell will lose water by osmosis.

Question 277: A
Stem cells have the ability to differentiate and produce other kinds of cells. However, they also have the ability to generate cells of their own kind and stem cells are able to maintain their undifferentiated state. The two types of stem cells are embryonic stem cells and adult stem cells. The adult stem cells are present in both children and adults.

Question 278: B
All of the following statements are examples of natural selection, except for the breeding of horses. Breeding and animal husbandry are notable methods of artificial selection, which are brought about by humans.

Question 279: C
Enzymes create a stable environment to stabilise the transition state. Enzymes do not distort substrates. Enzymes generally have little effect on temperature directly. Lastly, they are able to provide alternative pathways for reactions to occur.

Question 280: C
A negative feedback system seeks to minimise changes in a system by modulating the response in accordance with the error that's generated. Salivating before a meal is an example of a feed-forward system (i.e. salivating is an anticipatory response). Throwing a dart does not involve any feedback (during the action). pH and blood pressure are both important homeostatic variables that are controlled via powerful negative feedback mechanisms, e.g. massive haemorrhage leads to compensatory tachycardia.

Question 281: A
One of the major functions of white blood cells is to defend the body against bacterial and fungal infections. They can kill pathogens by engulfing them and also use antibodies to help them recognise pathogens. Antibodies are produced by white blood cells.

Question 282: B
The CV system does indeed transport nutrients and hormones. It also increases blood flow to exercising muscles (via differential vasodilatation) and also helps with thermoregulation (e.g. vasoconstriction in response to cold). The respiratory system is responsible for oxygenating blood.

Question 283: C
Adrenaline always increases heart rate and is almost always released during sympathetic responses. It travels primarily in the blood and affects multiple organ systems. It is also a potent vasoconstrictor.

Question 284: B
Protein synthesis occurs in the cytoplasm. Proteins are usually coded by several amino acids. Red blood cells lack a nucleus and, therefore, the DNA to create new proteins. Protein synthesis is a key part of mitosis, as it allows the parent cell to grow prior to division.

Question 285: F
Remember that most enzymes work better in neutral environments (amylase works even better at slightly alkaline pH). Thus, adding sodium bicarbonate will increase the pH and hence increase the rate of activity. Adding carbohydrate will have no effect, as the enzyme is already saturated. Adding amylase will increase the amount of carbohydrate that can be converted per unit time. Increasing the temperature to 100° C will denature the enzyme and reduce the rate.

Question 286: E
Taking the normal allele to be C and the diseased allele to be c, one can model the scenario with the following Punnett square:

		Carrier Mother	
		C	c
Diseased Father	c	Cc	cc
	c	Cc	cc

The gender of the children is irrelevant as the inheritance is autosomal recessive, but we see that all children produced would inherit at least one diseased allele.

Question 287: F
All of the organs listed have endocrine functions. The thyroid produces thyroid hormone. The ovary produces oestrogen. The pancreas secretes glucagon and insulin. The adrenal gland secretes adrenaline. The testes produce testosterone.

Question 288: A
Insulin works to decrease blood glucose levels. Glucagon causes blood glucose levels to increase; glycogen is a carbohydrate. Adrenaline works to increase heart rate.

Question 289: A
The left side of the heart contains oxygenated blood from the lungs which will be pumped to the body. The right side of the heart contains deoxygenated blood from the body to be pumped to the lungs.

Question 290: A
Since Individual 1 is homozygous normal, and individual 5 is heterozygous and affected, the disease must be dominant. Since males only have one X-chromosome, they cannot be carriers for X-linked conditions. If Nafram syndrome was X-linked, then parents 5 and 6 would produce sons who always have no disease and daughters that always do. As this is not the case shown in individuals 7-10, the disease must be autosomal dominant.

Question 291: C
We know that the inheritance of Nafram syndrome is autosomal dominant, so using N to mean a diseased allele and n to mean a normal allele, 5, 7 and 8 must be Nn because they have an unaffected parent. 2 is also Nn, as if it was NN all its progeny would be Nn and so affected by the disease, which is not the case, as 3 and 4 are unaffected.

Question 292: A
Since 6 is disease free, his genotype must be nn. Thus, neither of 6's parents could be NN, as otherwise 6 would have at least one diseased allele.

Question 293: A
Urine passes from the kidney into the ureter and is then stored in the bladder. It is finally released through the urethra.

Question 294: F
Deoxygenated blood from the body flows through the inferior vena cava to the right atrium where it flows to the right ventricle to be pumped via the pulmonary artery to the lungs where it is oxygenated. It then returns to the heart via the pulmonary vein into the left atrium into the left ventricle where it is pumped to the body via the aorta.

Question 295: E
During inspiration, the pressure in the lungs decreases as the diaphragm contracts, increasing the volume of the lungs. The intercostal muscles contract in inspiration, lifting the rib cage.

Question 296: D

Whilst A, B, C and E are true of the DNA code, they do not represent the property described, which is that more than one combination of codons can encode the same amino acid, e.g. Serine is coded by the sequences: TCT, TCC, TCA, TCG.

Question 297: B
The degenerate nature of the code can help to reduce the deleterious effects of point mutations. The several 3-nucleotide combinations that code for each amino acid are usually similar such that a point mutation, i.e. a substitution of one nucleotide for another, can still result in the same amino acid as the one coded for by the original sequence.

The degenerate nature of the code does little to protect against deletions/insertions/duplications, which will cause the bases to be read in incorrect triplets, i.e. result in a frame shift.

Question 298: D
The hypothalamus is the site of central thermoreceptors. A decrease in environmental temperature decreases sweat secretion and causes cutaneous vasoconstriction to minimise heat loss from the blood.

Question 299: A
The movement of carbon dioxide in the lungs and neurotransmitters in a synapse are both examples of diffusion. Glucose reabsorption is an active process, as it requires work to be done against a concentration gradient.

Question 300: F
Some enzymes contain other molecules besides protein, e.g. metal ions. Enzymes can increase rates of reaction that may result in heat gain/loss, depending on if the reaction is exothermic or endothermic. They are prone to variations in pH and are highly specific to their individual substrate.

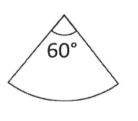

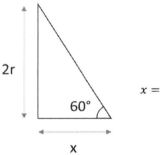

Question 301: C
Segment area $= \frac{60}{360}\pi r^2 = \frac{1}{6}\pi r^2$

$\frac{x}{\sin 30°} = \frac{2r}{\sin 60°}$

$\frac{2r}{\sqrt{3}}$

Total triangle area $= 2 \times \frac{1}{2} \times \frac{2r}{\sqrt{3}} \times 2r = \frac{4r^2}{\sqrt{3}}$

Proportion covered: $\frac{1}{6}\pi r^2 \Big/ \frac{4r^2}{\sqrt{3}} = \frac{\sqrt{3}\pi}{24} \approx 23\%$

Question 302: B
$(2r)^2 = r^2 + x^2$
$3r^2 = x^2$
$x = \sqrt{3}r$
$Total\ height = 2r + x = (2 + \sqrt{3})r$

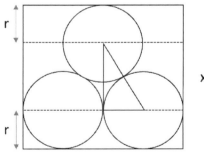

Question 303: A

$V = \frac{1}{3}h \times$ base area

Therefore base area must be equal if h and V are the same

Internal angle = 180° − external ; external = 360°/6 = 60° giving internal angle 120°

Hexagon is two trapezia of height h where:

$\frac{b}{\sin 90°} = \frac{h}{\sin 60°}$

$h = \frac{\sqrt{3}}{2}b$

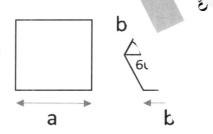

Trapezium area $= \frac{(2b+b)}{2}\frac{\sqrt{3}}{2}b = \frac{3\sqrt{3}}{4}b^2$

Total hexagon area $= \frac{3\sqrt{3}}{2}b^2$

So from equal volumes: $a^2 = \frac{3\sqrt{3}}{2}b^2$

Ratio: $\sqrt{\frac{3\sqrt{3}}{2}}$

Question 304: C

A cube has 6 sides so the Area of 9 cm cube = 6 x 9^2

9 cm cube splits into 3 cm cubes.

Area of 3 cm cubes = 3^3 x 6 x 9^2

$\frac{6 \times 3^2 \times 3^3}{6 \times 3^2 \times 3^2} = 3$

Question 305: C

$x^2 = (4r)^2 + r^2$

$x = \sqrt{17}r$

$\frac{\sqrt{17}r}{\sin 90°} = \frac{r}{\sin \theta}$

$\theta = \sin^{-1}\left(\frac{1}{\sqrt{17}}\right)$

Question 306: C

0 to 200 is 180 degrees so: $\frac{\theta}{180} = \frac{70}{200}$

$\theta = \frac{7 \times 180}{20} = 63°$

Question 307: A

Since the rhombi are similar, the ratio of angles = 1

Length scales with square root of area so length B = $\sqrt{10}$ length A

$\frac{angle\ A / angle\ B}{length\ A / length\ B} = \frac{1}{\sqrt{10}/1} = \frac{1}{\sqrt{10}}$

Question 308: E

$y = \ln(2x^2)$

$e^y = 2x^2$

$x = \sqrt{\frac{e^y}{2}}$

As the input is -x, the inverse function must be $f(x) = -\sqrt{\frac{e^y}{2}}$

Question 309: C

$log_8(x)$ and $log_{10}(x) < 0$; $x^2 < 1$; $\sin(x) \leq 1$ and $1 < e^x < 2.72$

So e^x is largest over this range

Question 310: C

$x \propto \sqrt{z}^3$

$\sqrt{2}^3 = 2\sqrt{2}$

Question 311: A

The area of the larger circle, radius x, must be 4x the smaller one so: $4\pi r^2 = \pi x^2$

$4r^2 = x^2$

$x = 2r$

The gap is $x - r = 2r - r = r$

Question 312: D

$x^2 + 3x - 4 \geq 0$

$(x - 1)(x + 4) \geq 0$

Hence, $x - 1 \geq 0$ or $x + 4 \geq 0$

So $x \geq 1$ or $x \geq -4$

Question 313: C

$\frac{4}{3}\pi r^3 = \pi r^2$

$\frac{4}{3}r = 1$

$r = \frac{3}{4}$

Question 314: B

When $x^2 = \frac{1}{x}$; $x = 1$

When $x > 1, x^2 > 1, \frac{1}{x} < 1$

When $x < 1, x^2 < 1, \frac{1}{x} > 1$

Range for $\frac{1}{x}$ is $x > 0$

Non-inclusive so: $0 < x < 1$

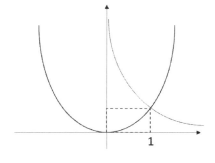

Question 315: D

Subtract line 2 from 3: $\begin{pmatrix} -1 & 2 & -1 \\ 2 & 1 & 3 \\ 0 & -2 & 1 \end{pmatrix} \begin{pmatrix} x \\ y \\ z \end{pmatrix} = \begin{pmatrix} 1 \\ 7 \\ 2 \end{pmatrix}$

Add 2x line 1 to line 2: $\begin{pmatrix} -1 & 2 & -1 \\ 0 & 5 & 1 \\ 0 & -2 & 1 \end{pmatrix} \begin{pmatrix} x \\ y \\ z \end{pmatrix} = \begin{pmatrix} 1 \\ 9 \\ 2 \end{pmatrix}$

Add 2xline 2 to 5x line 3: $\begin{pmatrix} -1 & 2 & -1 \\ 0 & 5 & 1 \\ 0 & 0 & 7 \end{pmatrix} \begin{pmatrix} x \\ y \\ z \end{pmatrix} = \begin{pmatrix} 1 \\ 9 \\ 28 \end{pmatrix}$

[Can be done via substitution from now onwards]: $\begin{pmatrix} -1 & 2 & -1 \\ 0 & 5 & 1 \\ 0 & 0 & 1 \end{pmatrix} \begin{pmatrix} x \\ y \\ z \end{pmatrix} = \begin{pmatrix} 1 \\ 9 \\ 4 \end{pmatrix}$

Subtract line 3 from line 2 and add line 3 to line 1:

$$\begin{pmatrix} -1 & 2 & 0 \\ 0 & 5 & 0 \\ 0 & 0 & 1 \end{pmatrix} \begin{pmatrix} x \\ y \\ z \end{pmatrix} = \begin{pmatrix} 5 \\ 5 \\ 4 \end{pmatrix}$$

$$\begin{pmatrix} -1 & 2 & 0 \\ 0 & 1 & 0 \\ 0 & 0 & 1 \end{pmatrix} \begin{pmatrix} x \\ y \\ z \end{pmatrix} = \begin{pmatrix} 5 \\ 1 \\ 4 \end{pmatrix}$$

Subtract 2 x line 2 from line 1:

$$\begin{pmatrix} -1 & 0 & 0 \\ 0 & 1 & 0 \\ 0 & 0 & 1 \end{pmatrix} \begin{pmatrix} x \\ y \\ z \end{pmatrix} = \begin{pmatrix} 3 \\ 1 \\ 4 \end{pmatrix}$$

$$\begin{pmatrix} 1 & 0 & 0 \\ 0 & 1 & 0 \\ 0 & 0 & 1 \end{pmatrix} \begin{pmatrix} x \\ y \\ z \end{pmatrix} = \begin{pmatrix} -3 \\ 1 \\ 4 \end{pmatrix}$$

Question 316: C

For two vectors to be perpendicular their scalar product must be equal to 0.

Hence, $\begin{pmatrix} -1 \\ 6 \end{pmatrix} \cdot \begin{pmatrix} 2 \\ k \end{pmatrix} = 0$

$\therefore\ -2 + 6k = 0$

$k = \frac{1}{3}$

Question 317: C

The point, q, in the plane meets the perpendicular line from the plane to the point p.

$q = -3i + j + \lambda_1(i + 2j)$

$\overrightarrow{PQ} = -3i + j + \lambda_1(i + 2j) + 4i + 5j$

$= \begin{pmatrix} -7 + \lambda_1 \\ -4 + 2\lambda_1 \end{pmatrix}$

PQ is perpendicular to the plane r therefore the dot product of $\overrightarrow{PQ}$ and a vector within the plane must be 0.

$\begin{pmatrix} -7 + \lambda_1 \\ -4 + 2\lambda_1 \end{pmatrix} \cdot \begin{pmatrix} 1 \\ 2 \end{pmatrix} = 0$

$\therefore\ -7 + \lambda_1 - 8 + 4 + \lambda_1 = 0$

$\lambda_1 = 3$

$\overrightarrow{PQ} = \begin{pmatrix} -4 \\ 2 \end{pmatrix}$

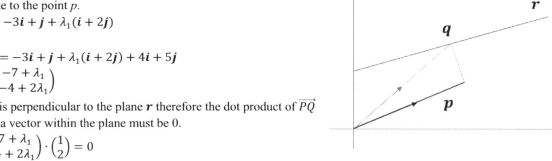

The perpendicular distance from the plane to point p is therefore the modulus of the vector joining the two $\overrightarrow{PQ}$:

$|\overrightarrow{PQ}| = \sqrt{(-4)^2 + 2^2} = \sqrt{20} = 2\sqrt{5}$

Question 318: E

$-1 + 3\mu = -7 \, ; \, \mu = -2$

$2 + 4\lambda + 2\mu = 2 \, \therefore \, \lambda = 1$

$3 + \lambda + \mu = k \, \therefore \, k = 2$

Question 319: E

$\sin\left(\frac{\pi}{2} - 2\theta\right) = \cos(2\theta)$

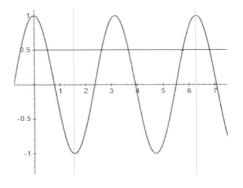

Root solution to $\cos(\theta) = 0.5$

$\theta = \frac{\pi}{3}$

Solution to $\cos(2\theta) = 0.5$

$\theta = \frac{\pi}{6}$

Largest solution within range is: $2\pi - \frac{\pi}{6} = \frac{(12-1)\pi}{6} = \frac{11\pi}{6}$

Question 320: A

$\cos^4(x) - \sin^4(x) \equiv \{\cos^2(x) - \sin^2(x)\}\{\cos^2(x) + \sin^2(x)\}$

From difference of two squares, then using Pythagorean identity $\cos^2(x) + \sin^2(x) = 1$

$\cos^4(x) - \sin^4(x) \equiv \cos^2(x) - \sin^2(x)$

But double angle formula says: $\cos(A + B) = \cos(A)\cos(B) - \sin(A)\sin(B)$

$\therefore$ if $A = B, \cos(2A) = \cos(A)\cos(A) - \sin(A)\sin(A)$

$= \cos^2(A) - \sin^2(A)$

So, $\cos^4(x) - \sin^4(x) \equiv \cos(2x)$

Question 321: C

Factorise: $(x + 1)(x + 2)(2x - 1)(x^2 + 2) = 0$

Three real roots at $x = -1, x = -2, x = 0.5$ and two imaginary roots at 2i and -2i

Question 322: C

An arithmetic sequence has constant difference d so the sum increases by d more each time:

$u_n = u_1 + (n - 1)d$

$\sum_1^n u_n = \frac{n}{2}\{2u_1 + (n - 1)d\}$

$\sum_1^8 u_n = \frac{8}{2}\{4 + (8 - 1)3\} = 100$

Question 323: E

$\binom{n}{k} 2^{n-k}(-x)^k = \binom{5}{2} 2^{5-2}(-x)^2$

$= 10 \times 2^3 x^2 = 80x^2$

Question 324: A

Having already thrown a 6 is irrelevant. A fair die has equal probability $P = \frac{1}{6}$ for every throw.

For three throws: $P(6 \cap 6 \cap 6) = \left(\frac{1}{6}\right)^3 = \frac{1}{216}$

Question 325: D

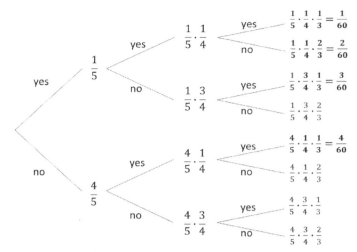

Total probability is sum of all probabilities:

$= P(Y \cap Y \cap Y) + P(Y \cap Y \cap N) + P(Y \cap N \cap Y) + P(N \cap Y \cap Y)$

$= \frac{1}{60} + \frac{2}{60} + \frac{3}{60} + \frac{4}{60} = \frac{10}{60} = \frac{1}{6}$

Question 326: C

$P[(A \cup B)'] = 1 - P[(A \cup B)]$

$= 1 - \{P(A) + P(B) - P(A \cap B)\}$

$= 1 - \frac{2+6-1}{8} = \frac{3}{8}$

Question 327: D

Using the product rule: $\frac{dy}{dx} = x \cdot 4(x + 3)^3 + 1 \cdot (x + 3)^4$

$= 4x(x + 3)^3 + (x + 3)(x + 3)^3$

$= (5x + 3)(x + 3)^3$

Question 328: C

$\int_1^2 \frac{2}{x^2} dx = \int_1^2 2x^{-2} dx =$

$\left[\frac{2x^{-1}}{-1}\right]_1^2 = \left[\frac{-2}{x}\right]_1^2$

$= \frac{-2}{2} - \frac{-2}{1} = 1$

Question 329: D

Express $\frac{5i}{1+2i}$ in the form $a + bi$

$\frac{5i}{1+2i} \cdot \frac{1-2i}{1-2i}$

$= \frac{5i+10}{1+4} \quad \frac{5i+10}{5}$

$= i + 2$

Question 330: B

$7\log_a(2) - 3\log_a(12) + 5\log_a(3)$

$7\log_a(2) = \log_a(2^7) = \log_a(128)$

$3\log_a(12) = \log_a(1728)$

$5\log_a(3) = \log_a(243)$

This gives: $\log_a(128) - \log_a(1728) + \log_a(243)$

$= \log_a\left(\frac{128 \times 243}{1728}\right) = \log_a(18)$

Question 331: E
Functions of the form quadratic over quadratic have a horizontal asymptote.
Divide each term by the highest order in the polynomial i.e. x^2:

$$\frac{2x^2 - x + 3}{x^2 + x - 2} = \frac{2 - \frac{1}{x} + \frac{3}{x^2}}{1 + \frac{1}{x} - \frac{2}{x^2}}$$

$$\lim_{x \to \infty} \left(\frac{2 - \frac{1}{x} + \frac{3}{x^2}}{1 + \frac{1}{x} - \frac{2}{x^2}}\right) = \frac{2}{1} \quad i.e. \, y \to 2$$

So the asymptote is $y = 2$

Question 332: A
$1 - 3e^{-x} = e^x - 3$
$4 = e^x + 3e^{-x} = \frac{(e^x)^2}{e^x} + \frac{3}{e^x} = \frac{(e^x)^2 + 3}{e^x}$
This is a quadratic equation in (e^x): $(e^x)^2 - 4(e^x) + 3 = 0$
$(e^x - 3)(e^x - 1) = 0$
So $e^x = 3, x = \ln(3)$ or $e^x = 1, x = 0$

Question 333: D
Rearrange into the format: $(x + a)^2 + (y + b)^2 = r^2$
$(x - 3)^2 + (y + 4)^2 - 25 = 12$
$(x - 3)^2 + (y + 4)^2 = 37$
$\therefore r = \sqrt{37}$

Question 334: C
$\sin(-x) = -\sin(x)$
$\int_0^a 2\sin(-x)\,dx = -2\int_0^a \sin(x)\,dx = -2[\cos(x)]_0^a = \cos(a) - 1$
Solve $\cos(a) - 1 = 0 \therefore a = 2k\pi$
Or simply the integral of any whole period of $\sin(x) = 0$ i.e. $a = 2k\pi$

Question 335: E
$\frac{2x+3}{(x-2)(x-3)^2} = \frac{A}{(x-2)} + \frac{B}{(x-3)} + \frac{C}{(x-3)^2}$

$2x + 3 = A(x - 3)^2 + B(x - 2)(x - 3) + C(x - 2)$
When $x = 3, (x - 3) = 0$, $C = 9$
When $x = 2, (x - 2) = 0, A = 7$
$2x + 3 = 7(x - 3)^2 + B(x - 2)(x - 3) + 9(x - 2)$

For completeness: Equating coefficients of x^2 on either side: $0 = 7 + B$ which gives: $B = -7$

Question 336: E
Forces on the ball are $weight = mg$ which is constant and tension T which varies with position.
$F = ma \, ; \, a = \frac{v^2}{r}$
$T + mg = m\frac{v^2}{r}$
If the ball stops moving in a circle it means there is no tension in the string (T=0) so:
$mg = m\frac{v^2}{r}$
$v = \sqrt{gr}$

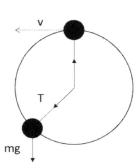

Question 337: E

To move at a steady velocity there is no acceleration so the forces are balanced. Resolve along the slope: $F + mg\sin(30) = T\cos(30)$

$$\frac{mg}{2} + F = \frac{T\sqrt{3}}{2}$$

$$T = \frac{2}{\sqrt{3}}\left(\frac{mg}{2} + F\right)$$

Work done in pulling the box W=Fd so: $P = vT\cos(30)$

$$P = \left(\frac{mg}{2} + F\right)v$$

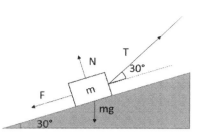

Question 338: C

This is a conservation of energy problem. In the absence of friction there is no dissipation of energy therefore the sum of the potential and kinetic energy must be constant: $\frac{1}{2}mv^2 + mgh = E$

At its highest the velocity and kinetic energy are 0 so $E = mgh_1$.
At the bottom of the swing the potential energy at h is converted to kinetic energy.

Therefore: $\frac{1}{2}mv^2 = E = mgh_1 \therefore v = \sqrt{2gh_1}$

$$h_1 = l(1 - \cos(\theta))$$

$$v = \sqrt{2gh_1} = \sqrt{2gl(1 - \cos(\theta))}$$

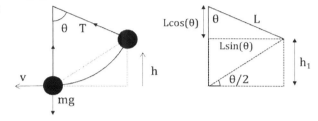

Question 339: E

Conservation of momentum. Before : $p = mu_1$

Afterward: $p = m(v_1 + v_2)$

Vertical components must cancel therefore: $v_2\sin(\theta) = 2v_2\sin(30°)$

$\sin(\theta) = 1$ giving $\theta = 90°$

Question 340: D

Elastic collision means kinetic energy is conserved so three balls will swing at a velocity equal to the velocity of the first to conserve both momentum and kinetic energy.

$$\frac{1}{2}mv^2 = \frac{1}{2}m_2u^2$$

But momentum is also conserved so $mv = m_2u$

Mass must therefore be equal i.e. 3 balls move at a velocity $u = v$

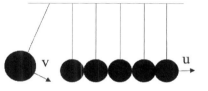

Question 341: A

The ball will follow a parabolic trajectory. The minimum angle is therefore given by the gradient of the parabola which goes through the points (0,3) and (-6,0). [**NB:** do not use a triangle, the ball lands 6m behind the fence so it takes a parabolic trajectory with the vertex directly above the fence. The smallest possible initial angle places the ball just passing over the fence.]

$y = -ax^2 + 3$

$0 = -36a + 3$

$a = \frac{1}{12}$

$y = -\frac{x^2}{12} + 3$

$\frac{dy}{dx} = -\frac{2x}{12} = -\frac{x}{6}$

$\frac{dy}{dx} = -\frac{6}{6} = -1 \therefore \tan(\theta) = -1 = 1$

$\theta = \arctan(1)$

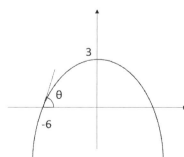

Question 342: B

Simple harmonic motion $m\frac{d^2x}{dt^2} = -kx$

Hence: $T \propto \sqrt{\frac{m}{k}}$.

Doubling k and halving m would therefore reduce time period T by a half. The frequency is the reciprocal of the time period and will therefore double.

Question 343: C

At the top of the bounce the kinetic energy is zero as velocity is zero. Highest velocity will be downwards before impact where $potential\ energy\ lost = kinetic\ energy\ gained$ (assuming no resistance).

$\frac{1}{2}mv^2 = mgh$

$v^2 = 2gh = 60$

$v = 2\sqrt{15}$

Question 344: D

Speed is close to c so need to consider Lorentz contraction in special relativity: $l' = l\sqrt{1 - \frac{v^2}{c^2}}$

$= l\sqrt{1 - \frac{\left(\frac{c}{10}\right)^2}{c^2}}$

$= l\sqrt{0.99}$

Question 345: B

Initial kinetic energy must equal work done to stop the car: $\frac{1}{2}mv^2 = Fd = \frac{mg}{2}d$

$v^2 = gd$

$d = \frac{v^2}{g}$

Question 346: D

Find the proportion of amplitude left, then use this to work out how many half-lives have passed: $\frac{25}{200} = \frac{1}{8} = \frac{1}{2^3}$

Therefore 12 seconds is three half-lives and t=4s.

Question 347: C

$f_{beats} = |f_1 - f_2| = \frac{1}{8}f = 10$

$f = 80$ Hz

Question 348: E

The two waves would interfere destructively as they are half a wavelength phase difference. A wave would reflect back onto itself in this way if reflected in a plane, perpendicular surface. These two waves travelling in opposite directions (incident and reflected) would produce a standing wave, with this exact point in time corresponding to zero amplitude. There are 5 nodes with two fixed ends making it the 4th harmonic of a standing wave. Thus, all the statements are true.

Question 349: C

Beta decay changes a neutron to a proton releasing an electron and an antineutrino (a doesn't change, b increases by one), then alpha decay emits an alpha particle which is two protons and two neutron (a decreases by 4, b decreases by two).

Question 350: A

Assume ideal gas: $PV = nRT$

$P_2 = \frac{nR2T}{1.1V}$

Therefore change in P is equal to $\frac{2}{1.1} = 1.818$ which is an 82% increase.

Question 351: E

Alpha particles are +2 and are deflected to the right. Were they a -1 charge they would follow path Q however electrons have a far smaller mass and will be deflected much more than an alpha particle.

Question 352: D

Assume brightness increases with current. Work out total resistance, then total current and then split between resistors within the circuit.

For three in parallel: $\frac{1}{R_T} = \sum \frac{1}{R} = \frac{3}{R}$ $\therefore$ $R_T = \frac{R}{3}$

$I_T = \frac{V}{R_T} = \frac{3V}{R}$

Therefore, current in each lamp is one third of this (split equally as equal resistance in each branch): $I_{1,2,3} = \frac{V}{R}$

For two in series and one in parallel, the two in series have resistance 2R so: $\frac{1}{R_T} = \frac{1}{2R} + \frac{1}{R}$ $\therefore$ $R_T = \frac{2R}{3}$

$I_T = \frac{V}{R_T} = \frac{3V}{2R}$

This is split with a third going to the branch with resistance 2R and two thirds going to the branch with resistance R: $I_6 = \frac{V}{R}$; $I_{4,5} = \frac{V}{2R}$

In series the total resistance is simple 3R so: $I_T = \frac{V}{R_T} = \frac{V}{3R}$

Current is equal in all and is equal to the total current so: $I_{7,8,9} = \frac{V}{3R}$

Current in 1,2,3 and 4 is the same and is greatest.

Question 353: A

Object is between f and the lens so rays will diverge on the other side producing a virtual image on the same side which is magnified.

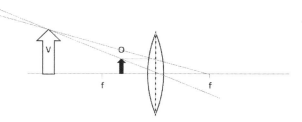

Question 354: B

Moments taken with the pivot at the wall must balance therefore: $\frac{2}{3} lT \sin \theta = lmg$

$T = \frac{3mg}{2 \sin \theta}$

Question 355: C

This process is known as the photoelectric effect (photons producing electron emission) and the presence of a work function arises due to wave particle duality. [n.b. thermionic emission uses heat not incident radiation to emit particles]. As the axis is kinetic energy and not potential, the intercept is the work function not the stopping potential.

Question 356: D

Huygens' principle states that every point on a wavefront is like a point source of a wave travelling at the same speed. This explains the first four but does not account for energy loss during propagation i.e. damping.

Question 357: A

Carnot cycle is the most efficient where: $\eta = \frac{work\ done}{heat\ put\ in} = 1 - \frac{T_{cold}}{T_{hot}} = 1 - \frac{280}{420} = \frac{3}{7} \approx 43\%$

Question 358: B

B is the only correct statement. NB- while generators can have a moving coil, they could equally have a moving magnetic field instead so this is not true.

Question 359: C

NAND (gives X), OR (gives Y) and AND (gives Z) gates

Question 360: E

Several almost synonymous terms. Those in bold are correct. E is the only line with all three.

	P	Q	R
A	**Elastic Modulus**	**Yield stress**	Fracture toughness
B	**Tensile Modulus**	**Plastic onset**	Yield stress
C	Hardness	**Stiffness**	**Ductile failure**
D	Ductility	**Elastic limit**	Brittle fracture
E	**Young's Modulus**	**Yield stress**	**Fracture stress**

Section 2: Worked Answers

Physics Question 1

a)

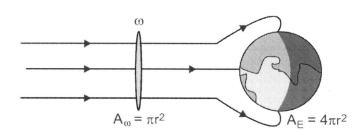

$$\omega_E = (A_\omega / A_E)\omega = \frac{\omega}{4}$$

b) Radiation reflected by the atmosphere $= a\Omega/4$

Radiation emitted as infrared from the Earth's surface $= \sigma T_s^4$, where T_s is the temperature of the Earth's surface

c) Total solar radiation that reaches the Earth = radiation reflected by the atmosphere + radiation emitted as infrared from the Earth's surface, i.e.

$\frac{\Omega}{4} = \frac{a\Omega}{4} + \sigma T_s^4$

Rearranging for T_s: $\Omega = a\Omega + 4\sigma T_s^4$

$T_s^4 = \frac{\Omega(1-a)}{4\sigma}$

$$T_s = \sqrt[4]{\frac{\Omega(1-a)}{4\sigma}}$$

d) When $\Omega = 1372$ Wm^{-2} and a = 0.3, **T_s = 255 K**

e) The black-body temperature of the Earth is far lower than the actual average surface temperature of the Earth (which is around 290 K). This is because the insulating effect of the atmosphere has not been considered in the calculations above. Effects of volcanism and other sources of heath within the Earth are also ignored in these calculations.

f) $d = 1.5 \times 10^{11}$ m, and $r_{sun} = 6.96 \times 10^8$ m and at d, $\Omega_E = 1372$ Wm^{-2}

The total power emitted per unit area from the sun = (ratio of the area of the sphere of radius d and r_{sun}) $\times \Omega_E$,

i.e. $\Omega_{Sun} = \left(\frac{4\pi d^2}{4\pi r_{sun}^2}\right)\Omega_E$

Therefore: $\Omega_{Sun} = \sigma T_{Sun}^4$

$T_{Sun} = \sqrt[4]{\frac{\Omega_{Sun}}{\sigma}}$

$T_{Sun} = \sqrt[4]{\left(\frac{4\pi d^2}{4\pi r_{sun}^2}\right)\frac{\Omega_E}{\sigma}}$

Using the values for d, r_{sun} & Ω_E, **T_{Sun} = 5790 K**

g) In this calculation, we have assumed a perfectly circular orbit and a constant solar power output.

Physics Question 2

a)

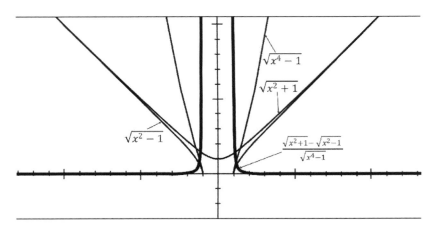

b) Evaluate: $\int \frac{\sqrt{x^2+1}-\sqrt{x^2-1}}{\sqrt{x^4-1}} dx$

Step 1 – Simplify the terms

The denominator is simplified as: $\sqrt{x^4-1} = (x^2+1)^{1/2}(x^2-1)^{1/2}$

Substituting this back into the original equation:

$$\int \frac{\sqrt{x^2+1}-\sqrt{x^2-1}}{\sqrt{x^4-1}} dx = \int \frac{\sqrt{x^2+1}-\sqrt{x^2-1}}{\sqrt{x^2+1}\sqrt{x^2-1}} dx$$

$$= \underbrace{\int \frac{1}{\sqrt{x^2-1}} dx}_{(I_1)} + \underbrace{\int \frac{1}{\sqrt{x^2+1}} dx}_{(I_2)}$$

Step 2 – Integration by substitution

I_1 and I_2 need to be integrated separately using different substitutions.

I_1 – Use the substitution $x = \tan(t)$

$$dx = \sec^2(t)dt = \frac{1}{\cos^2(t)} dt$$

Substituting $x = \tan(t)$ into $\sqrt{x^2+1}$ gives:

$$\sqrt{\tan^2(t)+1} = \sqrt{\sec^2(t)} = \sec(t) = \frac{1}{\cos(t)}$$

Putting this back into the original integral for I_1:

$$\int \frac{1}{\sqrt{x^2+1}} dx = \int \frac{1}{\sec(t)} \frac{1}{\cos^2(t)} dt = \int \cos(t) \frac{1}{\cos^2(s)} ds$$

$$I_1 = \int \frac{1}{\cos(t)} dt$$

I_2 – Use the substitution $x = \sec(s) = \frac{1}{\cos(s)}$:

$$dx = \sec(s)\tan(s)ds = \frac{1}{\cos(s)} \frac{\sin(s)}{\cos(s)} ds = \frac{\sin(s)}{\cos^2(s)} ds$$

Substituting $x = \sec(s)$ into $\sqrt{x^2-1}$ gives:

$$\sqrt{\sec^2(s)-1} = \sqrt{\tan^2(s)} = \tan(s) = \frac{\sin(s)}{\cos(s)}$$

Putting this back into the original integral for I$_2$:

$$\int \frac{1}{\sqrt{x^2-1}}dx = \int \frac{1}{\tan(s)}\frac{\sin(s)}{\cos^2(s)}ds = \int \frac{\cos(s)}{\sin(s)}\frac{\sin(s)}{\cos^2(s)}ds$$

$$I_2 = \int \frac{1}{\cos(s)}ds$$

Hence the total integral is : $I_1 + I_2 = \int \frac{1}{\cos(t)}dt - \int \frac{1}{\cos(s)}ds$

Using the Rule: $\int \frac{1}{\cos(A)}dA = ln|secA + tanA| + C$

$I_1 + I_2 = \int \frac{1}{\cos(t)}dt - \int \frac{1}{\cos(s)}ds = ln|\sec(t) + \tan(t)| - ln|\sec(s) + \tan(s)| + C$

Using the trig identity: $tan^2(A) + 1 = sec^2(A)$

We can express t and s in terms of x:
$x = tan(t)$
$tan^2(t) + 1 = sec^2(t)$
$x^2 + 1 = sec^2(t)$
$sec(t) + tan(t) = \sqrt{x^2 + 1} + x$

$x = sec(s)$
$sec^2(s) - 1 = tan^2(s)$
$x^2 - 1 = tan^2(s)$
$sec(s) + tan(s) = \sqrt{x^2 - 1} + x$

Hence:

$$\int \frac{\sqrt{x^2 + 1} - \sqrt{x^2 - 1}}{\sqrt{x^4 - 1}}dx = ln\left|\sqrt{x^2 + 1} + x\right| - ln\left|\sqrt{x^2 - 1} + x\right| + C$$

c)

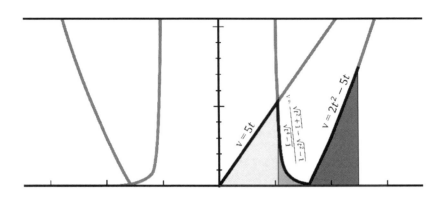

d)

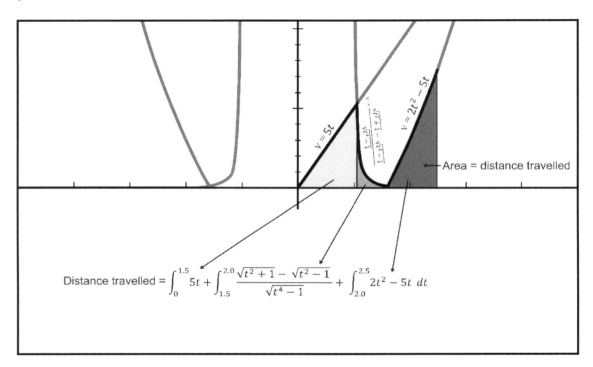

$$\text{Distance} = \int_0^{1.5} 5t + \int_{1.5}^{2.0} \frac{\sqrt{t^2+1} - \sqrt{t^2-1}}{\sqrt{t^4-1}} + \int_{2.0}^{2.5} 2t^2 - 5t \ dt$$

$$\text{Distance} = \left[\frac{5}{2}t^2\right]_0^{1.5} + \left[ln\left|\sqrt{x^2+1}+x\right| - ln\left|\sqrt{x^2-1}+x\right|\right]_{1.5}^{2.0} + \left[\frac{2}{3}t^3 - \frac{5}{2}t^2\right]_{2.0}^{2.5}$$

$$\text{Distance} = 5.625 + 0.106 + 10.703 = \mathbf{16.44 \ km}$$

Physics Question 3

a) At ∂N, $-\lambda \partial t$ atoms have decayed, $\frac{dN}{dt} = -\lambda N$ therefore $\int \frac{1}{N} dN = \int -\lambda dt$, $\ln(N) = -\lambda t + C$

When $t = 0$, $\ln(N_0) = C$ therefore $\ln(N) = -\lambda t + \ln(N_0)$ and $\boldsymbol{N = N_0 e^{-\lambda t}}$

b) $A = A_0 e^{-\lambda t}$

c) At $t = t_{1/2}$, $\frac{N_0}{2} = N_0 e^{-\lambda t_{1/2}}$ therefore $N_0 = 2 N_0 e^{-\lambda t_{1/2}}$ and $1 = 2 e^{-\lambda t_{1/2}}$

$-\lambda t_{1/2} = \ln\left(\frac{1}{2}\right)$

$t_{1/2} = \frac{1}{\lambda} \ln(2)$

i.e $t_{1/2} = \frac{0.693}{\lambda}$

di)

Parent Isotope	Daughter Isotope	Decay Products	λ (a^{-1})
^{238}U	^{206}Pb	$8 \propto +6\beta^-$	1.55×10^{-10}
^{235}U	^{207}Pb	$7 \propto +4\beta^-$	9.85×10^{-10}
^{232}Th	^{208}Pb	$6 \propto +4\beta^-$	4.95×10^{-11}
^{87}Rb	^{87}Sr	β^-	1.42×10^{-11}
^{147}Sm	^{143}Nd	$\propto$	6.54×10^{-12}
^{40}K	^{40}Ca and ^{40}Ar	β^- and electron capture	4.95×10^{-10} and 5.81×10^{-11}
^{39}Ar	^{39}Ar	β^-	2.57×10^{-3}
^{176}Lu	^{176}Hf	β^-	1.94×10^{-11}
^{187}Re	^{187}Os	β^-	1.52×10^{-11}
^{14}C	^{15}N	β^-	1.21×10^{-4}

dii) If the total number of daughter atoms present at time t is D, then the total number of atoms remaining, $N = N_0 - D$, and therefore $D = Ne^{-\lambda t}$

$N_0 - D = N_0 e^{-\lambda t}$

Becomes $D = N_0(1 - e^{-\lambda t})$

Using $N = N_0 e^{-\lambda t}$

$D = (e^{-\lambda t} - 1)$

Therefore $e^{-\lambda t} = \frac{D}{N} + 1$

$-\lambda t = \ln\left(\frac{D}{N} + 1\right)$

$\boldsymbol{t = -\frac{1}{\lambda} \ln\left(\frac{D}{N} + 1\right)}$

diii) Age of the Earth: ^{238}U (or any isotope with a half-life on the order of the age of the Earth)

Ancient artefacts: ^{14}C, due to its short half-life

e) Assuming that $[^{206}\text{Pb}] \gg [^{208}\text{Pb}]$, we can assume that all Pb present in the sample is due to the decay of ^{238}U
The amount of ^{238}U present now is

$$\left[^{238}U_T\right] = \frac{11.7 \times 10^{-5}}{238} = 4.92 \times 10^{-7} \text{ moles of } ^{238}\text{U}$$

When one mole of ^{238}U decays, one mole of ^{206}Pb is produced, therefore the total ^{206}Pb present = amount of ^{238}U that has decayed

$$\left[^{236}Pb_T\right] = \frac{3.58 \times 10^{-5}}{206} = 1.74 \times 10^{-7} \text{ moles of } ^{206}\text{Pb}$$

The total ^{238}U that was present at time $t = 0$ must be $\left[^{238}U_0\right] = \left[^{238}U_T\right] + \left[^{236}Pb_T\right] = 6.66 \times 10^{-7}$ moles

As $t_{1/2} = \frac{0.693}{\lambda_{238}}$ and $\lambda_{238} = \frac{0.693}{4.5 \times 10^9} = 1.54 \times 10^{-10}$
Hence as $N = N_0 e^{-\lambda t}$,
$t = -\frac{1}{\lambda} ln\left(\frac{N}{N_0}\right)$
Where $N = \left[^{238}U_T\right]$ therefore $t = -\frac{1}{1.54 \times 10^{-10}} ln\left(\frac{4.92 \times 10^{-7}}{6.66 \times 10^{-7}}\right)$

$\underline{\boldsymbol{t = 1.97 \times 10^9 \text{ years}}}$

Physics Question 4

ai) $V = -\frac{Gm_1m_2}{r}$

aii) $a = -\frac{\partial V}{\partial r} = -\frac{\partial}{\partial r}\left(\frac{Gm_1}{r}\right) = -\frac{Gm_1}{r^2}$

bi)

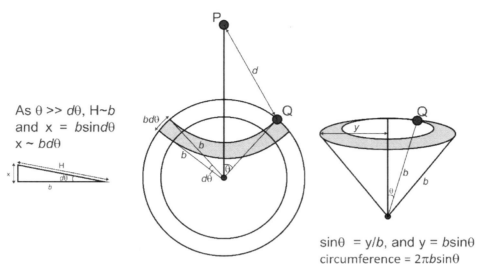

As $\theta \gg d\theta$, H~b
and $x = b\sin d\theta$
$x \sim bd\theta$

$\sin\theta = y/b$, and $y = b\sin\theta$
circumference $= 2\pi b\sin\theta$

Area of strip = circumference x width
Area $= (2\pi b\sin\theta)(bd\theta)$

$\boxed{\text{Area} = 2\pi b^2 \sin\theta d\theta)}$

bii) Mass of strip = area of strip x thickness x density

$M = 2\pi b^2 \sin\theta d\theta t\rho$
At point Q, as $V = -\frac{Gm}{r}$

$V = -\frac{2G\pi b^2 \sin\theta d\theta t\rho}{D}$
Distance D can be calculated as

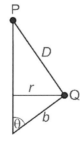

Using the cosine rule that
$a^2 = b^2 + c^2 - 2bc\cos A$,
$D^2 = b^2 + r^2 - 2br\cos\theta$

As $V = -G\int_m \frac{dm}{r}$ for a distribution of masses,

$V = -G\int_m = -\frac{2\pi b^2 \sin\theta d\theta t\rho}{D}$

$$V = -2G\pi b^2 t\rho \int_m = -\frac{sin\theta}{\sqrt{b^2+r^2-2rbCos\theta}} d\theta$$

However, $D^2 = b^2 + r^2 - 2brCos\theta$

$$2DdD = 2brSin\theta d\theta$$

$$sin\theta d\theta = \frac{D}{br} dD$$

Substituting this back into the original equation gives:

$$V = -2G\pi b^2 t\rho \int_m = -\frac{D}{Dbr} dD$$

$$V = -2G\pi b^2 t\rho \int_m = -\frac{1}{br} dD$$

$$V = -2G\pi b^2 t\rho \left[\frac{D}{br}\right]_{D_{min}}^{D_{max}}$$

There are two cases for point P, when P is inside and outside the hollow shell. When P is inside the shell, D_{max} and D_{min} are $b + r$ and $b - r$ respectively, therefore:

$$\boldsymbol{V_{inside}} = -2G\pi b^2 t\rho \left[\frac{D}{br}\right]_{b-r}^{b+r} = -4G\pi bt\rho$$

When P is outside the hollow shell, D_{max} and D_{min} are $r + b$ and $r - b$ respectively, therefore:

$$\boldsymbol{V_{outside}} = -2G\pi b^2 t\rho \left[\frac{D}{br}\right]_{r-b}^{r+b} = \frac{-4G\pi b^2 t\rho}{r}$$

biii) When P is inside the shell, the potential V is constant and independent of position

biv) As the potential V inside the shell is constant, acceleration a is zero

bv) $a = -\frac{\partial V_{outside}}{\partial r} = -\frac{\partial}{\partial r}\left(\frac{4G\pi b^2 t\rho}{r}\right)$

$$a = -\frac{G(4\pi b^2 t\rho)}{r^2}$$

$$\boldsymbol{a = -\frac{GM}{r^2}}$$

Physics Question 5

ai) The production of electromotive forces (emfs) and currents caused by a changing magnetic field through a metal coil is called electromagnetic induction

aii) In the upper case, as the N pole of a magnet approaches face A of the coil, face A becomes a North pole by inducing an anticlockwise current in the coil in order to oppose the forward motion of the magnet's N pole into the coil.

In the lower case, the N pole of a magnet moves away from face A of a coil. A clockwise current is induced in the coil, making face A South pole in order to oppose the motion of the magnet's N pole out of the coil.

aiii) Faraday's law states that when magnetic flux changes through a circuit, an emf is induced for as long as the change in magnetic flux continues. This causes an emf, F, to be produced when a metal coil spins inside a magnetic field as shown below

$$F = BACos\theta$$
For a coil with N turns, $FN = BANCos\theta$

Where B = magnetic field strength and A = area of coil. The magnetic flux is given by $\emptyset = BA$, and Lenz's law states $V = -N\frac{\Delta\emptyset}{\Delta t}$

Where V = voltage of induced current, and t = time. When motion of the coil ceases, $\frac{\Delta\emptyset}{\Delta t} = 0$ and the induced current becomes zero, therefore satisfying Faraday's law.

aiv) Area of the coil = 50 cm^2, and as $V = -N\frac{\Delta\emptyset}{\Delta t}$

$$V_{gen} = -35\frac{0.4\times(0.05\times0.1)}{50/60}$$

$$\boldsymbol{V_{gen} = -8.4\ mV}$$

bi) The dynamo theory describes the process through which a rotating, convecting and electrically conducting fluid acts to maintain a magnetic field. In the Earth, the conductive fluid is the Earth's metallic outer core, and is made of primarily Fe and Ni. Heat produced from the radioactive decay of isotopes in the core is the source of energy that keeps the temperature of the outer core above the melting temperature of Fe, Ni, etc.

bii) Incoming charged particles from the solar wind would not be deflected by the Earth's magnetic field, and would ionise on the Earth's surface. As a result, an atmosphere would not be stable, nor would the presence of liquid water on the Earth's surface.

The absence of a magnetic field indicates the absence of a rotating core of liquid metal (i.e. a metallic planetary outer core) required to generate a current. This will eventually occur when the activity of radioactive nuclides in the Earth's core is too low to sustain the temperatures required for a stable liquid outer core, causing the outer core to freeze and solidify. As a result, dynamo motion will cease and the planetary magnetic field will be lost.

biv) Io, a Jovian moon. Volcanism is caused by heat produced by tidal heating due to the gravitational attraction of Jupiter, and is not caused by an internally decaying metallic core as is the case in the Earth.

Chemistry Question 1

a) When at chemical equilibrium, the rates of both the forward and backward reactions are equal. The concentrations of the reactants and products may not necessarily be equal when the reaction is at equilibrium, i.e. equilibrium may lie on one side of the reaction.

b) $CO_{2(g)} \rightleftharpoons CO_{2(aq)}$ (1)

$H^+_{(aq)} + CO_3^{2-}{}_{(aq)} \rightleftharpoons HCO_3^-{}_{(aq)}$ (2)

$HCO_3^-{}_{(aq)} + H^+_{(aq)} \rightleftharpoons H_2CO_{3(aq)}$ (3)

The full reaction for the dissolution of CO_2 into seawater is actually:

$$CaCO_{3\,(s)} + CO_{2(aq)} + H_2O \rightleftharpoons Ca^{2+}_{(aq)} + 2HCO_{3(aq)}^-$$

Where $CaCO_{3(s)}$ is limestone/carbonates in the ocean

c) From the equation, $\frac{[H_2CO_3]}{p[CO_2]} = 10^{-1.47}$, we can write $[H_2CO_3] = 10^{-1.47} \, p[CO_2]$

Therefore $[H_2CO_3] = 10^{-1.47}(340 \times 10^{-6}) = \mathbf{10^{-4.94}}$

d)

$$[H^+] = [HCO_3^-] + 2[CO_3^{2-}] + [OH^-]$$

Using the answer for part c, we know that $[H_2CO_3] = 10^{-4.94}$, therefore

$$\frac{[H^+][HCO_3^-]}{[H_2CO_3]} = 10^{-6.35}$$

becomes

$$[H^+][HCO_3^-] = 10^{-6.35}[H_2CO_3] = (10^{-6.35})(10^{-4.94}) = 10^{-11.29}$$

Hence

$$[HCO_3^-] = \frac{10^{-11.29}}{[H^+]} \quad (1)$$

Using the equations in the table and the relationship given in part b, we can write:

And

$$\frac{[H^+][CO_3^{2-}]}{[HCO_3^-]} = 10^{-10.33} \quad (2)$$

Substituting the value of $[HCO_3^-]$ from (1) into (2) we get:

$$[H^+][CO_3^{2-}] = 10^{-10.33}[HCO_3^{2-}]$$
$$[CO_3^{2-}] = 10^{-10.33}\frac{10^{-11.29}}{[H^+]}$$
$$[CO_3^{2-}] = \frac{10^{-21.62}}{[H^+]^2} \quad (3)$$

From the table we can also write that:

$$[OH^-] = \frac{10^{-14}}{[H^+]} \quad (4)$$

Substituting (1), (3) and (4)into the original equation gives us

$$[H^+] = [HCO_3^-] + 2[CO_3^{2-}] + [OH^-]$$

$$[\mathbf{H^+}] = \frac{\mathbf{10^{-11.29}}}{[\mathbf{H^+}]} + \frac{\mathbf{10^{-21.32}}}{[\mathbf{H^+}]^2} + \frac{\mathbf{10^{-14}}}{[\mathbf{H^+}]}$$

e) Assuming that as $10^{-11.29} \ll 10^{-14} \ll 10^{-21.62}$, the answer for part d becomes

$$[H^+] \approx \frac{10^{-11.29}}{[H^+]}$$

Therefore

$$[H^+]^2 \approx 10^{-11.29}$$
$$[\mathbf{H^+}] \approx \mathbf{10^{-5.65}}$$

Or

$$[\mathbf{H^+}] \approx \mathbf{2.2ppm}$$

f) ph = -log([H⁺])

g) ph = -log($10^{-5.65}$) = **5.65**

h) Firstly, as

$$\frac{[H_2SO_3]}{p[SO_2]} = 10^{-0.096} \text{ and } [SO_2] = 0.2ppb(v), [H_2SO_3] = 10^{-0.096}p[SO_2] = 10^{-0.096}(0.2 \times 10^{-9})$$

$$[H_2SO_3] = 10^{-9.603}$$

Using the same method and answer to part d,

$$[H^+] = [HCO_3^-] + 2[CO_3^{2-}] + [HSO_3^-] + 2[SO_3^{2-}] + [OH^-]$$

becomes

$$[\mathbf{H^+}] = \frac{\mathbf{10^{-11.29}}}{[\mathbf{H^+}]} + \frac{\mathbf{10^{-21.32}}}{[\mathbf{H^+}]^2} + [\mathbf{HSO_3^-}] + 2[\mathbf{SO_3^{2-}}] + \frac{\mathbf{10^{-14}}}{[\mathbf{H^+}]}$$

Where $[HSO_3^-]$ and $2[SO_3^{2-}]$ are unknown. From the equations and values given in the table, we can write:

$$\frac{[H^+][HSO_3^-]}{[H_2SO_3]} = 10^{-1.77}$$

Therefore

$$[H^+][HSO_3^-] = 10^{-1.77}[H_2SO_3]$$

Substituting in the value of $[H_2SO_3]$ from above,

$$[H^+][HSO_3^-] = (10^{-1.77})(10^{-9.603})$$
$$[H^+][HSO_3^-] = 10^{-11.37}$$
$$[HSO_3^-] = \frac{10^{-11.37}}{[H^+]} \quad (1)$$

And

$$\frac{[H^+][HSO_3^{2-}]}{[SO_3^{2-}]} = 10^{-7.21}$$

Therefore

$$[H^+][SO_3^-] = 10^{-7.21}[HSO_3^-]$$
$$[H^+][SO_3^-] = 10^{-7.21}\frac{10^{-11.37}}{[H^+]}$$

And

$$[SO_3^-] = 10^{-7.21} \frac{10^{-11.37}}{[H^+]^2}$$

$$[SO_3^-] = \frac{10^{-18.58}}{[H^+]^2} \quad (2)$$

Finally, substituting (1) and (2) into the equation

$$[H^+] = \frac{10^{-11.29}}{[H^+]} + \frac{10^{-21.32}}{[H^+]^2} + [HSO_3^-] + 2[SO_3^{2-}] + \frac{10^{-14}}{[H^+]}$$

Gives:

$$[H^+] = \frac{10^{-11.29}}{[H^+]} + \frac{10^{-21.32}}{[H^+]^2} + \frac{10^{-11.37}}{[H^+]} + \frac{10^{-18.26}}{[H^+]^2} + \frac{10^{-14}}{[H^+]}$$

As $10^{-11.29} + 10^{-11.37} \gg 10^{-14} \gg 10^{-18.26} \gg 10^{-21.32}$,

$$[H^+] \approx \frac{10^{-11.29}}{[H^+]} + \frac{10^{-11.37}}{[H^+]}$$

Hence

$$[H^+]^2 \approx 10^{-11.29} + 10^{-11.37}$$
$$[H^+] \approx 10^{-5.51}$$

Therefore

$$\underline{\boldsymbol{pH \approx 5.51}}$$

i) The main sources of atmospheric SO_2 are volcanoes and anthropogenic sources

Chemistry Question 2

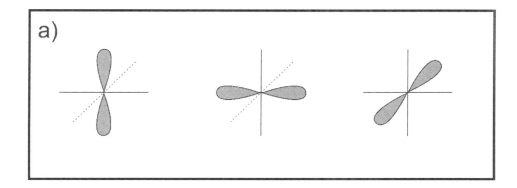

bi)

$$XH_3 + H^- \longrightarrow XH_4^- \quad i.e. \quad \text{H:X} + [:H]^- \longrightarrow \left[\text{H:X:H} \right]^-$$

$$XH_3 + H^- \longrightarrow XH_4^+ \quad i.e. \quad \text{H:X} + H^+ \longrightarrow \left[\text{H:X:H} \right]^+$$

$$XH_3 + H \longrightarrow XH_4 \quad i.e. \quad \left[\text{H:X} \right]^- + \cdot H \longrightarrow \text{H:X:H}$$

bii)

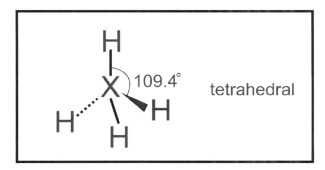

tetrahedral

biii) X can be C, N or Br

ci)

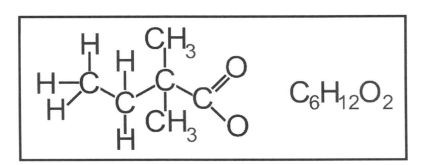

cii)

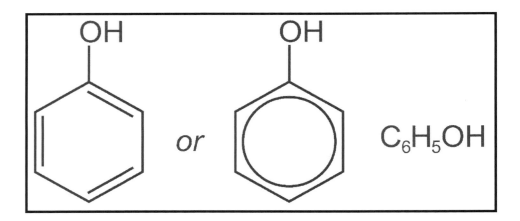

For this solution, $\frac{[H^+][C_6H_{12}O_2]}{[C_6H_{12}OH]} = 10^{-pk_a}$ therefore $-\log_{10}\left[\frac{[H^+][C_6H_{12}O_2]}{[C_6H_{12}OH]}\right] = pk_a$ and

$$-\log_{10}\left[\frac{[C_6H_{12}O_2]}{[C_6H_{12}OH]}\right] -\log_{10}[H^+] = pk_a$$

$$pH = \log_{10}\left[\frac{[C_6H_{12}O_2]}{[C_6H_{12}OH]}\right] + pk_a$$

$$pH = \log_{10}\left[\frac{3}{1}\right] + 7.5 = \mathbf{10.5}$$

Chemistry Question 3

a)

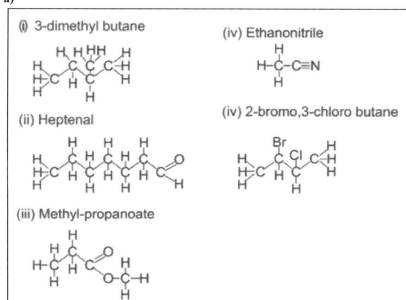

bi) (Thermal) Cracking

bii) $H_3C - CH_2 - CH_2 - CH_2 - CH_2 - CH_2 - CH_2 - CH_2 - CH_2 - CH_3 \rightarrow H_3C - CH = CH_2 + H_3C - CH_2 - CH_2 - CH_2 - CH_2 - CH_2 - CH_2$
i.e. decane $\rightarrow$ ethane + heptane

biii) Gasoline, diesel oil, bitumen, lubricants, petroleum gases, kerosene

biv) Zeolites

bv)

① Initiation

   $CH_3CH_3 \longrightarrow 2CH_3\bullet$

② Hydrogen abstraction

   $CH_3\bullet + CH_3CH_3 \longrightarrow CH_4 + CH_3CH_2\bullet$

③ Radical decomposition

   $CH_3CH_2\bullet \longrightarrow CH_2{=}CH_2 + H\bullet$

④ Radical addition

   $CH_3CH_2\bullet + CH_2{=}CH_2 \longrightarrow CH_3CH_2CH_2CH_2\bullet$

⑤ Termination

   $CH_3CH_2\bullet + CH_3\bullet \longrightarrow CH_3CH_2CH_3$
   $CH_3CH_2\bullet + CH_3CH_2\bullet \longrightarrow CH_2{=}CH_2 + CH_3CH_3$

bvi) The most common impurity found in hydrocarbons is sulphur. The greatest risk during the thermal cracking process is combustion/explosion

Chemistry Question 4

ai) Isomerism is the phenomenon whereby certain compounds with the same molecular formula, exist in different forms due to different organisations of atoms.

aii)

There are 6 isomers of C_4H_8

aiii) Molecules (i), (ii), (iii), (iv), (v) and (vi) are all structural isomers as they are all the same chemical formula however atoms are arranged differently. Molecules (ii) and (iii) are stereoisomers, as atoms are in the same order but in a different arrangement, i.e. (ii) = cis and (iii) = trans.

bi) and **bii)**

(i) Ethene + Hydrogen Bromide

(ii) Cycloheane + Hydrogen Bromide

biii) Electrophilic addition

Chemistry Question 5

a) The bond strength of H-X compounds varies and depends on X. The reactivity of H-X molecules is inversely proportional to the bond strength, such that molecule reactivity decreases from H-I, H-Br, H-Cl to H-F, where H-I has the weakest bond (therefore most reactive) and H-F has the strongest bond (therefore least reactive).

bi,bii)

(i)

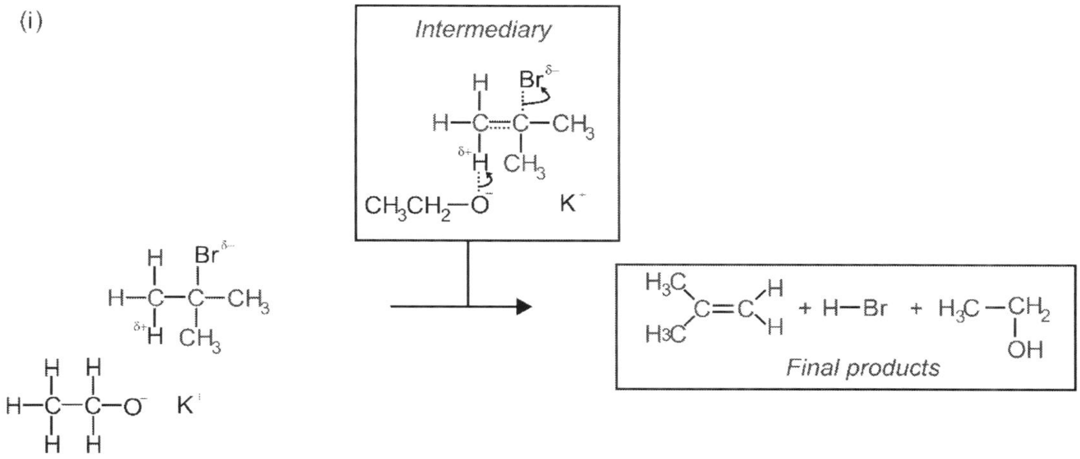

(ii)

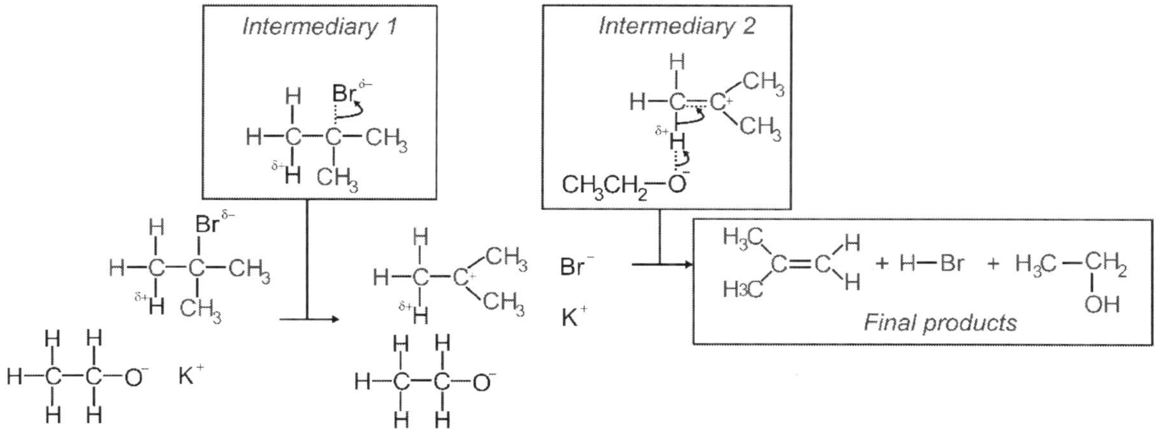

ci)

$$k_a = \frac{[CH_3COO^-][H^+]}{[CH_3COOH]}$$

$$pk_a = -log_{10}[k_a]$$

cii) Because there are only two components, $[CH_3COO^-] \sim [H^+]$ and therefore

$$k_a = \frac{[CH_3COO^-][H^+]}{[CH_3COOH]} \sim \frac{[H^+]^2}{[CH_3COOH]}$$

Therefore

$[H^+] = \sqrt{10^{-pk}[CH_3COOH]} = \sqrt{10^{-4.76} \times 0.017} = 5.435 \times 10^{-4}$

and $pH = -log_{10}(5.435 \times 10^{-4}) = \mathbf{3.26}$

ciii)

Ethanol

$H_3C-CH_2-OH \rightleftharpoons H_3C-CH_2-O^- + H^+$

Ethanoic acid

Both reactions involve ionising an O-H bond, however for CH_3COO^- the O^- anion is stabilised by resonance/delocalisation

Equilibrium therefore lies on the RHS of this reaction. This is not the case for O^- anions in alcohols, this making carboxylic acids more acidic than alcohols

Biology Question 1

a) DNA has to be translated to mRNA, pairing the 3' DNA strand with a 5' mRNA strand. This leads to the following:

DNA: 3' GAC ACG CCG AGT 5'
mRNA: 5' CUG UGC GGC UCA 3'
AA: Leu Cys Gly Ser

b) Yes, a mutation of this base could retain the same amino acids as according to the decoding wheel, the UUG base triplet also encodes Leucine.

c) Using splicing the gene sequence can be extracted from human genome and inserted into bacteria as a plasmid using bacteriophages. Using appropriate promoters will result in production of gene product, i.e insulin.

d) The mutation must occur in the amplification protein as this is responsible for controlling the response amplitude. The more amplification occurs, the larger the amount of insulin that is released.

e) Type 2 diabetes is marked by cells lack of sensitivity to insulin. This means that due to high levels of insulin in the blood, the cells become desensitized to insulin requiring increasing amounts of insulin to achieve the same degree of stimulation and GLUT4 translocation. At some point the pancreas can no longer keep up with insulin production and this will result in a decreased translocation of Glut 4 transporter to the cell surface which in turn will reduce the amount of glucose that enters the cell upon stimulation.

f) Glucagon opposes the action of insulin. With regards to the liver, this means that glucagon increases the mobilisation of glucose from hepatic storages. As glucose is stored in form of glycogen, glucagon will cause an increase in glycogenolysis which will allow glucose to be released raising the blood sugar levels.

Biology Question 2

a) Vertebrates have myelinated nerves, this increases the transmission speed of information.

b)

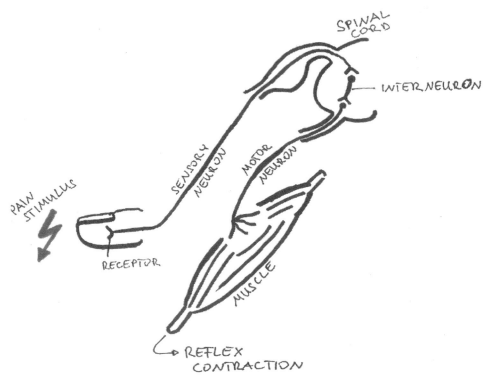

c) The
   purpose of reflexes is protection of the individual. It serves to que the body to act quickly to withdraw the affected body part from danger. The purpose of transmission of the information to the brain lies in the higher computing ability of the brain thereby allowing for more precise analysis of the stimulus.

d) Mimicry is the idea that non-toxic species copy the eternal attributes of toxic species as defence mechanisms. This serves to protect them from predators. Usually mimicry involves adoption of bright colours in distinctive patterns.

e) Action potentials are generated by the coordinated opening of different voltage-gated ion channels. Closed at resting potential, they open under depolarization of the membrane allowing entry of sodium ions which further depolarizing the membrane. After a certain voltage threshold is reached, the channels close and potassium channels open to bring the voltage potential back to the normal level. After this, potassium is pumped into the axon in exchange for sodium.

f) Lidocaine blocks the sodium channels thereby blocking the progress of the action potential along the nerve fibre as the sodium channels are needed to generate the electric current to produce depolarisation of the nerve membrane.

Biology Question 3

a) In large units, leadership becomes essential. There is a strict separation between alpha animals and other members of the group. With the alpha status comes the primary right for breeding as well as other advantages with regards to food acquisition etc. The hierarchical order is maintained by constant competition meaning that only the strongest individuals remain in power.

b) Organisation of individuals into groups leads to a variety of advantages including protection from predators as well as separation of labour as exemplified here in the success rates of hunting depending on hunting party size. There is also the evolutionary advantage resulting from the constant competition for the leadership positions which ensures that only the strongest individuals proliferate leading to propagation of beneficial genes through the population.

c) Communication allows for the control of large groups of individuals as it allows transmission of orders as well as communication of emotions etc. Generally speaking, one has to differentiate between different types of communication. There is chemical communication in insects and then there are forms of verbal communication in higher apes. The complexity of communication processes requires an increasing degree of cerebral complexity.

d) The reproductive pressure is important as it again ensures that the strongest individuals in the herd have the greatest proliferative success. In addition to that, proliferation is always connected to external environments with breeding periods being timed to ensure the maximal likelihood of offspring survival.

e) Genetic diversity helps maintain genetic adaptability and protects the population from accumulation of negative genetic traits such as genetic diseases. Maintenance of genetic adaptability is important as it allows populations to adjust to a variety of different environments.

f) Female dominance exists in several animal species such as lions, elephants and bonobo apes. However, male dominance is more common. This could be due to factors such as physical superiority and aggression.

Biology Question 4

a) Ruminants regurgitate their food and therefore digestion of food matter is more complete meaning that toxins accumulate to a higher degree than it does in monogastriers.

b)

➤ Heart: Increase of rate and contractility, also increase of energy demand
➤ Lungs: bronchodilation, increase of respiratory rate, increase of energy demand
➤ Gut: reduction in peristalsis, reduction in perfusion, reduction in nutrient absorption
➤ Blood vessels: increase in blood pressure, centralisation of blood, contraction of peripheral blood vessels, dilation of blood vessels in skeletal muscle and heart

c) N-Methyltyramine acts by competing with adrenaline for breakdown by MAO-A. Increase in adrenergic stimulation causes a general increase in energy demand. Paired with the inhibition of citric acid cycle by fluoroactate this leads to complete consumption of energy reserves leading to death.

d) Competitive agonists act by occupying the enzyme and thereby displacing a proportion of the original substrate from the active site. This leads to a proportional increase in the concentration of the original substrate. In this case adrenaline.

e) Main focus would be to increase activity of MAO-A as this would maintain appropriate breakdown adrenaline. This could for example be done by exogenous administration of MAO-A.

f) Fight or flight acts to increase the body's readiness to physical performance either with regards to fighting or to running away to withdraw from the danger. This is aided by the selective increase in performance of all systems supporting skeletal muscle contraction (Increased heart rate, vasodilation in skeletal muscle and bronchodilation) and the shut-down of all non-performance oriented process.

Biology Question 5

a)

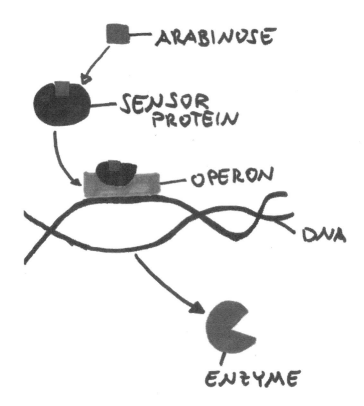

b) The response arc works along the same lines. A protein complex senses the presence of lactose in the environment and through that triggers the expression of lactase.

c) A gain of function mutation in the operon would lead to constantly activated expression of the associated digestive enzyme. This would result in the permanent production of this enzyme which is problematic as is will cause continuous energy consumption.

d) Bacteria are unable to control the general make up of their environment. For this reason, they life in a feast to famine type existence. Being adaptable to the nutrients provided by the environment ensures that no resources are wasted on unnecessary enzymes.

e) This means that certain bacterial species have acquired or developed sensing mechanisms that monitor the concentration of antibiotics in the environment leading to the expression of countermeasures in response to antibiotic presence. This is important as it shifts the sensitivity patterns of bacteria to antibiotics in sometimes unpredictable directions.

f) As humans, we can influence their environment due to the complex nature of our interaction with it. This means that we can take control over what resources we are provided with making facultative expression less necessary. One example of facultative expression in humans would be lactase expression in the gut. Deactivation of expression will lead to lactose intolerance.

Past Paper Worked Solutions

THE BASICS

Hundreds of students take the NSAA exam each year. These exam papers are then released online to help future students prepare for the exam. Since the NSAA is such a new exam, past papers have become an invaluable resource in any student's preparation.

Where can I get NSAA Past Papers?

This book does not include NSAA past paper questions because it would be over 500 pages long if it did! However, all NSAA past papers since 2016 (including the specimen paper) are available for free from the official NSAA website. To save you the hassle of downloading lots of files, we've put them all into one easy-to-access folder for you at **www.uniadmissions.co.uk/NSAA-past-papers**.

How should I use NSAA Past Papers?

NSAA Past papers are one the best ways to prepare for the NSAA. Careful use of them can dramatically boost your scores in a short period of time. The way you use them will depend on your learning style and how much time you have until the exam date but here are some general pointers:

Four to eight weeks of preparation is usually sufficient for most students.

Make sure you are completely comfortable with the NSAA syllabus before attempting past papers – they are a scare resource and you shouldn't 'waste them' if you're not fully prepared to take them.

Its best to start working through practice questions before tackling full papers under time conditions.

You can find two additional mock papers in the *NSAA Practice Papers* Book (flick to the back to get a free copy).

How should I use this book?

This book is designed to accelerate your learning from NSAA past papers. Avoid the urge to have this book open alongside a past paper you're seeing for the first time. The NSAA is difficult because of the intense time pressure it puts you under – the best way of replicating this is by doing past papers under strict exam conditions (no half measures!). Don't start out by doing past papers (see previous page) as this 'wastes' papers.

Once you've finished, take a break and then mark your answers. Then, review the questions that you got wrong followed by ones which you found tough/spent too much time on. This is the best way to learn and with practice, you should find yourself steadily improving. You should keep a track of your scores on the next page so you can track your progress.

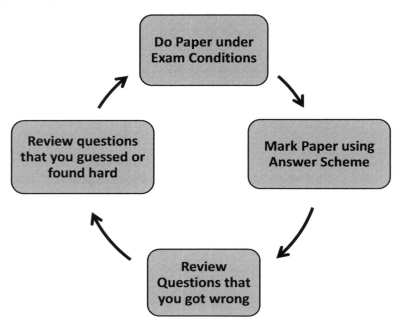

Scoring Tables

Use these to keep a record of your scores – you can then easily see which paper you should attempt next (always the one with the lowest score).

SECTION	1A	1B	1C	1D	1E
Specimen					
2016					
2017					
Mock Paper A					
Mock Paper B					

SECTION 2	1st Attempt	2nd Attempt	3rd Attempt
Specimen			
2016			
2017			
Mock Paper A			
Mock Paper B			

Specimen

Section 1A

Question 1:A

The area of the metallic piece can be written in terms of the radius of the semicircle (x), which is equal to half of the side square (2x). Therefore:

Area of the piece= area of the square –area of the semicircle

$$100 = (2x)^2 - \frac{\pi x^2}{2} = x^2 \left(4 - \frac{\pi}{2} \right)$$

The equation can therefore be rearranged to obtain the value of radius (x) and then the side of the square (2x). The answer is A.

Question 2: E

A drawing of the triangle can help to solve this question. If PQ=20, then RQ=10 and the hypotenuse PR ($10\sqrt{5}$) can be obtained by Pythagoras. The perpendicular bisects the hypotenuse at point T and it forms a new right-angled triangle PQT which is similar to PRQ and therefore:

$$\frac{QT}{10} = \frac{20}{10\sqrt{5}}$$

Otherwise, Pythagoras can be used again for the PQT triangle as the hypotenuse (20) and the side PT ($10\sqrt{5}/2$) are known. The answer is E

Question 3: A

A drawing of the cube can be useful to solve this question. The base of the cube is a square of side of unit length. Therefore, the diagonal (x) that divides such square into two right-angled triangles can be calculated by Pythagoras to obtained the hypothenuse (the diagonal x). A second triangle is formed with the height of the cube, the dashed line and half of x. Therefore, Pythagoras can be used again to obtain the value of the dashed line (the hypotenuse of the second triangle). The answer is A.

Question 4: D

When the clock marks 9:45, the hour hand has moved ¾ between 9 and 10 hours. If the angle between each hour is 360/12=30°, then at 9:45 the angle would be (¾)(30°)=22.5°. The answer is D

Question 5: B

The area of the triangle is 0.5xbasexheight. Then the values provided by the figure are used in the previous equation and the simplification lead to the answer: B.

Question 6: D

Because the length of the cylinder (l) is equal than the diameter of the sphere, then l=2r (r=radius of the sphere). If the volume of the cylinder is the area of the circle times its length, then its volume can be calculated in terms of the radius (r): $(\pi r^2)(2r)$. Finally, the fraction volume of sphere/volume of cylinder is obtained. The answer is D

Question 7: A

The answer of this question can be obtained by inspection. In the selected range, the values of option B and E falls in the range between 0 and 1, while option C produces values smaller than 1. On the other hand, A and D gives values bigger than one, where A gives the biggest value for each value of x. Therefore, the answer is A.

Question 8: C

Because both triangles are similar, then:

$$\frac{AB}{AD} = \frac{BC}{DE} \rightarrow \frac{4}{x} = \frac{x}{x+3}$$

This leads to a quadratic equation of roots -2 and 6, from which only 6 makes sense. Therefore, DE=6+3=9 and the answer is C.

Question 9: C

A proportionality constant (k) is necessary to eliminate the proportionality and therefore $P=k/Q^2$. Make the values of k=1, Q_1=1 and Q_2=1.4 (40% increase), then P_1=1 and P_2=1/1.96. Finally, the change of P=(1-P_1/P_2)100=(1-1/1.96)100≈49%. The answer is C

Question 10: D

The proportionalities can be written as equation such as: $x = bz^2$ $y = \frac{c}{z^3}$

Where "b" and "c" are constants. If both equation can be express in terms of z^6, then

$$x^3 = b^3 z^6 \qquad y^2 = \frac{c^2}{z^6}$$
$$x^3 = b^3 \frac{c^2}{y^2}$$
$$x^3 \propto \frac{1}{y^2}$$

The answer is D

Question 11: C

Let's make QX=2. Therefore, it is possible to find the values of PX=12, XR=3 and PR=12+3=15. Then, the value of PM=15/2=7.5 and MX=12-7.5=4.5. Finally, the value of QX/MX is obtained and the answer is C.

Question 12: D

The inequality can be rearrange to:

$$x^2 + 2x - 8 \geq 0$$
$$(x + 4)(x - 2) \geq 0$$

Finally, to satisfy the latter inequality x≤-4 and x≥2. The answer is D

Question 13: A

If the units are ignored, then:

Surface area of cylinder=volume of cylinder
$$2\pi r^2 + 2\pi rh = \pi r^2 h$$

Therefore, the latter equation can be divided by πr and rearrange to obtain h in terms of r and the answer: A.

Question 14: D

To have a difference less than one:

$$6 < 2\sqrt{n} < 8$$
$$36 < 4n < 64$$
$$9 < n < 16$$

This means that there are 6 integers that satisfy the inequality. The answer is D

Question 15: B

The easiest way to find the solution is a drawing of the transformations. The answer is B.

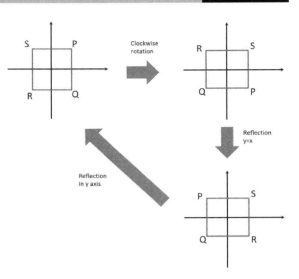

Question 16: C

If we make the sides of the external square equal to 3, then the sides of the inscribed square can be found by Pythagoras' theorem ($\sqrt{1^2 + 2^2} = \sqrt{5}$). Now a scale factor (f) can be calculated by:

$$f = \frac{area\ of\ incribed\ square}{area\ of\ external\ square} = \frac{(\sqrt{5})^2}{3^2} = \frac{5}{9}$$

Therefore, the area of the fourth squared (third inscribed square) is $(5/9)^3 = 125/729$. The answer is C

Question 17: C

The variables in the equation can be substitute by the variable times the factor that determines its change in value and then we obtain the new equation:

$$M = \frac{(1.5x + 1.5y)^2 0.8z}{2P} Q = 0.9\frac{(x+y)^2 z}{P} Q$$

Therefore, the value of M decreases by 10%. The answer is C.

Question 18: B

It is possible to obtain the probability of getting a 6 on the unfair dice (Pu_6) from the probability of getting a 12 (P_{12}) and the probability of getting a 6 from the fair dice:

$$P_{12} = Pf_6 * Pu_6$$

$$Pu_6 = \frac{\frac{1}{18}}{\frac{1}{6}} = \frac{1}{3}$$

Therefore, the probability to get a number from 1 to 5 in the unfair dice is 2/3. In order to get a 2 requires the probability to get a 1 from the fair (1/6) and unfair dice (1/5 * 2/3=2/15). Then, the result is (1/6)*(2/15)=1/45 and it is given as option B.

Section 1B

Question 19: C
The resultant force is 300N upwards and from Newton's second law F=ma. Then the acceleration can be obtained as 5ms^{-2} upwards. The answer is C

Question 20: C
The period (P) of the wave is obtained from the graph and then the frequency (f) can be obtained as f=1/P. Finally, the speed of the wave (v) can be calculated by v=fλ (λ=wavelength). The answer is C

Question 21: B
From the equation of momentum (p) it is possible to rearrange the equation to get the speed in terms of the momentum and then substitute this on the equation kinetic energy. As a result, an equation for the mass is obtained as:

$$m = \frac{p^2}{2KE} = \frac{900}{300} = 3$$

The answer is B.

Question 22: E
If the potential difference can be obtained by V=IR and V=P/I, then volts can be define as ampere*ohm and watt per ampere as well as joule per coulomb. Therefore, by inspection of the option A, B and C do not produce any of the aforementioned definition. On the other hand, if newton can be expressed as joule per metre, then newton per coulomb (option D) is equal to volt per metre. Therefore, the only correct option is E

Question 23: D
The number of half-lives that each source decays over 24 hrs is obtained by 24hrs/half-life time. This means that source X and Y decays 5 and 3 half-lives respective and therefore, after 24hrs, source X have decay: 320-160-80-40-20-10 Bq while source Y: 480- 240-120-60 Bq. Then, the combined count rate can be obtained as 10+60=70 Bq. The answer is D

Question 24: B
Because the object falls from rest, then all the potential energy (PE) is transformed into kinetic energy (KE) and therefore PE=KE or mgh=0.5mv^2. By rearranging the equation and using the values of the g and v, it is possible to obtain the value of the height (h) as 20m. The value of m is not necessary. The answer is B

Question 25: C
The potential energy lost (PE) can be calculated by PE=mgh to obtain a value of 100 000J. Therefore, if F=W/s and the work done (W) is equal to 100000J, and the distance travelled (s) is 100*10=1000m, the force is 100N. The answer is C

Question 26: D
The work performed by the motor (W) is equal to the potential energy gained by the load and then W=mgh=150J and the power P=W/t=150/1.5=100W. Because the motor is 100% efficient, I=P/V=4A. The answer is D

Question 27: A
Because all the kinetic energy is transformed into potential energy, then mgh=0.5mv^2. The masses cancel out and the equation can be rearranged to obtain the height of the ball 7.2m. The answer is A.

Question 28: C
To stop the lorry, the resistive forces must be perform a work (W) equal to the kinetic energy of the lorry and therefore, W= ½mv^2. Because, W=F*s, then the distance travelled (s) can be obtained as s=W/F=(½ mv^2)/F= mv^2/2F. The answer is C.

Question 29: B
The emission of an alpha particle (2 neutrons and 2 protons) reduces the proton number by 2 (R-2) and the nucleon number by 4 (N-4). Therefore, the first decay can be expressed as $^{P=N-4}_{R-2}Y$. On the other hand, the emission of a beta particle (an electron) transforms a neutron into a proton, changing the proton number (R-2+1) without a change in the nucleon number (P) and therefore Z can be expresses as $_{Q=R-1}^{P}Z$. The answer is B.

Question 30: B
If the distance (s) travelled by the pulse is 2x10cm=20cm=0.2m, then the time (t) can be obtained from the speed (v) t=s/v=0.2/500=0.0004s=0.4ms. The answer is B.

Question 31: B
Options R and S are distance-time graphs, which gradient is the speed of the object. Because the gradient is constant, the speed is constant and therefore the no acceleration is shown in these graphs. On the other hand, P and Q are velocity-time graphs, which constant gradient is equal to the acceleration of the object. However, a quick calculus of the gradient for both graphs demonstrate that P has a gradient of 10/24 while Q has a gradient of (58-10)/20=2.4ms^{-1}. The answer is B

Question 32: D
The graphs is a straight line with a gradient of 20/100=0.2, which units depends of the values of x and y. All the option can be expressed in terms of a physics equation with a gradient as seen below:

Option	Equation	Gradient
A	a=F/m	1/m=1/5=0.2Kg^{-1}
B	I=V/R	1/R=1/5=0.2Ω^{-1}
C	KE= ½mv²	½m=(0.5)(0.4)=0.2Kg
D	λ=v/f	v=0.2ms^{-1}
E	W=Fd	F=0.2N

As it is seen all the graphs are correct except for D, which need to graph λ against 1/f to give a straight line not against f. Therefore, the answer is D

Question 33: D
A) This is not correct because nuclear fission is a process where the nucleus split into smaller parts, while gamma emission do not produce split in the nucleus.

B) Half-life is the time taken for a radioactive substance to decay half of its amount. Therefore, this option is not correct

C) The number of neutrons in a nucleus can be obtained by the nucleon number minus the atomic number. This option is not correct

D) A beta particle is an electron that is emitted due to the transformation of a neutron into a proton without changing the nucleon number. This option is correct

E) The transformation of a neutron into a proton produces beta decay. Therefore, this option is not correct

The answer is D

Question 34: D

The total resistance is the sum of the individual resistance R_1+R_2. This resultant resistance is used to obtain the current of the circuit $I=V/(R_1+R_2)$ and then the voltage across R_1: $V_1=IR_1=V*R_1/(R_1+R_2)$. Finally, the equation for the power dissipated in R_1 can be obtained by the substitution of the valued of V_1 and I on the equation $P_1=V_1I$. The answer is D

Question 35: D

Because it is a speed-time graph, the area under the curve represents the travelled distance. Such area can be obtained by calculating the area under the different section of the graph. The section from 0-1, 4-5, 5-6 and 6-7 must be calculated using $[(v_1+v_2)/2]*t$, while from 1-4 the area of the rectangle must be obtained. The sum of all the areas gives a result of $100(ms^{-1})min$. This result must be multiplied by $(60s/1min)$ to obtain the value of the distance in m. The answer is D.

Question 36: D

Statement P cannot be deduced due to the lack of information about the wavelength, which cannot be deduced either. Therefore, statement P and Q are not correct. The maximum distance of oscillation is 5.0 mm, which means that the amplitude, distance from equilibrium position to maxima, is the half of such distance and therefore, statement Q is not correct. Statement S is possible to deduce because frequency=1/period, where period=0.2miliseconds. The answer is B.

Section 1C

Question 37: E

Given that the pH is 5.0 and equal volumes of the indicators are added, the overall colour can be worked out by determining what the colour of each of the indicators would be at pH 5.0. Methyl orange would be yellow, bromothymol blue would be yellow and phenolphthalein would be colourless. Therefore, overall the colour of the mixture would be yellow.

Question 38: A

It is important to notice in this question it asks for the products of aqueous sodium chloride, not just sodium chloride. The positive electrode attracts the negative ions – in this case chlorine is discharged in preference to oxygen. The negative electrode attracts the positive ions – in this case hydrogen is discharged in preference to sodium.

Question 39: A

Giant covalent structures have high melting and boiling points and do not conduct electricity when solid nor when molten. Only substance A fulfils these criteria.

Question 40: A

In this question we are shown as series of graphs that show how the concentration of the reactant A, and the product Z, change over time. The reaction is said to go to completion with equimolar samples of A and B added. Since two moles of A react with one mole of B, all of reactant A would be used up when the reaction goes to completion and so would reach a final concentration of 0. Moreover, one mole of product forms for every two moles of reactant A used. You would expect, therefore, the concentration of A to decrease at twice the rate that the concentration of Z increases. These lines of evidence support graph 1 as the only correct possibility.

Question 41: B

Firstly, you need to write the molecular formula for the two different ions in iron oxide. Fe^{2+} forms FeO, whilst Fe^{3+} forms Fe_2O_3. What you can spot is that Fe_3O_4 would be the overall formula is equal amounts of FeO and Fe_2O_3 were present. However, whilst the mixture ratio of the two compounds is 1:1, the molar ratio of the iron ions is 1:2 (Fe^{2+}: Fe^{3+}). Therefore, $1/(2+1) = 1/3$, of the fraction of the iron ions are Fe^{2+}.

Question 42: E
Statement 1 is incorrect since the molecular mass is 40, not 20. The electron configuration of the element is 2,8,8,2, so the element is in Group 2, and is not a noble gas. This element would form an ion by losing its outer electrons – it would therefore form an ion with a positive, not a negative charge. Group 2 contains metals. Therefore, statements 2, 3 and 5 are incorrect and statement 4 is correct.

Question 43: E
Bond breaking is endothermic and requires energy, so the bond enthalpy is positive. Bond making is exothermic and releases energy, so the bond enthalpy has a negative value. Therefore, for the overall reaction to be exothermic, the bond enthalpy of the products has to be greater than the reactants (since energy is given out overall). 6 N-H bonds form in the products, whilst 1 Nbond and 3 H-H bonds are broken. Therefore, 6(N-H) > Nbond + 3(H-H), so the answer is; $6z > x + 3y$.

Question 44: C
Oxidising agents get reduced during a reaction (i.e the oxidation state decreases). This is true of equation 2, where the oxidation state of Cr decreases from +6 in $Cr_2O_7^{2-}$, to +3 in Cr^{3+}. It is also true in equation 3 where the oxidation state of copper decreases from +2 to +1 from Cu^{2+} to CuI. Mg in equation 1 gets oxidised, not reduced. Similarly, sulfur in H_2SO_4 gets oxidised, not reduced.

Question 45: D
Firstly, calculate the number of moles of water by dividing the mass, by the Mr of water (6 g/18). Then multiply this value by the molar gas constant, 24 dm^3, to get the volume of water vapour produced; $(6/18)*24 = (1/3)* 24 = 8\ dm^3 = 8000\ cm^3$.

Question 46: E
To get the empirical formula, you first need to calculate the molar ratio of iodine and oxygen. Iodine = 63.5 g/127 which equals ½. Oxygen = 20.0 g/16 = 5/4. Multiply both fractions by 4 to get an integer molar ratio of iodine: oxygen of 2:5. Hence, the empirical formula is I_2O_5.

Question 47: C
Non-metals are found on the right-hand side of the periodic table. They react by gaining electrons to complete their outer shell of electrons. More reactive non-metals are non-metals that can more easily fill their outer shell of electrons. A more reactive non-metal must therefore more strongly attract an electron and have less electrons to gain, before their outer shell is complete. You therefore need to look for a group 7 element with a lower number of electron shells. This is true of element C.

Question 48: C
Firstly, you need to work out what isotopes are present to form CH_2BrCl with a relative molecular mass of 128. Subtracting the molecular mass of CH_2 (14) leaves 114. 114 can only be formed by the bromine 79 isotope and the chlorine 35 isotope. The probability a compound has bromine 79 is ½. The probability a compound has chlorine 35 is ¾. Therefore, the probability a compound has both bromine 79 and chlorine 35 is $(1/2) * (3/4) = 3/8$.

Question 49: A
Fractionating columns operate by heating the bottom of the flask, therefore the temperature in the flask will be greater than at the top of the column. Since the liquid contains only hexane and heptane, and hexane has the lower boiling point, hexane will be distilled first and thus the conditions in answer A are the most likely temperatures.

Question 50: D
The first thing you can calculate in this question is the number of moles of carbon in stage 2; 12 g/12 = 1 mole. From the balanced equation in stage 2, you can then deduce that 12g of carbon forms 2 moles of CO. From the balanced equation in stage 3, you can deduce that 3 moles of CO react to form 3 moles of CO_2. Hence, 2 moles of CO (from stage 2), allow the production of 2 moles of CO_2 in stage 3. Given the Mr of CO_2 is 44, the mass of CO_2 produced = 2 * 44 = 88g.

Question 51: E

Statement A is incorrect since pressure does affect the position of equilibrium as there are more moles of gas on the reactant than product side. The reaction is exothermic so raising the temperature will shift the equilibrium to the left, not right. At equilibrium sulfur dioxide is being changed into sulfur trioxide, it is just that the rate of this forward reaction matches that of the reverse reaction. Catalysts do not alter the position of equilibrium. Statements B,C and D are thus incorrect. Statement E is correct as the forward reaction rate is initially greater when the concentration of reactants is higher.

Question 52: E
Firstly, write out the balanced equation for the reaction; NaOH + HCl → NaCl + H_2O. Thus 1 mole of NaOH reacts with 1 mole of HCl. The number of moles of HCl used in the reaction = 50.0 cm^3 * 0.50 mol dm^{-3} = 0.025. Therefore, 0.025 moles of NaOH reacted. Use the A_r values to calculate the Mr of NaOH as 40, then calculate the mass of NaOH = 0.025 * 40 = 0.025 * 4 = 1g. The percentage purity is then 1g/1.20g = 5/6 = 0.833 = 83.3 %.

Question 53: C
Firstly, calculate the number of moles of sulfuric acid = 12.5 cm^3 * 2.0 mol dm^{-3} = 25/1000 moles. Using the balanced chemical equation you can deduce that 50/1000 moles of XOH were dissolved in water. Given that the mass of XOH dissolved was 2.8g you can calculate the Mr of XOH as 2.8 /(50/1000) = 280/5 = 56. Subtracting 17 from 56 (the Mr of OH) leaves the relative atomic mass of X as 39.

Question 54: D
This question can be solved by forming a series of algebraic equations.

Hydrogen atoms:
r = 2s

Oxygen atoms
3r = 6 + s + 2t

Nitrogen
r = 2 + t
Substituting (r = 2 + t) into the oxygen atom algebraic equation gives;
6 + 3t = 6 + s + 2t, which rearranged gives s=t.
Therefore, the answer is either A or D. You can either use trial and error to check both answers or further use the algebraic equations by using s=t;
2s = 2 + t, to 2s = 2 + s, therefore s = 2. If s = 2, then t = 2.

Section 1D

Question 55: D

Statement 1 is incorrect since gametes are produced by the process, meiosis, not mitosis. Statement 2 is incorrect since growth of cells is required for cells to go through mitosis, but not a role of mitosis per se. Mitosis is a process of cell division and therefore does not repair cells but by providing two new daughter cells can replace skin cells. Therefore, statement 3 is incorrect and statement 4 is correct.

Question 56: D

Between 0 and 11 minutes, the oxygen demand is greater than the oxygen supply – there is therefore insufficient oxygen for only aerobic respiration. There is however oxygen present so both aerobic and anaerobic respiration will occur. So, answer D is correct.

Question 57: F

Natural selection, often referred to as 'survival of the fittest', is the process by which organisms that are better adapted to their environment survive to reproduce and produce more offspring. The organism can be 'better adapted than' other members of their species and/or 'better adapted than' other species. This results in the differential survival of 'fitter' organisms which can then reproduce to pass on their traits. This can result in evolution, a gradual change in characteristics over time, and extinction of species that are outcompeted by the better adapted species. Therefore, all four statements are correct.

Question 58: D

Statement 1 is correct. Temperature is the limiting factor up to 22 °C since increasing the temperature increased the rate of photosynthesis (the rate of the reaction). When the rate peaks at 22 °C, other factors such as light intensity and carbon dioxide concentration are now limiting the rate. As the temperature is further increased the rate of photosynthesis drops, hence statement 3 is incorrect. The reason this happens is due to denaturation of enzymes that thus no longer work, so statement 2 is correct.

Question 59: F

From the karyogram you can tell that the person is not healthy as there are three copies of chromosome 21 whilst a healthy individual has two copies of each chromosome. Indeed, the presence of three chromosome 21's can cause Down's syndrome. Otherwise, there are no visible differences in the size and banding patterns in each chromosome pair. The exception is the X and Y chromosome, where Y is smaller, but this is normal. Only males have a Y chromosome, hence statement 2 is correct. White blood cells contain a diploid nucleus which is where the chromosomes can be isolated. Therefore, statement 3 is also true.

Question 60: F

Statement 1 is incorrect since meiosis does not result in genetically identical offspring. Stem cells from the bone marrow are diploid which means they have two copies of each chromosome – as the cell is human, which have 23 pairs of chromosomes, 46 chromosomes are most likely to be present. Stem cells are undifferentiated but have the potential to differentiate – since the stem cell is from the bone marrow, where white blood cells are derived, it is likely that the stem cell could differentiate into a white blood cell. Hence, statements 2 and 3 are correct.

Question 61: C

The frequency of occurrence refers to the percentage of quadrats that contain at least one daisy species. 10 out of 25 quadrats contain at least one daisy, so the frequency of occurrence is $10/25 = 0.40$

Question 62: F

A heterozygous individual would contain one allele for attached ear lobes and one allele for unattached ear lobes. This would be the genotype. The pedigree displays the phenotypes of the individuals. We are told that the allele for attached ear lobes is recessive, therefore the allele for unattached ear lobes is dominant and would be the phenotype of heterozygous individuals. You should recall that offspring inherit one allele from each parent. Given this information you can write the potential genotypes for each individual;

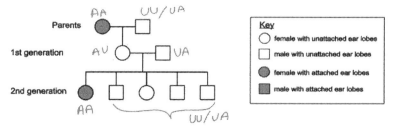

The 2nd generation individual with attached ear lobes must have a homozygous genotype (both attached ear lobe alleles) so each parent must have at least one attached ear lobe allele as seen in the labelled pedigree above. Therefore, all of the individuals with unattached ear lobes could be heterozygous and so the maximum number is 7.

Question 63: A

Mark on the graph the y value at x values of 0.12 and 0.084. When x=0.12, y=2%. When x=0.084, y=72%. Therefore, following the statements set the effect on percentage haemolysis increases by 70%. This increase is due to uptake of water. This is because water moves by osmosis from solutions with a greater water potential to a solution with a lower water potential. Water potential increases as solute concentration, in this case NaCl, decreases. Therefore, as the NaCl concentration decreases from $0.12 \rightarrow 0.084$ mol dm^{-3}, the water potential of the solution increases so more water moves into the red blood cells which have a lower water potential.

Question 64: H

A positive phototropic response describes growth towards the light source. Not all uncovered shoots showed a positive phototropic response since the shoot with the tip cut off showed no phototropic response, hence statement 1 is incorrect. Statement 2 is incorrect as the shoot covered with an opaque sheath with tip exposed showed a phototropic response even though part of the shoot was covered. Statement 3 is incorrect since the shoot enclosed by an opaque box still grew as tall as the control shoot.

Question 65: D

Trend 1 is incorrect since there is not enough evidence to support it. For example, from 1959 to 1964, both populations are increasing simultaneously. Trend 2 is correct – this becomes obvious once you have observed that the number of wolves and moose are plotted against y axis with different scales. Trend 3 is incorrect since, as stated by trend 2 and from the graph, the population of wolves is always less than the population of moose. Trend 4 is correct; for example, the moose population increases from 1985 to 1993 when the wolf population is low.

Question 66: G

	XAA	XYAA	XXAA	XXYAA	XXYYAA
X:A	0.5:1	0.5:1	1:1	1:1	1:1
Sex	Male	Male	Female	Female	Female

Question 67: H

Digestive enzymes catalyse catabolic reactions – they break down organic matter. Respiratory enzymes are involved in the production of ATP/energy through the breakdown of organic matter. Process 1 = photosynthesis (neither digestive or respiratory enzymes). Process 2= digestion of plant matter by animals (use digestive enzymes). Process 3 = digestion of animal matter by decomposers (use digestive enzymes). Process 4 = respiration and production of CO_2 (use respiratory enzymes). Hence, H is the correct answer.

Question 68: B
The y axis is the enzyme-substrate complex concentration. Over time, the concentration would increase as substrate binds the active site of the enzymes. The concentration plateaus when all enzyme active sites become full. The concentration then decreases as substrate is used up and so less is left to bind the enzyme. The concentration reaches zero when the reaction comes to completion and no substrate is left. Answer A is wrong as enzyme concentration does not change during a reaction. Answer C is wrong as the pH would not change in this way. Answer D is wrong since the product concentration would increase until it plateaus – there would not be a decrease. Answer E is wrong since the substrate concentration would only decrease.

Question 69: B
Statement 1 is correct – the enzymes used are restriction enzymes. Statement 2 is incorrect as bacteria do not contain nuclei. Statement 3 is correct as the bacteria are cultured to produce insulin. The insulin is then purified from the bacteria before use in humans. Hence statement 4 is incorrect.

Question 70: E
Mutations cause changes in the DNA sequence or structure. Statement 1 is correct since altering the genetic code could change the amino acids that the triplet of nucleotides code for. Statement 2 is incorrect since the mutation in a cheek cell would not be passed on to offspring of that organism – this could only happen if the mutation was in a gamete. Statement 3 is correct since mutating DNA could have many affects including the protein produced, the levels of transcription and processing of mRNA all of which could change essential cell processes that could result in cell death.

Question 71: D
We are told that the condition is caused by the presence of at least one allele for the condition. Hence, it is likely that the allele is dominant. T is a male and could pass on the allele for the condition (would always happen if T was homozygous for the condition, or there would be a 50% chance if T was heterozygous). Alternatively, the condition could arise de novo via a mutation in the egg of S during gamete production. Therefore, all three statements are correct.

Question 72: F
A liver cell is an animal cell – starch is found in plant cells, not animal cells. A liver cell is a somatic cell and so is diploid, containing the full complement of the genome. Therefore, is would contain two X chromosomes if the cell was female and one X chromosome if the cell was male (in humans). Since, the full genome complement is present, the gene for amylase would also be present, although the gene is unlikely to be expressed in liver cells. Only statements 2 and 3 are therefore correct.

Section 1E

Question 73: F

The key to solve this question is the properties of the logarithms. If the $\log_{10}$ is taken for both sides, then the equation can be rearrange to

$$x\log_{10}(a) + 2x\log_{10}(b) + 3x\log_{10}(c) = \log_{10}(2)$$
$$x\log_{10}(ab^2c^3) = \log_{10}(2)$$
$$x = \frac{\log_{10}(2)}{\log_{10}(ab^2c^3)}$$

The answer is F

Question 74: C

The momentum before and after the collision is the same, therefore:

$$m_{p1}v_{p1} + m_{q1}v_{q1} = m_{p2}v_{p2} + m_{q2}v_{q2}$$
$$(2)(3) + (-5)r = -(2)(1) + (5)(0.5)r$$

Attention must be paid to the sign of the momentum from each particle before and after the collision. The latter equation can be rearrange to obtained the value of r=16/15. The answer is C.

Question 75: D

From the unit circle, it clear that the value of option A is equal to -1, while the $\log_{10}(100)$=2. Sin ($\pi/2$)=1, therefore option C is equal to 1, meanwhile log
$_2(10)$ produces a value no much bigger than $\log_2(8)$=3. Finally, if $0<\sqrt{2}-1<1$, therefore $(\sqrt{2}-1)^{10}<1$. Hence, the answer is D

Question 76: A

The parachutist reaches two terminal velocities, one at high speed before opening the parachute and another a low speed after the parachute is opened. At such terminal velocities, the drag force is equal and opposite to the weight. Therefore, the acceleration and resultant force are zero. However, at the moment the parachute is open, there is a rapid deceleration and upwards resultant force action over the parachutist. This means that the drag force rapidly increases and overcomes the weight.

The only graph that follow such description is A.

Question 77: E

The key to solve this question is to transform 2^x=y. Therefore the resultant is a quadratic equation $y^2-8y+15=0$, which roots are 3 and 5. If 2^x=3 and 2^x=5, then x=$\log_{10}(3)$/ $\log_{10}(2)$ and x=$\log_{10}(5)$/ $\log_{10}(2)$. Hence, the sum of both roots gives the answer: option E.

Question 78: C

The stationary state of the block plus the coefficient of friction bigger than zero implies that block remains stationary until the force overcome the friction. After that, the block will move with an increasing acceleration equivalent to the increase of the horizontal force. Hence, the answer is C.

Question 79: E

The change of sign from both sides of the inequality requires the inversion of the inequality. Therefore, statement 1 is true. Statement 2 can be rearrange as a quadratic equation with factors $(a-b)^2{\geq}0$, which is true. However, statement 3 can be false if c=-1. Hence, the answer is E

Question 80: C

The momentum before and after the collision is the same, therefore:

$$m_{w1}v_{w1} + m_{r1}v_{r1} = m_{w2}v_{w2} + m_{r2}v_{r2}$$
$$(0.2)(3) + 0 = (0.2)(1) + (0.2)v_{r2}$$

Then, the speed of the red ball after the collision can be obtained as 2ms^{-1}. The answer is C.

Question 81: A
The sequence rule is formed in such a way that if n=odd then n+1=1, and n=even then n+1=2. Therefore, the first 100 terms gives a sum: 50x1+50x2=150. The answer is A.

Question 82: A
The initial potential energy of the ball transforms into the kinetic energy (KE) and therefore, KE=mgh=16mg. Such kinetic energy is lost during the first bouncing to 0.5*16mg, which is converted to potential energy to reach a height of 0.5*16=8m. This means that every bouncing produces a half in the height of the ball, therefore for the second bouncing and later the height is 4m, 2m, 1m=100 cm. Hence, after the 4th bouncing the height of the rebound falls below 160 cm. The answer is A

Question 83: C
The first derivative of the equation is a cubic equation which roots represent the turning points of the curve. Because the curve has roots at x=0,1,2 and turning points at (0,-10), (1,-9) and (2,-10). Then it is possible to say that the graph has two distinct real roots. The answer is C.

Question 84: B
Because the weight of the man is bigger than the lecture on the scales, this means that the normal force acting on the man has decreased. Therefore, there is a resultant downward force acting on the man that provides him a downwards acceleration. The only statement that satisfy this description is shown as option E

Question 85: D
The fact that graph log y – log x is a straight line means that the log of the parent function must produce a logarithmic equation where the log x (=X), log y (=Y) and the constants have the form Y=mX+c. After applying log to all the options, only log y = b*log x +log a have the form of a straight line with log x and log y as variables. The answer is D.

Question 86: B
The distance travelled to stop the tram can be obtained from the equation of motion: $v^2 = u^2 + 2as$. Alternatively, the average speed and time to stop the tram can be obtained with the data provided and their multiplication provides the total distance travelled by the tram. The answer is B

Question 87: D
In a quadratic equation the discriminant condition to obtain real values indicates that:
$$b^2 > 4ac$$
$$(a - 2)^2 > 4a(-2)$$
This inequality can be rearrange to
$$a^2 + 4a + 4 > 0$$
$$(a + 2)^2 > 0$$
Therefore, this is true for all values except a=-2. The answer is D

Question 88: C
A force diagram can be helpful to solve this question. The tension on the diagonal rope (T) has a vertical (T_y) and a horizontal (T_x) component. Because the horizontal rope (H) has only an horizontal component, then:
$$T_y = w$$
$$Tcos(60) = 5$$
If cos (60)=0.5, then T=10N. Once the value of T is obtained the value of T_x and H can be obtained because T_x=H= T*sin (60)=5$\sqrt{3}$. The answer is C.

Question 89: D

If properties of tan (x) and sin (x) indicate that:

  A) $-1 \leq \tan(x) \leq 1$ is satisfied when $0 \leq x \leq \pi/4$ and $3\pi/4 \leq x \leq \pi$

  B) $\sin(2x) \geq 0.5$ is true when $\pi/6 \leq 2x \leq 5\pi/6$ then $\pi/12 \leq x \leq 5\pi/12$

Therefore, the range to satisfy both expressions is $\pi/12 \leq x \leq \pi/4$ and the length interval is $\pi/6$. The answer is B

Question 90: A

The tension T is a horizontal force acting on the carriage 2. Therefore, such force can be calculating by $T = m_2 a$ (m_2=mass of second carrier). The acceleration of the carriage is the same for all the train, which is provide by the thrust force (F). Therefore, $a = F/m_T$, where the total mass (m_T) can be obtained by the sum of the individual masses.

Section 2

Question 1

a) The distance is the area under the curve and although there is no such thing as a negative speed, the change of direction of the velocity vector produces a negative value of velocity. This means that from 0 to C the train moves away the station, from C to D the train remains stationary, and from D to G the train moves towards the station.

For the intervals where the train maintains a constant speed, the area can be calculated by:
$$s = \Delta v * \Delta t$$
When the train accelerates and decelerates, the area under the line can be obtained by:

$$s = \frac{\Delta v * \Delta t}{2}$$

The sum of all the areas provides the distance

Interval	0-A	A-B	B-C	C-D	D-E	E-F	F-G	Sum
Time	180	720	200	200	200	720	180	/////
Speed	0/40	40	40/0	0	0/-40	-40	-40/0	/////
Distance	3600	28800	4000	0	-4000	-28800	-3600	0

If t=40min=2400s, the train will be back at the station

b) The graph shows that such line is a straight line with a negative gradient (a). Therefore, the equation can be obtained as: $v - v_0 = a(t - t_0)$

$$a = \frac{v_c - v_B}{t_c - t_B} = \frac{0 - 40}{1100 - 900} = \frac{-40}{200} = -\frac{1}{5} ms^{-2}$$

Therefore if V_0 =0 and t_0=1100 then:

$$v - 0 = -\frac{1}{5}(t - 1100)$$

$$v = 220 - \frac{1}{5}t$$

c)i) The integral

$$\int_{1300}^{1500} v(t)dt$$

represents the area under the graph under the interval 1300-1500, points D to E, which were calculated in the table above. Therefore, the answer is -4000

ii) The area under the graph, as it was stated above, is the distance travelled from point D to E.

d) The gradient (a) of the line BC is the deceleration of the train, which produces a force equal to:

$$F = ma = 10000 * \left(-\frac{1}{5}\right) = -2000N$$

The force surges due to the deceleration of the train because the breaking and friction resistance

e) At 90s the train has a constant acceleration. Therefore, such acceleration and corresponding force can be calculated as previously:

$$a = \frac{v_A - v_0}{t_A - t_0} = \frac{40}{180} = \frac{2}{9}ms^{-2}$$

$$F = ma = 10000 * \left(\frac{2}{9}\right) = 2222.22N$$

At 90s the speed of the train is:

$$v - v_0 = a(t - t_0)$$

$$v = \frac{2}{9}t = \frac{2}{9}(90) = 20ms^{-1}$$

Finally, the mechanical power is obtained by:

$$P = Fv = 2222.22 * 20 = 44444.44 \ W$$

f)

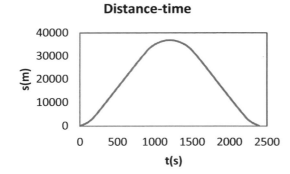

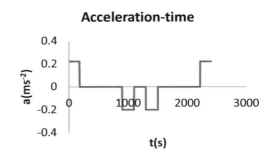

Question 2

a) The best way to approach this question is to look at the system of forces acting on the stone. The drag force is the only horizontal force acting on the stone which depends and opposites the velocity. Due to its opposition to the velocity, the drag force must have a negative sign. Additionally, the faster the stone, the bigger the drag force. Because, this is a system of forces there is a resultant force determined by the Newton's second law: F=ma

b)i) The velocity integral can be evaluated as:

$$\int_{v_0}^{v} \frac{1}{v^3} dv = \int_{v_0}^{v} v^{-3} dv = -\frac{1}{2v^2} + \frac{1}{2v_0^2} = \frac{1}{2v_0^2} - \frac{1}{2v^2}$$

On the other hand, the integral for the time contains "b" and "m" which are constants and therefore, the integral simplifies to:

$$\int_{0}^{t} -\frac{b}{m} dt = -\frac{b}{m} \int_{0}^{t} dt = -\frac{bt}{m}$$

Therefore, the final equation can be written as:

$$\frac{1}{2v^2} - \frac{1}{2v_0^2} = \frac{bt}{m}$$

ii) It was previously stated that:

$$\frac{1}{2v^2} - \frac{1}{2v_0^2} = \frac{bt}{m}$$

Therefore, this can be rearranged to:

$$\frac{1}{v^2} - \frac{1}{v_0^2} = \frac{2bt}{m}$$

$$\frac{1}{v^2} = \frac{2bt}{m} + \frac{1}{v_0^2} = \frac{2btv_0^2 + m}{mv_0^2}$$

$$v^2 = \frac{mv_0^2}{m + 2bv_0^2 t}$$

c) If v= ½v₀, then the previous equation can be used to obtain the time as:

$$\left(\frac{v_0}{2}\right)^2 = \frac{mv_0^2}{m + 2bv_0^2 t}$$

$$\frac{v_0^2}{4} = \frac{mv_0^2}{m + 2bv_0^2 t}$$

$$\frac{v_0^2}{v_0^2} = \frac{4m}{m + 2bv_0^2 t}$$

$$m + 2bv_0^2 t = 4m$$

$$2bv_0^2 t = 4m - m = 3m$$

$$t = \frac{3m}{2bv_0^2}$$

Therefore, the time for a half speed can be expressed in terms of the initial velocity, the mass and the constant b.

d) To graph the functions, it is important to have in mind the previous equations:

$$v^2 = \frac{mv_0^2}{m + 2bv_0^2 t}$$

$$ma = -bv^3$$

Therefore, the equation for the velocity and the acceleration in terms of time are the following:

$$\frac{v^2}{v_0^2} = \frac{m}{m + 2bv_0^2 t}$$

$$v = v_0 \sqrt{\frac{m}{m + 2bv_0^2 t}}$$

$$a = \frac{-bv^3}{m} = -\frac{bv_0^3}{m}\left(\frac{m}{m + 2bv_0^2 t}\right)^{\frac{3}{2}}$$

$$a = -bv_0^3 \sqrt{\frac{m}{(m + 2bv_0^2 t)^3}}$$

This means that both graphs will show an square root behaviour respect to time. However, an importance difference can be seen in both graphs. The velocity is positive and shows a decrease approaching to zero (inverse square root), while the acceleration starts as a negative value which have tendency to zero as time approach to infinity:

Acceleration-time

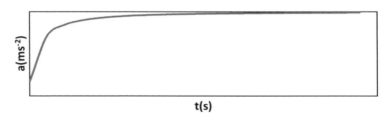

Velocity-time

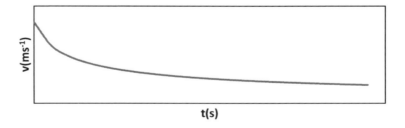

Question 3a

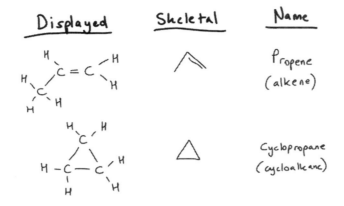

Question 3b

Alkenes react readily with bromine via electrophilic addition reactions to form a single product.

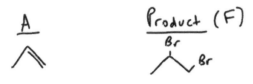

Question 3c

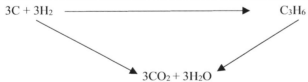

Question 3di

$C_3H_6 + 9/2 \, O_2 \rightarrow 3CO_2 + 3H_2O$

Question 3dii

Recall that the standard enthalpy change of formation is the enthalpy change when 1 mole of a compound forms from its elements. Then use Hess's law to draw the following calculation;

$3C + 3H_2 \xrightarrow{\hspace{4cm}} C_3H_6$

$3CO_2 + 3H_2O$

Use the enthalpies of combustion to calculate ΔH_1 and ΔH_2.

ΔH_1: $3(-393.5) + 3(-241.8) = -1905.9$

ΔH_2: -2058

$\Delta_f H$ (A): $-1905.9 - -2058 = (+)152.1 \text{ kJ mol}^{-1}$

Question 3diii
Use the above information swapping the combustion enthalpy of A to B.
$\Delta_f H$ (B): -1905.9 - -2091 = (+)185.1 kJ mol^{-1}

Question 3div
Using the principles of Hess's law again, the standard enthalpy change for the reaction = $\Delta_f H$ (A) - $\Delta_f H$ (B)
= 152.1 – 185.1
= -33 kJ mol^{-1}, the value is negative, so this reaction is exothermic.

Question 3e
The average contribution $\Delta_c H°$ per CH_2 groups can be found by dividing the enthalpy of combustion by the number of CH_2 groups. C_6H_{12} has 6 CH_2 groups so the average $\Delta_c H°$ per CH_2 group = -3920/6 = -653.3 kJ mol^{-1}
For B (C_3H_6) there are 3 CH_2 groups, so the average $\Delta_c H°$ per CH_2 group = -2091/3 = -697 kJ mol^{-1}
These results show that more energy is released on combustion of B than C_6H_{12} per CH_2 group. Therefore, it can be deduced that B is more unstable; the molecule has extra strain.

Question 4ai
Oxygen has an oxidation state of -2. As there are three oxygen atoms (net -6), two arsenic atoms and there is no overall charge on As_2O_3, the oxidation state of arsenic must be +3.

Question 4aii
The molecular formula for iron(III) oxide = Fe_2O_3. The balanced equation is;
$2FeAsS + 5O_2 \rightarrow Fe_2O_3 + 2SO_2 + As_2O_3$

Question 4bi
Arsenic is in group 5 so has 5 electrons in its outer shell. To complete the outer shell it can form three bonds with oxygen.
Geometry = trigonal pyramidal (as 4 electron pairs; one lone pair and three bonding pairs)

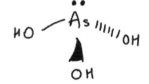

Question 4bii
$As_2O_3 + 3H_2O \rightarrow 2H_3AsO_3$

Question 4biii
Firstly, calculate the Mr of As_2O_3; (74.92*2) + (16*3) = 197.84. The number of moles of As_2O_3 dissolved in water
= 20.6g/197.84 = 0.104
From the balanced equation in 4bii you can deduce that 2 moles of arsenous acid forms from 1 mole of As_2O_3. Therefore, the number of moles of arsenous acid = 0.104*2 = 0.208 moles. Since, As_2O_3 was dissolved in one dm^3, the concentration of arsenous acid = 0.208 mol dm^{-3}.

Question 4ci
So, one way to think about this question is that if we have 20.6g in one dm^3, diluting by a factor of 10^{30}, now means we have 20.6g in 10^{30} dm^3. 100 cm^3 = 0.1 dm^3, so the mass in 0.1 dm^3 of the diluted solution = 20.6/10^{31} = 2.06 x 10^{-30}g.

Question 4cii
20.6g is present in 10^{30} dm^3. Therefore, 0.1g is present in;
[(10^{30}/20.6)*0.1] 4.854 x 10^{27} dm^3.
1 m^3 = 1000 dm^3
Therefore, 0.1g is present in 4.854 x 10^{24} m^3.
1 m^3 = 1 x 10^{-9} km^3
Therefore, 0.1g is present in 4.854 x 10^{15} km^3.
Fraction of the volume of the earth = 4.854 x 10^{15}/1.08 x 10^{12} which is ~ 40,000/9

Question 4ciii

Given the M_r of As_2O_3 = 197.84, one mole of As_2O_3 = 197.84g.

Given also that there are 6.02×10^{23} molecules per mole, one molecule of As_2O_3 has a mass of $197.84/(6.02 \times 10^{23})$ = 3.286×10^{-22} g.

Each molecule of As_2O_3 contains two atoms of As.

Therefore, the mass of As_2O_3 in solution for there to be one atom of As =

$3.286 \times 10^{-22}/2 = 1.64 \times 10^{-22}$g.

In part ci it was calculated that 2.06×10^{-30}g is present in 100 cm^3. Therefore, 1.64×10^{-22}g is present in $[(100/2.06 \times 10^{-30})*1.64 \times 10^{-22}]$ which =

7.98×10^9 cm^3.

With 28 cm^3 per bottle, this equates to 2.85×10^8 bottles.

Question 4di

pH of pure water = 7. Therefore, $[H^+]$ = 10^{-7} = 1.0×10^{-7} mol dm^{-3}.

Question 4dii

(1) Dilution by factor of 10^2
 - Concentration = 1×10^{-2} mol dm^{-3}
 - pH = 2
(2) Dilution by factor of 10^6
 - Concentration = 1×10^{-6} mol dm^{-3}
 - pH = 6
(3) Dilution by factor of 10^{10}
 - Concentration = 1×10^{-10} mol dm^{-3}
 - pH = 7 (note, the reason the answer is not pH 10 is because this is an acidic solution and therefore the pH cannot be greater than 7).

Question 5a

A sequence of DNA. You can tell this by the numbers on the first row that show it is a sequence and by the four different letter; A, T, C and G representing adenine, thymine, cytosine and guanine, respectively.

Question 5b

Transcription involves the copying of a DNA sequence into an RNA sequence. RNA contains uracil (U) instead of thymine (T) and contains ribose instead of deoxyribose. The transcribed sequence is single stranded, whereas DNA is double stranded. We do not know if the sequence in the table is the coding (sense) DNA strand or the non-coding (antisense) DNA strand – the transcribed RNA sequence would match the coding DNA strand (with U, not T) and be complementary to the non-coding DNA strand.

Question 5c

Organism 3. The fact that the DNA sequences from the different organism are very well conserved suggests that the sequence encodes a protein. The organism's sequence that is most different from the rest is least likely to lead to a functional part of a protein. Organism 3 is most different due to a deletion of nucleotide 326 for guanine – this deletion could result in a frameshift mutation. Due to the fact amino acids are coded for by triplets of RNA (from the DNA sequence), a deletion could cause all subsequent triplets to be misread – this would lead to the production of an incorrect protein.

Question 5d

(i)   Most closely related are organisms 4 and 5. There is only one base difference between them. This is at position 322

(ii)   Least related organisms are 6 and 7. There are 6 base differences between them.

Question 5e

Archaea and bacteria

Question 5f

How the differences in these sequences might have arisen – this is the process of natural selection. The 'how' includes both how the mutations/changes in the DNA sequence arose and then how the changes were selected for to be kept in the organisms' population. How the mutations arose could come from intrinsic sources such as errors during DNA replication that are not recognised and repaired, or from extrinsic sources such as exposure to UV light or carcinogens such as nicotine. The extrinsic sources can damage the bases in the DNA sequence. For the mutations to be kept in the organism's population there must have been a selection pressure, with individuals with the mutation being fitter and reproducing more, passing on the mutation to future generations. The selection pressure would depend in what the protein the DNA sequence is coding for and how the mutation affects the protein. The mutation may not affect the protein function, in which case the mutation may be kept in the population by genetic drift. Genetic drift could have been enhanced if the population of the organism decreased greatly.

The possible evolutionary consequences could involve speciation, whereby the two organisms are too genetically different to reproduce to produce fertile offspring. It could lead to extinction – this is most likely with organism 3 whose protein encoded by the sequence in the table is most likely non-functional. If this protein was essential for survival it would greatly reduce the fitness of the organism. It would be equally valid to say that there would be minor evolutionary consequences without knowing further information about the rest of the genome and knowing which part/which protein the DNA sequence actually codes for.

Question 6a

DNA/protein/mRNA sequencing
Mate them together to see if they produce fertile offspring

Question 6b

Natural selection, often referred to as survival of the fittest, is one process of evolution whereby individuals with advantageous alleles (provide higher fitness) have a higher chance of survival so they are more likely to reproduce and pass on their beneficial alleles. The frequency of the beneficial allele increases. It is common for one allele to be responsible for the phenotypic characteristic with one allele dominant and one recessive. Stable polymorphisms can involve multiple alleles at different genomic locations – there must be several selection pressures to maintain the alleles which makes stable polymorphisms rare in nature.

Question 6c

When the frequency of a snail shell polymorphism increases in the population, their fitness decreases (they are less likely to survive since they are more easily recognised by birds). The population of this polymorphism will therefore decrease. As it decreases their survival rate will increase. As their survival rate increases, the population of the polymorphism will increase – this then decreases their survival. The end results are oscillating cycles in the population size of the different polymorphisms.

Question 6d

Alleles		Unbanded (UU)	
		U	U
Banded (uu)	u	Uu	uU
	u	Uu	uU

All the F1 genotypes will be heterozygous (Uu). Since unbanded (U) is dominant, the phenotype of the F1 progeny are unbanded.

Question 6e

Alleles (F1 generation cross)		Unbanded (Uu)	
		U	u
Unbanded (Uu)	U	UU	uU
	u	Uu	uu

The genotypic ratio= 1:2:1 of homozygous dominant:heterozygous:homozygous recessive (UU:Uu:uu). Estimated numbers = (240/4)*n, where n=the ratio value. Therefore, there would be an expected number of 60 homozygous dominant, 120 heterozygous and 60 homozygous recessive.
The phenotypic ratio = 3:1 unbanded:banded, where unbanded is the phenotype of both UU and Uu. The estimated populations are 180 unbanded and 60 banded.

Question 6f

There are many factors to consider. Once the two habitats are chosen you need to choose which areas to sample to measure the individual of pink, banded snails. As snails, although motile, are slowing moving, random samples could be taken using a frame quadrat. Random points can be chosen by selecting random coordinates. Random samples avoid bias. Repeat this process and take as many samples as possible – the more samples, the more reliable the data is. Then, to get the population for the habitat, multiply the size of the whole area by the average number of pink, banded snails in one quadrat. Note, depending on the habitat, a belt transect may be more ideal.

To further avoid bias, repeat at different times of the day, different seasons.
A more advanced study would consider the distribution of the pink, banded snails in the two habitats and correlate them with additional measurements such as soil acidity and plant species present.
You could also take it a step further by measuring the size and age (if possible) of the pink, banded snails.

END OF PAPER

2016

Section 1A

Question 1: G

In this question the key is the change on sign, which produce an inversion in the inequality an therefore 8>(x/2)-6. The rest is resolve as a nomal equation and the answer is G

Question 2: B

The general form for the square of a binary addition is $a^2 \pm 2ab + b^2$. This produces the elimination of the square roots and allows the addition of terms to 5. Attention must be play in the sign inside of the brackets which gives the sign of the second term to $-2\sqrt{2}\sqrt{3}$.

Question 3: C

An easy way to solve this problem is to look the ratio as equations. Then 5Q=2R and 3R=10S. The substitution of the second equation into the first and the reduction of term lead to the answer C.

Question 4: E

If 20 members produce a mean of 28 years, then the product of these values is equal to the sum of all the ages of the members. When the number of members raises to 22 with an average of 30 a new and larger sum of all ages is obtain. The subtraction of the second result minus the first divided by two gives the average age of the new member seen as answer E.

Question 5: C

After one year the scanner has depreciate £3000 to £12000 and a further depreciation of £2400 occurs for the second year. The answer is C.

Question 6: B

The points ABC forms a triangle of angles 30° (=90°-60°) in A, 60° (=330°+30°-90°) in B and 90°in C. Therefore, it is possible to find the distance BC by trigonometry using AB=4 and sin(60) = cos(30) =√3/2 angle. The answer is B

Question 7: F

The addition of a proportionality constant (k) allows writing an equation of x in function of y: $x=k/\sqrt{y}$. where the value of k can be obtained when x=8 and y=9. Then y is written in function of x: $y=(k/x)^2$ and its value is obtained. The answer is F.

Question 8: E

The trapezium can be divided into a rectangle of sides x and x-1, and a triangle with sides x and (x+5)-(x-1). The addition of their areas is equal to the area of the trapezium. Equally the area is also equal to half area of a regular trapezium of equation (a+b)h/2 with a and b sides. In both cases, this leads to a quadratic equation $X^2+2x-120$ with roots 10 and -12. The root 10 is taken to calculate the value of RS equal to 15. The answer is E

Question 9: B

The equation cannot be simplified any further. Therefore the obvious step is to multiply both sides by the denominator $3b^2-1$, then group common terms and factorise to $b^2(3a-1)=2+a$. The simplification of this equation leads to the answer B

Question 10: C

The value of the side PQ and SR is equal to the perimeter of the circle in the cylinder (p=2πr), which allows to calculate value of radius r of the cylinder. Then, the volume is obtained by multiplying the area of the circle times the high of the cylinder (side PS). The answer is C

Question 11: A

In this question the key is factorisation and the elimination of term in the denominator. The denominator can be factorised to x(x-2). The numerator can be separated to factors: -(x-2)(x+2). Attention must be paid to the negative sign, which change the sign of the whole fraction. Then, the (x-2) factor is cancel by the one in the numerator. Then, the fraction can be simplified, paying attention to changes in sign, and the terms can be reduced to the value seen in answer A.

Question 12: D

In this question, the key is on selecting the necessary information. The question tells you that a boy is required so the total number of boys is necessary. The number of swimming boys is not given but it is possible to calculate it by finding out the number of total swimmers. Then the total of swimming boy is divided by the total number of boys and the answer is D.

Another way is creating a table as you read the information as seen below:

	Swimming	Archery	Tennis	Total
Boys	_32_		(2/3)*36=23	_74_
Girls	25			46
Total	57	27	36	120

Once the table have the necessary information, it is not necessary to fill it up, the total number of boys and swimming boys is easily visible and the probability is obtained as mentioned above and answer D is obtained

Question 13: D

The numbers can be expressed as 3^n, then the properties of exponentials: $(3^n)^m = 3^{n*m}$, $3^n*3^m = 3^{n+m}$ and $3^n/3^m = 3^{n-m}$, can be used to simplified the given equation to 3^{4n}. The answer is D

Question 14: E

The points RQT forms an isosceles triangle with x as one of the angles. Because it is an isosceles triangle the other two angles are equal to (180-x)/2. This is the value of the external angle (α) of the polygon and used in the equation $\alpha=360/n$ to find the equation. The answer is E

Question 15: B

The required probability is the sum of the probability of an overweight person having Type 2 diabetes plus an non-overweight person with the same disease. The first term is the product of a person being overweight (3/5) times its probability of having diabetes (9/50). Similarly, for a non-overweight person, 2/5 of the population, whose probability is 1/6 of 9/50. The addition of both products lead to the answer B.

Question 16: A

The substitution of the values of x in the linear equation gives the values of y. Then, the values of x and y can be used in the quadratic equation to create a system of two linear equations with two variables "a" and "b". The solution of such system with a selected method provides the answer A.

Question 17: C

The diagonals of a rhombus generate four triangles of the same dimensions, whose hypotenuse can be calculated by the Pythagorean theorem as the other sides are 5/2 and 3/2. Then, the scale factor is obtained from simplification of $\sqrt{68}$ over the hypotenuse found. The answer is C.

Question 18: F

The slope of a line is determined by $\Delta y/\Delta x$. The equation of the slope for this line is generate with the coordinate of the two point provided. Once the equation $(6-2p)/(2-p)$ is obtained, it is visible that values of 2 and 3, and between them, do not fulfil the conditions, then set of values are given in answer F

Section 1B

Question 19: B

The energy of a photon is directly proportional to the frequency of the electromagnetic wave according to the Planck's equation. if the highly energetic gamma rays have a higher frequency than the less energetic microwave, the frequency decrease. Additionally, the speed of an electromagnetic wave is preserved, regardless of its change in frequency and wavelength. If $c=f\lambda$, where c is the speed of the wave, f the frequency and λ the wavelength. Therefore, to preserve the speed a decrease in the frequency produces an increase wavelength and the answer is B.

Question 20: D

The production of Pb with a 210 nucleon number requires a loss of 4 nuclear particles (neutron and protons), which is equivalent to one alpha decay, and the generation of two protons to preserve the atomic number, which is represented by two beta decay. Then the answer is D.

Question 21: H

Heat transfer is driven by ΔT. Therefore, any two changes in temperatures that leave ΔT the same, produces the same rate of heat transfer. Although, changes in A and l can also be varied, these are more difficult to determine. Then, the answer is H.

Question 22: F

In this question, the key can be found in the shape of the graph and the values on it. Kinetic energy have a quadratic equation with the velocity. Therefore, a parabolic graphs must be expected. The potential energy of a 20 kg mass at 2 m is 100J and not 10 as seen in the graph. Therefore, the answers that satisfy both conditions are 3 and 4, and the answer is F.

Question 23: C

In this question the key can be found by looking changes in the nucleon number. The addition of the nucleon number of products plus the number of free neutrons must be equal to the nucleon number of uranium plus the number of protons or neutron colliding against the uranium nucleus. This only occurs in answer C.

Question 24: D

. To obtain the maximum power lost in the 5Ω resistor, it is necessary to calculate the current at minimum resistance of the variable resistor. Then , the total resistant of a series circuit is equal to the addition of all the resistors. Once the current is calculated by $I=V/R$, the loss power is obtained from $P=I^2R$. The answer is D.

Question 25: E

The key to answer this question consist in calculating the intensity of a parallel circuit before and after switching on. The total resistance of a series circuits is the addition of all the individual resistances (30+30) when the switch is off but only 30 Ω when it is on. Then, the total resistance of a parallel circuit is $1/R_T=1/R_1+1/R_2$. The intensities before and after switching on can be calculated by $I=V/R$ and the difference between them provide the answer: E.

Question 26: D

The radius and temperature of the old sun can be written in terms of the present values as 100R and T/2. The substitution of this values in the equation can gives an equation that provides the proportion of power between the old and the present sun as (10000/16). This value multiplied by the current power of the sun provides the answer of the question: D

Question 27: E

The distance travelled by a particle in the middle is a bit difficult to calculate as it is equivalent to the area under the curve. To approximate this, it is possible to multiply the amplitude, frequency, wavelength and time (in seconds). The answer is E

Question 28: E

The tension on the rope holding the mass is equal to the weight of the mass plus the force to accelerate such mass. Such tension is the same on the side of the motor. Therefore, the tension of the coupling is twice the tension on the rope holding the mass. The answer is H.

Question 29: F

The current (I) of a series circuit is constant along the circuit and calculated by $I=V/R_{total}$. The current is the charge (C) that flow over time (t) and therefore charge can be obtained by $C=I*t$. On the other hand, the power loss in the heater (P) is equal to $P=Energy/t$ and $P=V*I$. Then the voltage and charge can be obtained providing the answer F

Question 30: D

The volume of the cube is equal to the cube of one of its sides (10^3), while the volume of the inner cuboid is equal to the area of the small square times the length of the side of the cube (5^2*10). The difference of this volumes provides the final volume of the figure while the product of the gravitational field times the weight provide the mass. Then, the density, mass over volume, can be calculated giving the answer F

Question 31: D

The driving force in heat transfer is the difference in temperatures if such difference do not exist the system is in equilibrium. Therefore, convection can only occur in P and Q, as R and S are in equilibrium. All objects emit radiation but this is increase with the increase in temperature. Additionally, dull bodies can absorb and emit radiation more efficiently. Then S has the greatest rate of emission. The answer is D

Question 32: A

The distance travelled is the area below the line (d_1) until 20s plus the area above the line from 20 to 30s (d_2). On the other hand, the distance from the travel position is the difference between the aforementioned areas (d_1-d_2). Finally, average speed is equal to the total travel distance over the time elapsed. Then the answer of the question is A.

Question 33: A

After the first half lives the values of X and Y must be the same and therefore the graph must shows an intersection. For the second half life time, the value of Y must be greater than X but never bigger or equal to the original value of X. Finally, the values must become lower in the following in the next half-lives. Then the answer is A

Question 34: G

The mass percentage is equal to the mass of tin (m_1) over the total mass (m_1+m_2) times 100: $(m_1)(100)/(m_1+m_2)$. Additionally the mass of both materials is equal to the density (X or Y) times the volume (V): $m_1= XV$. The substitution of the second equation into the first gives an equation of X, Y and the volume. If hypothetical total volume of 100cm^3 and the percentage of material in volume give a hypothetical volumes of tin and copper of 10 and 90 cm^3. These values can be substituted in the last equation and reduced to the equation seen in answer G.

Question 35: D

If the uranium atom is at rest before the decay, then the total momentum before and after decay is equal to zero and therefore, the momentum (P) of the Thorium atom and alpha particle is the same. If the kinetic energy (E_K) of both particles is related to the momentum (P) and mass (m) by $E_K =P^2/2m$ and the sum of both energies is equal to the total kinetic energy, then it is possible to obtain an equation of momentum in terms of the total energy and the mass of the uranium (mass of alpha particle + thorium) and the mass of thorium. Finally, this value of the momentum is substitute in the equation of kinetic energy and the answer is obtained: D

Question 36: G

The loud speaker generates waves that are reflected by the buildings creating standing waves with fundamental length $L.=\lambda/2$ ($\lambda=$ wavelength). In order to make each echo to coincide with the click, L must be equal to the highest common factor (16m) between the two distances. Then, the wavelength is 32m and the frequency can be calculated using the equation of the velocity of a wave. The answer is G.

Section 1C

Question 37: D

$^{40}_{20}Ca^{2+}$ contains 18 electrons (20 – 2) and 20 neutrons (40 – 20). A has 18 electrons but 18 neutrons. B has 17 electrons and 20 neutrons. C has 18 electrons and 22 neutrons. D has 18 electrons and 20 neutrons, so is the correct answer. E has 19 electrons and 20 neutrons.

Question 38: D

Statement 1 is incorrect since titanium is not a noble gas and will have its usual electron configuration with an incomplete outer shell of electrons. Statement 2 is incorrect since it is true for a metal, not an ionic compound which titanium oxide is. Statement 3 is correct. 7.2g of Ti equates to 7.2/48 moles which can be simplified to 1.2/8. 3.6 dm^3 of O_2 using the molar gas constant equates to 3.6/24 moles of O_2. 3.6/24 can be simplified to 1.2/8. Hence, one mole Ti is present for every mole of O_2. Thus, the empirical formula is TiO_2.

Question 39: C

The question asks in which reactions are covalent bonds broken and formed. The only bonds formed in reaction 1 are between sodium and oxygen ions, but these are ionic, not covalent bonds. Likewise, ionic bonds are broken and formed in reaction 3. Only in reaction 2 are covalent bonds broken and formed - the reaction at the cathode; $H_2O + 2e^- \rightarrow H_2 + 2OH^-$; involves the breaking of covalent bonds in the water molecule and forming covalent bonds to form H_2.

Question 40: C

We are told increasing the temperature increases the yield at equilibrium, therefore the forward reaction must be endothermic (+ve enthalpy change). This eliminates D, E and F. Increasing the pressure did not change the equilibrium position, therefore the number of moles of gas must be equivalent for reactants and products. Only for C is this the case.

Question 41: C

If 1.6g of the compound is bromine, then (2.4 – 1.6) 0.8g of the compound is oxygen. To get the empirical formula you need to calculate the ratio of moles of bromine:oxygen. For bromine the number of moles is 1.6g/80, whilst for oxygen it is 0.8g/16. You can simplify the fractions by dividing (1.6/80) by 1.6 and (0.8/16) by 0.8 to get 1/50 for bromine and 1/20 for oxygen. (1/50):(1/20) can be simplified to 20:50 and subsequently 2:5 showing that 2 moles of bromine form with 5 moles of O. Hence, the empirical formula = Br_2O_5.

Question 42: D

Firstly, you need to calculate the number of protons. Since Sb^{3+} has 48 electrons, Sb must have 51 (48 + 3) electrons and hence 51 protons. The isotope with 70 neutrons therefore has an atomic mass of 121 (51 + 70), whilst the isotope with 72 neutrons has an atomic mass of 123 (51 + 70). The relative atomic mass is therefore (0.6*121) + (0.4*123) = 72.6 + 49.2 = 121.8.

Question 43: D

Statement 1 is incorrect since the distance migrated by a spot on the chromatogram depends on how fast the dye moves in the mobile and stationary phase, not on their concentration. Statement 2 is incorrect since the stationary phase is the filter paper, whilst the mobile phase is the solvent. Using the ratio of the solvent font in chromatogram 1 & 2, which has halved in chromatogram 2 and given that the solvent and filter paper have remained the same, you can tell that dye W migration distance should now be 8.2 cm/2 = 4.1 cm and for dye Y, 6.4 cm/2 = 3.2 cm, both of which can be seen in chromatogram 2.

Question 44: E

Initially by looking at the graph you can see that experiment W produce twice the volume of oxygen compared to experiment Z, thus twice as many moles must be produced. Therefore, you can eliminate answers B, C and D which do not alter the number of moles in the reaction. It is then a matter of calculating if A or E is correct. You can do this by calculating the number of moles of hydrogen peroxide, the number of which is double the number of moles of oxygen ($2H_2O_2 \rightarrow O_2 + 2H_2O$). In A, experiment Y has (100 cm^3 * 1.0 mol dm^{-3}) 0.1 moles and experiment Z has (50 cm^3 * 2.0 mol dm^{-3}) 0.1 moles – there would therefore be 0.05 moles of O_2 produced in both experiments, which from the graphs is not the case. Instead, E is correct since 0.1 moles of hydrogen peroxide (100 cm^3 * 1.0 mol dm^{-3}) are used in experiment Y, which is double the number of moles in experiment Z (25 cm^3 * 2.0 mol dm^{-3}). These conditions fit those seen in the graph.

Question 45: C

A redox reaction must have both oxidation and reduction. Reaction1 is a redox reaction. The oxidation state of chlorine decreases from 0 to -1 (reduction), whist the oxidation state of iodine increases from -1 to 0 (oxidation). Reaction 2 only shows reduction – chlorine gains electrons. Reaction 3 shows neither oxidation or reduction since the oxidation state of all elements remains the same. Reaction 4 is a redox reaction. The oxidation state of chlorine decreases from 0 to -1 from $Cl_2 \rightarrow HCl$ (reduction), whist the oxidation state of chlorine also increases from -1 to 0 from $Cl_2 \rightarrow HClO$ (oxidation).

Question 46: A

The first thing to do is to write a balanced equation. This involves noticing that copper(II) nitrate = $Cu(NO_3)_2$ as you have Cu^{2+} reacting with NO_3^-. The equation is therefore; $3Cu + (?)HNO_3 \rightarrow (?)Cu(NO_3)_2 + 4H_2O$ + compound X. Since compound X does not contain copper or hydrogen you can deduce that there must be 3 moles of $Cu(NO_3)_2$ and $8HNO_3$ (the 8 hydrogens from $4H_2O$). The balanced equation is then; $3Cu + 8HNO_3 \rightarrow 3Cu(NO_3)_2 + 4H_2O$ + compound X. Adding the number of the different elements you are left with 2 nitrogen and 2 oxygen on the product side, so compound X is NO and the final equation is;

$3Cu + 8HNO_3 \rightarrow 3Cu(NO_3)_2 + 4H_2O + 2NO$

Question 47: C

During the electrolysis of sodium chloride you should be able to recall that hydrogen is produced at the negative electrode (cathode), where the following reduction reaction occurs; $2H_2O + 2e^- \rightarrow H_2 + 2OH^-$. Therefore, straight away you can eliminate answers B, D, and G. Chlorine is produced at the positive electrode, where the following oxidation reaction occurs; $2Cl^- \rightarrow Cl_2 + 2e^-$. You can therefore also eliminate answer E. This leaves answers A, C and F. We are told that 2.4 dm^3 of H_2 is produced – using the molar gas constant this equates to 0.1 moles of H_2. Answer A is therefore incorrect since 0.1g of H_2 equals 0.05 moles (0.1g/2). From the two half equations you can see that for every mole of H_2 produced 1 mole of Cl_2 is. There must therefore also 2.4 dm^3 of chlorine produced, which fits the answer C.

Question 48: F

The forward reaction is exothermic, as heat is given out (-100 kJ mol^{-1}). Therefore, the products are at a lower energy state than the reactants. For the reaction to go in reverse, the activation energy therefore requires this difference in energy plus the activation energy of the forward reaction – hence, 100 kJ mol^{-1} + 150 kJ mol^{-1} = 250 kJ mol^{-1}. This is easier to understand if you sketch out an energy diagram.

Question 49: F

Statement 1 would show HX was a stronger acid, since stronger acids react have a faster rate of reaction than weak acids, so measuring the time taken would differ between the acids. Statement 2 is incorrect since the same amount of sodium hydroxide is required to neutralise the same amount of both acids. This is because both acids react with sodium hydroxide in a 1:1 molar ratio; $HX/HY + NaOH \rightarrow Na(X/Y) + H_2O$. Statement 3 is correct since strong acids dissociate fully in solution whereas weak acids dissociate partially. Dissociation involves the release of H^+ ions which can be detected using a conductivity meter.

Question 50: A

Firstly, write out a balanced equation using the knowledge that carbonates and acids react to give a salt, carbon dioxide + water, and that sodium carbonate = Na_2CO_3. The balanced equation is; $Na_2CO_3 + 2HCl \rightarrow 2NaCl + H_2O + CO_2$. From the equation we can tell that the 240 cm^3 gas released is CO_2 and can now work out the number of moles of CO_2 using the molar gas constant. 240 cm^3/24 000 cm^3 = 0.01 moles of CO_2. There is a 1:1 ratio of CO_2: Na_2CO_3 so 0.01 moles of Na_2CO_3 must have reacted. Using the A_r values given you can calculate the Mr of Na_2CO_3 = 106. Then, to find the mass of Na_2CO_3 that reacted you do 106 * 0.01 = 1.06 g. Since, 1.50 g of impure Na_2CO_3 was added in the reaction (1.50-1.06) 0.44 g is the mass of the impurity.

Question 51: F

First, write the balanced equation; $2Li + 2H_2O \rightarrow 2LiOH + H_2$. You can then tell that H_2 is the gas produced in this reaction and one mole forms for every 2 moles of lithium that reacts. 0.35 g of lithium equals 0.05 moles (0.35/7), so 0.025 moles of H_2 must have been collected. 0.025 moles of gas = (0.025 * 24 000 cm^3) 600 cm^3.

Question 52: D

First, write the balanced equation; $2NaOH + H_2SO_4 \rightarrow Na_2SO_4 + 2H_2O$. This tells us that 2 moles of NaOH react with 1 mole of H_2SO_4. Next, calculate the number of moles of NaOH used. This is 25.0 cm^3 * 0.1 mol dm^{-3} = 1/400. Therefore, 1/800 moles of sulfuric acid reacted. Convert moles to g by multiplying 1/800 by 98 (can take 98 as 100 for an easier calculation). Therefore, 1/8 g of sulfuric acid was used. Concentration is then, (1/8)/0.05 = 5/2 = 2.5 g dm^{-3}, which due to rounding is closest to 2.45 g dm^{-3}.

Question 53: C

To test deduction 1 you need to use the half equations to form a full balanced equation. This is done by making the number of electrons in each reaction equivalent (in this case, by multiplying the reaction at the cathode by 2) and combining the equations as follows; $2H_2O + 4H_2O + 4e^- \rightarrow O_2 + 4H^+ + 4e^- + 2H_2 + 4OH^-$. You can cancel out the electrons and simplify the equation by combining $4H^+ + 4OH^-$ to form 4 water molecules; $6H_2O \rightarrow O_2 + 4H_2O + 2H_2$, and further simplify to $2H_2O \rightarrow O_2 + 2H_2$. It is then clear that the ratio of hydrogen: oxygen is 2:1 not 1:1. Also from the full equation you can see that two water molecules are used up and hence deduction 2 is correct since the sodium sulfate solution would become more concentrated as the amount of water decreases. The full equation also shows that there is no accumulation of H^+ and so deduction 3 is incorrect.

Question 54: C

The easiest step to take first is to form an algebraic equation for you to calculate the C-O bond energy knowing that bond breaking is endothermic so positive and bond making is exothermic so negative;

$4(C-H) + (C=C) + 2(O-H) - 5(C-H) - (C-C) - (C-O) - (O-H) = -45$

Simplify;

$(C=C) + (O-H) - (C-H) - (C-C) - (C-O) = -45$

Put in values;

$611 + 464 - 413 - 346 - (C-O) = -45$

$316 - (C-O) = -45$

$\underline{361 = (C-O)}$

Section 1D

Question 55: C

Since copper ions are poisonous, the presence of copper ions would greatly decrease the fitness of the fish since they will most likely die. Copper ions therefore act as a selection pressure, since only fish that have the capability of surviving in the presence of copper ions will be able to reproduce to pass of their genetic characteristics to future offspring. This ability to survive in the presence of copper ions requires a fish to be well adapted to their presence. Hence statement 1 and 3 could be correct. Statement 2 is incorrect – genetic variation can occur in traits other than survival to copper ions and so a lack of genetic variation is unlikely to be true and wouldn't necessarily explain why the other types of fish died.

Question 56: F

Osmosis is the process by which water moves from an area of high water potential to an area of lower water potential. When the cell is surrounded by a solution that it more concentrated this means that the solution has a lower water potential. Therefore, the net movement of water is from the interior of the cell to the surroundings. The consequence of this is that the water potential of the cell cytoplasm decreases, such that it is lower than the water potential of the vacuole. Therefore, there is also net water movement from the vacuole to the cell cytoplasm as depicted by arrow 4.

Question 57: A

The only single-celled organisms listed are algae, bacteria and fungi. Of these organisms, only algae have chloroplast – the organelle that carries out photosynthesis. Algae also have a cell wall.

Question 58: C

Percentage decrease =(difference in the number of bubbles at 30 and 60 °C)/(number of bubbles at 30 °C) = (32-8)/32 = 24/32 = ¾ = 75 %. This narrows down the answer to either C or D. Student C is correct since high temperatures cause enzymes to denature which occurs when bonds in the enzymes break resulting in the loss of enzyme structure.

Question 59: E

We are told that albinism is a recessive genetic condition. This means that an albino must have two copies of the albinism allele. A symptomless carrier would contain one albinism allele and one normal allele. Therefore, the total number of albinism alleles = (29 * 2) + 81,200 = 58 + 81,200 = 81,258.

Question 60: B

The reaction is being catalysed by a human enzyme. To decrease the time it takes for the solution to become clear, the rate of the enzyme-catalysed reaction must be increased. Enzymes denature at high temperatures (>37 °C), therefore increasing to 70 °C would decrease the rate of the reaction since the enzyme no longer works. Extreme pH values such as pH 13 also cause enzymes to denature preventing them from functioning. Increasing or decreasing the amount of protein and enzyme solution by the same amount would have no affect on the time taken for the solution to become clear since the ratio of enzyme: protein remains constant. Statement B could decrease the time taken for the reaction to occur since stirring increases the frequency of successful collisions between enzymes and substrates.

Question 61: B

Capillary tubes are cylindrical. Volume of gas produced = area of circular face * distance gas bubble moves. Therefore, the volume = $\pi r^2 d$. The radius = diameter/2 = 1.0 mm/2 = 0.5 mm. Distance = 16 mm. Volume = $\pi(0.5*0.5)(16) = (16\pi/4) = 4\pi$. This narrows the answers to either A or B. Photosynthesis involves the conversion of water and carbon dioxide to oxygen and glucose. The reason the rate reduces after 3 minutes is due to a reduction in carbon dioxide, one of the reactants.

Question 62: B

The presence of a large central vacuole tells us that the cell is likely a plant cell. The single, stained round structure is most likely the nucleus. This cell would contain a cell wall, mitochondria and chromosomes. However, at a magnification of 40x only the cell wall would be visible.

Question 63: H

Plant shoots show positive phototropism to light, which means that plants grow towards the direction of light. The curving of the shoot seen in the diagram suggests that the light is unidirectional. The curving occurs due to increased cell divisions and cell growth of cells further from the direction of light (area Q in this case which is in the shade). This increased elongation and division of cells is due to a higher concentration of the hormone auxin in area Q than area P. Hence, all three statements are correct.

Question 64: E

In DNA, complementary base pairing occurs between A and T, and C and G. Therefore, if strand 1 contains 26% A, then strand 2 must contain 26% T. Similarly, if strand 1 contains 14% T, then strand 2 must contain 14% A. To get to the final answer, you must also calculate the percentage of cytosine present in strand 1. Since, only A,T, C and G are present the percentage of cytosine = $100 - 26 - 28 - 14 = 32\%$. Using this knowledge the correct values for P,Q,R and S are;

P = 14%

Q = 28%

R = 32%

S = 26%

Question 65: G

Cystic fibrosis is a recessive condition so both alleles must be defective for the child to have the condition. The female carrier contains one allele that is defective and one allele that is normal. The male carrier also contains one allele that is defective and one allele that is normal. Therefore, there is a 50% chance that the female will pass on the defective allele and there is a 50% chance that the male will pass on the defective allele. The probability that a child will get cystic fibrosis = $(1/2) * (1/2) = ¼$. The probability that a child won't get cystic fibrosis is therefore ¾. From the punnet square below ½ would be carriers;

CF=normal cf=defective		Female	
	Genotype	CF	cf
Male	CF	CF CF	CF cf
	cf	CF cf	cf cf

The probability that the couple have a male or a female is ½.

The probability that a child is a male **and** with cystic fibrosis = $¼ * ½ = 1/8$

The probability of a female child without cystic fibrosis = $½ * ½ = 1/4$

The answer is therefore G.

Question 66: E

Intraspecific competition refers to competition within a species (i.e between members of the same species). Statements 4 and 5 only are examples of intraspecific competition. Statement 4 is an example of competition for a sexual partner. Statement 5 is an example of competition for space.

Question 67: D

Sperm cells are haploid since they are produced via meiosis. The sperm cell would therefore contain 4 chromosomes. Each chromosome contains 2 strands of DNA, so there would be 8 strands of DNA in each sperm cell. Meiosis involves two cell divisions and so 4 cells would be produced. Hence, the answer is D.

Question 68: B

Actively contracting muscle cells would be using high levels of glucose for respiration and producing high levels of carbon dioxide (from aerobic respiration) and lactic acid (from anaerobic respiration). Therefore, the correct answer is B.

Question 69: D

To get the ratio of males: females add up the number of circles (females) which is 9 and the number of squares (males) which is 5. The ratio is therefore 5:9 (males: females). One Y chromosome is found only in healthy male humans. Since this genotype matches that of the females of species Q, 9 females would have a total of 9 Y chromosomes.

Question 70: C

Answer A is incorrect since anaerobic respiration does not use up oxygen. Answer B is incorrect since photosynthesis produces oxygen so the concentration wouldn't decrease. For these reasons and the fact that the population of algae and bacteria is high at point 3, answer C is correct. There is still oxygen present at point 4, so answer D is incorrect. Fish are not competing with algae for oxygen – algae produce oxygen via photosynthesis. Therefore, answer E is incorrect.

Question 71: H

The value of the Y axis remains constant as the substrate concentration increases. Label 1 could be correct if the enzyme concentration is high so that the active sites are not saturated. Therefore, increasing substrate concentration would result in a greater rate of substrate loss. However, this value would remain constant when rate of substrate loss is normalised by the mass in mg. Label 2 could be correct. Complexes could be either enzyme-substrate or enzyme-product. Loss of enzyme-product complexes would have the same rate regardless of substrate concentration. So, the number of complexes would vary depending on the rate of formation. Therefore, both the rate of enzyme-substrate complex formation and the number of complexes would increase as substrate concentration is increased giving a constant y value. Label 3 could be correct assuming the enzymes are not saturated with substrate. This is because the rate of product formed per enzyme would increase with increasing substrate concentration which is then normalised to a constant y value by the increasing mass in mg.

Question 72: E

DNA sequence after the first mutation = CXG CAG T…
CXG codes for arginine when X=G. The probability that X=G is ¼. Therefore, the probability that the first codon does not code for arginine = $1 - ¼ = ¾$.

DNA sequence after the second mutation (possibilities) =
XGC AGT, CGC AGT, CXC AGT, CXG AGT, CXG CGT, CXG CAT, CXG CAG.
Could both triplets code for arginine:
XGC AGT: no, AGT = serine
CGC AGT: no, AGT = serine
CXC AGT: no, AGT = serine
CXG AGT: no, AGT = serine
CXG CGT: yes (1/4 for CXG, when X=G) and CGT = arginine
CXG CAT: no, CAT = histidine
CXG CAG: no, CAG = glutamine
The probability the DNA sequence is CXG CGT = 1/7. The probability therefore that the DNA sequence is CGG CGT = $(1/7 * ¼) = 1/28$.
The answer is therefore E.

Section 1E

Question 73: C
The substitution of values of x and result leads to two equation with p and q as variables. An equation for q can be expressed in terms of p and substitute this in the other equation. The result after simplification is a quadratic equation of only one root p=1. The answer is C

Question 74: C
At terminal speed the resultant force is zero and the parachutist falls a constant speed. However, it doesn't imply that all the forces are newton's third law pair of forces. The only pair of forces under Newton's third law is the force than the parachutist exert over the parachute and vice versa. The answer is C

Question 75: C
A drawing can be helpful to solve this question. The coordinates of P and Q are used to determine the diameter, radius and coordinates of the centre of the circle. Such values can be substitute in the equation of the circle. Then, the equation is simplified to obtain the answer: C

Question 76: A
The force that the surface exert is equal to the weight of the trolley plus the vertical component of the force (F), calculated as $F\sin(\theta)$. On the other hand, the horizontal component of the force times the distance travelled provides the work done. The answer is A.

Question 77: C
If n_{th} term=$a*r^{n-1}$, then it is possible to determine the value of the common ratio ($r=1/\sqrt{2}$). The value of the common ration is substituted in the equation for the sum to infinity and then after rationalising denominator and factorising the answer is obtained: C

Question 78: H
The magnitude of the force between the pivot and the plank is the weight of the plank. Because the system is in equilibrium, the sum of moments on the left is equal to those on the right. Each side composed by the moment from the child and the moment of 1.2m of plank. This balance and the mass of the plank are used to calculate the weight of each side of the plank. Then, those weight are used in another equilibrium of forces without the children to find the centre of mass and relocate the pivot. The answer is H.

Question 79: B
The key to solve this question is the geometry inside of the circle. Drawing on the figure can be helpful to understand the solution. The points where the tangents touch the circle, the centre of the circle and the middle of the PC line form two equilateral triangles or one rhombus of sides equal to the radius. The largest diagonal of the rhombus is the base of the shaded triangle and its used to obtain the area of the shaded triangle. The area covered by the circle is 1/3 of the area of the circle, indicated by the 120° angle in the rhombus or 2x60° of the equilateral triangles, minus half the area of the rhombus. Once the area of the triangle and the covered area from the circle are calculated, the shaded area is obtained as answer B

Question 80: B
The difference in total energy, potential energy plus kinetic energy, between point X and Y is equal to the energy lost. Therefore, the kinetic and potential energies on both points are calculate and the difference on total energy obtained. The answer is B.

Question 81: D
The $\tan(\theta)$ can be expressed in terms of $\sin(\theta)/\cos(\theta)$. The product $\sin(\theta)\sin(\theta)$ can expressed as $1-\cos^2(\theta)$. Then, the equation is simplified to a quadratic equation in terms of $\cos(\theta)$. The roots of the equation give the answer: D

Question 82: B

If the frictional force were non-existent or in direction of the force P, the system were not in equilibrium. On the other hand, the clockwise moment would be produce by the force P times the total height of the object (base to edge P). Therefore, the answer is B

Question 83: G

The equation can be rearrange as the general form of a quadratic equation for which b^2-4ac needs to be bigger or equal to zero to have real roots. If $b=-(a+2)$, $a=3$ and $c=3$, then b^2-4ac can be expressed as a quadratic equation in terms of a for with roots -8 and 4. Therefore, values smaller than-8 and bigger than 4 produce positive values of b^2-4ac. The answer is G

Question 84: G

The object lose kinetic energy in the way up and therefore, the difference in kinetic energy (E_k) is equal to the object's potential energy (E_P): $K_{E1}-K_{E2}=E_p$. Such balance and the use of the equations of kinetic and potential energy provides the height of the object. Similarly, all the kinetic energy is transform to potential energy ($E_k=E_p$) when the object achieve the maximum height. Then, the suvat equations are used to obtain the time to reach such heights, which are used to get the final time. The answer is G

Question 85: D

At $y=0$, $m=-3/x_1$ and $p=-2/x_2$ and $x_2=x_1+5$. If the lines are perpendicular to each other, then $m*p=-1$. The values of p, m and x_2 are substituted in the latter equation to form an equation in terms of x_1 only. Here, by inspection of the resultant equation, it is possible to see that the value that make $m>1$ and $m*p=-1$ is $x_1=-2$. Otherwise, the equation can be rearrange in a quadratic equation of roots $x_1=-2$ and $x_1=-3$, where only $x_1=-2$ fulfill the requirement of $m>1$. Therefore, the value of x_1 is used to obtain m, p and m+p. The answer is D.

Question 86: E

The moment before and after the collision must be preserved. Then, the sum of the momentum before and after the collision is the same. Notice that the momentum of Q is equal to zero. Using the equation of momentum, the velocity of P can be obtained. The sum of the kinetic energies before and after the collision is calculated and the difference between the sums are the kinetic energy lost. The answer is E

Question 87: E

The first derivative of the equation can be used to find the range of an increasing or decreasing function. Therefore, the second derivative of the function is a quadratic equation, when equal to zero, can be rearrange to obtain the roots of x in terms of a. Using the roots of x, the set of values can be determined as answer G

Question 88: A

A resultant force can be calculated because the system is not equilibrated and there is acceleration. Then, the interaction of two horizontal forces produces a third force which can be calculated using the Pythagorean theorem (15 N). On the other hand, if the frictional force is equal to the normal times the friction coefficient and the normal force equal to the weight of the object, then all the forces are calculated to get the resultant force. Once the resultant force is obtained the acceleration is determined. The answer is A.

Question 89: E

A graph of the curve, the translation and the reflection can help to solve the problem. The y component of the vector shifts the graph up 3 places, while the x component moves the graph 4 to the right. Therefore, the equation modifies to $y=(x-4)^2+3$. On the other hand, the reflection does not only invert the graph and the signs on the equation but also move it two places towards –y. Therefore, $y=-(x-4)^2-3-2$. The answer is E.

Question 90: C

The acceleration on the body implies a resultant force is acting over the body and the mass. Such force is equal to the sum of the masses between the object and the mass times the acceleration. Such force is also the resultant of the sum of all the forces acting on the body: frictional force, downward force and pull-up force. The downward force can be calculated using the sin(30) times the weight of the object, while the pull up force is the equal to the weight of the mass. Once the resultant, downward and pull-up forces are calculated, the frictional force is obtained. The answer is C.

Section 2

Question 1a

i) If one revolution has 360° and each disc rotates at 160 revolutions per second, then it will rotate (360°/revolution)(160 revolutions/s)=57 600°/s. Therefore, the time to move one second 1/(57600°/s) = 1.74×10^{-5} s/°.

ii) For 160 revolutions, the time taken to rotate 30° is t=(30°)(1.74×10^{-5} s/°)=5.22×10^{-4} s. Then, the speed of the molecule must be v=d/t=0.24m/5.22×10^{-4} s =461ms^{-1}.

iii) The first slit allows passing molecules with a full range of speeds. However, the second split only allows molecules with a set of discrete speed that arrives at θ and those that made one or more extra rotations: θ+2π and θ2nπ respectively.

iv) If the maximum speed of a molecule was calculated in ii), the second fastest speed of a molecule to pass the two slits is when the second slit given an extra rotation then: θ+360 (or θ+2π). Therefore, a new time (t) is for the first slit to the second must be calculated t=(360+30°)* (1.74×10^{-5} s/°)=6.77×10^{-3} s. Finally, the distance d=24 cm is used to calculate the speed as before: v=d/t=0.24m/6.77×10^{-3} s =35.4 ms^{-1}.

v) The 0.3°angluar width in each side of the 30° centre for each slit allows faster molecules to pass at smaller angular displacement: 30°-0.3°-0.3°=29.4° and slower molecules at larger angular difference: 30°+0.3°+0.3°=30.6°. These new angles are used to calculate the v_{max} and v_{min}, respectively, using the same equations used above:

t_{max}=29.4*(1.74×10^{-5} s/°)=5.12×10^{-4} s v_{max}=0.24m/5.12×10^{-4} s=469 ms^{-1}

t_{min}=30.6*(1.74×10^{-5} s/°)=5.32×10^{-4} s v_{min}= 0.24m/5.12×10^{-4} s=451 ms^{-1}

b)i) The time (t) required for the particle to fall into the hole is the same than the time required to reach the angle θ. Therefore, the angular speed provides the relation between the angle and the time t=θ/ω while the angular speed can be obtained by the equation: ω=360°*f. On the other hand, the time also be by the equation of Newtonian free fall without air resistance h=v₀t+h₀+gt²/2, where the initial speed (v₀) and height (h₀) are equal to zero and then t=√((2g/h)). Because both times are the same, it is possible to equate both equation and rearrange the result to have expression for θ.

$$\theta = 2\pi f \sqrt{\frac{2h}{g}}$$

ii) If the hole is vertically under the particle when it is released, then the disk needs to give one revolution to allow the particle to pass. The time to get one revolution is t=1/f=1/20 s. Such time is the same that the particle need to fall into the hole so the equation of free fall is used to get the height h=gt²/2=9.81/(2*20²)= 1.23x10⁻²m

iii) Similarly to the previous questions the key to solve this problem is the equations of free fall mentioned in question b.i. However, the time (t') needed in this question is such time required for the particle to fall between both discs. However, opposite to the previous case the particle would have an initial speed v₀, which can be calculated by the free fall from the initial point to the first disc:

$$v_0 = \sqrt{2gh}$$

$$v_0 = \sqrt{2(9.81)(0.1)} = 1.96ms^{-1}$$

Then:

$$h' = v_0 t' + \frac{1}{2}gt^2$$

$$0.15 = 196t' + \frac{1}{2}(9.81)t'^2$$

This can be rearrange as a quadratic equation where only the positive root t'=0.083s has a physical meaning. Such time t' is required for a full rotation and therefore f=1/t'=1/0.083s = 12 rotations

Question 2

a) Circuit (i) is an arrangement in series and therefore, the total potential difference is the sum of the individual potential difference V=1.5V+1.5. On the other hand, the current remains the same in the whole circuit and then $A_1=A_2=V/R=30V/10\Omega=3A$.

The second circuit is an arrangement in parallel and the potential difference will remain the same and therefore V=3.0 V. However, the current in A_1 must be twice $2A_2$ due to first Kirchhoff's law. Therefore, $A_1=V/R=3/10=3$ A and $A_2=A_1/2=3/2=1.5$ A.

b) A new drawing of the circuit showing the new internal resistances (r) can be helpful to solve the problem. To solve the problem a new total resistance (R_T) must be calculated. In series the total resistance is sum of the individual resistances: $RT=R+2r=10+(2*0.1)=1.2\Omega$. Once the total resistance is obtained, the readings in the ammeter and voltmeter can be obtained using Ohms law, where the effects on the internal resistance are taken into account by using the total resistance:

i) $$A_1 = A_2 = \frac{V}{R_T} = \frac{1.5+1.5}{1.2} = 2.5A$$
$$V=IR=(2.5A)(1.0)=2.5 \text{ V}$$

In parallel, the $A_1=2A_2$ and because the potential difference is preserved in the whole circuit $V=IR=(\varepsilon-Ir)$, where the equation can be rearrange to obtain A_1 and therefore V and A_2:

ii) $$A_1 = \frac{\epsilon}{R+\frac{r}{2}} = \frac{3}{1+\frac{0.1}{2}} = 2.86A$$
$$A_2 = \frac{2.86}{2} = 1.43 \text{ A}$$
$$V = A_1 R = (2.86)(1) = 2.86 \text{ V}$$

c) The total amount of energy provided by each cell will be related by its power and the time taken to release such energy: E=Pt. If each cell has the same energy, then cells with lower rate of energy transfer will last longer. Power per cell can be calculated as follow in each circuit:

a.i) $P = \frac{VA_1}{2} = \frac{(3)(3)}{2} = 4.5W$

a.ii) $P = VA_2 = (3)(1.5) = 4.5W$

b.i) $P = \frac{\varepsilon A_1}{2} = \frac{(3)(2.5)}{2} = 3.75W$

b.ii) $P = \epsilon A_2 = (3)(1.43) = 4.29W$

Therefore, the cells in b.i will last the longest due to their smaller energy rate transfer.

d) If the fan requires a power (P) of 0.96W and a potential difference (V) of 2.4 V then the total amount of current is calculated as I=P/V=0.96/2.4=0.4A. If the loss of potential due to the internal resistance is not taken into account and because the potential is preserve in a parallel circuit, then the number of solar cell in series (N) can be obtained by N=2.4V/0.5V=4.8 solar cells. This means that 5 solar cell in series are required with two parallel sections with a current (i) in each section equal to i = I/2=0.4/2=0.2A. Because the current in a series circuit is conserved, then current in each solar cell is 0.2A.

e)i) The total resistance (R_T) in a parallel circuit can be calculated as the sum of the reciprocal of the individual resistances:

$$\frac{1}{R_T} = \frac{1}{R_1} + \frac{1}{R_2} = \frac{1}{1} + \frac{1}{2} = \frac{3}{2}$$

$$R_T = 2/3$$

Once the total resistance is calculated, the current of the cell is obtained using Ohm's law: I=V/R=1.5/(2/3)=2.25A

ii) Although the resistor(r), R1 and R2 are in parallel with each other, the resultant resistance (R_T mentioned above) is in series with the internal resistant. Therefore, the total resistance (R_{T2}) can be calculated as R_{T2}=R_T+r=2/3+0.1=0.766. Then, the current is I=V/R_{T2}=(3/2)/0.766=1.96A. Then, the current (I_2) through R_2 is obtained I_2=I/3 =1.96/3=0.65A and the dissipated power P=$I_2^2 R_2$=(0.65)^2(2)=0.85W

iii) Similar to the previous question, the total resistant (R_{T1}) in parallel is calculated and then the internal resistance in series is added to get the total resistance of the circuit (R_{T2}).Then:

$$\frac{1}{R_T} = \frac{1}{R_1} + \frac{1}{R_2} + \frac{1}{R_3} = \frac{1}{1} + \frac{1}{2} + \frac{1}{4} = \frac{7}{4}$$

$$R_T = \frac{4}{7}$$

$$R_{T2} = R_T + r = \frac{4}{7} + 0.1 = 0.67$$

$$I = \frac{V}{R_{T2}} = \frac{1.5}{0.67} = 2.23A$$

iv) The reciprocal of the total resistance of a parallel circuit of infinite resistors is the sum of a geometric series of initial value a=1 and ratio of ½ :

$$\frac{1}{R_T} = \frac{1}{R_1} + \frac{1}{R_2} + \frac{1}{R_3} + \cdots = 1 + \frac{1}{2} + \frac{1}{4} + \cdots = \frac{a}{1-r} = \frac{1}{1-\frac{1}{2}} = 2$$

$$R_T = 1/2$$

The rest is calculated as in the previous case:

$$R_{T2} = R_T + r = \frac{1}{2} + 0.1 = 0.6\Omega$$

$$I = \frac{V}{R_{T2}} = \frac{1.5}{0.6} = 2.5A$$

Question 3a

Use the periodic table to recall the number of electrons in the outer shell of sulfur, carbon and nitrogen. When the negative charge is on sulfur or nitrogen, the atom will have an additional electron.
Negative charge on sulfur:

Negative charge on nitrogen:

Question 3bi

Constant = absorbance/ [FeSCN^{2+}]. Constant = 1.85/(2.5 x 10^{-4} mol dm^{-3})
= 7400 mol^{-1} dm^3.

Question 3bii

[FeSCN^{2+}] = [Fe^{3+}] = absorbance/constant = 0.519/7400
= 7.0135 x 10^{-5} mol dm^{-3}.

Question 3biii

10 cm^3 of the solution was mixed with 10 cm^3 of a solution of thiocyanate. The solution was therefore diluted 2x. Therefore, the Fe^{3+} concentration in the solution prepared from the cereal = 7.0135 x 10^{-5} mol dm^{-3} * 2
= 1.403 x 10^{-4} mol dm^{-3}.

Question 3iv

100g of the breakfast cereal was dissolved in 250 cm^3 solution with a [Fe^{3+}] of 1.403 x 10^{-4} mol dm^{-3}. The number of moles in this solution = (250/1000) dm^3 * 1.403 x 10^{-4} mol dm^{-3} = 3.507 x 10^{-5}.
Using the A$_r$ of Fe as 55.85, the mass of Fe = (55.85 * 3.507 x 10^{-5})
= 1.96 x 10^{-3} g.

Question 3ci

The oxidation state of hydrogen = +1, as it can only lose one electron. Therefore, with two hydrogens, the total oxidation state is +2. Since H$_2$O$_2$ has no net charge, the oxidation state of oxygen must be -1.

Question 3cii

Acidic solutions contain abundant H$^+$ ions. When H$_2$O$_2$ reacts with H$^+$, water is produced. H$_2$O has no net charge; with two hydrogens, both with an oxidation state of +1, the oxidation state of oxygen must be -2.

Question 3ciii

We have just worked out that H$_2$O$_2$ gets reduced to water by reacting with H$^+$. Now, add the oxidation of Fe to the equation, ensuring that the net charges of the reactants and products are the same;
2Fe^{2+}$_{(aq)}$ + H$_2$O$_2$ $_{(aq)}$ + 2H$^+$$_{(aq)}$ → 2H$_2$O$_{(l)}$ + 2Fe^{3+}$_{(aq)}$

Question 4a

Question 4b

When the alkenes react with hydrogen, the double bond gets saturated forming two different alkanes;

The chlorination of the alkanes results in the addition of one chlorine in replacement of a hydrogen. There are four isomers from chlorination alkane A;

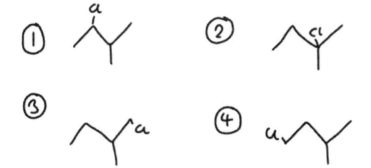

There are three isomers of alkane B;

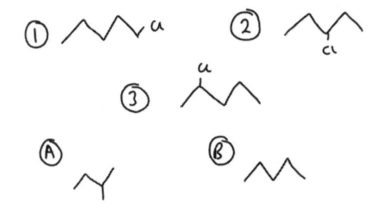

Question 4c

Alkenes S,T and U form alkane B , the straight chain alkane. The three alkenes in question are therefore;

The reaction with HBr results in the formation of a carbocation intermediate bound to hydrogen before the bromine binds. The cation can arise on only the second carbon of the first alkene listed above. However, the cation can arise on either the second or third carbon of the second and third alkenes listed above. When only one cation can

form, there will be no structural isomers of the final product, $C_5H_{11}Br$. Alkene U is therefore;

Question 4d

Alkenes P,Q and R form alkane A , the branched chain alkane. The three alkenes in question are therefore;

R has the most negative enthalpy of formation. Therefore, R has the greatest number of carbons attached to the double bond. R is therefore;

Question 4e

To deduce the structure of alkene P and Q, the enthalpy of formation of both alkenes needs to be calculated. Using the principal that the more negative the enthalpy of formation is, the greater the number of carbons directly attached to the double bond, the alkene with the more negative enthalpy of formation must be;

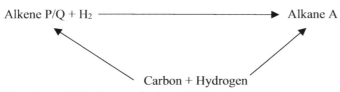

You can recall Hess's Law to work out an equation to give the enthalpy of formation.

Alkene P/Q + H$_2$ ⟶ Alkane A

Carbon + Hydrogen

Therefore, ΔH(hydrogenation) = Δ_fH(A) - Δ_fH(P/Q)

Δ_fH(P/Q) = Δ_fH(A) - ΔH(hydrogenation)

Δ_fH(A) will be the same for both alkene P and Q, since it is the same alkane.

Therefore, the more negative the ΔH(hydrogenation), the greater the value of Δ_fH for the alkene will be. The alkene with the more negative enthalpy of formation will therefore have a less negative ΔH(hydrogenation). The value of ΔH(hydrogenation) for alkene P = -113 kJ mol^{-1}, whereas the value of ΔH(hydrogenation) for alkene Q = -119 kJ mol^{-1}. Since, the ΔH(hydrogenation) for alkene P is less negative, alkene P will have a more negative

enthalpy of formation. Hence, alkene P is;

Whereas, alkene Q =

Question 4f

The equation for the combustion of alkene P is;

C_5H_{10} + 15/2 O_2 → 5H$_2$O + 5CO$_2$ (0)

With the information given, we know the enthalpy of hydrogenation;

C_5H_{10} + H$_2$ → C_5H_{12} ΔH = -113 (1)

We know the enthalpy change of formation of H$_2$O, so can deduce that;

H_2O → H$_2$ + 1/2O$_2$ ΔH = +286 (2)

We know the enthalpy change of combustion for alkane A;

C_5H_{12} + 8O$_2$ → 6H$_2$O + 5CO$_2$ ΔH = -3528 (2)

Summing equations (1), (2) and (3) gives the reactants and products of equation (0). Therefore, the energy change of combustion = -113 + 286 – 3528

= -3355 kJ mol^{-1}.

Question 5a

Protein (enzyme)

Question 5b

Phosphodiester bond

Question 5c

All the sequences are palindromic. This is evident when you consider that DNA is double stranded with complementary base pairing between the nucleotides G and C, and T and A. This can be seen below for each sequence;

GAATTC   GGATCC   AGCT

CTTAAG   CCTAGG   TCGA

This means that either DNA strand can be recognised to be cut by the restriction enzyme. Therefore, it allows the same restriction enzyme to cut both strands of DNA at the same site instead of just one.

Question 5d

Defence mechanism to degrade foreign DNA such as from viruses.

Question 5e

You may find it helpful to draw out plasmids that are only cut with a single restriction enzyme first before drawing the diagram representing both BamH1 and EcoR1 treatment;

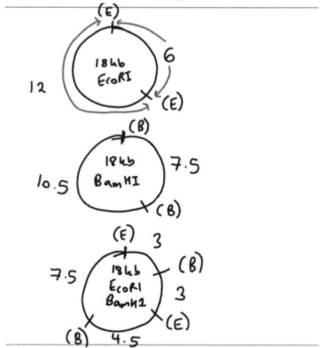

Question 5f

Genetic engineering involves the genetic modification of DNA. Restriction enzymes can be used to cut out a segment of DNA, such as a gene. The same restriction enzymes can be used to cut open a segment of DNA in a plasmid/different genetic location. The two DNA sequences have complementary sticky ends so allow for insertion of the DNA fragment. For example, genes can be cut out and transferred between organisms. Provide a specific example; e.g the human gene for insulin can be inserted in bacteria so that the bacteria can produce insulin.

Question 5g

EcoRI is an enzyme with an active site where DNA cleavage is catalysed. The shape of this active site is critical for the enzyme to function. The active site is part of the final tertiary/quaternary structure of the enzyme. The tertiary/quaternary structure is held together by van der Waals interactions, hydrogen bonds, electrostatic interactions and covalent disulphide bonds. Except the disulphide bonds, these bonds can be broken by changes in temperature and pH which alters the shape of the active site – this is enzyme denaturation.

Temperature:
Initially increasing temperature increases the rate if the reaction as there is more kinetic energy increasing the frequency of successful collisions between substrate and enzyme. The rate will increase until the optimum temperature (~37°C as in humans).

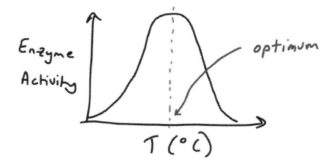

Increasing the temperature further increases the kinetic energy of the protein causing it to vibrate more. Increased vibration causes the weak bonds holding the protein together to break. Enzyme denaturation and loss of activity.

pH:
Altering the pH has a strong effect on the electrostatic interactions within the enzyme due to the presence of either H^+ or OH^- ions which alters the charge on individual amino acids. The rate is maximum at the optimum pH when the enzyme structure and active site matches the substrate.

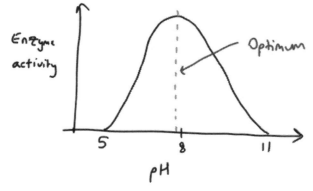

Question 6a

Use a ruler to measure the length of each organism and calculate how many times longer than the scale bar it is. Be careful to note the answers must be in mm.

A: 60 mm +/- 15 mm

B: 0.6 mm +/- 0.15 mm

C: 0.005 mm +/- 0.0015 mm

Question 6b

B: Light microscope

C: Transmission electron microscope (TEM)

Question 6c

Surface area of a cylinder (S)= 2(area of circle) + (circumference of circle * length)

$S = 2\pi R^2 + 2\pi RL = 2\pi R(R+L)$, where R=radius and L=length

Volume $(V) = \pi R^2 L$

Ratio (S:V); $2\pi R(R+L)$: $\pi R^2 L$ which can be simplified to 2(R+L): RL

In this organism L >> R, so the ratio can be further simplified to 2L: RL and 2:R

Therefore, the ratio of S/V = 2/R.

R ~ 1.5 mm, therefore the ratio = 2/(1.5) = 1.3 mm^{-1}. (Values between 1 mm^{-1} and 2 mm^{-1} are accepted).

Question 6d

Larger organisms have smaller surface area:volume ratios.

Question 6e

Oxygen, carbon dioxide, glucose, urea

Question 6f

Larger organisms have a smaller surface area:volume ratio, but often require greater amounts of substances e.g oxygen to survive. Adaptations are therefore essential.

However, even smaller organisms may require additional adaptations. For example, exchanging substances across a surface can be affected by dehydration and concentration gradients of substances may oppose that required. Adaptations;

It is important to point out in the examples used how they help to overcome the constraints of size. This includes increasing the surface area, providing a shorter diffusion distance, having a counter-current exchange, maintaining a strong concentration gradient (by having nearby capillaries to take substance to/away and lungs are ventilated) Examples; lungs and blood vessels in animals, gills in fish, root hair/microvilli to increase surface area, tubules in insects

END OF PAPER

2017

Section 1A

Question 1: F
In this question the key can be found by separating 12 into factors 3 and 4. Then, $\sqrt{4}$ is 2 and $\sqrt{3}$ is a common term that can be factorised in both the denominator and the numerator. The operations in both the numerator and the denominator can be performed, providing the answer seen in letter F.

Question 2: E
To solve the problem, it is necessary to find the roots of the quadratic equation of that can be form from the inequality. The factorisation of the equation $2x^2+x-15$ provides the roots -3 and 2.5. Then, the substitution of x= -3 ± 1 and x=2.5 ± 1 leads to the answer E.

Question 3: B
The key to answer this question is two rearrange the equation by terms. First, 5 must be added in both sides of the equation. Then, the equation is divided by 3, followed by the square root. Finally, the terms inside the parenthesis must be rearrange to the other side of the equation to give the answer B.

Question 4: E
The number of apples and pears times their respective price for both people can be arrange into two linear equations: $2x+5y=P$ and $3x+5y=Q$. The solution of the linear system of equation gives an equation of y in terms of P and Q. Then the answer is G

Question 5: B
If P is directly proportional to Q^2 and Q inversely proportional to R, then proportional constants ("a" and "b") are needed to express both proportions as equations such as $P=aQ^2$ and $Q=b/R$. The value of the constants can be obtained with the values of P, Q and R. Then, an expression of P in terms of R is obtained as answer: E

Question 6: C
By inspection of the sequences it is clear that values of above 10 would produce negative values of sequence T. These leave 6,7, 8 as possible answers. Therefore substitution of these on the sequences shows that 7 produce equal values on both sequences. Then, n=8 and the answer is C

Question 7: D
The numerator in the equation can be simplified by factorising the term in the parenthesis to $-x^2(2-3x)(2+3x)$.attention must be paid to the change of sign in the division. Therefore, common terms can be eliminated to simplified the equation to $2+(2+3x)/x$. The equation is simplified further to the answer showed in letter D

Question 8: B
Drawing a parallelogram in the Cartesian coordinates can help to solve this question. The inspection of the figure, shows that the height of the parallelogram is the y coordinate of point Q (a+1) and the base is the x coordinate of point R (3a/2). Then the equation of the area of the parallelogram leads to a quadratic equation in terms of "a", which roots are -3 and 2. However, a=2 is only consider as -3 leads to coordinates in a different quadrant. The y coordinate of point P is the same as the one in Q (a+1=2+1=3) while the x coordinate is equal to the difference between Q and R in the x coordinate: (3a/2)-2a. Therefore the answer is B

Question 9: D
The numbers 4 and 8 can be factorised to 2^2 and 2^3. Then the properties of the exponents can be used $(2^n)^m=2^{n*m}$, $2^n*2^m=2^{n+m}$ and $\sqrt{2}=2^{1/2}$. When $\log_2$ is applied in both sides of the equation, an equation in term of x is obtained and solved for x. Then, the answer is obtained as seen in letter D
Question 10: C

There are different ways to calculate the number of students taking German. One is calculating the number of girls studying Spanish and German, and then the total of students taking German. Similarly, it is possible to find the answer using the total number of boys. A quick way to find the answer is using a table as below:

	French	German	Spanish	Total
Girls	X	3X-X+Y-35	35-Y	3X
Boys		2Y	Y	
Total		2X+3Y-35	35	100

It is not necessary to fill the table to find the equation. The answer is C

Question 11: C
The exterior angle of a regular polygon is 360/n, then two equations can be form for n and n+4. If the difference between external angles 4°, therefore the difference of such equation will equally be 4°. This leads to a quadratic equation, which positive root is the answer: C

Question 12: B
The ship, lighthouse and canoe form an isosceles triangle, where the bearing of L from R is the repeated angle of the triangle. Such angle is obtained from the bearing of R from L and the properties of parallel lines. Then, the bearing of C from L can be obtained (220+40). Then, such angle and the properties of parallel lines allows to determine the answer: B

Question 13: B
The clock is a circle of 360° with 6° per minute and 30° per hour (360/60 and 360/12 respectively). Then, at 4:40, the minute hand will be at 40*6=240°. However, the hour angle must be at between the 5 and 4 hrs. Therefore, the position of the hrs hand can be obtained by (30°/hr)(4rs)+(240°/360°)(30°)=140°. Finally, the difference between the angles of both hands leads to the answer B.

Question 14: D
If the percentage profit can be obtained by:
$$\%profit = \left(\frac{profit}{cost}\right)(100) = \left(\frac{price - cost}{cost}\right)(100)$$
Then, the cost of producing the large cake can be found and because the production is proportional to the volume, it is possible to find the cost of the six pack (3/4 cost of a large cake) and then the profit.

Question 15: C
The probability of two dependent event is P(A and B)=P(A)*P(B|A). The probability that the first rabbit is male can be written as x/(x+4) while the probability of the second is (x-1)/(4+x-1). The first probability times the second is equal to the probability of two male rabbits (1/3). This equation can be rearrange and simplify to a linear equation which gives the value of x. Then, the answer is C.

Question 16: F
The key to this question consist to find the radius of the circle. The radius of the circle is equal to the diagonal that goes from the upper corner of the square to the centre of the circle. Such diagonal forms a right triangle inside of the square with sides x, (x/2) and r (the radius of the circle). Then "r" or "r²" can be found by the Pythagorean theorem and used to calculate the area of the semicircle A=πr². Finally, the area of the square is subtracted from the area of the semicircle in order to obtain the answer: F.

Question 17: C
In this question, the key is the volume of the pipe, which is equal to the difference between the volume of the inner and outer cylinder. The volume (V) of both cylinders can be calculated by V=π*r²*h, where r is the radius and h the height. Then, the mass is equal to the volume of the pipe times the density of the metal. Therefore, the answer is G.
Question 18: E

The diagonals that bisect the vertices of a regular hexagon form six equilateral triangles. Each triangle is divided by the apothem (c) into two right triangles. The apothem is half the distance mention in the question (c=6). If the sides of the right triangle are c(=6), "x" and "x/2", the value of x can be obtained by the Pythagorean theorem $c^2=x^2+(x/2)^2$. Then, the area of the right triangle can be obtained and 12 times that value is equal to the area of the triangle. Therefore, the answer is E.

Section 1B

Question 19: B
The total travelled distance is the area under the curve. When it decelerate for 20s (130-110), such area is composed by ten squares seen in the graph. If each square has an area 5m/s*10s, then area under the curve and total distance is 500m. This results can also be obtained by using the suvat equations: s=[(v-u)/2t]+ut. The answer is B.

Question 20: D
In any heat transfer process the mass is unaffected. However, an increase in temperature of a body produces a separation between the molecules of the body, which lead to an increase in volume for the same amount of mass. If the density is mass of a body per unit of volume, the increase of temperature of the body would reduce the density of the body. Therefore, the answer is G.

Question 21: E
The key to answer this question is the equation for the speed of a wave (c) in terms of the wavelength (λ) and frequency (f): $c=\lambda f$. In order to detect an electromagnetic wave, this must be in the visible light range. On the other hand, to hear a wave it must be below 20KHz. Then, the transformation of the frequencies into wavelength with the aforementioned equation provides one of the answers. The answer is E

Question 22: E
The current in a circuit (I) is equal to the flow of charge per second (60C/3s), while the resistance (R) can be expressed in terms of current (I) and voltage (V): R=V/I. Therefore, the resistance can be calculated providing the answer in letter E

Question 23: D
The energy (Ec) to lift the car can be obtained by the equation of potential energy: Ec=mgh. Therefore, the total energy loss, including the 25% from the motor, can be obtained by the difference between the total energy input (28000J) and the calculated potential energy given to the car (Ec). The answer is D.

Question 24: D
The time difference (Δt) times the speed of the wave ($c=3 \times 10^8 ms^{-1}$) provides the difference in distance travelled by the both gamma rays (Δs). To produce such difference (Δs) the source must be away from Q half of the distance Δs. This means that the answer is D.

Question 25: B
A balance equation for the number of protons must include only 94, 54, (or their difference) and x. Although a balance equation for the nucleon number can be more complicated by including the proton number, this would require more than 4 terms. Therefore, a balanced equation for the nucleon number must include numeric values (1, 239 or 240), w, y and z. Therefore, the only equation that fulfil this requirements is B

Question 26: F
The key to answer this equation are the basic equations of potential energy, power and efficiency. The potential energy provided to the system is equal to the weight of the object times the gravitational strength times the height lifted. Such value of energy divided by the time provides the theoretical power, while the power over the efficiency gives the total power used by the circuit. If the power of a circuit (P) is related to the current (I) and the potential difference (V) by $P=VI$, then the value of the current can be calculated. Therefore, the answer is F

Question 27: C
If only alpha particles and β^- particles are emitted, the loss of proton requires a lost in the atomic mass. This is not fulfilled in the answer A.

Question 28: E
If the density (ρ) is equal to the mass (m) over the volume (V): $\rho=m/V$ and the mass of the atoms is equal to the mass of the nucleus, then the ratio of densities is equal to the ratio between the volume or radius (r) of the nucleus and the one of the atom: $\rho_{atom}/\rho_{nucleus}=V_{nucleus}/V_{atom}=r_{atom}/r_{atom}$. Then the ratio of densities can be calculated and answer A is obtained.

Question 29: E
The speed of the wavelength (c) can be determined by the frequency (f) and wavelength (λ) of the wave: $c=f\lambda$. According to the graphs, the wavelength is
twice the distance x_2-x_1, while the period (= 1/frequency) is 3/2 the difference of time t_2-t_1. The substitution of these values provides the equation for the speed of the wave and the answer is E.

Question 30: C
If the power of a circuit (P) can be expressed in terms of the current (V) and potential difference (V) by $P=VI$ and the current (I) in terms of the charge flow (C) and the time (t) in seconds by $I = C/t$. Then the values of time, potential difference and power can be substitute into the equations and the answer is obtained: C

Question 31: C
The question is related to the conservation of momentum. The momentum before and after the collision are equal to zero. Therefore, momentum of the freight train is equal to the momentum of the passengers train. If the momentum (M) is related to the mass (m) and velocity (v): $M=mv$ and the mass of the train (m) can be expressed in terms of the number of carriages (n) and its individual mass $m=n*m_{carriage}$. Then, an expression with for the number of passangers carriers can be obtained. The answer is C

Question 32: C
The inspection of the resultant units in the solution is the key for this question. It is clear the option 3 would leave units of Kgm^{-6}, while option 2 would produce units of $Kgms^{-2}$ as $J= Kgm^2s^{-2}$. On the other hand, option 1 clearly provides the result of 40Kg as well as option 2 because $N = Kgms^{-2}$. The answer is **C**.

Question 33: C
Although the kinetic energy must remain constant, this is not equal to 1800J and option one is not correct. Although the resultant force is zero when the parachutist reaches constant speed, it doesn't imply that all the forces are Newton's third law pair of forces and the forces on option three are not a pair. On the other hand, the parachutist loose gravitational potential as it comes down by the rate: $3600Js^{-1}$ according to the equation $\Delta E_P/\Delta t=mgv$ ($\Delta Ep=$ change in energy potential, $\Delta t=$ change in time, m= mass, g= gravitational field strength, v=velocity). The answer is C

Question 34: D
If the material were composed of 120g of X and 120 g of Y, this indicates that X would decay to 30g and Y to 15 g in 6hrs. Therefore the amount fraction of Z generated for each compound can be calculated and their addition provides the answer D

Question 35: E

The kinetic energy (E) of both cars is related to their mass (m) and their velocity (v) by $E= 0.5mv^2$. Therefore, $E_x/E_y =(0.5m_xv_x^2)/(0.5m_yv_y^2)$ provides the ratio of kinetic energies. The substitution of the values of v_x and m_x in terms of y and the elimination of common terms provides the answer of the question: E

Question 36: E

The potential difference in a parallel circuit is the same for all the resistance. Then, the potential difference can be obtain from the 12Ω resistor by equation $P=V^2/R$ (P=power, V=potential difference, R= resistance). Then, the potential of the 4Ω resistor can be obtained from the same equation. The answer is E

Section 1C

Question 37: F

For this question statements 1 and 3 are correct. In statement 1, both O^{2-} and Mg^{2+} have 10 electrons and so both have the same electron configuration; 2,6. In statement 2, sulphur has $(32 - 16)$ 16 neutrons, whilst oxygen has $(18 - 8)$ 10 neutrons – so sulphur does not have double the number of neutrons. In statement 3, there are 10 electrons in $^{16}_8O^{2-}$ and 8 electrons in $^{18}_8O$, the sum of which equals 18, which is the same number of electrons in $^{32}_{16}O$.

Question 38: B

Only reactions 1 and 3 show oxidation. In reaction 1, calcium is oxidised (oxidation state increases from 0 in Ca, to +2 in Ca^{2+}. In reaction 2, chlorine is reduced, not oxidised. In reaction 3, carbon is getting oxidised (oxidation state increases from +2 in CO to +4 in CO_2. In reaction 4, the oxidation states for all elements stays the same.

Question 39: H

All three statements are true for 1.00 mol dm^{-3} of ethanoic acid. Weak acids can turn blue litmus paper red. Weak acids also react with sodium carbonate to produce CO_2 (acid + carbonate → salt + CO_2 + H_2O). HCl and ethanoic acid both react with sodium hydroxide in a 1:1 ratio, so the name number of moles of both acids is required for the neutralisation reaction ($HCl/CH_3COOH + NaOH → Na(Cl/CH_3OO) + H_2O$).

Question 40: A

None of the answers actions can both increase the rate of reaction and increase product yield for both reactions Q and R. Increasing the pressure would increase the rate of reaction for both Q and R, but would only increase the product yield of Q where there are fewer moles of gas on the product side. Increasing the temperature would increase the rate of reaction for both Q and R, but would only increase the product yield of R which is an endothermic reaction. A suitable catalyst would increase the rate of reaction but have no effect on the position of equilibrium, so neither product yields would increase.

Question 41: D

From the chromatogram you can tell that only statement 3 is correct. Since the same solvent (mobile phase) and paper (stationary phase) is used in each sample you can directly compare the distance migrated by the spot in each sample. For example, the spot in R matches the distance of spot (i) so you can assume they are the same. Likewise, the spot in S matches spot (ii) and (iv). Using this knowledge, you can tell that sweet 1 contains both additives whilst sweet 2 contains additive S, not R. R_f = (distance moved by a spot)/(solvent font distance). Counting 1 square as 1, the solvent font = 10 in this chromatogram. Therefore, the R_f value for (iv) = 0.4, (iii) = 0.2 and (v) = 0.7. Thus, statement 2 is wrong as the R_f value is double, not half, and statement 3 is correct.

Question 42: C

From the atomic number, 20, you can deduce the electronic configuration, (2,8,8,2) which tells you element X is in group 2. Therefore, the ion charge of X would = +2. As oxygen has an oxidation state of -2, the simple oxide that forms is XO. Since, this is a metal (X) and a non-metal (O) interacting, the bonding is ionic. The character of the oxide is basic since the oxide dissociates in water to produce X^{2+} and OH^- ions, the latter which makes the solution alkaline.

Question 43: D
Ionic equations include the reacting particles of a balanced chemical equation. In this case, it includes the ions that are producing the precipitate copper(II) phosphate(V). The written precipitate informs us that the oxidation state of copper $= +2$, whilst for it is $+5$ for phosphorus. Since the oxidation state of oxygen is -2 we can work out that copper(II) phosphate(V) $= Cu_3(PO_4)_2$. Therefore, we need $3Cu^{2+}$ and $2PO_4^{3-}$ ions to produce the precipitate and so answer D is correct.

Question 44: D
Statement 1 is correct and is a redox reaction, as in the reaction,
$2Li + 2H_2O \rightarrow 2LiOH + H_2$,
lithium is oxidation state decreases from $0 \rightarrow +1$, whilst hydrogens oxidation state decreases from $+1 \rightarrow 0$. Statement 2 is incorrect since 7g of lithium equates to 1 mole of lithium, which from the balanced equation above, equates to 0.5 moles of hydrogen. 0.5 moles of H_2 (Mr=2) equals a mass of 1g, not 2g. Statement 3 is correct since the pH increases on production of the hydroxide ions. Statement 4 is correct as 14g of lithium equals 2 moles of lithium. 2 moles of lithium reacts with 2 moles of water. 2 moles of water equals 36g (2*18).

Question 45: D
During the electrolysis of aqueous copper(II) chloride Cu^{2+} ions are attracted to and reduced at the cathode (negative electrode) whilst Cl^- ions are attracted to and oxidised at the anode (positive electrode). The correct equations for the electrodes are those seen in answer D.

Question 46: E
57g of the compound is fluorine, therefore, $(81 - 57)$ 24g of the compound is carbon. You can then work out the number of moles of fluorine and carbon. Number of moles of $F = 57/19 = 3$ moles. Number of moles of $C = 24/12 = 2$ moles. The empirical formula mass is therefore C_2F_3. Since the relative molecular mass is double the empirical formula mass, the molecular formula $= C_4F_6$.

Question 47: E
To work out the change in volume in each reaction, you first need to work out the change in the number of moles of gas for each reaction. You can do this by working out the number of moles of the gas where the mass has been given and using the balanced equation to work out the number of moles of the other gases.
(1): 56g of CO (Mr=28) $= 56/28 = 2$ moles. Therefore, there are 3 moles of gaseous reactants (2 CO and 1 O_2) and 2 moles of gaseous products (2 CO_2). This is a difference of 1 mole $= 24$ dm^3.
(2): 36g of $H_2O = 36/18 = 2$ moles. Therefore, there are 2 moles of gaseous reactants (2 H_2O) and 3 moles of gaseous products (2 H_2 and 1 O_2). This is a difference of 1 mole $= 24$ dm^3.
(3): 30g of NO $= 30/30 = 1$ mole. Therefore, there are 1.5 moles of gaseous reactants (1 NO and 0.5 O_2) and 1 mole of gaseous product (1 NO_2). This is a difference of 0.5 moles $= 12$ dm^3.
Hence, only reactions 1 and 2 show a difference of 24 dm^3.

Question 48: D
This question tests your understanding of limiting reactants. From the equation you can see that 1 mole of Mg reacts with 1 mole of H_2SO_4 which produces 1 mole of the product H_2. In each experiment 1.2g of Mg is used which equates to (1.2/24) 0.05 moles. Line P shows the volume of H_2 produced when (40 cm^3 * 1.0 mol dm^{-3}) 0.04 moles of sulfuric acid is used. Therefore, the four squares in H_2 volume seen for Line P represent 0.04 moles of H_2 produced.

In experiment Q, (40 cm^3 * 2.0 mol dm^{-3}) 0.08 moles of sulfuric acid are used. Since, Mg is now the limiting reactant, only 0.05 moles of sulfuric acid can react producing 0.05 moles of H_2, representing 5 squares – so the answer is line 2.

In experiment R, (40 cm^3 * 0.5 mol dm^{-3}) 0.02 moles of sulfuric acid are used. Now, sulfuric acid is the limiting reactant so only 0.02 moles of sulfuric acid and Mg can react producing 0.02 moles of H_2, representing 2 squares – so the answer is line 5.

Question 49: E

This question involves calculating the bond energy of nitrogen. You can either do this precisely using the values given or more easily through rounding the values. Either approach requires you to create the initial equation to work out the bond energy knowing that bond breaking is endothermic so positive and bond making is exothermic so negative;

Nitrogen bond + 3(H-H) – 6(N-H) = -93

Rounding the values gives the following calculation

Nitrogen bond + 3(450) – 6(400) = -100

N bond + 1350 – 2400 = -100

N bond + 1450 -2400 = 0

N bond = 950 → answer is 945 kJ mol^{-1}

Question 50: B

Statement 1 is correct as the negative electrode is where ions gain electrons and get reduced.

To test statement 2 you first need balanced equations for the half reactions for both reactions;

Molten lead(II) chloride

Negative: $Pb^{2+} + 2e^- \rightarrow Pb$ Positive: $2Cl^- \rightarrow Cl_2 + 2e^-$

Brine

Negative: $2H_2O + 2e^- \rightarrow H_2 + 2OH^-$ Positive: $2Cl^- \rightarrow Cl_2 + 2e^-$

Both reactions produce 1 mole of Cl_2 for every mole of product forming at the negative electrode. 20g of Pb (20g/207) equates to ~0.1 mole of Pb, thus ~0.1 moles of Cl_2, whereas 20g of H_2 (20g/2) equates to 10 moles of H_2 and 10 moles of Cl_2. Therefore, the volume of Cl_2 gas produced is not the same for the two reactions. Statement 3 is incorrect since hydrogen is produced at the negative electrode during the electrolysis of brine and is not a metal.

Question 51: A

At position Y, the graph changes from a linear increase to being stationary as the mass of zinc. Thus, position Y marks the mass when the mass of zinc is no longer the limiting reactant. At Y therefore, the mass of zinc must react fully with 50 cm^3 of 0.100 mol dm^{-3} of silver nitrate solution. The number of moles of silver nitrate solution = 50 cm^3 * 0.100 mol dm^{-3} = 0.005 moles. From the balanced equation provided you can see that 2 moles of silver nitrate react with 1 mole of Zn, therefore, 0.005/2 = 0.0025 moles of Zn are reacting at position Y. 0.0025 moles of Zn, given its A_r of 65 equates to 0.163g (65*0.0025).

Question 52: D

The easiest way to solve this question is to first draw a number line to work out how far the isotopes 62.93 and 64.93 are from 63.55

62.93----------------63.55----------------------64.93

      ←--0.62-------→←--------1.38--------→

Therefore, the ratio of isotopes ^{63}Cu:^{65}Cu in the sample= 1.38:0.62. To work out the percentage of the isotopes we need the sum of the ratio to equal 1. Currently the sum is 1.38 + 0.62 = 2. Therefore, to get to 1, divide the ratio by 2 to give a ratio of 0.69:0.31. The percentage of ^{63}Cu is then 69% and for ^{65}Cu 31% which matches answer D.

Question 53: C

8.8g of carbon dioxide = 0.2 moles (8.8g/44). From the balanced equation you can tell that 0.2 moles of carbon dioxide is produced when 0.2 moles of $CaCO_3$ reacts with 0.4 moles of HCl.

The Mr of $CaCO_3$ = 100, therefore at least (0.2*100) 20g of $CaCO_3$ is required to produce 8.8g of carbon dioxide. Similarly, answer B can be eliminated since the number of moles of HCl is not enough to produce 8.8g of carbon dioxide.

A greater mass of $CaCO_3$ and more moles of HCl will produce carbon dioxide faster, thus you can narrow the options down to C or E. Although the number of moles of both reactants are the same for C and E, C has a smaller volume (thus higher pressure) and so would react to produce carbon dioxide faster than the conditions in E.

Question 54: D

0.05 nanometres = 0.05 $x10^{-9}$. The radius of the nucleus is therefore 0.05 $x10^{-9}$/ 50 000 = 0.01 $x10^{-13}$. 0.01 $x10^{-13}$ = 1 $x10^{-15}$ = 1 fm.

Section 1D

Question 55: A

Oxygen debt refers to the amount of oxygen required to oxidise the lactic acid that accumulates during anaerobic respiration to carbon dioxide and water. Statement 3 is incorrect since fit people are better able at carrying out physical exercise and whose pulse rate are more likely to return to normal after exercising faster. From the graph, student Q lactic acid concentration returns to normal before student P so it could be argued that student Q is fitter. Hence, student Q repays the oxygen debt faster than student P so statement 1 is incorrect. As student P produces more lactic acid, more oxygen is required to oxidise the lactic acid and so student P has a higher oxygen debt than student Q. Therefore, statement 2 is incorrect.

Question 56: B

Only ~1% of the human genome codes for proteins. The rest of the genome contains non-coding elements and are important for maintaining the structure of the genome or have a function that we are not yet certain of. Of the small percentage of the genome with a known function, more mutations are likely to be harmful than beneficial since deletion/substitution mutations are more likely to alter a gene sequence resulting in the non-functional production of proteins than a beneficial mutation. However, majority of mutations will have no effect at all. Pie chart B is the only chart that represents these facts.

Question 57: C

The frequency of occurrence refers to the percentage of quadrats that contain at least one occurrence of a particular species.
Species X: 9 quadrats/10 quadrats have at least one individual. So the frequency is 0.9.
Species Y: 7/10 quadrats have at least one individual. So the frequency is 0.7.
Species Z: 8/10 quadrats have at least one individual. So the frequency is 0.8.
Species Y therefore is the lowest value.

Question 58: E

Stem cells are undifferentiated cells. The difference between a stem cell and an epithelial cell from the same healthy female is not due to a different genome, but due to different genes being expressed. Therefore, like female epithelial cells, the stem cells will also contain two X chromosomes and the same genes. Therefore, statements 1 and 2 are correct. Statement 3 is incorrect since when a stem cell divides only 2 cells are produced, not 3.

Question 59: A

The key of this question is to notice that they have highlighted the word 'always'. All three statements might result in an increase in the size of a population, but not always. This is because there are many variables that influence population size that need to be considered. For example, in statement 2, whilst supplying more of the nutrient that is at the lowest concentration may reduce competition within a species allowing more of them to survive, it may also provide more food for predators or other competing species.

Question 60: D

Bacteria and fungi both have a cell wall, whilst animal cells do not. Bacteria, fungi and animals all use enzymes to release energy for cell processes. The membrane-bound structure that contains DNA refers to the nucleus – this is present in fungi and animals, but not bacteria.

Question 61: B

The primary consumer is the rat. The secondary consumer is the rattlesnake. Assuming 10% of the energy from each stage is passed on, then the rat receives 150,000 * 0.1 = 15,000 units of energy. Therefore, the rattlesnake receives 15,000 * 0.1 = 1,500 units of energy. So, the energy lost between the primary and secondary consumer = 15,000 – 1,500 = 13,500 units of energy.

Question 62: D

Statement 1 is incorrect since daughter cells are genetically identical in bacterial cell division. Statement 2 is incorrect since the process of bacterial cell division is through binary fission, not mitosis. Statement 3 is correct – bacteria do not have a nucleus, so their chromosomes are found in the cytoplasm where replication must occur before the bacterium divides.

Question 63: G

Roots show a positive tropic response to gravity (as with the positive phototropism seen with shoots and light). Therefore, when the clinostat motor is running, the effect of gravity is lost so the root will grow straight – in this set up, horizontally. When the motor is stationary, the effect of gravity will be felt by the root, which as it shows positive tropism to gravity will grow down.

Question 64: B

One of the sons in the family tree has the condition. Since the condition is recessive, the son must have received one allele for the condition from each parent. Therefore, the mother has a genotype Aa (when A=normal allele, a=condition allele). This means that both daughters have Aa as their genotype.

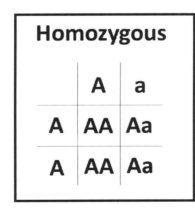
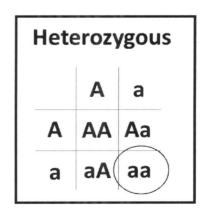

By drawing out punnet squares for both situations in the table no children have the condition if the father is homozygous dominant (AA), whilst ¼ of the children have the condition is the father is heterozygous. Since the probability of a daughter is ½, the probability that the first child will be a girl who has the condition when (i) the father is homozygous dominant = 0*1/2 = 0, and (ii) the father is heterozygous = ¼* ½ = 1/8 = 0.125.

Question 65: C
Water moves via osmosis from regions of high water potential to regions of lower water potential. The concentrated sucrose solution has a very low water potential whilst the water the glass tube is suspended in has the highest possible water potential. Therefore, water will move through the partially permeable membrane into the glass tube down the water potential gradient causing a linear increase in the height of level P.

Question 66: C
Mitosis is the process of cell division that involves one round of cell division after the genome has been replicated. Therefore, it maintains the copy number of the genome. Only stages 1 and 4 maintain the copy number, in this case, the copy number, n, is maintained.

Question 67: F
The number of floating discs is being used as a measure of the rate photosynthesis. This is valid since photosynthesis results in the production of oxygen. As gas is less dense than the liquid solution, the discs will float when sufficient oxygen has accumulated. Therefore, the sooner the disc floats, the greater the rate of photosynthesis. Statement 1 is correct as all 16 discs float first for the dark green leaf discs. This is due to there being more chloroplasts in the darker green leaves. Statement 2 is incorrect since at 5 minutes, 25% of the light green discs are floating, whilst 75% (12/16) remain at the bottom of the beaker. Statement 3 is correct as the reciprocal would mean that a longer time for the discs to float would give a smaller value as a measure of the relative rate of photosynthesis, which makes sense, as it would take longer for sufficient oxygen to accumulate.

Question 68: H
You can tell from the table that changing the concentration of amylase alters the diameter of the clear area so factor 3 is correct. Factor 1 and 3 are also both correct since pH and temperature can alter the rate of the reaction catalysed by amylase. Amylase is an enzyme and is a protein and so at high temperatures and extreme pH levels can become denatured preventing starch from being broken down. This would result in a decrease in diameter of the clear area that forms.

Question 69: A
Plant shoots show positive phototropism which means that they grow towards the light source. Therefore, shoots P and R, that have the tip exposed, grow towards the light source as auxin accumulates on the shaded side of the root tip so the distance between the top of each shoot and the light source decreases over time. This is represented in graph 1. Shoot Q, without a shoot tip, does not show a phototropic response and so the distance between the light source and the shoot will not change over time.

Question 70: H
The mutations could be deletion or substitution. First identify where the mutations occur;
ATG **X**GA GAC ATG TTA AGG T**X**G GAC CCC CGA GTC
The maximum number of triplets is 11, so the sequence could code for 11 amino acids. However, if the mutation at position 20 changed G to A, so that the codon is TAG, then it would now code for a stop codon and so the sequence could be only 6 amino acids long. So, statement 1 is correct. Statement 2 is also correct – if the mutation at position 4 changed C for A, the triplet would still code for arginine so the protein sequence would remain the same. Statement 3 is correct since 7 different amino acids could be present if the mutation at position 4 changes from C to G coding for Glycine. The sequence would be; Met, Gly, Asp, Met, Leu, Arg, Trp, Asp, Pro, Arg, Val.

Question 71: C
Statement 1 is incorrect since it was the oxygen required for survival that was the dependent variable (the one being measured) and so a better conclusion would be; as the temperature of the water increased, greater levels of oxygen were required for survival. Statement 2 is correct as you can see from graph 2, the dissolved oxygen level decreases at higher temperatures. Statement 3 is incorrect graph 1 shows the oxygen levels required for survival, it does not measure oxygen uptake. Indeed, oxygen dissolves more poorly at higher temperatures as evident from graph 2.

Question 72: F

Two heterozygotes could have the genotype Aa, with allele A representing the dominant phenotype. The expected phenotypic ratio from the monohybrid cross;

	A	a
A	AA	aA
a	Aa	aa

AA, Aa and aA would have the dominant phenotype, whilst aa would have the recessive phenotype. The expected phenotypic ratio is therefore 3:1.

The fact that the resulting offspring had a 2:1 phenotypic ratio could therefore be explained by a low number of offspring since the larger the number of offspring the more likely the actual phenotypic ratio would match the expected. Statement 1 is therefore correct. Statement 2 is wrong since if the recessive condition was lethal prior to birth you would expect the ratio to be greater than 3:1, not less (2:1). Hence, if homozygous dominant (AA) was lethal before birth, this could explain the 2:1 ratio.

Section 1E

Question 73: E
The denominator of the fraction can be factorised to $2(3-\sqrt{3})$ and then the fraction can be multiplied by $(3+\sqrt{3})/(3+\sqrt{3})$. In this way the dominator is reduced to $2(9-3)$ and the numerator to $(3+\sqrt{3})^2$. When the square is performed in the numerator, the fraction is left in terms multiples of 3 and the expression can be reduced to answer E.

Question 74: B
The sum of moment of forces on the left is equal to the sum of forces on the right, before moving the load. Therefore, the balance of moments before moving the load is used to calculate the moment created by the weight of the load. Because such moment remains constant before and after moving the load, this is used on the equilibrium of moments after moving the load to calculate the new distance of the counterweight. The answer is B

Question 75: C
The key to this question is the unit circle. It is possible to rearrange the equations to that $\sin(x)= -½$ and $\cos(2x)= ½$. Therefore, $x=(7/6)\pi$ or $210°$ and $2x= (7/3)\pi$. No other smaller value of x between 0 and $(7/6)\pi$ can produce $\sin(x)= -½$ but $x= \pi/6$ and $(5/6)\pi$ produces $\cos(2x)= ½$. The answer is C

Question 76: C
A moving object with zero resultant force keeps moving at the same speed and direction. Therefore, the resultant force must be zero to preserve the speed of the aircraft, otherwise the aircraft would be accelerating. The answer is C

Question 77: B
The equation can be rearrange to $(3^{(2x+1)})/3^x=6$. Then, the properties of the exponent can be used to simplify the fraction and $\log_3$ is applied to both sides of the equation. Therefore, the answer is B

Question 78: D
The speed is equal to the magnitude of the velocity, which is calculated by the suvat equation: $v^2=u^2+2as$ (v=final velocity, u=initial velocity, a= acceleration and s=distance). Then, the answer is D.

Question 79: D

The first derivative of the equation is a quadratic equation whose roots provide the local maximum and the minima of the cubic equation. Therefore, when the derivative is set to zero and the values provided of x are substituted, a two linear equations are obtained. The system of equation can be solve and the values of p and q are obtained. The answer is D

Question 80: F
As the system is balanced, the friction of the rough surface to keep the system in balance and the force meter would measure the down force provided only by the hanging mass. Therefore, the answer is F.

Question 81: E
The derivative of y is equal to $n(a+bx)^{n-1}d(a+bx)/dx$. Once the derivative is obtained, the expression for $(2+3x)^5$ is displayed using Pascal triangle to obtain the coefficients for the term $(3x)^3 2^2$. The product of the coefficients with all the numerical values, including 6 and 3 obtained from the derivative, leads to the answer: E.

Question 82: A
The final kinetic energy of the apple and the initial potential energy of the apple can be calculated with the values provided and the respective equations. Therefore, the work done is equal to the difference between both energies. The answer is A.

Question 83: A
The sum to infinity in a geometric progression can be described by the equation $a_1/(1-r)$ where a_1 and r are the first term and the common ratio, respectively. Therefore, the values of a_1 and r can be substitute into the equation and this can be rearrange and simplify to $\frac{1}{2}=\sin(2x)$. If $\sin(30)=0.5$, then $2x=30°=(1/6)\pi$ in the range from 0 to $\pi/2$. However, this will be true in the range of π to 2π at $\pi+x$ and $(3/2)\pi-x$. The answer is A.

Question 84: A
The key to solve the question is the equation of potential and kinetic energy. The total kinetic energy of the stone transformed to potential energy when the stone is lost all its velocity. Then, the equations of energy are used to calculate the height of the stone at zero velocity and again to calculate the final velocity. Once such velocity is obtained the time can be calculated using the suvat equations. The answer is A

Question 85: E
The equation for the sequence is used to calculate the values of u_2-u_4 such as:
$$u_2 = p(2) + 3$$
$$u_3 = p(2p + 3) + 3$$
$$u_4 = p(2p^2 + 3p + 3) + 3 = -7$$
$$2p^3 + 3p^2 + 3p + 10 = 0$$
The cubic equation is solved with only one real root p=-2. Then, the values for u_2 and u_3 are obtained using the new value of p and finally the value of the sum. The answer is C.

Question 86: B
If the work done by the force of the bowstring is equal to the kinetic energy of the bow, then the area under the force-distance graph is the kinetic energy. Once the arrow loss its velocity, all the kinetic energy is transform in potential energy. Then, the maximum height of the arrow can be calculated. The answer is B

Question 87: B
The cubic equation on the denominator can be factorised in (x-1)(x-1)(x-4). This mean that any negative number would produce a negative result in the numerator and denominator, then the fraction would be positive and bigger than zero. Equally, the factorised denominator indicates that any number from zero to 4 would lead to fraction lower or equal than zero. Therefore, the answer is A.

Question 88: H

When the book slides a constant speed the resultant force and acceleration are equal to zero and therefore, the component of the weight (mg*sin(20°)) and the friction (μ*mg*cos(20°)) are equal but opposite. Then, the value of the coefficient of friction (μ) is obtained as tan(20°). At 25° there is a resultant force and acceleration (F=m*a) which is equal to the sum of the component of the weight (mg*sin(20°)) and the friction (μ*mg*cos(20°)). Therefore, the substitution of the value of the coefficient of friction provides the answer: H

Question 89: E

The product of the gradient of two perpendicular lines must be equal to -1. Therefore:
$$m_1 * m_2 = -1$$
$$(2p^2 - p) * (p - 2) = -1$$
$$2p^3 - 5p^2 + 2p + 1 = 0$$
The cubic equation is solve with roots of p=1, 3/4±√17/4. Because √17/4≈1 then p≈3/4+1≈1.75. The answer is B.

Question 90: C

The area under the graph is the impulse and it is equal to the change in the momentum of the ball. Because the ball has an initial momentum opposite to the momentum leaving the racket, the impulse is equal to the sum of momentums. Therefore, the momentum of the ball as it leaves the racket is equal to the impulse minus the initial momentum. The answer is B.

Section 2

Question P1

a) For relatively small deformations of an object, the displacement or size of deformation (x) is directly proportional to the deforming force (F).

An equation must be written such as:

$$F = kx$$

Elastic potential energy (EPE) is the potential energy store as a result of a deformation of an elastic object and it is equal to the work done (W) against the bonds between the atoms of the material.

$$EPE = \frac{kx^2}{2}$$

b) The force applied to the rope can be obtained by using the mass of Alice then F=mg=(50)(9.81)=490.5N. Then it's possible to calculate the rope's elastic constant (k) and the EPE using the equations described above:

$$k = \frac{F}{x} = \frac{490.5}{26 - 10} = 30.65 Nm^{-1}$$
$$EPE = \frac{kx^2}{2} = \frac{(30.65)(26 - 10)^2}{2} = 3924\,J$$

c) The bungee jump can be described in three steps:

1) Free fall. Alice accelerate downwards with constant acceleration of g=9.81ms^{-2} and increasing speed described by v^2=2gx.
2) Stretching of the rope. At a distance of x=10m the rope is starting to stretch, which creates and upward force of tension that reduced the downward acceleration until the weight equals the tension and the accelerations becomes equal to zero.
3) Lowest point. At this point the tension exceeds Alice's weight and her speed decreases due to the upward acceleration. Then, her speed reduces to zero at the maximum tension of the rope and lowest point of her fall.

d) Because the only data know about system correspond to the Alice's potential energy and the elastic properties of the rope. Then, the velocity can be calculated using the conservation of energy between the Alice's kinetic energy (KE) and EPE of the rope at 15m, and the initial potential energy (PE).

$$EPE + KE = PE = \frac{1}{2}k(x - 10)^2 + \frac{1}{2}mv^2 = mgx$$
$$\frac{1}{2}(30.65)(15 - 10)^2 + \frac{1}{2}(50)v^2 = (50)(9.81)(15)$$
$$383.13 + 25v^2 = 7357.5$$
$$v = \sqrt{\frac{7357.5 - 383.13}{25}} = 16.7 ms^{-1}$$

e) At instantaneous rest, Alice's speed (v) and kinetic energy (KE) are equal to zero. Therefore, the balance of energy reduces to:

$$EPE = PE = \frac{1}{2}k(x - 10)^2 = mgx$$
$$\frac{1}{2}(30.65)(x - 10)^2 = (50)(9.81)(x)$$
$$15.33x^2 - 797x + 100 = 0$$

This is a quadratic expression with roots of 2 and 50. Where only the 50m result make physical sense. Therefore, the result is x=50m

f) The maximum speed is achieved when the tension balance the weight. At this point, the resultant force and the acceleration are equal to zero. Therefore, the balance of forces can be written as:

$$F = W$$
$$kx = mg$$
$$x = \frac{mg}{k} = \frac{(50)(9.81)}{30.65} = 16m$$

However, the initial 10m of the rope must be included so the total value of x is x=16+10=26m.

g) Alice experiences the maximum acceleration in the upward direction after reaching the bottom of the fall. This upward acceleration and corresponding upward force (F_R) are the result of the greater tension force than weight. This means that the balance of forces can provide the acceleration by:

$$F_R = F - W$$
$$ma = k(x - 10) - mg$$
$$a = \frac{k(x - 10) - mg}{m} = \frac{(30.65)(40) - (50)(9.81)}{50} = 14.71ms^{-2}$$

h) The key for this question is the description made in c). During free fall, Alice grabs speed at constant acceleration. After 10m, the tension produces a deceleration (or upward acceleration) until Alice reaches the lowest point at 50m and the upward acceleration becomes a=14.71ms^{-2}.

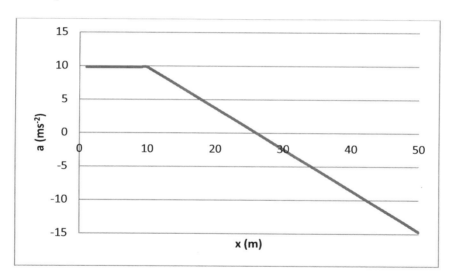

Question P2

a) The light that passes through the slits diffracts and therefore they spread out as they pass the slits. The two spread out beams interfere constructively and destructively when they travel in and out of phase, respectively. This produces a band of fringes made on the screen. This diffraction experiment proved the wave nature of light.

b)

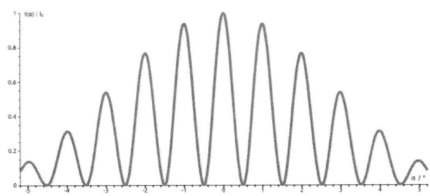

Each fringe is of the same size and equally spaced with the maximum peak at the centre of the graph with x=0. This graph must be a smooth sinusoidal curve.

c) The path difference is how much further ray 2 has travel compared with ray 1. Such difference must be at least a wavelength difference and can be describe with the triangle showed in the figure. (Perpendicular line must be shown)

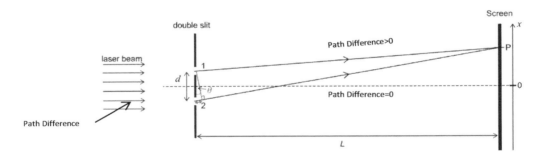

d) The previous diagram shows that the split separation, the path difference and the perpendicular forms a triangle of angle θ. Therefore, for the first minimum (destructive interference) the path difference is λ/2, and then:

$$\sin(\theta) = \frac{\lambda/2}{d}$$

Because the distance travelled by the second ray, the distance to the screen (L) and distance of the projection in the screen (x) forms a triangle, it is possible to obtain an equation based on trigonometry. If the angle of such triangle is the same as the one formed by the path difference (θ), and because at small angles sin(θ)≈ tan(θ) =x/L, then:

$$\frac{dx}{L} = \frac{\lambda}{2}$$

$$x = \frac{\lambda L}{2d}$$

e) At point P the amplitude for each light wave is

$$A_1 = A_0 cos\left(\omega t - \frac{2\pi(L - \Delta L)}{\lambda}\right) = A_0 cos(B)$$
$$A_2 = A_0 cos\left(\omega t - \frac{2\pi(L + \Delta L)}{\lambda}\right) = A_0 cos(C)$$

Then the total amplitude:

$$A = A_1 + A_2 = A_0 cos(B) + A_0 cos(C) = A_0[cos(B) + cos(C)]$$
$$A = 2A_0 \cos\left(\frac{B - C}{2}\right)\cos\left(\frac{B + C}{2}\right)$$

$$A = 2A_0 \cos\left(\frac{\omega t - \frac{2\pi(L - \Delta L)}{\lambda} - \omega t + \frac{2\pi(L + \Delta L)}{\lambda}}{2}\right)\cos\left(\frac{\omega t - \frac{2\pi(L + \Delta L)}{\lambda} + \omega t - \frac{2\pi(L + \Delta L)}{\lambda}}{2}\right)$$

$$A = 2A_0 \cos\left(\frac{2\pi\Delta L}{\lambda}\right)\cos\left(\omega t - \frac{2\pi L}{\lambda}\right)$$

Therefore

$$F = 2A_0$$
$$G = \frac{2\pi\Delta L}{\lambda}$$
$$H = \omega t - \frac{2\pi L}{\lambda}$$

f) If t=0 and A=0. This means that the value of each cosine is zero. Values of 90° and 270° or π/2 and 3π/4 produces cosines equal to zero. Therefore:

$$\frac{2\pi\Delta L}{\lambda} = \frac{\pi}{2}, \quad and \quad \frac{2\pi\Delta L}{\lambda} = \frac{3\pi}{2}$$

$$\Delta L = \frac{\lambda}{4}, \quad and \quad \Delta L = \frac{3\lambda}{4}$$

g) Note that the equation in d) can be used to calculate the wavelength, taking care of the units used:
$$\lambda = \frac{2dx}{L} = \frac{(2)(0.015)(0.1)}{5} = 0.0006mm = 600nm$$
Because the value of ΔL was established in f), then:
$$L = \frac{\lambda}{4} = \frac{600}{4} = 150nm$$

Question B1a

(i)   Plant (note the nucleus, cell wall and vacuole)

(ii)   Bacterial (note, there is no nucleus)

Question B1b

High resolution and magnification with an electron microscope enables organelles and other structural features to be recognised.

Question B1c

(i)   Magnification = Measured size/Actual size

        Measured = 3 cm, Actual = 20 μm

        Magnification = $3 \times 10^{-2}/20 \times 10^{-6}$

        = 1500x

(ii)   Magnification = Measured size/Actual size

        Measured = 3 cm, Actual = 0.5 μm

        Magnification = $3 \times 10^{-2}/0.5 \times 10^{-6}$

        = 60 000x

Question B1d

Ribosomes are a protein/RNA complex that catalyse translation required for protein synthesis. Proteins are present in mitochondria and chloroplast, suggesting that Ribosomes evolved first. Moreover, Ribosomes are present in both chloroplast and mitochondria. Mitochondria are present in all eukaryotes, whilst chloroplasts are only present in algae. This suggests mitochondria arose before chloroplast.

Question B1e

Percentage = (volume of the nucleus/volume of the cell)*100

= $[(4/3\pi R_n^3)/(4/3\pi R_c^3)]*100$, where radius of nucleus (R_n) = ~20 μm and radius of cell (R_c) = ~50 μm

= $(R_n^3/R_c^3)*100$

= $(20^3/50^3)*100$ = 6.4% (values from 6-20% are accepted)

Question B1f

Fig (i) = plant, Fig(ii) = bacteria

DNA replication

For plants DNA replication occurs in the nucleus, whilst it occurs in the cytoplasm of bacteria.

Transcription

For plants transcription occurs in the nucleus, whilst it occurs in the cytoplasm of bacteria. This allows bacteria to couple transcription with translation/protein synthesis, whilst for plants the mRNA needs to be exported across the nuclear membrane to be translated.

Aerobic respiration

For plants aerobic respiration takes place in the mitochondria. Bacteria do not have mitochondria, so respiration occurs on the external membrane.

However, in both, glycolysis occurs in the cytoplasm

Photosynthesis

For plants photosynthesis takes place in the chloroplasts. Bacteria do not have chloroplasts, so photosynthesis occurs on the external membrane.

Others

More membranes in eukaryotes enables compartmentalisation of reactions and a greater surface area for reactions. E.g eukaryotes also possess membrane-bound lysosomes where protein degradation occurs, which are not present in bacteria.

Question B2a

    (i)   3- *Escherichia coli*

    (ii)   2- Strawberry

Question B2b

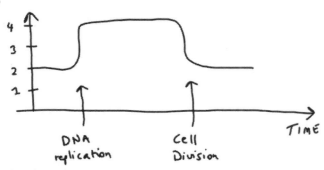

Mitosis;

Meiosis:

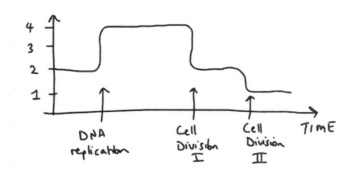

Question B2c

Humans have 23 sets of chromosomes, one paternally derived and one maternally derived. One of each copy is present in each gamete. There are essentially 23 events (for each homologous chromosome) of which the outcome is either maternal or paternal. The number of possible combinations is therefore $2^{23} = 8388608$.

Question B2di

¼. There is a probability of ½ that the female will pass on the disease-causing allele. There is a probability of ½ that the male will pass on the disease-causing allele. Therefore, the probability the child will have the disease (have two copies of the disease-causing allele) = probability get the disease-causing allele from the male <u>and</u> female = ½ * ½ = ¼.

Question B2dii

Given above there is a probability that the child will have the disease of ¼. The probability that a child won't have the disease = 1- ¼ = ¾.

The probability of a male = ½

Therefore, the probability the child is male and does not have the disease = ½ * ¾ = 3/8.

Question B2e

   (i)   Different mechanisms of reproduction

          Asexual reproduction:

          Binary fission (bacteria) – genetically identical, no variation (besides mutations). Note generation can be generated in bacteria through conjugation and uptake of DNA from their environment

          Mitosis – genetically identical, no variation (besides mutations)

          Budding (yeast) – genetically identical, no variation (besides mutations)

          Sexual reproduction:

          Meiosis – variation from independent assortment, recombination and random fertilisation

          Both asexual/sexual reproduction variation influenced by mutation rate and the environment

   (ii)   How variation affects the likelihood of survival

          Variation leads to differential survival so that the best adapted survive to pass on their characteristics

          Marks for specific examples

          If sexual organisms cannot adapt quickly enough they may be prone to extinction

Question C1ai

$2Li + H_2 \rightarrow 2LiH$

Question C1aii

Ionic. First clue is the presence of a metal and a non-metal in LiH. LiH also has a high melting point and conducts when molten, which are features of ionic compounds.

Question C1aiii

Combined hydrogen always has an oxidation state of $+1$, except when it is in a metal hydride, as is the case here where the oxidation state is -1. Lithium therefore is $+1$. To form lithium and hydrogen, they must be reduced and oxidised, respectively, Therefore, lithium appears at the cathode and hydrogen appears at the anode.

Question C1b

$4LiH + AlCl_3 \rightarrow LiAlH_4 + 3LiCl$

Question C1c

To determine the formula for substance B, it is expected that calculations are conducted using the information given, as opposed to trying to fill in a formula with leftover atoms.

Lithium aluminium hydride is the only reactant. It has a $M_r = (6.941 + 26.98 + 4(1.008)) = 37.953$. 3.8g were heated. The number of moles of $LiAlH_4 = 3.8g/37.953 = 0.1$ moles.

1.8g of Al was produced. The number of moles of Al produced $= 1.8g/26.98 = 0.067$

Considering the reactant, the likely flammable gas is hydrogen (the hint was that the question says the gas is flammable). 2.4 dm^3 of H_2 was produced. Given 1 mole of a gas $= 24$ dm^3, 0.1 moles of H_2 was produced.

The number of moles of H_2 matches the number of moles $LiAlH_4$ which $=0.1$ moles. To get the molar ratio of the reactants and products divide the number of moles by 0.067 to give a ratio 1.5:1 and then multiply by 2. The molar ratio is therefore 3 moles of $LiAlH_4$ decomposes to give 2 moles of Al and 3 moles of H_2;

$3LiAlH_4 \rightarrow 2Al + 3H_2 +$ substance B. Given this, substance B must be Li_3AlH_4.

Question C1d

Intermediates of electrophilic addition reactions are always such that a secondary carbocation forms in preference to a primary carbocation.

Given the reaction steps above, the structures R and Y are as follows where deuterium is added at the second stage;

Question C1ei

There are four isomers with the formula C_3H_5D

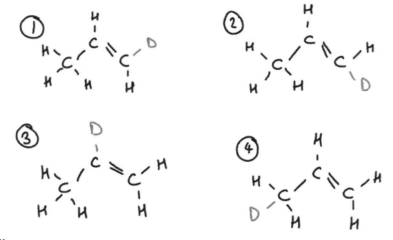

Question C1eii

2,2-dideuterated propane has both deuterium atoms attached to the second carbon. From the answers in question C1d, the only structure with deuterium attached to the second carbon is structure Y. Therefore, the reagents to get 2,2-dideuterated propane are HCl followed by $LiAlD_4$. To get the second deuterium attached to the second carbon of propane, the isomer of propene Z with deuterium attached to carbon 2 (structure 3 above) must be used. The reaction is as follows;

Question C2a

N=3, $Z_+ = 2$, $Z_- = 1$

Lattice enthalpy = $\dfrac{-1.07 \times 10^5 \times 3 \times 2 \times 1}{(73+133)}$

= -3116.5 kJ mol⁻¹

Question C2b

N=4, $Z_+ = 3$, $Z_- = 1$

Lattice enthalpy = $\dfrac{-1.07 \times 10^5 \times 4 \times 3 \times 1}{(54+133)}$

= -6866.3 kJ mol⁻¹

Question C2c

The oxidation state of copper in CuF_2 is +2

The oxidation state of copper in CuF_3 is +3

In this reaction, copper is oxidised. However, the oxidation state of fluorine decreases from 0 in F_2 to -1 in CuF_3. Fluorine is reduced. The reaction is therefore a redox reaction.

Question C2d

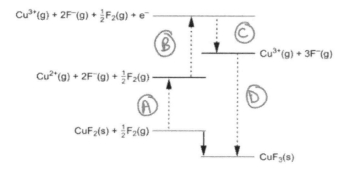

The enthalpy change A is the reverse lattice enthalpy for CuF_2 = -(-3116.5)

The enthalpy change B involves the oxidation of Cu^{2+} to Cu^{3+} which is provided in the question as 3555.

The enthalpy change C is for the reduction of fluorine which is given in the question as -540. As ½ a mole of fluorine is reduced, the enthalpy change is (-540/2) = -270.

The enthalpy change D is the lattice enthalpy for the formation of CuF_3, calculated in part b as -6866.3.

The overall enthalpy change = 3116.5 + 3555 - 270 – 6866.3 = -464.8 kJ mol⁻¹.

Question C2e

Start by constructing a diagram similar to that in part d for the new reaction. Note that out of the two M^{2+}, one if oxidised to M^{3+} to eventually form MF_3, whilst the other is reduced to M^+ to eventually form MF. The appropriate Hess's law cycle can be seen below;

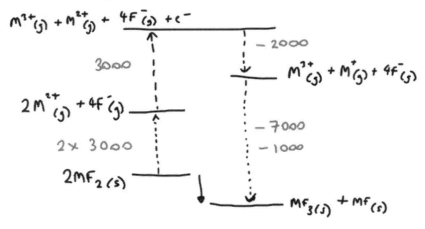

The overall enthalpy change = 6000 + 3000 − 2000 − 7000 − 1000 = -1000 kJ mol⁻¹

END OF PAPER

NSAA SECTION 1 (2018)

Part A Mathematics (All candidates)

Question 1: E

It is easiest to present the information from the question in a table:

	Men	Women	**Total**
Passed 1st attempt			*167*
Failed 1st attempt		*143*	
Total	*300*	*200*	

The number of women who passed their first attempt can be calculated as total women – women who failed $= 200 - 143 = 57$

The number of men who passed their first attempt is total people who passed 1st attempt – women who passed 1st attempt $= 167 - 57 = \mathbf{110}$

Question 2: B

It may help to draw a diagram:

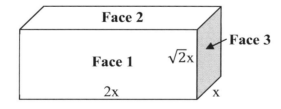

Volume $= (2x)(\sqrt{2}x)(x) = 2\sqrt{2}x^3$

There are 6 faces in total, but 3 different proportions, so surface area is:

$$2(2x)(\sqrt{2}x) + 2(2x)(x) + 2(\sqrt{2}x)(x) = 2x^2(2\sqrt{2} + 2 + \sqrt{2})$$

Volume = 2 x S.A

$$2\sqrt{2}x^3 = 4x^2\left(3\sqrt{2} + 2\right)$$

$$2\sqrt{2}x^3 - 12\sqrt{2}x^2 - 8x^2 = 0 \qquad \text{(factorise out } x^2\text{)}$$

It is possible to disregard the $x^2 = 0$ soln. *in this case* because this is the solution for the cuboid having no dimensions, no volume and no surface area. It is not always possible to disregard this solution – take care not to 'divide' by x without good reason, as it may cause solutions to be 'lost'.

$$2\sqrt{2}x - 12\sqrt{2} - 8 = 0$$

Rearranging for x gives: $x = \frac{12\sqrt{2}+8}{2\sqrt{2}} = 6 + \frac{8}{2\sqrt{2}} = 6 + 2\sqrt{2}$

Question 3: H

Find gradient of line joining the two points in terms of p using $m = \frac{\Delta y}{\Delta x}$:

$$m = \frac{2p - (p-1)}{(1-p) - p} = \frac{p+1}{1-2p}$$

Rearrange the equation of the line to $y = mx + c$ form, to find m:

$$y = -\frac{2}{3}x - \frac{1}{3} \qquad m = -\frac{2}{3}$$

'Parallel' means the two gradients are equal: $\frac{p+1}{1-2p} = -\frac{2}{3}$

Rearranging for p gives: $3(p+1) = -2(1-2p)$

$$3p + 3 = -2 + 4p$$

$$p = 5$$

Question 4: D

Let $QR = x$. Draw a labelled diagram:

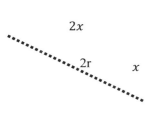

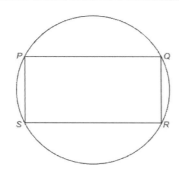

Use area to find 'x': $96 = (2x)(x)$

therefore $x = \sqrt{\dfrac{96}{2}} = \sqrt{48} = 4\sqrt{3}$

The Pythagorean theorem gives

$$(2r)^2 = (2x)^2 + (x)^2$$

$$4r^2 = \left(8\sqrt{3}\right)^2 + \left(4\sqrt{3}\right)^2 = 240$$

Rearranging for 'r' gives: $r = \sqrt{60} = 2\sqrt{15}$

Question 5: C

Define variables: T = temperate (C), b = expected number of bottles sold

Form general expression $b \propto T^2$ and equation $b = kT^2$.

Form specific equations with information $64 = k(16^2)$ and solve for the constant of proportionality, $k = \dfrac{1}{4}$.

Form the equation with the second set of information: $256 - 31 = \dfrac{1}{4}T^2$

Solve for T to get $T = 30°C$

Question 6: E

If the ratio of the heights is $4:5$, the ratio of volumes is $4^3:5^3$.

Multiplying 320 by a ratio of $64:125$ gives $\dfrac{320}{64}(125) = 625\text{cm}^3$.

Question 7: A

Mean = 'total of all numbers included' / 'number of numbers included'

Working through the information from the question step-by-step tells us:

1. The sum total of all the numbers $= np$
2. The sum total of two of the numbers $= 2q$

3. The sum total of all numbers (minus the two) = $(n-2)(10)$

These expressions can then be combined as $(1) = (2) + (3)$

$$np = 2q + 10(n-2)$$

giving $n(p-10) = 2q - 20$

so $n = \dfrac{2(q-10)}{p-10}$.

Question 8: C

Draw a diagram, labelling the y-intercepts.

Find P by substituting y=3x-23 into 5x+2y=20:

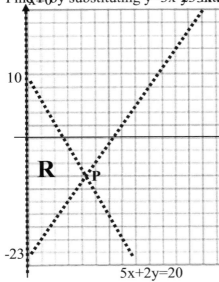

5x+2y=20

$5x + 2(3x - 23) = 20$

Rearranging give x=6 at P.

Use $area = \frac{1}{2}base \times height$ with

base equal to the distance along the

y-axis and height equal to the x-

coordinate of P.

$$Area = \frac{1}{2}(33)(6) = 99$$

Question 9: E

Length scale of $1:40$ means volume scale of $1^3 : 40^3$.

Convert mass of full-sized pillar into cm³: $12\pi \times 10^6$

Volume of model is therefore $\dfrac{full-sized\ pillar}{40^3} = \dfrac{12\pi \times 10^6}{64 \times 10^3} = \dfrac{3\pi \times 10^3}{16}$

Mass = density x volume $= \dfrac{4}{3} \cdot \dfrac{3\pi \times 10^3}{16} = \dfrac{1000\pi}{4} = 250\pi$

Question 10: D

The internal angles in a regular pentagon are all 108°. RSU is equilateral so ∠RSU=60°. Therefore ∠UST is 48°. As RSU is equilateral, SU=RS. All sides are the same length in a regular pentagon so SU=ST and therefore STU is isosceles. This means ∠STU can be found by:

$$\angle STU = \frac{1}{2}(180 - 48) = 66°$$

Question 11: C

The original price is p. An increase of 125% gives a price of 2.25p. A decrease of 40% gives a price of (0.6)(2.25p) = 1.35p = q.

Question 12: F

Form expressions, letting the first number be 'a' and the second, 'b':

$$0.8a = \frac{2b}{3}$$

This can be rearranged and simplified to give $1.2a = b$, or in the smallest whole number ratio, $x : y = 5 : 6$.

Therefore $x - y = -1$.

Question 13: E

Draw a diagram. Arrows show North (N).

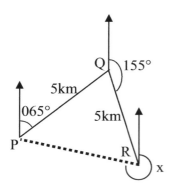

Using 'C-angles' (interior angles)

gives $\angle PQN = 180-65 = 115°$

and $\angle QRN = 180-155 = 25°$

At point Q the angle inside the

triangle is $360-155-115 = 90°$

Because PQR is isosceles, once the interior angle at Q is know the angles QPR and QRP can be calculated as $\frac{1}{2}(180-90) = 45°$

Finally, the bearing at R can be calculated as $360-25-45 = 290°$.

Question 14: A

First, use the probability given: $\frac{1}{3} = \frac{3n-1}{7n+5}$

This can be rearranged to find $n = 4$.

Then find the expression (in terms on 'n'), for the number of students choosing tomato sauce only. This may be clarified with a diagram:

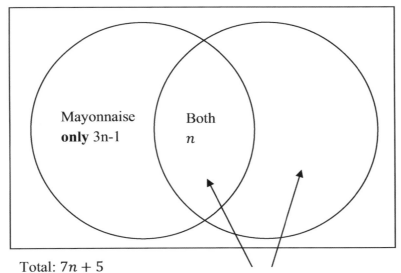

As total selecting tomato sauce = both + tomato sauce **only**, tomato sauce only = $3n + 1 - n = 2n + 1$.

The probability is therefore $\frac{2n+1}{7n+5} = \frac{2(4)+1}{7(4)+5} = \frac{9}{33} = \frac{3}{11}$.

Question 15: C

The alternate segment theorem means $\angle PST = \angle PQS = 75°$.

Because the angle between a tangent and a radius is a right angle, $\angle PSO = 90\text{-}75 = 15°$.

As PQS is isosceles $\angle QSP = \frac{1}{2}(180 - 75) = 52.5°$

$\angle QSO$ is therefore 52.5-15=37.5°.

Question 16: C

From the question: $h = b + 3$ and $area = \frac{hb}{2} = 14$

Combine as simultaneous equations to get $\frac{b(b+3)}{2} = 14$

This gives the quadratic $b^2 + 3b - 28 = 0$, the only appropriate solution of which is $b = 4$cm. Therefore $h = 7$cm.

Use Pythagoras on half the triangle: $s^2 = h^2 + \left(\frac{b}{2}\right)^2 = (b+3)^2 + \left(\frac{b}{2}\right)^2$

Combining terms gives: $s^2 = b^2 + 6b + 9 + \frac{1}{4}b^2 = \frac{5}{4}(4^2) + 6(4) + 9$

$s^2 = 53$ and so s must lie between 7 and 8.

Question 17: G

For the 1st term (n=1): $2 = p(1^2) + q = p + q$

For the 2nd term (n=2): $17 = p(2^2) + q = 4p + q$

Solve as simultaneous equations (subtract) to give: $3p = 15$ so $p = 5$ and $q = -3$.

Therefore $\frac{p-q}{p+q} = \frac{5-(-3)}{5+(-3)} = \frac{8}{2} = 4$

Question 18: B

The number of red sweets taken will always be exactly 1, because at the point that the child has taken one red sweet, they stop taking any more. Therefore, the options which give more green sweets than red are:

2, 3, 4, 5, or 6 green sweets followed by a red.

Considering the opposite scenarios (fewer green than red) reduces the number of calculations required:

The chance of the child picking a red sweet on their first pick is ½.

The chance of the child picking one green and then red is $\left(\frac{1}{2}\right)\left(\frac{6}{11}\right) = \frac{3}{11}$.

All remaining scenarios give more green than red, so the probability can be worked out as $1 - \frac{1}{2} - \frac{3}{11} = \frac{5}{22}$.

Part B: Physics (Optional)

Question 19: B

Alpha particles: atomic number (Z) = 2, mass number (A) = 4

Beta particles: atomic number (Z) = -1, mass number (A) = 0

Particles released: $5\alpha+2\beta$: $\Delta Z = 5(2) + 2(-1) = \mathbf{8}$

Question 20: B

Combining resistors in series using $R_{total} = R_1 + R_2 + R_3 = 30\Omega$

Calculate terminal voltage using $V = IR$. $V = 0.2(30) = 6V$

After removal of resistor R₃: $R_{total} = 27\Omega$

Calculate new current using $I = \frac{V}{R}$. $I = \frac{6}{27} = \frac{2}{9} \approx 0.22$

Question 21: G

UV has higher frequency, lower wavelength than visible light.

Convert minimum wavelength of visible light to frequency using $f = \frac{c}{\lambda}$. $f = \frac{3\times10^8}{400\times10^{-9}} = 7.5 \times 10^{14} Hz$

This is the minimum frequency of UV, as it is the boundary between UV and visible light.

Question 22: E

$$Average\ speed = \frac{total\ distance}{total\ time}$$

Find the total distance as the area under the graph (splitting into 3 sections: triangle, rectangle, triangle). Use $area\ of\ triangle = \frac{1}{2}bh$.

Area $= \frac{1}{2}(20)(12) + (80 - 20)(12) + \frac{1}{2}(120 - 80)(12) = 1020m$

Therefore average speed $\frac{1140}{120} = 9ms^{-1}$

Question 23: E

Energy transferred (J) = Power (W) x time (s):

$100 \times (10 \times 60) = 60,000J$ total energy transferred.

Efficiency of 5% means 95% of the energy is wasted.

Energy wasted $= 0.95 \times 60,000 = 57,000J$.

Question 24: C

Heat flow will be directly proportional to both the cross-sectional area (greater cross section = more energy transfer), and the difference in temperatures.

It will be inversely proportional to the length between the two ends (a longer bar means a shallower temperature gradient, and the shallower the gradient the less energy will be transferred).

Question 25: C

Electrical energy transferred (J) = current (A) x voltage (V) x time (s)

$= 1250 \times 400 \times 4 = 2,000,000J$

Efficiency of 45% means 45% of the energy input is converted to useful energy (kinetic) output.

Kinetic energy $= 0.45 \times 2,000,000 = 900,000J$

Question 26: A

$momentum = mass \times velocity$ and $K.E. = \frac{1}{2} \times mass \times velocity^2$

Divide KE by momentum to find velocity: $\dfrac{K.E.}{momentum} = \dfrac{\frac{1}{2}mv^2}{mv} = \dfrac{1}{2}v$

$\frac{1}{2}v = \frac{96}{24}$ therefore $v = 8$m/s

Sub back into momentum or KE equations to find mass: $m = \frac{24}{8} = 3$kg

Question 27: A

The background count-rate is the value the count tends towards once the isotope has decayed – in this case 20cpm.

The half-life is calculated as the time taken for the isotope to fall to half the previous value, but an adjustment must be made to remove the background count rate. Therefore the initial reading of 120 on the graph corresponds to an activity of 100cpm for the sample, and so the half-life should be measured to a sample activity of 50cpm (70 on the graph). This gives 40 seconds.

Question 28: C

Resultant force down = weight – air resistance = mass x acceleration

$10m - 12 = 2m$ therefore $m = 1.5$kg

Question 29: E

A frequency of 10Hz means a particle in the rope completes 10 full cycles per second, or 200 full cycles in 20 seconds. An amplitude of 4 means the particle travels a distance of 16cm for each full cycle (rest-top-rest-bottom-rest is a full cycle). The total distance travelled is therefore 20 x 16 = 3200cm.

The speed is unnecessary and is included to obscure the solution!

Question 30: C

Overall equation: $mass\ balance\ reading = m_{cyl} + \rho_{fluid}V$

Forming equation for addition of water: $290 = m_{cyl} + V$

Form equation for addition of oil: $270 = m_{cyl} + 0.9V$

Solving as simultaneous equations gives: $20 = 0.1V$ so $V = 200\text{cm}^3$

Substituting this back into either equation gives $m_{cyl} = 90$g

Question 31: B

At terminal velocity (the straight-line/constant-gradient section of the graph) weight downwards = air restance upwards, giving:

$1000 = kv^2$ so $k = \frac{1000}{v^2}$

The velocity is the gradient of the distance-time graph, and is found to be 50m/s. Therefore $k = \frac{1000}{50^2} = 0.4$.

Question 32: E

Form equations from the information in the question using $v = f\lambda$.

For the waves in deep water: $v = f(1.5)$

For the waves in shallower water: $(v - 18) = f(1.2)$

Rearranging to solve for f, $18 = 0.3f$, gives $f = 60$Hz

Then solve for speed in shallower water $(1.2f) = 72$ cm/s.

Question 33: H

Nucleons in = 235 (Uranium) + 1 (thermal neutron) = 236

Nucleons out = 236 = 88 (Bromine) + 145 (Lanthanum) + ? (neutrons)

Rearrange to find the number of neutrons out as 236-88-145=3.

Protons in = 92 (Uranium)

Protons out = 92 = 35 (Bromine) + ? (Lanthanum)

Rearrange to find atomic number of Lanthanum is 57.

Beta decay involves a neutron turning into a proton and an electron, therefore when when Lanthanum decays the proton number goes from 57 to 58.

Question 34: C

Let the resistance of X, Y and Z = R.

Create an expression for the total resistance of X and Y: $\frac{1}{R_{total}} = \frac{1}{R} + \frac{1}{R}$

$$R_{total} = \frac{R}{2}$$

The circuit can therefore be considered as a resistor, Z, of resistance R, in series with a resistor, 'XY', of resistance R/2.

The power dissipated is proportional to the resistance, and therefore two-thirds of the power (12W) will be dissipated through Z, with the other third (6W) dissipated in the combination of X and Y.

The power will split between X and Y equally (3W each).

Question 35: E

As the circuit involves the lamp and variable resistor connected in series, the current in the lamp and resistor will be equal, and the total circuit voltage will be the sum of the voltages across the two components.

The circuit voltage can therefore be found (using the information given when the variable resistor is set to 4Ω, and the graph):

$$Circuit\ Voltage = V_{res} + V_{lamp} = 4(2) + 6 = 14V$$

When the resistance of the variable resistor is set to 0, all 14V are dropped across the lamp. Using the table, the current would be 3A.

The power is therefore $IV = 3(14) = 42W$

Question 36: A

Distance = speed x time so as wave is travelling at the same speed in all directions, and the time taken to detection is the same for X and Y the distance between the epicentre and X must equal the distance between the epicentre and Y. This doesn't mean that '1' must be true, however, as the epicentre could be equidistant but lie to one side of XY, rather than on the line.

'2' isn't necessarily true, as Z needn't be equidistant from X and Y. For example the scenario below would give the detection pattern seen:

'3' also needn't be true in all cases. The distance travelled between detection by X or Y, and Z is

$$distance = speed \times time = 4(60) = 240\text{km}$$

However, as shown in the diagram, while Z must be no more than 240km from one of X or Y – it could be considerably further from the other (if it was on the opposite side of the epicentre).

Part C: Chemistry (Optional)

Question 37: C

Protons = atomic number = 29

Neutrons = mass number – number of protons = 64 - 29=35

The ion has lost two electrons so although normally the number of protons and electrons are equal, this one would be 29-2=27.

Question 38: C

1. Increasing the temperature will favour the endothermic reaction and move the equilibrium position to the left.
2. Adding water (a product) will favour the backwards reaction and move the equilibrium position to the left.
3. Adding a catalyst does not affect equilibrium – as it has the same effect on both directions of reaction.
4. Adding ethanol (a reaction) will favour the forward reaction and move the equilibrium position to the right.

Question 39: A

The two equations taking place during the electrolysis of dilute aqueous sodium sulfate are the oxidation and reduction of oxygen and hydrogen as sodium is more reactive than hydrogen, and there are no chlorine ions. They are:

Anode: $O^{2-} \rightarrow \frac{1}{2}O_2 + e^-$

Cathode: $H^+ + e^- \rightarrow \frac{1}{2}H_2$

Question 40: D

Atomic number of 5 means electron configuration of 2,3. It is therefore period 2, group 13 (on simple periodic tables the groups 3-12 for the transition metals are omitted, and so this may be more familiarly referred to as group '3').

Relative atomic mass = weighted isotopic average = $10(0.2) + 11(0.8) = 10.8$. *This could be deducted without working, as the average will be closer to 11 than 10 given the distribution in the graph.*

Question 41: B

The melting points are irrelevant, in fractional distillation the liquefied air will have the fractions progressively turn into gases as they reach their boiling points.

The gas with the lowest boiling point will therefore evaporate first, and the gas with the highest boiling point will evaporate last.

Question 42: E

As chlorine ions are present they will react at the anode to form chlorine gas. As sodium is more reactive than hydrogen, hydrogen gas will be formed at the other electrode. The solution remaining will be sodium hydroxide, which is alkaline.

Question 43: F

Determinations of oxidation or reduction should use the **OIL RIG** system: **O**xidation **I**s **L**oss (of electrons), **R**eduction **I**s **G**ain. Although quicker deductions using gain or loss of oxygen may be applicable if obvious.

The carbon dioxide is losing oxygen and therefore being reduced.

The calcium carbonate is neither gaining nor losing electrons and nor is CaO.

Question 44: A

As Y is a monatomic anion it will have gained electrons to get to the electron configuration. (It will therefore have a smaller atomic number than X).

As Z is a monatomic cation it will have lost electrons to get to the electron configuration. (It will therefore have a larger atomic number than X).

Statement A is **always** correct. (B is false, C could be true, but not always, D could be true, but not always, E could be true, but not always).

Question 45: E

Drawing a table sorts the question information (in bold).

	SO_2	O_2	SO_3
Before (mol)	5.00	11.0	0.00
	-4.00 (80%)	-2.00	+4.00
After (mol)	1.00	9.00	4.00

The gaps can then be filled in:

- If 4 moles of sulfur dioxide have reacted, half that many moles of oxygen will have reacted.
- If 4 moles of sulfur dioxide have reacted, that many moles of sulfur trioxide will have been produced.

This means there are 14 moles of gas at equilibrium, each of which takes up $60dm^3$, the total is then found by multiplying the number of moles by the volume per mole.

Question 46: C

When a simple molecular substance changes state, the energy is required to break (or released in the formation of) the intermolecular forces. The covalent bonds within the molecules aren't affected or involved. Therefore 1 and 3 are incorrect.

Question 47: A

Moles of anhydrous copper sulfate required $= \frac{250}{1000} \times 0.2 = 0.05 \text{moles}$

Mass of anhydrous copper sulfate $= 0.05(64 + 32 + 16 \times 4) = 8g$

The mass of hydrated copper sulfate used by mistake was 8g.

Moles of hydrated copper sulfate $= \frac{8}{64+32+16\times4+5(18)} = 0.032 \text{moles}$

Concentration of solution made $= \frac{0.032}{0.25} = 0.128 \text{mol/dm}^3$

Question 48: D

1. Bromine is less electronegative than chlorine and so would lose electrons to chlorine (and be oxidised), rather than acting as an oxidising agent.
2. Boiling point increases down group 17 (7) due to the increased size of the molecules.
3. Bromine reacts with calcium to form calcium bromide, $CaBr_2$. The percentage of bromine (by mass) is $\frac{80\times2}{80\times2+40} = \frac{160}{200} = 80\%$

Question 49: B

1. There are spots at 0.26 and 0.61 so this is correct.
2. There is no spot at 0.71 in mixture P so this is incorrect.
3. Glycine has a lower Rf value than glutamic acid, so glutamic acid is not the least mobile in this solvent.
4. There is a spot at 0.50 in both P and Q so this is correct.

Question 50: A

Rate of reaction in first 2 seconds (in cm³/s): $\frac{24}{2} = 12cm^3/s$

Convert to moles per second: $\frac{12}{24,000} = 0.5 \times 10^{-3} \text{moles/s}$

Convert to grams per second (Mg): $(0.5 \times 10^{-3})(24) = 12 \times 10^{-3} g/s$

Question 51: C

$$3Cu + a\,HNO_3 \rightarrow b\,Cu(NO_3)_2 + c\,H_2O + dNO$$

Balance Cu: $b = 3$

$$3Cu + a\,HNO_3 \rightarrow \mathbf{3}\,Cu(NO_3)_2 + c\,H_2O + dNO$$

Balance H: $a = 2c$ (1)

Balance N: $a = 3 \times 2 + d$ (2)

Balance O: $3a = 3 \times 3 \times 2 + c + d$ (3)

Solve as simultaneous equations. Sub (1) and (2) into (3) to get an equation only including 'a':

$$3a = 18 + \frac{a}{2} + a - 6$$

Rearranging for a gives $\frac{3}{2}a = 12$, so $a = 8$

Question 52: C

Work backwards from the end of the question to the start.

Moles of sodium hydroxide required to neutralise the hydrochloric acid remaining in solution $= \frac{12.5}{1000} \times 0.1 = 1.25 \times 10^{-3}$ moles.

Hydrochloric acid and sodium hydroxide neutralise in a 1:1 ratio, so the moles of hydrochloric acid remaining in solution is also 1.25×10^{-3}.

The moles of hydrochloric acid added initially $= \frac{50}{1000} \times 0.1 = 5 \times 10^{-3}$.

This means that 3.75×10^{-3} moles of HCl reacted (the difference).

Using the balanced equation, the number of moles of calcium hydroxide which react with hydrochloric acid will be half, 1.875×10^{-3} moles.

Mass of calcium carbonate $= 1.875 \times 10^{-3} \times 100 = 0.1875$g

Question 53: B

The balanced equation is: $2Li + \frac{1}{2}O_2 \rightarrow Li_2O$

This means that the stoichiometric ratio of lithium:oxygen is 4:1.

Moles of lithium $= \frac{2.8}{7} = 0.4$ moles

Moles of oxygen $= \frac{1.2}{24} = 0.05$ moles.

Therefore oxygen is the limiting reagent.

The maximum moles of lithium oxide will be twice the moles of oxygen. This means the maximum mass will be $0.1 \times (30) = 3$ g.

Question 54: E

Draw a table if necessary to visualise:

	NO	O_2	NO_2
Before (mol)	excess	'y'	0
	-z/2	-z/2	+ 'z'
After (mol)		y-z/2	'z'

- If 'z' moles of NO_2 form, then half that many moles of oxygen must have reacted.

If z/2 moles of oxygen have reacted, then the energy released will be the number of moles multiplied by the energy per mole.

Part D: Biology (Optional)

Question 55: F

Stonefly are indicative of clean, well oxygenated water (at points 1 and 3), whereas bloodworms are adapted for surviving in heavily polluted water with low oxygen content (at point 2).

Question 56: D

1. Sickle cell anaemia affects oxygen supply, it would therefore be likely to increase the amount of anaerobic respiration, not decrease it.
2. This is probably untrue – there isn't enough information to tell – but it is unlikely that there would be more significant medical intervention due to the area having malaria.
3. This is true – carrying the sickle cell gene is likely to have a positive impact on survival.

Question 57: E

1. Both cells appear to be in a single layer of tissue within the oesophagus (they have the same structure).
2. As they aren't reproductive cells they will be formed by mitosis.
3. Animal cells don't have a cell wall.

Question 58: E

1. $0.1 \times 0.2 \times 1 = 0.02 m^3$ of water sampled.
2. Occurrence of the tadpoles just means what proportion of the samples they appeared in, which is 9/10 or 90%.
3. An estimate could be calculated, but it is unlikely to be accurate given that the samples taken are only representative of the shoreline of the pond.

Question 59: E

Expected ratio of male to female is half and half.

1st generation= 2 rats

1st generation of offspring= 8 rats (assume 4 are female, 4 are male)

2nd generation (offspring)= 4 females with litters of 8 = 32 (16 female)

3rd generation (offspring)= 16 females with litters of 8 = 128 (64 female)

4th generation (offspring)=64 females with litters of 8 = 512 (256 male)

Question 60: E

There are 3 divisions into 2 cells: $1 \rightarrow 2 \rightarrow 4 \rightarrow 8$ (mitosis).

In meiosis producing haploids, the cells divide into 4 – so the final number would be 8x4.

Question 61: H

1 and 3 are required for any growth. 2 is required if the tip is to grow towards light (in a shoot) or away from light (in roots). An even distribution of hormone would cause the plant to grow in a straight line.

Question 62: G

1 is incorrect – the concentrations would tend towards an equilibrium rather than simply adding together.

2 is correct – although at equilibrium there is no net movement of water, the movement still happens in all directions.

3 is correct – the amount of osmosis is directly proportional to the difference in concentrations, which will be greatest when the cell is first placed in the solution.

Question 63: A

Adenine and thymine form a complementary pair, and cytosine and guanine form a complementary pair.

2 strands of 25 means 50 total bases, of which 14% are adenine.

Therefore, there will be 7 adenine and 7 thymine bases, with the remaining 36 bases split evenly (18 each) between C and G.

Question 64: B

1 is correct, it is likely that if changing the section has resulted in the mutated lipase being 'unreactive' that the section is part of its active site (note: it might not be, but the statement says 'could be').

2 is incorrect, there are a range of different types of mutation (deletions, insertions, replacements) which may have different effects.

3 is incorrect, lipase enzymes will breakdown the lipids into glycerol and fatty acids, meaning the pH will drop.

Question 65: F

The mutation couldn't have occurred in Q's father, because it would have had to have been passed on to Q and all people who carry the mutation show symptoms. The mutation could have happened in R, or in P during the formation of the 'R' embryo.

Question 66: E

Meiosis must have occurred in the production of the egg cell, with mitosis and differentiation occurring during Dolly's development. The genes weren't altered at any stage, so genetic engineering did not have to occur.

Question 67: A

1. Kinetic energy of reaction molecules will increase as temperature increases (this will happen at all points).
2. In section Y, despite increasing temperature the rate of oxygen production is constant – this is indicative of the fact that another factor is limiting.
3. If the plant's enzymes had denatured the rate of oxygen released would drop back to zero. The rate has not fallen, it has merely levelled out – so this is incorrect.

Question 68: C

The bacteria containing the original plasmid would grow on both the petri dish containing penicillin and the dish containing tetracycline, as it is resistant to both of these antibiotics.

The bacteria with the recombinant plasmid is still resistant to penicillin (and so would grow on that dish), but is no longer resistant to tetracycline due to the disruption to that gene caused by the insertion of the gene for herbicide resistance.

Question 69: H

1. The gene does not code for chlorophyll as it is found across a range of kingdoms.
2. This is correct as it is found in both organisms which contain their genetic information in a nucleus and those which don't.
3. This is correct – there are only 4 genes different between the oak tree and mushroom sequences.

Question 70: G

1. This is incorrect. When mitosis takes place the cell mass will halve – which takes place at 24 and 48 hours.

2. The mass halves twice (the vertical sections) – so this is correct.
3. The divisions are taking place every 24 hours.

Question 71: F

1. As a recessive allele causes resistance, both of the alleles must code for resistance in order for the insect to be resistant. If a resistant insect (rr) breeds with an insect which does not have the allele (RR), all offspring will be 'Rr' (and therefore sensitive).
2. Mutations occur randomly – the likelihood of those being positively selected for may vary due to exposure to environmental factors, but not the number of mutations.
3. Maintaining genetic variation means that other mutations may be favoured.

Question 72: B

1. This is true – the mutation has no effect on the phenotype of the plant or the number of length of chromosomes – and so genes have not 'disappeared' there has been a replacement.
2. This is untrue – due to the mutation.
3. This is untrue – due to the mutation.

Part E Advanced Mathematics and Advanced Physics

Question 73: A

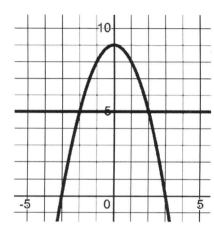

Draw a diagram.

The area between C and L is equal to the area below C (between the two points of intersection) minus the rectangular area below L.

Find the points of intersection:

$9 - x^2 = 5$ gives $x = \pm 2$

Find the area below C by integrating:

$$\int_{-2}^{2} 9 - x^2 \, dx = \left[9x - \frac{x^3}{3} \right]_{-2}^{2} = \left[9(2) - \frac{2^3}{3} \right] - \left[9(-2) - \frac{-2^3}{3} \right]$$

$$= \frac{92}{3}$$

The area below L is base x height $= 4 \times 5 = 20$

The area between C and L is therefore $\frac{92}{3} - 20 = \frac{32}{3}$.

Question 74: E

SUVAT: $s = 1{,}600$m, $u = 0$m/s, $v = 80$m/s, $a = ?$

Use $v^2 = u^2 + 2as$: $80^2 = 2(1600)a$. Therefore $a = \frac{6400}{3200} = 2$m/s^2.

Question 75: D

Rearranging gives: $2 \sin^3 \theta - \sin \theta = 0$

Factorise (dividing would lose solutions): $\sin\theta (2 \sin^2 \theta - 1) = 0$

Solutions are $\sin\theta = 0$ or $\sin\theta = \pm \frac{1}{\sqrt{2}}$

Considering the graph of $y = \sin\theta$ (overlayed with $y = 0$, $y = \frac{1}{\sqrt{2}}$, and $y = -\frac{1}{\sqrt{2}}$) shows 5 solutions in the interval $-\frac{\pi}{2} \leq \theta \leq \pi$:

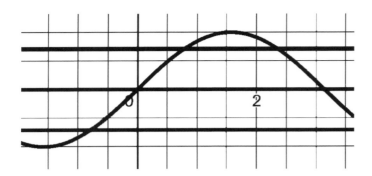

Question 76: F

A: Not necessarily true – balanced overall doesn't mean 'equal'.

B: There will likely be more than 3: normal reaction, friction, weight, driving force.

C: Not true – the driving force up the slope will be balanced by both friction and the component of the weight parallel to the slope.

D: Not true – mass is straight down, contact is perpendicular to plane.

E – Not enough information to know.

F – This must be correct. Constant speed means no overall resultant force (Newton's First Law).

Question 77: C

The tangent to the curve has gradient found by differentiation:

$\frac{dy}{dx} = 6x - 2$

The gradient of the curve is equal to the gradient of the tangent, so:

$6x - 2 = 1$ therefore $x = \frac{1}{2}$

The y-coordinate is found by substituting x back into the equation of the curve: $y = 3\left(\frac{1}{2}\right)^2 - 2\left(\frac{1}{2}\right) + 1 = \frac{3}{4}$

The value of k can then be found as $\frac{3}{4} = \frac{1}{2} + k$, giving $k = \frac{1}{4}$.

Question 78: D

All blocks have the same acceleration, calculated using Newton's 2nd Law (N2L): $30 = (3 + 4 + 6 + 2)a$ giving $a = 2\text{m/s}^2$.

Considering N2L on 'Z' alone: $30 - T_1 = 2(2)$ gives $T_1 = 26\text{N}$

Then considering N2L on 'Y' alone: $T_1 - T_2 = 6(2)$

Therefore $26 - T_2 = 12$, so $T_2 = 14\text{N}$.

Question 79: E

n^{th} term of A.P $= a + (n - 1)d$

13th term $= 6 \times 1^{\text{st}}$ term: $a + 12d = 6[a]$

11th term $= 2 \times 5^{\text{th}}$ term $- 1$: $a + 10d = 2[a + 4d] - 1$

Combine terms: $5a = 12d$ and $a - 1 = 2d$

Solve simultaneously: $5 = 2d$ so $d = \frac{5}{2}$ and $a = 6$

3rd term $= a + 2d = 6 + 2\left(\frac{5}{2}\right) = 11$

Question 80: F

Let contact force at X $= F_x$.

Take moments around Y: $10g(2) + 40g(3) = F_x(4)$

Solve for $F_x = 35g = 350\text{N}$.

Question 81: C

In general $\log(a) + \log(b) = \log(ab)$

$$\log_2\left(\frac{5}{4}\right) + \log_2\left(\frac{6}{7}\right) + \cdots + \log_2\left(\frac{64}{63}\right) = \log_2\left(\frac{(5)(6)\dots(64)}{(4)(5)\dots(63)}\right)$$

As an aside: $n! = n \times (n-1) \times (n-2) \dots \times 3 \times 2 \times 1$.

In this case, not all terms are included, so instead of $64!$ the expression for the numerator is $\frac{64!}{4!}$. Similarly, instead of $63!$ the expression for the denominator is $\frac{63!}{3!}$.

The expression is therefore equal to $\log_2\left(\frac{64!}{4!} \cdot \frac{3!}{63!}\right)$ which simplifies to $\log_2\left(\frac{64}{4}\right) = \log_2(16) = 4$

Question 82: D

Change in momentum = Impulse = Force x time

Change in momentum of X when force is applied = 5 x 3 = 15 kgm/s

$\Delta mv = m(v_f - v_1)$ gives $15 = 2(v_f - 4.5)$ and therefore $v_f = 12$m/s

Conservation of momentum:

Momentum of X+Y before = Momentum of XY after

$2(12) + 3(0) = (3 + 2)v_{combined}$ which can be rearranged to give the speed of the combined 'XY' as $\frac{24}{5}$m/s.

Question 83: C

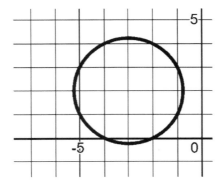

Draw a diagram.

Consider the simplest case, when the tangent is horizontal (or vertical).

The co-ordinates of P would therefore be:

$x = -3 - 5\sqrt{3}$ and $y = 2 + \sqrt{5}$.

The shortest distance between the point P and the circle can then be generalised as the length of the line marked 'L' minus the radius.

Shortest distance $= \sqrt{(x_p - x_c)^2 + (y_p - y_c)^2} - r$ where the point P has coordinates (x_p, y_p) and the circle has centre (x_c, y_c).

Substituting in the values above gives $shortest\ distance = 3\sqrt{5}$.

Question 84: F

Conservation of momentum:

(Momentum of X+ Momentum of Y) before = Momentum of 'XY' after

After: XY both have velocity '-v', and therefore momentum = -3mv

Before: X has momentum 'mv'

Rearrange to find the momentum of Y before = -3mv – mv = -4mv

Speed of Y before is therefore -2v.

Question 85: D

'Brute force' method:

Binomial expansion: $(a + x)^n = a^n + na^{n-1}x + \frac{n(n-1)}{2!}a^{n-2}x^2 + \cdots$

Expansion of $(1 - 2x)^5 = 1 + 5(-2x) + \frac{5(4)}{2}(-2x)^2 + \frac{5(4)(3)}{(3)(2)}(-2x)^3$

$= 1 - 10x + 40x^2 - 80x^3 + \cdots$

Expansion of $(1 + 2x)^5 = 1 + 5(2x) + \frac{5(4)}{2}(2x)^2 + \frac{5(4)(3)}{(3)(2)}(2x)^3 + \cdots$

$= 1 + 10x + 40x^2 + 80x^3 + \cdots$

When multiplied together the x^3 terms would be:

$1(80x^3) - 10x(40x^2) + 40x^2(10x) - 80x^3(1) = 0$

Alternative 'clever' method:

$(1 - 2x)^5(1 + 2x)^5 = [(1 - 2x)(1 + 2x)]^5 = [1 - 4x^2]^5$

Because the bracket to be expanded contains only an x^2 term, there will be no terms in the expansion with x raised to an odd power.

Question 86: A

Resolve horizontally: $P = T\sin30$ $(\sin(30) = \frac{1}{2})$

Question 87: E

$$\int_0^2 x^m dx = \left[\frac{x^{m+1}}{m+1}\right]_0^2 = \left[\frac{2^{m+1}}{m+1}\right] = \frac{16\sqrt{2}}{7}$$

$$\int_0^2 x^{m+1} dx = \left[\frac{x^{m+2}}{m+2}\right]_0^2 = \left[\frac{2^{m+2}}{m+2}\right] = \frac{32\sqrt{2}}{9}$$

$$\left[\frac{2^{m+2}}{m+2}\right] = \left[\frac{2^{m+1}}{m+1}\right]\left[\frac{2(m+1)}{m+2}\right] \text{ giving } \frac{32\sqrt{2}}{9} = \frac{16\sqrt{2}}{7}\left[\frac{2(m+1)}{m+2}\right]$$

Which can be rearranged for $\frac{1}{9} = \frac{m+1}{7(m+2)}$ giving $m = \frac{5}{2}$.

Question 88: A

Although this looks like SHM, the angle is not small enough for the equations to be appropriate.

Find the vertical distance between 'pivot' and pendulum at the 'amplitude position' using Pythagoras: $\sqrt{50^2 - 30^2} = 40$cm.

This means between 'amplitude' and 'equilibrium' the bob loses '10cm' of GPE: $0.01(10)(0.1) = 0.01$

It will gain KE = GPE lost, and therefore $0.01 = \frac{1}{2}mv^2$ can be rearranged to give $v = \sqrt{\frac{0.02}{0.01}} = \sqrt{2}$m/s.

Question 89: C

It may help to draw a diagram:

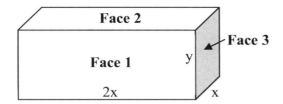

Volume of the cuboid $= 2x^2y = 576$ this can be rearranged to give $y = \frac{288}{x^2}$.

S.A of the cuboid $= 2(2xy + xy + 2x^2) = 4x^2 + 6xy$

Substitute to eliminate y: $S.A = 4x^2 + \frac{1728}{x}$

If this is a maximum value then the differential of the surface area with respect to x (or y) is equal to 0.

$\frac{dSA}{dx} = 8x - \frac{1728}{x^2} = 0$ can be rearranged to find $x = 6$.

When $x = 6$, $y = 8$ and the largest face therefore has surface area $= 12\text{x}8 = 96$ cm^2.

Question 90: B

SUVAT (1st object): $s = 0$m, $a = -10$m/s^2, $u = 40$m/s, $t = T$

Use $s = ut + \frac{1}{2}at^2$ for both objects.

For object 1 this gives: $0 = 40T - 5T^2$ which can be solved to give $T = 0$ which isn't a relevant solution, or $T = 8s$.

SUVAT (2nd object): $s = -h$m. $a = -10$m/s^2, $u = 0$m/s, $t = 8 - 2$s

This gives $-h = -5(6^2)$ therefore $h = 180$m.

END OF SECTION

NSAA SECTION 2 (2018)

Physics

Question P1

a) At the time t_0 the vertical velocity of the ball is zero, and this is reflected in the initially 'flat' gradient of the graph.

The ball then accelerates towards the ground, which can be seen in the curvature giving an increasingly negative gradient (meaning increasing velocity towards the ground) until time t_1.

After t_1 the gradient of the graph remains constant, indicating the ball has reached terminal velocity.

b) $mg - F_d = ma$

Therefore $a = g - \frac{F_d}{m}$

c) Terminal speed means 'a' is zero, so $g = \frac{F_d}{m}$ or $gm = F_d$

Therefore $gm = \frac{1}{4}\pi\rho r^2 v_t^2$

This can be rearranged to give $v_t^2 = \frac{4gm}{\pi\rho r^2}$ and $v_t = \sqrt{\frac{4gm}{\pi\rho r^2}}$.

d) Substituting in the numbers in the question (remembering to convert units where necessary) gives $v_t = 2.04$m/s.

e)

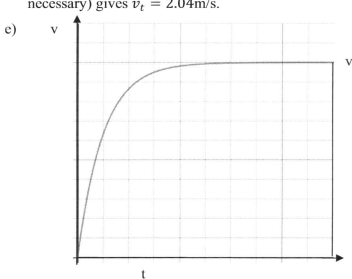

The ball initially accelerates with acceleration due to gravity. As the ball's velocity increases its acceleration decreases (shown by the decreasing gradient of the graph), until it reaches terminal velocity (shown by the flat section of the graph).

f) The question states $\frac{v}{v_t} = 0.99$

$0.99^2 = 1 - 10^{-\frac{0.051y}{0.025}}$

Rearrange: $1 - 0.99^2 = 10^{-\frac{0.051y}{0.025}}$

Take logarithms $\log_{10}(0.0199) = -2.04y$

Rearrange for $y = 0.83$m

Question P2

a) i) The voltage across components in parallel is the same – therefore the voltage will be 1.4V (the same as the LED).

   ii) The current through the resistor is $I = \frac{V}{R} = \frac{1.4}{30} = 0.047$A

b) i) The current through the variable resistor will be the sum of the two currents it splits into (through the 30Ω resistor and the LED) – it is therefore 55mA.

   ii) The voltages around a series circuit must sum to the terminal voltage of the power supply. The voltage of the variable resistor is therefore the terminal voltage minus the voltage dropped across the LED-resistor section. 4.6V

   iii) $R = \frac{V}{I} = \frac{4.6}{0.0546} = 84\Omega$

c) i) When the variable resistor is 20ohms, the total resistance of the two resistors in parallel is 10ohms. The circuit can then be considered a series circuit between a 10ohm and 20ohm component – which will (as a potential divider) split the voltage proportionally into 2V and 4V. The voltage on the voltmeter will therefore be 4.0V.

   ii)

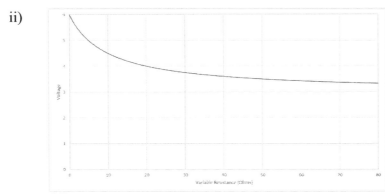

iii) It can be helpful to draw a table:

Rvar (ohms)	R of variable & 20Ω resistor (ohms).	Voltage across var & 20 ohm	Power (W)
0	0 (short)	0	0
5	4	1	0.2
20	10	2	0.2
50	14.29	2.5	0.125
80	16	2.66	0.09

Combining resistances in parallel uses $\frac{1}{R_T} = \frac{1}{R_1} + \frac{1}{R_2}$

Finding the voltage uses $V = \frac{R}{R_T} V_T$

Finding power uses $P = \frac{V^2}{R}$.

iv)

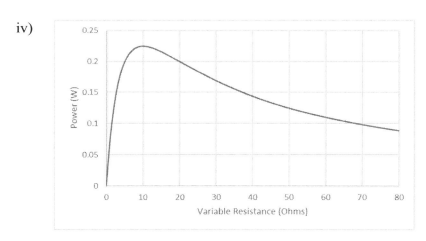

d) From the graph the equation $\log R_{AB} = k\theta + c$ is formed.

Using the points given in the question gives the equations:

$\log(1000) = c$ so $c = 3$

$\log(2{,}000{,}000) = 270k + 3$ so $k = 0.0122$

The equation can then be used to find R_{AB}:

$\log R_{AB} = 0.0122(110) + 3$

So $R_{AB} = 10^{0.0122(110)+3} = 22.1 k\Omega$

Chemistry

Question C1

a) i) The reaction appears to be a condensation reaction, which has eliminated an oxygen and some hydrogen atoms – so a good suggestion is water.

ii) Using the example given initially, the cycle shouldn't change but the double-bond-O should be swapped for nitrogen bonded to OH:

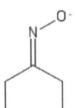

iii) The hydrogen atom attached to the oxygen will be the most acidic as oxygen is electronegative and so the oxygen-hydrogen bond will be weaker. The resulting anion formed would be:

b) The structures would turn into (in order):

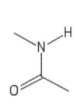

c) $Ni(C_4O_2N_2H_7)_2 = NiC_8O_4N_4H_{14} \rightarrow Mr = 288.922$

d) Moles of dry precipitate $= \dfrac{0.368}{288.922} = 1.2737 \times 10^{-3}$ mol

Moles of nickel $=$ moles of precipitate (using the structural formula in (c)) $= 1.2737 \times 10^{-3}$ mol

Mass of nickel $= 1.2737 \times 10^{-3} \times 58.69 = 0.07475g$

Nickel content % by mass $= \dfrac{0.07475}{1.5} = 4.98\%$

e) Palladium or platinum in the alloy would cause the precipitate to increase in mass, and would therefore increase the calculated number of moles of nickel in the precipitate. This would lead to an overestimate for the nickel content.

Question C2

a) $CO_{2(g)} + 2OH_{aq}^- \rightarrow CO_{3(aq)}^{2-} + H_2O_{(l)}$

b) i) Mass drop = mass of water = 0.0931g

Moles of water $= \frac{0.0931}{18.016} = 5.17 \times 10^{-3}$ mol

ii) Moles of acid added $= 1 \times \frac{14.7}{1000} = 14.7 \times 10^{-3}$ mol

Moles of NaOH in titration = moles of HCl $= 14.7 \times 10^{-3}$ mol

Moles of NaOH before bubbling $= 1 \times \frac{25}{1000} = 25 \times 10^{-3}$ mol

Moles in reaction with CO_2 = before - remaining for titration

$25 \times 10^{-3} - 14.7 \times 10^{-3} = 10.3 \times 10^{-3}$ moles

Using the equation in part (a), each mole of OH reacts with half than amount of carbon dioxide, so the moles of carbon dioxide absorbed is 5.15×10^{-3} moles.

iii) A 0.1g sample is burnt and produces 5.15×10^{-3} moles of CO_2 and 5.17×10^{-3} moles of water (from part (iii)). This can be more easily shown in a table (initial values in **bold**).

	C	H	O	Total
Moles	5.15×10^{-3}	5.17×10^{-3}	1.74×10^{-3}	
Mr	12	1.008	16	
Mass	61.8×10^{-3}	10.3×10^{-3}	0.02778	**0.1**
Ratio	6	3	1	

The masses of carbon and hydrogen can be calculated using $m = Mr \times n$.

The mass of oxygen is then the remaining mass between the total of carbon and hydrogen and the total mass put in.

The moles of oxygen can then be calculated.

Then find the lowest common ratio, by dividing each of the number of moles through by the smallest value (in this case, oxygen).

The empirical formula is therefore C_3H_6O.

c) i) Oxygen has an oxidation number of -2, so Mn must be +6 to give an overall charge of -2.

ii) K is +1, O is-2, so Cr must be +6 to give no overall charge.

d) Write both half equations:

$$Fe^{2+} \rightarrow Fe^{3+} + e^-$$
$$MnO_4^- + 5e^- + 8H^+ \rightarrow Mn^{2+} + 4H_2O$$

Multiply the first equation by 5 in order to ensure the electrons will cancel out, and then combine:

$$MnO_4^- + 8H^+ + 5Fe^{2+} \rightarrow Mn^{2+} + 4H_2O + 5Fe^{3+}$$

Biology

Question B1

a)

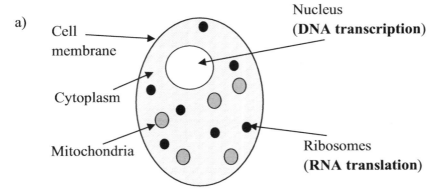

b) There are 20 amino acids which need coding for, and as genetic material is read in triplets (with 4 base options for each position) there are 64 possible triplets. Therefore the redundancy is 44/64.

c) Multiple triplets can code for the same amino acid, which means mutations may end up coding for the amino acid planned for originally – reducing the effect of the mutation.

d) 299 amino acids = 897 bases

897 bases at 18 bases per second = 49.8 seconds

e) 50 amino acids to code for means that there must be a minimum of 50 possible configurations of pair. The number of configurations for a pair is just the number of bases squared. The smallest square number larger than 50 is 64, and therefore the smallest number of bases is 8.

f) There are a range of changes which can occur in DNA sequences including substitution, deletion and insertion.

If substitution takes place this will change an amino acid sequence – while this may have no effect (if the substitution leads to a triplet which codes for the same amino acid as the unsubstituted code), it can also have very significant consequences. One of the main consequences is in the premature termination of the chain, if the new triplet codes for a 'stop' point. This can disrupt protein synthesis (in producing proteins with the incorrect shape, reducing the effectiveness of the enzymes they make up), or even prevent a given protein being synthesised.

Substitution based genetic diseases include sickle cell anaemia. The point mutation which takes place alters the shape of the red blood cells causing them to block blood supply, and giving significantly reduced oxygen saturation levels.

If a deletion or insertion takes place this can have even more significant effects than point mutations, due to the knock on effect of the single mutation on the entirety of the rest of the chain. This 'frameshift' means that the remainder of the genetic code will be read in triplets which have all been shifted forwards or backwards by one base, and therefore may code from completely different proteins.

Frameshift mutations can increase the risks of various cancers, as well as genetic predisposition to extreme high cholesterol.

Question B2

a) A benefit of using quadrats is that deductions can be made about large areas without the effort and investment of resources needed to study the entire area.

A problem is that the validity of such deductions can vary, particularly if inadvertent bias is brought into the sample (eg. people only want to walk on dry areas of grass and so don't sample muddy areas without realising their bias).

b) $\frac{6}{8} = 75\%$

c) Total number of plants = 12

Total square metres covered = 8x4 =32

Plants per square metre $= \frac{12}{32} = 0.375$

d) 2 plants per square metre in a field of 140 square metres, means a total of 280 plants. There are currently 30 plants, so an increase of 250 is required. The plants increase by 70 per week (or 10 per day), so this will take 25 days.

e) Plants produce flowers in order to allow pollination to occur, given they reproduce asexually.

They may only flower on very long timescales if their main pollinator has a cycle of population growth. It may be optimum for the plants to synchronise the expenditure of energy required to flower with the highest population of pollinators.

f) There are a number of factors which may affect the spread and photosynthetic rate of the plant. Some factors which may play a part include:

- Light level – higher light intensity will lead to a greater rate of photosynthesis, up to the point at which other factors become limiting. While this is unlikely to be a significant factor in an open field, it may be that as crowding begins light is one of the first 'resources' to become scarce. As such, light level may play a part in limiting the spread of the plant, as new plants will not grow if they cannot very quickly absorb the light they require, as well as being limited by the photosynthetic rate.

- Competition with other species. As the plant is an invasive species, it may not be adapted to the environment as effectively as many of the species already present. This would lead to a limit on the water and nutrients available to the new plants.

- It is also less likely to have developed adequate defence mechanisms for common insects or animals found in the environment. This may mean that after the initial rapid increase in the number of individuals, the widespread competition and lack of resilience in the environment causes a quick levelling out and lack of significant ongoing population growth.

- There are also internal factors which affect the ability of the plant to spread. Although asexual reproduction means that plants can often reproduce quickly there will still be a minimum time required which is limited by the rate of growth of the plants.

- Though it depends on the environment, the effect of carbon dioxide level on photosynthetic rate is unlikely to be a significant factor, given the comparative availability and the likelihood that other limitations will become significant long before carbon dioxide level would be limiting.

NSAA Practice Papers
Introduction

Already seen them all?

So, you've run out of past papers? Well hopefully that is where this book comes in. It contains two full mock papers with worked solutions - each compiled by natural sciences tutors at *UniAdmissions* and not available anywhere else.

Having studied natural sciences at Cambridge, our tutors are intimately familiar with the NSAA and its associated admission procedures. So, the novel questions presented to you here are of the correct style and difficulty to continue your revision and stretch you to meet the demands of the NSAA.

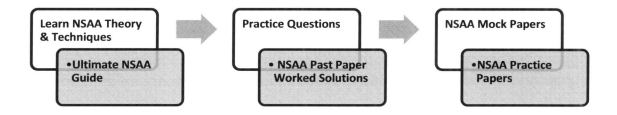

Start Early

It is much easier to prepare if you practice little and often. Start your preparation well in advance; ideally 10 weeks but at the latest within a month. This way you will have plenty of time to complete as many papers as you wish to feel comfortable and won't have to panic and cram just before the test, which is a much less effective and more stressful way to learn. In general, an early start will give you the opportunity to identify the complex issues and work at your own pace.

Prioritise

Some questions in sections can be long and complex – and given the intense time pressure you need to know your limits. It is essential that you don't get stuck with very difficult questions. If a question looks particularly long or complex, mark it for review and move on. You don't want to be caught five questions short at the end just because you took more than three minutes in answering a challenging multi-step question. If a question is taking too long, choose a sensible answer and move on. Remember that each question carries equal weighting and therefore, you should adjust your timing in accordingly. With practice and discipline, you can get very good at this and learn to maximise your efficiency.

Positive Marking

There are no penalties for incorrect answers; you will gain one for each right answer and will not get one for each wrong or unanswered one. This provides you with the luxury that you can always guess should you absolutely be not able to figure out the right answer for a question or run behind time. Since each question provides you with 4 to 6 possible answers, you have a 16-25% chance of guessing correctly. Therefore, if you aren't sure (and are running short of time), then make an educated guess and move on. Before 'guessing' you should try to eliminate a couple of answers to increase your chances of getting the question correct. For example, if a question has five options and you manage to eliminate 2 options- your chances of getting the question increase from 20% to 33%!

Avoid losing easy marks on other questions because of poor exam technique. Similarly, if you have failed to finish the exam, take the last 10 seconds to guess the remaining questions to at least give yourself a chance of getting them right.

Practice

This is the best way of familiarising yourself with the style of questions and the timing for this section. Although the exam will essentially only test GCSE level knowledge, you are unlikely to be familiar with the style of questions in all sections when you first encounter them. Therefore, you want to be comfortable at using this before you sit the test.

Practising questions will put you at ease and make you more comfortable with the exam. The more comfortable you are, the less you will panic on the test day and the more likely you are to score highly. Initially, work through the questions at your own pace, and spend time carefully reading the questions and looking at any additional data. When it becomes closer to the test, **make sure you practice the questions under exam conditions**.

Repeat Questions

When checking through answers, pay particular attention to questions you have got wrong. If there is a worked answer, look through that carefully until you feel confident that you understand the reasoning, and then repeat the question without help to check that you can do it. If only the answer is given, have another look at the question and try to work out why that answer is correct. This is the best way to learn from your mistakes, and means you are less likely to make similar mistakes when it comes to the test. The same applies for questions which you were unsure of and made an educated guess which was correct, even if you got it right. When working through this book, **make sure you highlight any questions you are unsure of**, this means you know to spend more time looking over them once marked.

Use the Options:

Some questions may try to overload you with information. When presented with large tables and data, it's essential you look at the answer options so you can focus your mind. This can allow you to reach the correct answer a lot more quickly. Consider the example below:

The table below shows the results of a study investigating antibiotic resistance in staphylococcus populations. A single staphylococcus bacterium is chosen at random from a similar population. Resistance to any one antibiotic is independent of resistance to others.

Calculate the probability that the bacterium selected will be resistant to all four drugs.

A   1 in 10^6
B   1 in 10^{12}
C   1 in 10^{20}
D   1 in 10^{25}
E   1 in 10^{30}
F   1 in 10^{35}

Antibiotic	Number of Bacteria tested	Number of Resistant Bacteria
Benzyl-penicillin	10^{11}	98
Chloramphenicol	10^9	1200
Metronidazole	10^8	256
Erythromycin	10^5	2

Looking at the options first makes it obvious that there is **no need to calculate exact values**- only in powers of 10. This makes your life a lot easier. If you hadn't noticed this, you might have spent well over 90 seconds trying to calculate the exact value when it wasn't even being asked for.

In other cases, you may actually be able to use the options to arrive at the solution quicker than if you had tried to solve the question as you normally would. Consider the example below:

A region is defined by the two inequalities: $x - y^2 > 1 \ and \ xy > 1$. Which of the following points is in the defined region?
A. (10,3)
B. (10,2)
C. (-10,3)
D. (-10,2)
E. (-10,-3)

Whilst it's possible to solve this question both algebraically or graphically by manipulating the identities, by far **the quickest way is to actually use the options**. Note that options C, D and E violate the second inequality, narrowing down to answer to either A or B. For A: $10 - 3^2 = 1$ and thus this point is on the boundary of the defined region and not actually in the region. Thus the answer is B (as $10-4 = 6 > 1$.)

In general, it pays dividends to look at the options briefly and see if they can be help you arrive at the question more quickly. Get into this habit early – it may feel unnatural at first but it's guaranteed to save you time in the long run.

Manage your Time:

It is highly likely that you will be juggling your revision alongside your normal school studies. Whilst it is tempting to put your A-levels on the back burner falling behind in your school subjects is not a good idea, don't forget that to meet the conditions of your offer should you get one you will need at least one A*. So, time management is key!

Make sure you set aside a dedicated 90 minutes (and much more closer to the exam) to commit to your revision each day. The key here is not to sacrifice too many of your extracurricular activities, everybody needs some down time, but instead to be efficient. Take a look at our list of top tips for increasing revision efficiency below:

1. Create a comfortable work station
2. Declutter and stay tidy
3. Treat yourself to some nice stationery
4. See if music works for you → if not, find somewhere peaceful and quiet to work
5. Turn off your mobile or at least put it into silent mode
6. Silence social media alerts
7. Keep the TV off and out of sight
8. Stay organised with to do lists and revision timetables – more importantly, stick to them!
9. Keep to your set study times and don't bite off more than you can chew
10. Study while you're commuting
11. Adopt a positive mental attitude
12. Get into a routine
13. Consider forming a study group to focus on the harder exam concepts
14. Plan rest and reward days into your timetable – these are excellent incentive for you to stay on track with your study plans!

Keep Fit & Eat Well:

'A car won't work if you fill it with the wrong fuel' - your body is exactly the same. You cannot hope to perform unless you remain fit and well. The best way to do this is not underestimate the importance of healthy eating. Beige, starchy foods will make you sluggish; instead start the day with a hearty breakfast like porridge. Aim for the recommended 'five a day' intake of fruit/veg and stock up on the oily fish or blueberries – the so called "super foods".

When hitting the books, it's essential to keep your brain hydrated. If you get dehydrated you'll find yourself lethargic and possibly developing a headache, neither of which will do any favours for your revision. Invest in a good water bottle that you know the total volume of and keep sipping through the day. Don't forget that the amount of water you should be aiming to drink varies depending on your mass, so calculate your own personal recommended intake as follows: 30 ml per kg per day.

It is well known that exercise boosts your wellbeing and instils a sense of discipline. All of which will reflect well in your revision. It's well worth devoting half an hour a day to some exercise, get your heart rate up, break a sweat, and get those endorphins flowing.

Sleep

It's no secret that when revising you need to keep well rested. Don't be tempted to stay up late revising as sleep actually plays an important part in consolidating long term memory. Instead aim for a minimum of 7 hours good sleep each night, in a dark room without any glow from electronic appliances. Install flux (https://justgetflux.com) on your laptop to prevent your computer from disrupting your circadian rhythm. Aim to go to bed the same time each night and no hitting snooze on the alarm clock in the morning!

Revision Timetable

Still struggling to get organised? Then try filling in the example revision timetable below, remember to factor in enough time for short breaks, and stick to it! Remember to schedule in several breaks throughout the day and actually use them to do something you enjoy e.g. TV, reading, YouTube etc.

MONDAY	
TUESDAY	
THURSDAY	
FRIDAY	
SATURDAY	
SUNDAY	
EXAMPLE DAY	School Chemistry Pure

seconds on a section 1 question – move on regardless of how close you think you are to solving it.

Getting the most out of Mock Papers

Mock exams can prove invaluable if tackled correctly. Not only do they encourage you to start revision earlier, they also allow you to **practice and perfect your revision technique**. They are often the best way of improving your knowledge base or reinforcing what you have learnt. Probably the best reason for attempting mock papers is to familiarise yourself with the exam conditions of the NSAA as they are particularly tough.

Start Revision Earlier

Thirty five percent of students agree that they procrastinate to a degree that is detrimental to their exam performance. This is partly explained by the fact that they often seem a long way in the future. In the scientific literature this is well recognised, Dr. Piers Steel, an expert on the field of motivation states that *'the further away an event is, the less impact it has on your decisions'*.

Mock exams are therefore a way of giving you a target to work towards and motivate you in the run up to the real thing – every time you do one treat it as the real deal! If you do well then it's a reassuring sign; if you do poorly then it will motivate you to work harder (and earlier!).

Practice and perfect revision techniques

In case you haven't realised already, revision is a skill all to itself, and can take some time to learn. For example, the most common revision techniques including **highlighting and/or re-reading are quite ineffective** ways of committing things to memory. Unless you are thinking critically about something you are much less likely to remember it or indeed understand it.

Mock exams, therefore allow you to test your revision strategies as you go along. Try spacing out your revision sessions so you have time to forget what you have learnt in-between. This may sound counterintuitive but the second time you remember it for longer. Try teaching another student what you have learnt, this forces you to structure the information in a logical way that may aid memory. Always try to question what you have learnt and appraise its validity. Not only does this aid memory but it is also a useful skill for Oxbridge interviews and beyond.

Improve your knowledge

The act of applying what you have learnt reinforces that piece of knowledge. A question may ask you to think about a relatively basic concept in a novel way (not cited in textbooks), and so deepen your understanding. Exams rarely test word for word what is in the syllabus, so when running through mock papers try to understand how the basic facts are applied and tested in the exam. As you go through the mocks or past papers take note of your performance and see if you consistently under-perform in specific areas, thus highlighting areas for future study.

Get familiar with exam conditions

Pressure can cause all sorts of trouble for even the most brilliant students. The NSAA is a particularly time pressured exam with high stakes – your future (without exaggerating) does depend on your result to a great extent. The real key to the NSAA is overcoming this pressure and remaining calm to allow you to think efficiently.

Mock exams are therefore an excellent opportunity to devise and perfect your own exam techniques to beat the pressure and meet the demands of the exam. **Don't treat mock exams like practice questions – it's imperative you do them under time conditions.**

Things to have done before using this book

Do the ground work

➤ Read in detail: the background, methods, and aims of the NSAA as well logistical considerations such as how to take the NSAA in practice. A good place to start is a NSAA textbook like *The Ultimate NSAA Guide* (flick to the back to get a free copy!) which covers all the groundwork.

➤ It is generally a good idea to start re-capping all your GCSE maths and science.

➤ Practice substituting formulas together to reach a more useful one expressing known variables e.g. $P = IV$ and $V = IR$ can be combined to give $P = V^2/R$ and $P = I^2R$. Remember that calculators are not permitted in the exam, so get comfortable doing more complex long addition, multiplication, division, and subtraction.

➤ Get comfortable rapidly converting between percentages, decimals, and fractions.

➤ Practice developing logical arguments and structuring essays with an obvious introduction, main body, and ending.

➤ These are all things which are easiest to do alongside your revision for exams before the summer break. Not only gaining a head start on your NSAA revision but also complimenting your year 12 studies well.

➤ Discuss scientific problems with others - propose experiments and state what you think the result would be. Be ready to defend your argument. This will rapidly build your scientific understanding for section 2 but also prepare you well for an oxbridge interview.

➤ Read through the NSAA syllabus before you start tackling whole papers. This is absolutely essential. It contains several stated formulae, constants, and facts that you are expected to apply - or may just be an answer in their own right. Familiarising yourself with the syllabus is also a quick way of teaching yourself the additional information other exam boards may learn which you do not. Sifting through the whole NSAA syllabus is a time-consuming process so we have done it for you. **Be sure to flick through the syllabus checklist** later on, which also doubles up as a great revision aid for the night before!

Ease in gently

With the ground work laid, there's still no point in adopting exam conditions straight away. Instead invest in a beginner's guide to the NSAA, which will not only describe in detail the background and theory of the exam, but take you through section by section what is expected. *The Ultimate NSAA Guide* is the most popular NSAA textbook – you can get a free copy by flicking to the back of this book.

When you are ready to move on to past papers, take your time and puzzle your way through all the questions. Really try to understand solutions. A past paper question won't be repeated in your real exam, so don't rote learn methods or facts. Instead, focus on applying prior knowledge to formulate your own approach.

If you're really struggling and have to take a sneak peek at the answers, then practice thinking of alternative solutions. It is unlikely that your answer will be more elegant or succinct than the model answer, but it is still a good task for encouraging creativity with your thinking. Get used to thinking outside the box!

Accelerate and Intensify

Start adopting exam conditions after you've done two past papers. Don't forget that **it's the time pressure that makes the NSAA hard** – if you had as long as you wanted to sit the exam you would probably get 100%. If you're struggling to find comprehensive answers to past papers then NSAA *Past Papers Worked Solutions* contains detailed explained answers to every NSAA past paper question and essay (flick to the back to get a free copy).

Doing all the past papers from 2016 – present twice is a good target for your revision. In any case, choose a paper and proceed with strict exam conditions. Take a short break and then mark your answers before reviewing your progress. For revision purposes, as you go along, keep track of those questions that you guess – these are equally as important to review as those you get wrong.

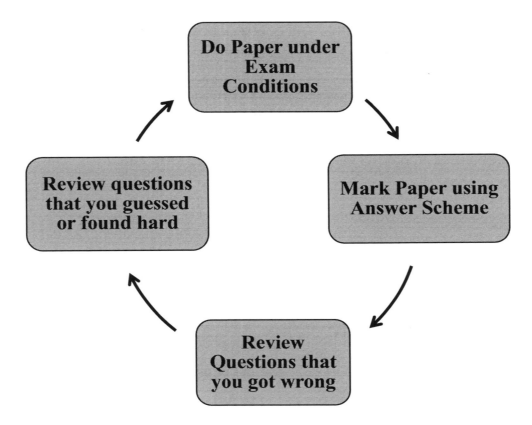

Once you've exhausted all the past papers, move on to tackling the unique mock papers in this book. In general, you should aim to complete one to two mock papers every night in the ten days preceding your exam.

Section 1: An Overview

What will you be tested on?	No. of Questions	Duration
1A: Maths 1B: Physics 1C: Chemistry 1D: Biology 1E: Advanced Maths + Physics	18 MCQs per section You must complete section 1A and two other sections	80 Minutes

Section 1 is the most time-pressured section of the NSAA. As part of section one, you have to pick two sections from biology, chemistry, physics or advanced maths & physics. You have to answer 54 questions in 80 minutes. The questions can be quite difficult and it's easy to get bogged down. However, it's possible to rapidly improve if you prepare correctly so it's well worth spending time on it.

In most cases it will be immediately obvious to you which section will suit you best. Generally, applicants for physical natural sciences will choose physics/maths whilst those for biological sciences will choose the biology and chemistry. However, like the natural sciences Tripos, this is by no means a hard and fast rule – it is extremely important that you choose the section you want to do ahead of time so that you can focus your preparation accordingly.

If you're unsure, take the time to review the content of each section and try out some questions so you can get a better idea of the style and difficulty of the questions. In general, the biology and chemistry questions in the NSAA require the least amount of time per question whilst the maths and physics are more time-draining as they usually consist of multi-step calculations.

Maths

NSAA maths questions are designed to be time draining- if you find yourself consistently not finishing, it might be worth leaving the maths (and probably physics) questions until the very end. Good students sometimes have a habit of making easy questions difficult; remember that section 1A is pitched at GCSE level so you are not expected to know or use calculus or advanced trigonometry in it.

Physics

Physics Questions in the NSAA are challenging as they frequently require you to make leaps in logic and calculations. Thus, before you go any further, ensure you have a firm understanding of the major principles and are confident with commonly examined topics like Newtonian mechanics, electrical circuits and radioactive decay as you may not have covered these at school depending on the specification you did.

Chemistry

Most students don't struggle with NSAA chemistry - however, there are certain questions that even good students tend to struggle with under time pressure e.g. balancing equations and mass calculations. It is essential that you're able to do these quickly as they take up by far the most time in the chemistry questions. Balancing equations intuitively or via trial and error will only get you so far in the NSAA as the equations you'll have to work with will be fairly complex. To avoid wasting valuable time, it is essential you learn a method that will allow you to solve these in less than sixty seconds on a consistent basis.

Biology

The biology questions tend to be fairly straightforward and require the least amount of time. You should be able to do the majority of these within the time limit (often far less). This means that you should be aiming to make up time in these questions. In the majority of cases – you'll either know the answer or not i.e. they test advanced recall so the trick is to ensure that there are no obvious gaps in your knowledge.

Advanced Maths

Section 1E Maths requires a much broader knowledge of the A level Maths curriculum and you're highly advised to revise the topics below before proceeding further with the practice questions in this book. The main concepts include algebra, graphing functions, laws of logarithms, differentiation, integration, logic arguments, geometry, series and Trigonometry.

Advanced Physics

Advanced Physics requires a much broader understanding of the A level Physics and the main concepts include but not limited to vectors and scalars, difference between normal and frictional components of contact forces, simple harmonic motion and oscillations, gravitational forces, electricity and magnetism and radioactivity.

Section 2: An Overview

What will you be tested on?	No. of Questions	Duration
2 questions of 6 covering Biology, Chemistry and Physics	2 questions	40 Minutes

Section two questions are designed to stretch you by putting you out of your comfort zone. In addition to the core knowledge required for section one, you will need to apply core scientific principles in unfamiliar contexts.

All section two questions require you to have the knowledge from section 1A maths as well as the corresponding subject knowledge from section one. For example biology section two questions require 1A maths and 1D Biology. Similarly, physics Section two questions require 1A maths, 1B physics and 1E advanced maths/physics. Each question is out of 25 marks.

Physics

Trying to answer section 2 physics questions without first learning all the core formulas is like trying to run before you can walk – ensure you're completely confident with all the formulas given in sections 1B + 1E before starting the practice questions.

Physics is a very varied subject, and the questions you may be asked in an exam will reflect this variety. Many students have a preferred area within physics, e.g. electronics, astrophysics or mechanics. However, it is important to remember not to neglect any subject area in its entirety on the basis that you will answer questions on another subject. Finally, it is very important to show all working clearly, and not just write the final answer.

Chemistry

Chemistry is dominated by applications in the real world and you can expect the questions to reflect this. If you design your revision round this idea, it will help you not only prepare better as you are more likely to retain the information, but it will also make sure that you are not thrown off by challenging application questions.

There are two main types of chemistry questions: organic and inorganic. Organic chemistry questions often involve drawing and naming molecules, whilst inorganic chemistry questions can be more mathematical. It is paramount that you analyse each question in advance to ensure that you are aware of what is coming up. You do not want to be halfway through a question and realise that you would rather have answered another question!

Biology

Biology questions are heavily knowledge based and require you to apply a principle in order to get to the correct answer. Thus, it essential you're familiar with concepts like genetics, natural selection, cells, organs systems and species interaction. It will make your life a lot easier if you feel comfortable with all the different aspects of biology. Specialisation here can go a long way.

The very nature of the exam is designed to throw you off guard and force you to use your knowledge to come to conclusions you might not have been taught at school. This is what separates good and great students. Applying the principles you have learned, securely and efficiently, will allow you to answer most questions correctly, even if you have never addressed them before.

Biology is a very logical science that is largely based on the idea that the goal is always to reach the maximum amount of effect with a minimum of energy expenditure. Thus, it is obvious that you need to have a sound scientific basis in order to recognise the different connections between topics.

Revision Checklist

MATHS

Syllabus Point	What to Know
1. Number	Understand and use BIDMAS Define; factor, multiple, common factor, highest common factor, least common multiple, prime number, prime factor decomposition, square, positive and negative square root, cube and cube root Use index laws to simplify multiplication and division of powers Interpret, order and calculate with numbers written in standard index form Convert between fractions, decimals and percentages Understand and use direct and indirect proportion Apply the unitary method Use surds and π in exact calculations, simplify expressions that contain surds. Calculate upper and lower bounds to contextual problems Rounding to a given number of decimal places or significant figures
2. Algebra	Simplify rational expressions by cancelling or factorising and cancelling Set up quadratic equations and solve them by factorising Set up and use equations to solve problems involving direct and indirect proportion Use linear expressions to describe the nth term of a sequence Use Cartesian coordinates in all four quadrants Equation of a straight line, $y=mx+c$, parallel lines have the same gradient Graphically solve simultaneous equations Recognise and interpret graphs of simple cubic functions, the reciprocal function, trigonometric functions and the exponential function $y=kx$ for integer values of x and simple positive values of k Draw transformations of $y = f(x)$ [$y=af(x)$, $y=f(ax)$, $y=f(x)+a$, $y=f(x-a)$ only]
3. Geometry	Recall and use properties of angle at a point, on a straight line, perpendicular lines and opposite angles at a vertex, and the sums of the interior and exterior angles of polygons Understand congruence and similarity Use Pythagoras' theorem in 2-D and 3-D Use the trigonometric ratios, between 0° and 180°, to solve problems in 2-D and 3-D Understand and construct geometrical proofs, including using circle theorems: a. **the angle subtended at the circumference in a semicircle is a right angle** b. **the tangent at any point on a circle is perpendicular to the radius at that point** Describe and transform 2-D shapes using single or combined rotations, reflections, translations, or enlargements, including the use of vector notation
4. Measures	Calculate perimeters and areas of shapes made from triangles, rectangles, and other shapes, find circumferences and areas of circles, including arcs and sectors Calculate the volumes and surface areas of prisms, pyramids, spheres, cylinders, cones and solids made from cubes and cuboids (formulae given for the sphere and cone) Use vectors, including the sum of two vectors, algebraically and graphically Discuss the inaccuracies of measurements Understand and use three-figure bearings
5. Statistics	Identify possible sources of bias in experimental methodology Discrete vs. continuous data Design and use two-way tables Interpret cumulative frequency tables and graphs, box plots and histograms Define mean, median, mode, modal class, range, and inter-quartile range Interpret scatter diagrams and recognise correlation, drawing and using lines of best fit Compare sets of data by using statistical measures
6. Probability	List all the outcomes for single and combined events Identify different mutually exclusive outcomes and know that the sum of the probabilities of all these outcomes is 1 Construct and use Venn diagrams Know when to add or multiply two probabilities, and understand conditional probability Understand the use of tree diagrams to represent outcomes of combined events Compare experimental and theoretical probabilities Understand that if an experiment is repeated, the outcome may be different

PHYSICS

	Syllabus Point	What to Know
1.	Electricity	Electrostatics: charging of insulators by friction, gain of electrons induces negative charge, uses in paint spraying and dust extraction Conductors vs. insulators **Current = charge/ time** **Resistance = voltage/ current**, how to connect ammeters and voltmeters V–I graphs for a fixed resistor and a filament lamp Series vs. parallel circuits Resistors in series (but not parallel) **Voltage = energy/ charge** Basic circuit symbols and diagrams **Power = current x voltage** **Energy = power x time** $\left(\frac{V_p}{V_s} = \frac{n_p}{n_s}\right)$ thus when 100% efficient $V_p I_p = V_s I_s$ Method of electromagnetic induction, applied to a generator
2.	Motion and Energy	**Speed = distance/time**, difference between speed and velocity **Acceleration = change in velocity/time** Distance-time vs. velocity-time graphs (including calculation and interpretation of gradients and average speed) Newtons laws: -First: **momentum = mass x velocity**, conservation of momentum -Second: **force = mass x acceleration**, **force = rate of change of momentum**, resultant force, **W = mg**, gravitational field strength (~10N/kg on Earth), free fall acceleration, terminal velocity -Third = every action has an equal and opposite reaction **Work = force x distance** = transfer of energy **Potential energy = mgh** **Kinetic energy = $\frac{1}{2}mv^2$** Crumple zones and road safety **Power = energy transfer/time** Conservation of energy, forms of energy, useful and wasted energy, % efficiency
3.	Thermal physics	Conduction: factors affecting rate of conduction Convection: temperature and density of fluids Radiation: infrared, absorption and re-emission Particle models of solids, liquids, gases, and state changes **Density = mass/volume** Experimental methods of determining densities
4.	Waves	Transfer of energy without net movement of matter, transverse (electromagnetic) vs. longitudinal (sound) Define amplitude, wavelength, frequency (1Hz = 1 wave/second), and period **Wave speed = frequency x wavelength** Reflection and refraction (including ray diagrams), and Doppler effect Application of ultrasound
5.	Electromagnetic Spectrum	Properties of electromagnetic waves (speed of light, transverse) Distinguished by wavelength, longest to shortest: radio, microwaves, infrared, visible light, ultraviolet, x-ray, gamma Applications and dangers
6.	Radioactivity	Atomic structure, charges and mass of subatomic particles, ionisation Radioactive decay: alpha vs. beta vs. gamma emission, decay equations, define activity of a sample Ionising radiation: penetrating ability, ionising ability, presence of background radiation (including origin), applications and dangers Define half-life and interpret from graphs Nuclear fission: absorption of thermal neutrons, uranium-235 (decay equation), chain reaction Nuclear fusion: hydrogen to form helium, requires significant temperature and pressure, significance as a possible energy sauce

CHEMISTRY

Syllabus Point	What to Know
1. **Atomic Structure**	Structure of the atom Relative masses and charges of protons, neutrons, and electrons Atomic vs. mass number, electron configurations Isotope definition Define A_r, calculate M_r Mass spectrometry
2. **Periodic Table**	Organisation of periods vs. groups and metals vs. non-metals Displacement reactions and reactivity, extraction of metals from their ores Position of the alkali metals, halogens, noble gases, and transition metals, relate position to electron configuration Reactivity increases down a metal group but decreases down a non-metal group Properties of transition metals Calculate A_r from isotopic mass and abundance.
3. **Reactions & Equations**	Conservation of matter Endothermic vs. exothermic Charges of common polyatomic cations (e.g. CO_3^{2-}) Formulate equations describing redox reactions Factors that affect the position of equilibrium in reversible reactions
4. **Calculations**	Define the mole, convert grams to moles, **1 mole of gas = 24dm^3** Percentage composition by mass of a compound, empirical vs. molecular formulae Calculate reactants in excess Calculate molar concentration: **moles = (volume cm^3/1000) x concentration mol dm^{-3}** Titration calculation, define saturated **Percentage yield = (actual yield/predicted yield) x 100**
5. **Redox**	Describe oxidation vs. reduction Recognise disproportionation Transfer of electrons, determine oxidation states
6. **Bonding**	Define elements vs. compounds Ionic vs. covalent vs. metallic bonding, simple and giant covalent structures
7. **Groups**	Alkali metals: group 1, electron donors, low melting/boiling points, store in oil, describe reaction with water, oxygen, and halogens Halogens: most reactive non-metals, establishing reactivity series with displacement reactions, reactions with silver nitrate Noble gases: least reactive elements Transition metals: position in the periodic table, properties and uses
8. **Separation techniques**	Compounds vs. mixtures Miscible liquid separation: fractional distillation, chromatography Immiscible liquid separation: separating funnel Dissolving, filtering, distillation, and crystallisation
9. **Acids and Bases**	Definitions and properties of strong and weak acids and bases
10. **Rates of Reaction**	Effects of concentration, temperature, particle size, catalyst presence, and pressure Calculate loss of reactant over time, predict measurable variables from chemical equation Collision theory and activation energy Function of catalysts
11. **Energetics**	Exothermic vs. endothermic
12. **Electrolysis**	Define electrode, cathode, anode, and electrolyte Why DC not AC? Electrolysis of brine and electroplating using copper sulfate
13. **Organic**	Alkanes vs. alkenes (general formulae, IUPAC terminology, saturated vs. unsaturated, combustion) Polymers: method of alkene polymerisation, define monomer, identify biodegradable and non-biodegradable polymers General formulae, chemical properties, and uses of alcohols and carboxylic acids

BIOLOGY

Syllabus Point	What to Know
1. Cells	Differences in cellular structure and function between: -Animals: cell membrane, cytoplasm, nucleus, mitochondrion -Plants: cell membrane, cytoplasm, nucleus, cell wall, chloroplast, mitochondrion, vacuole -Bacteria: cell membrane, cytoplasm, cell wall, no true nucleus Multiple cells form tissues, several tissues form an organ
2. Movement Across Membranes	Difference between diffusion, osmosis, and active transport Role of cellular proteins Need for mitochondria in active transport
3. Cell Division & Sex	Define mitosis vs. meiosis Asexual vs. sexual reproduction Sex determination: females XX, males XY Calculate gender ratio
4. Inheritance	Role of nucleus in cell function Define genes, alleles, dominant, recessive, heterozygous, homozygous, phenotype, and genotype Use monohybrid crosses and family trees to calculate ratios/percentages Cystic fibrosis, polydactyly, and Huntington's
5. DNA	Chromosomes Structure of DNA Protein synthesis from DNA base triplets
6. Gene Technologies	Methods of experimental gene insertion Roles of stem cells: embryonic vs. adult
7. Variation	Natural selection: variation, differential survival based on adaptation, only those best adapted survive to reproduce Antibiotic resistance (MRSA) Genetic vs. environmental causes of variation Extinction occurs when organisms can't adapt quickly enough
8. Enzymes	Define biological catalyst Mechanism of action: lock and key vs. induced fit Effects of temperature and pH The role of amylase, protease, and lipase
9. Animal Physiology	Define and describe aerobic and anaerobic respiration Define homeostasis Negative vs. positive feedback Regulation of blood glucose, water, and temperature Function of white blood cells Hormones: travel in blood to target organs Structure (anatomy), organisation, and function of the: -Nervous system: sensory vs. motor vs. relay neurons, reflex arcs, synapses -Respiratory system: thorax, process of ventilation and gas exchange -Circulatory system: sinoatrial node, atrioventricular node, heart rate and ECGs, differences between arteries, veins, and capillaries, blood groups -Digestive system: digestive enzymes, pH -Kidney: the nephron, role in homeostasis
10. Environment	Food chains, energy flow Pyramids of biomass Define niche Factors affecting population growth Carbon cycle: photosynthesis, respiration, combustion, decomposition Nitrogen cycle: bacteria, nitrification, decomposition, nitrogen fixation, denitrification

ADVANCED MATHS

Syllabus Point	What to Know
1. **Algebra**	Laws of Indices and manipulation of Surds Quadratic Functions: Graphs, use of discriminant, completing the square Solving Simultaneous Equations via Substitution Manipulation of polynomials e.g. expanding brackets, factorising Use of Factor Theorem + Remainder Theorem
2. **Differentiation**	First order and second order derivatives Familiarity with notation: $\frac{dy}{dx}, \frac{d^2y}{dx^2}, f'(x), f''(x)$ Differentiation of functions like $y = x^n$
3. **Geometry**	Equations for a circle: 1. $(x-a)^2 + (y-b)^2 = r^2$ 2. $x^2 + y^2 + cx + dy + e = 0$ Equations for a straight line: $y - y_1 = m(x - x_1)$ & $Ax + by + c = 0$ Circle Properties - The angle subtended by an arc at the centre of a circle is double the size of the angle subtended by the arc on the circumference - The opposite angles in a cyclic quadrilateral summate to 180 degrees - The angle between the tangent and chord at the point of contact is equal to the angle in the alternate segment - The tangent at any point on a circle is perpendicular to the radius at that point - Angles in the same segment are equal - The Perpendicular from the centre to a chord bisects the chord
4. **Graphing Functions**	Sketching of common functions including lines, quadratics, cubics, trigonometric functions, logarithmic functions and exponential functions Manipulation of functions using simple transformations Graph of $y = a^x$ series
5. **Integration**	Definite and indefinite integrals for $y = x^n$ Solving Differential Equations in the form: $\frac{dy}{dx} = f(x)$ Understanding of the Fundamental Theorem of Calculus and its application: $\int_a^b f(x)dx = F(b) - F(a)$, where $F'(x) = f(x)$ $\frac{d}{dx}\int_a^x f(t)dt = f(x)$
6. **Law of Logarithms**	$a^b = c \leftrightarrow b = log_a c$ and $log_a a = 1$ $log_a x + log_a y = log_a(xy)$ and $log_a x - log_a y = log_a\left(\frac{x}{y}\right)$ $k\, log_a x = log_a(x^k)$ and $log_a \frac{1}{x} = -log_a x$
7. **Logic Arguments**	Terminology: True, false, and, or not, necessary, sufficient, for all, for some, there exists Arguments in the format: -If A then B, -A if B -A only if B -A if and only if B
8. **Series**	Arithmetic series and Geometric Series Summing to a finite and infinite geometric series Binomial Expansions and Factorials
9. **Trigonometry**	Solution of trigonometric identities Values of sin, cost, tan for 0, 30, 45, 60 and 90 degrees Sine, Cosine, Tangent graphs, symmetries, periodicities Sin Rule: $\frac{a}{SinA} = \frac{b}{Sin\,B} = \frac{c}{Sin\,C}$ Cosine Rule: $c^2 = a^2 + b^2 - 2ab\,cosC$ $Area\ of\ Triangle = \frac{1}{2}ab\sin C$ $\sin^2\theta + \cos^2\theta = 1$ $tan\theta = \frac{sin\theta}{\cos\theta}$

ADVANCED PHYSICS

Syllabus Point	What to Know
1. **Vector**	Calculate, manipulate and resolve Vectors and their components & resultants Graphical interpretations of vectors + scalars
2. **Mechanics & Motion**	Calculate the moment of a force Difference between normal and frictional components of contact forces Understand how to use the coefficient of Friction including $F = \mu R$ and $F \leq \mu R$ Use of the equations of Motion -Force $F = \frac{\Delta mv}{t}$ Derivation + Integration of physical values e.g. Velocity from an acceleration-time graph Principle of conservation of momentum (including coalescence)+ Linear Momentum -Conservation of momentum $\Delta mv = 0$ Application of Newton's laws e.g. -Linear Motion of point masses -Modelling of objects moving vertically or on a planet -Objects connected by a rod or pulleys Principle of conservation of energy and its application to kinetic/gravitational potential energy
3. **Gravitational Forces**	Gravitational Force: $F = \frac{Gm_1 m_2}{r^2} = \frac{GMm}{r^2}$ Gravitational Potential: $V = \frac{Gm}{r}$ Gravitational Acceleration: $a = \frac{GM}{r^2} = \frac{\partial V}{\partial r}$
4. **Simple Harmonic Motion & Oscillations**	Angular velocity: $\omega = \frac{v}{r} = 2\pi f$ Angular acceleration: $a = -(2\pi f)^2 x = -(2\pi f)^2 A Cos(2\pi ft)$ -Speed $v = \pm 2\pi f \sqrt{A^2 - x^2}$ Angular Displacement: $x = A Cos(2\pi ft)$ Concept of Wave: - Speed $c = f\lambda$ - Period $T = \frac{1}{f}$ - Snell's law $n_1 sin\theta_1 = n_2 sin\theta_2$
5. **Electricity & Magnetism**	Current and Electricity Concepts: -E.m.f $\varepsilon = \frac{E}{Q} = I(R + r)$ -Resistivity $\rho = \frac{RA}{l}$ -Resistors in series $R = \sum_{i=1}^{n} R_i$ -Resistors in parallel s $R = \sum_{i=1}^{n} \frac{1}{R_i}$ Magnetic Field Concepts: -Magnetic flux $\emptyset = BA$ -Magnetic flux linkage $\emptyset N = BAN$ -Magnitude of induced e.m.f $\varepsilon = N\frac{\Delta\emptyset}{\Delta t}$
6. **Radioactivity**	Radioactivity Concepts: -Decay $N = N_0 e^{-\lambda t}$ -Half life $T_{1/2} = \frac{ln2}{\lambda}$ -Activity $A = \lambda N$ -Energy $E = mc^2$

How to use this Book

If you have done everything this book has described so far then you should be well equipped to meet the demands of the NSAA, and therefore **the mock papers in the rest of this book should ONLY be completed under exam conditions**.

This means:

➤ Absolute silence – no TV or music
➤ Absolute focus – no distractions such as eating your dinner
➤ Strict time constraints – no pausing half way through
➤ No checking the answers as you go
➤ Give yourself a maximum of three minutes between sections – keep the pressure up
➤ Complete the entire paper before marking
➤ Mark harshly

In practice this means setting aside two hours in an evening to find a quiet spot without interruptions and tackle the paper. Completing one mock paper every evening in the week running up to the exam would be an ideal target.

➤ Tackle the paper as you would in the exam.
➤ Return to mark your answers, but mark harshly if there's any ambiguity.
➤ Highlight any areas of concern.
➤ If warranted read up on the areas you felt you underperformed to reinforce your knowledge.
➤ If you inadvertently learnt anything new by muddling through a question, go and tell somebody about it to reinforce what you've discovered.

Finally relax… the NSAA is an exhausting exam, concentrating so hard continually for two hours will take its toll. So, being able to relax and switch off is essential to keep yourself sharp for exam day! Make sure you reward yourself after you finish marking your exam.

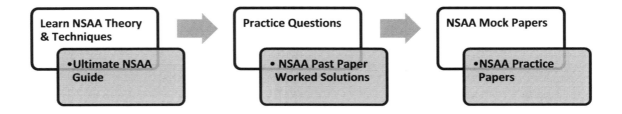

Scoring Tables

Use these to keep a record of your scores from past papers – you can then easily see which paper you should attempt next (always the one with the lowest score).

SECTION 1	1st Attempt	2nd Attempt	3rd Attempt
Specimen			
2016			
2017			

SECTION 2	1st Attempt	2nd Attempt	3rd Attempt
Specimen			
2016			
2017			

And the same again here but with our mock papers:

SECTION 1	1st Attempt	2nd Attempt	3rd Attempt
Mock A			
Mock B			

SECTION 2	1st Attempt	2nd Attempt	3rd Attempt
Mock A			
Mock B			

Mock Paper A

Section 1A: Maths

Question 1 $1 + \cancel{4\cancel{14}\cancel{18}} - \cancel{6\sqrt{2}} + 1 \quad +9 + \cancel{6\sqrt{2}} + 2$

Simplify fully: $1 + (3\sqrt{2} - 1)^2 + (3 + \sqrt{2})^2$

A $30 + 6\sqrt{2} - 2\sqrt{18}$ C $3[2(\sqrt{2} - 1) + 2]$ (F)   31
B $30 + 6\sqrt{2} + 2\sqrt{18}$ D   22
                                            E   29

Question 2

Calculate the radius of a sphere which has a surface area three times as great as its volume.

A   0.5   D   2   F   More information is
(B)   1   E   2.5   needed
C   1.5

 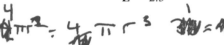

Question 3

There are 1200 international airports in the world. If 4 flights take off every hour from each airport, calculate the annual number of commercial flights worldwide, to the nearest 1 million.

A   28 million   C   42 million   E   48 million
(B)   36 million   D   44 million   F   56 million

365
96
2190
33050

⮞ F + G − H = 2
⮞ F − G − H = 3

A   -2
B   -0.5
C   0
D   0.5
E   2

Calculate the value of FGH.

35240000

Question 4

Given that:

⮞ F + G + H = 1   5240

35240 × 1000
1 2

Question 5

How many seconds are there in 66 weeks? [n! = 1 x 2 x 3 x... x n].

$66 \times 7 \times 24 \times 60 \times 60$

A   7!   C   9!   E   11!
B   8!   D   10!   (F)   12!

Question 6

The diagram to the right shows a series of regular pentagons. What is the product of angles **a** and **b**?

A   580°   (C)   3,888°   E   9,255°
B   1,111°   D   7,420°

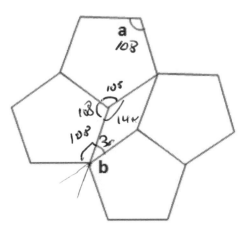

108
36
6 48
108   3 2 48
2   3 888
216

360 − 216 = 144

144×2 = 288
360 − 288 = 72/2 = 36

Question 7

The table below shows the results of a study investigating antibiotic resistance in staphylococcus populations.

Antibiotic	Number of Bacteria tested	Number of Resistant Bacteria
Benzyl-penicillin	10^{11}	98
Chloramphenicol	10^{9}	1200
Metronidazole	10^{8}	256
Erythtomycin	10^{5}	2

A single staphylococcus bacterium is chosen at random from a similar population. Resistance to any one antibiotic is independent of resistance to others. Calculate the probability that the bacterium selected will be resistant to all four drugs.

A   1 in 10^{12}
B   1 in 10^{6}
C   1 in 10^{20}
D   1 in 10^{25}
E   1 in 10^{30}
F   1 in 10^{35}

$$\frac{98}{10^{11}} \times \frac{1200}{10^{9}} \times \frac{256}{10^{8}} \times \frac{2}{10^{5}}$$

$$\frac{98}{90 \times 1200 \times 250 \times 2}{10^{33}}$$

Question 8

Evaluate: $\dfrac{3.4 \times 10^{11} + 3.4 \times 10^{10}}{6.8 \times 10^{12}}$

$3.4 + 3.14 \quad x(10^{4}$

A 5.5×10^{-12}
B 5.5×10^{-2} (circled)
C 5.5×10^{1}
D 5.5×10^{2}
E 5.5×10^{10}
F 5.5×10^{12}

$\dfrac{x \times 10^{10}(10+1)}{x \times 10^{10} \times 2 \times 100}$

$\dfrac{11}{2000}$

$\frac{1}{2} \times 10^{-3}$ $\dfrac{9 \times 12 \times 25 \times 2}{10^{29}}$

Question 9

Find the values of angles b and c.

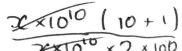

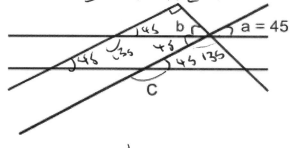

$a = 45$

100

$2300 = 5000$

10^{26}

A   45° and 135°
B   45° and 130°
C   50° and 135°
D   55° and 130°
E   More information needed.

Question 10

Calculate the perimeter of a regular polygon which has interior angles of 150° and sides of 15cm.

A   75 cm
B   150 cm
C   180 cm
D   225 cm
E   1,500 cm
F   More information is needed.

$\dfrac{360}{n} = 30$

$n = 12$

15
12
30
150
180

Question 11

A tangent line to a circle of radius 3 metres intersects with another line 4 metres from its tangent point. How far is this point of intersection from the centre of the circle?

A   1 metres
B   3 metres
C   5 metres
D   7 metres
E   9 metres

Question 12
Simplify and solve: (e - a) (e + b) (e − c) (e + d)...(e - z)?

A   0
B e^{26}

C e^{26} (a-b+c-d...+z)
D e^{26} (a+b-c+d...-z)

E e^{26} (abcd...z)
F   None of the above.

Question 13
Each vertex of a square lies directly on the edge of a circle with a radius of 1cm. Calculate the area of the circle that is not occupied by the square.

A $0.25cm^2$
B $0.5cm^2$

C $0.75cm^2$
D $1.0cm^2$

E $1.25cm^2$
F $1.5cm$

Question 14
The diagram below shows a series of identical sports fields:

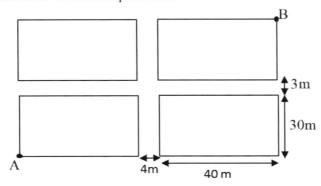

Calculate the shortest distance between points A and B.
A   100 m
B   105 m

C   146 m
D   148 m

E   154 m
F   None of the above.

Question 15
Calculate $\dfrac{1.25 \times 10^{10} + 1.25 \times 10^9}{2.5 \times 10^8}$

A   0
B   1

C   55
D   110

E 1.25×10^8
F 5.5×10^7

G 5.5×10^8

Question 16
Evaluate the following expression: $\left(\frac{6}{8} \times \frac{7}{3}\right) \div \left(\frac{7}{5} \times \frac{2}{6}\right) \times 0.40 \times 15\% \times 5\% \times \pi \times \left(\sqrt{e^2}\right) \times 0.20 \times (e\pi)^{-1}$

A $\dfrac{4}{55}$

B $\dfrac{8}{770}$

C $\dfrac{9}{4,000}$

D $\dfrac{8}{54,321}$

E $\dfrac{9}{67,800}$

Question 17

Rearrange the following to make m the subject: $T = 4\pi \sqrt{\dfrac{(M+3m)l}{3(M+2m)g}}$

A $m = \dfrac{16\pi^2 lM - 3gMT^2}{48\pi^2 l - 6gT^2}$

C $m = \dfrac{3gMT^2 - 16\pi^2 lM}{6gT^2 - 48\pi^2 l}$

E $m = \left(\dfrac{16\pi^2 lM - 3gMT^2}{6gT^2 - 48\pi^2 l}\right)^2$

B $m = \dfrac{16\pi^2 lM - 3gMT^2}{6gT^2 - 48\pi^2 l}$

D $m = \dfrac{4\pi^2 lM - 3gMT^2}{6gT^2 - 16\pi^2 l}$

Question 18

The mean of a set of 11 numbers is 6. Two numbers are removed and the mean is now 5. Which of the following is not a possible combination of removed numbers?

A   1 and 20   C   10 and 11   E   19 and 2

B   6 and 9   D   15 and 6

END OF SECTION

Section 1B: Physics

Question 19

Element $^{188}_{90}X$ decays into two equal daughter nuclei after a single alpha decay and the release of gamma radiation. What is the daughter element?

A	$^{91}_{45}D$	**C**	$^{184}_{88}D$	**E**	$^{186}_{45}D$
B	$^{92}_{44}D$	**D**	$^{186}_{90}D$		

Question 20

An unknown element has two isotopes: ^{76}X and ^{78}X. $A_r = 76.5$. Which of the statements below are true of X?

1. ^{76}X is three times as abundant as ^{78}X.
2. ^{78}X is three times as abundant as ^{76}X.
3. ^{76}X is more stable than ^{78}X.

A	1 only	**C**	3 only	**E**	2 and 3
B	2 only	**D**	1 and 3	**F**	None of the above.

Question 21

A crane is 40m tall. The lifting arm is 5m long and the counterbalance arm is 2m long. The beam joining the two weighs 350kg, and is of uniform thickness. The lifting arm lifts a 2000kg mass. What counterbalance mass is required to balance exactly around the centre point?

A	4,220kg	**C**	5,013kg	**E**	10,525kg
B	4,820kg	**D**	5,263kg		

Question 22

A ball of radius 2 m and density 3 kg/m^3 is released from the top of a 20m frictionless ramp and rolls down. What is its speed at the bottom? Take $g = 10$m^{-2}.

A	1 ms^{-1}	**C**	7 ms^{-1}	**E**	14 ms^{-1}
B	4 ms^{-1}	**D**	9 ms^{-1}	**F**	20 ms^{-1}

Question 23

Which of the following statements is true regarding the Doppler Effect?

A   The Doppler Effect applies only to sounds.
B   The Doppler Effect makes ambulances appear to have a higher frequency when driving towards you.
C   The Doppler Effect makes ambulances sound higher-pitched when driving away from you.
D   The Doppler Effect means you never hear the real siren sound as an ambulance drives past.

Question 24

A 1.2 V battery is rated at 2500 mA hours and is used to power a 30 W light. How many batteries will it take to power the light for 1 hour?

A	1	**C**	10	**E**	100
B	6	**D**	60		

Question 25
A funicular railway like the one illustrated lifts a full carriage weighing 3600kg up an incline. The distance travelled is 200m, and the vertical ascent, **v**, is 80m. Ten passengers weighing an average of 72kg disembark, then the carriage descends. As a result of efficient design, the energy from the descent is stored to drive the next ascent. Assuming the same load of 10 passengers then enters the car, how powerful an engine is required to move the carriage at 4ms⁻¹?

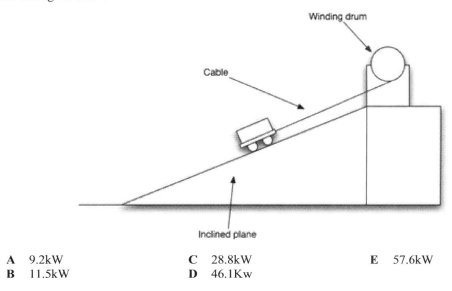

A	9.2kW	C	28.8kW	E	57.6kW
B	11.5kW	D	46.1Kw		

Question 26
For Christmas, Mr James decorates his house with 20 strings of 150 bulbs each. Each 150-bulb string of lights is rated at 50 Watts. Mr James turns the lights on at 8pm and off at 6am each night. The lights are used for 20 days in total.

If 100 kJ of energy costs 2p, how much is the total cost Mr James has to pay?

A	£2160.00	C	£14.40	E	£0.24
B	£144.00	D	£0.72		

Question 27
Which of the following statements is true regarding waves?

A	Waves can transfer mass in the direction of propagation.	C	All light waves have the same energy.
B	All waves have the same energy.	D	Waves can interfere with each other.
		E	None of the above.

Question 28
A mechanical winch lifts up a bag of grain in a mill from the floor into a hopper.

Which of the following statements are TRUE?
1. This increases gravitational potential energy
2. The gravitational potential energy is independent of the mass of the grain
3. The work done is the difference between the gravitational potential energy at the hopper and when the grain is on the floor
4. The work done is the difference between the kinetic energy of the grain in the hopper and on the floor

A	1 only	C	1 and 4	E	1, 2 and 4
B	1 and 3	D	1, 2 and 3	F	None of the above

Question 29

Rearrange $\frac{(7x+10)}{(9x+5)} = 3z^2 + 2$, to make x the subject.

A. $x = \frac{15\,z^2}{7 - 9(3z^2+2)}$

B. $x = \frac{15\,z^2}{7 + 9(3z^2+2)}$

C. $x = -\frac{15\,z^2}{7 - 9(3z^2+2)}$

D. $x = -\frac{15\,z^2}{7 + 9(3z^2+2)}$

E. $x = -\frac{15\,z^2}{7 + 3(3z^2+2)}$

F. $x = \frac{15\,z^2}{7 + 3(3z^2+2)}$

Question 30

A barometer records atmospheric pressure as 10^5 Pa. Recalling that the diameter of the Earth is 1.2×10^7 m, estimate the mass of the atmosphere. [Assume $g = 10$ ms^{-2}]

A 4.5×10^8 kg

B 4.5×10^{10} kg

C 4.5×10^{12} kg

D 4.5×10^{13} kg

E 4.5×10^{19} kg

F   More information is required

Question 31

A 6kg missile is fired and decelerates at 6ms^{-2}. What is the difference in resistive force compared to a 2kg missile fired and decelerating at 8ms^{-2}?

A   8N

B   12N

C   16N

D   20N

E   24N

Question 32

Which will have a greater current, a circuit with two identical resistors in series or one with the same two resistors in parallel?

A   Series more than parallel.

B   Parallel more than series.

C   Same in both.

D   More information needed.

Question 33

A 2,000 kg car is driving down the road at 36 km per hour. A deer runs out into the road 105 m in front of the car. It takes the driver 0.5 seconds to react to the deer and hit the brakes. The car stops just in time. What is average braking force exerted?

A   20 N

B   100 N

C   200 N

D   1,000 N

E   2,000 N

Question 34

A man cycles along a road at the rate shown in the graph below:

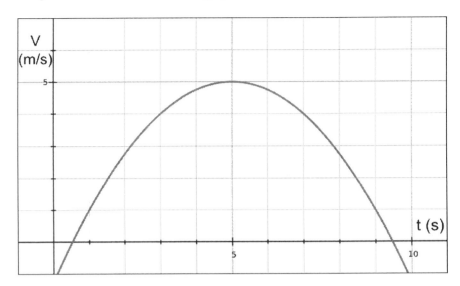

Calculate his displacement at t = 10 seconds.

A 5 m	**C** 25 m	**E** 35 m
B 10 m	**D** 30 m	**F** 40 m

Question 35

Put the following types of electromagnetic waves in ascending order of wavelength:

	Shortest - Longest			
A	Visible Light	Ultraviolet	Infrared	X Ray
B	Visible Light	Infrared	Ultraviolet	X Ray
C	Infrared	Visible Light	Ultraviolet	X Ray
D	Infrared	Visible Light	X Ray	Ultraviolet
E	X Ray	Ultraviolet	Visible Light	Infrared
F	X Ray	Ultraviolet	Infrared	Visible Light
G	Ultraviolet	X Ray	Visible Light	Infrared

Question 36

In a lights display, a 100W water fountain shoots 1L of water vertically upward every second. What is the maximum height attained by the jet of water, as measured from where it first leaves the fountain? Assume that there is no air resistance, that the fountain is 100% efficient and g=10 ms^{-2}

A 2m	**C** 10m	**E**	The initial speed of the jet is required to
B 5m	**D** 20m		calculate the maximum height

END OF SECTION

Section 1C: Chemistry

Question 37

A is a group 3 element and *B* is a group 16 element. Which row best describes what happens to *A* when it reacts with *B*?

	Electrons are	Atom Size
A	Gained	Increases
B	Gained	Decreases
C	Gained	Unchanged
D	Lost	Increases
E	Lost	Decreases
F	Lost	Unchanged

Question 38

Which of the following correctly describes the product of the polymerisation of chloroethene molecules?

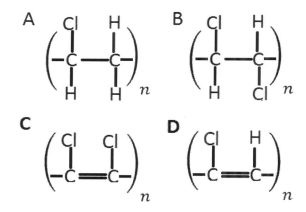

Question 39

Which of the following are true about the reaction between alkenes and hydrogen halides?

1. The product formed is fully saturated.
2. The hydrogen halide binds at the alkene's saturated double bond.
3. The hydrogen halide forms ionic bonds with the alkene.

A	Only 1	C	Only 3	E	2 and 3	G	All of the
B	Only 2	D	1 and 2	F	1 and 3		above.
						H	None of the
							above.

Question 40

Which of the following correctly describes the product of the reaction between propene and hydrofluoric acid (HF)?

A	$C(F)H_3$-CH_2-CH_3	C	CH_3-$C(F)H_2$-CH_2	E	None of the above.
B	CH_3-$C(F)H$-CH_3	D	CH_3-$C(F)H_2$-CH_3		

Question 41
For the following reaction, which of the statements below are true?

$$N_{2(g)} + 3\ H_{2(g)} \rightleftharpoons 2\ NH_{3(g)}$$

1. Increasing pressure will cause the equilibrium to shift to the right.
2. Increasing pressure will form more ammonia gas.
3. Increasing the concentration of N_2 will create more ammonia.

A 1 only	C 3 only	E 2 and 3	G None of the
B 2 only	D 1 and 2	F All of the above.	above.

Question 42
When sodium and chlorine react to form salt, which of the following best represents the bonding and electron configurations of the products and reactants?

	Sodium (s)		Chlorine (g)		Salt (s)	
	Intra-element bond	Element electron configuration	Intra-element bond	Element electron configuration	Compound bond	Compound electron configuration
A	Ionic	2, 8, 1	Covalent	2, 8, 8, 1	Ionic	2, 8, 1 : 2, 8, 8, 1
B	Metallic	2, 7	Covalent	2, 8, 1	Ionic	2, 8 : 2, 8
C	Covalent	2, 8, 2	Ionic	2, 8, 8	Covalent	2, 8 : 2, 8, 8
D	Ionic	2, 7	Ionic	2, 8, 8, 7	Covalent	2, 7 : 2, 8, 8, 7
E	Metallic	2, 8, 1	Covalent	2, 8, 7	Ionic	2, 8 : 2, 8, 8

Question 43
A cylindrical candle of diameter 4cm burns steadily at a rate of 1cm per hour. Assuming the candle is composed entirely of paraffin wax ($C_{24}H_{52}$) of density 900 kgm^{-3} and undergoes complete combustion, how much energy is transferred in 30 minutes? You may assume the molar combustion energy is 11,000 $kJmol^{-1}$, and that $\pi=3$.

A 140,000 J	C 185,000 J	E 215,000 J
B 175,000 J	D 200,500 J	F 348,000 J

Question 44
On analysis, an organic substance is found to contain 41.4% Carbon, 55.2% Oxygen and 3.45% Hydrogen by mass. Which of the following could be the chemical formula of this substance?

A $C_3O_3H_6$	C $C_4O_2H_4$	E $C_4O_2H_8$
B $C_3O_3H_{12}$	D $C_4O_4H_4$	F More information needed

Question 45
200 cm^3 of a 1.8 $moldm^{-3}$ solution of sodium nitrate ($NaNO_3$) is used in a chemical reaction. How many moles of sodium nitrate is this?

A. 0.09 mol	B. 0.36 mol	C. 0.42 mol	D. 0.85 mol	E. 0.92 mol

Question 46
Which of the following correctly describes the product of the reaction between hydrochloric acid and but-2-ene?

A $CH_3-CH_2-C(Cl)H-CH_3$	C $C(Cl)H_2-CH_2-CH_2-CH_3$	E None of the above
B $CH_3-C(Cl)-CH_2-CH_3$	D $CH_3-CH_2-CH_2-C(Cl)H_2$	

Question 47

The electrolysis of brine can be represented by the following equation: $2\,NaCl + 2\,X = 2\,Y + Z + Cl_2$
What are the correct formulae for X, Y and Z?

	X	Y	Z
A	H_2O	H_2	O_2
B	H_2O	NaOH	O_2
C	H_2O	NaOH	H_2
D	H_2	H_2O	O_2
E	H_2	NaOH	O_2
F	H_2	NaOH	H_2
G	NaOH	H_2O	H_2
H	NaOH	H_2O	O_2

Question 48

Which of the following statements is true regarding electrolysis?

A   Using an AC-current is most effective.
B   Using a DC-current is most effective.
C   An AC-current causes cations to gather at the cathode.
D   A DC-current would plate the anode in copper from a copper sulphate solution.
E   No current is used in electrolysis.

Question 49

Which of the following in NOT a polymer?

A   Polythene
B   Glycogen
C   Collagen
D   Starch
E   DNA
F   Triglyceride

Question 50

Place the following substances in order from most to least reactive:

1	Sodium
2	Potassium
3	Aluminium
4	Zinc
5	Copper
6	Magnesium

A   1 » 2 » 6 » 3 » 4 » 5
B   1 » 2 » 6 » 3 » 5 » 4
C   » 1 » 6 » 3 » 4 » 5
D   » 1 » 6 » 3 » 5 » 4
E   » 6 » 1 » 3 » 4 » 5

Question 51

A cup has 144ml of pure deionised water. How many electrons are in the cup due to the water? [Avogadro Constant = 6×10^{23}]

A 8.64×10^{24}
B 8.64×10^{25}
C 1.2×10^{24}
D 4.8×10^{24}
E 4.8×10^{25}

Question 52

Steve's sports car requires 2.28kg of octane to travel to Pete's house 10 miles away. Calculate the mass of CO_2 produced during the journey.

A   0.88 kg
B   1.66 kg

C   2.64 kg
D   3.52 kg

E   5.28 kg
F   7.04 kg

Question 53

Which of the following are true about the formation of polymers?

1.   They are formed from saturated molecules.
2.   Water is released when polymers form.
3.   Polymers only form linear molecules.

A   Only 1
B   Only 2

C   Only 3
D   1 and 2

E   1 and 3
F   2 and 3

G   All of the above.
H   None of the above.

Question 54

Balance the following chemical equation. What is the value of **x**?

$$\textbf{w}\ HIO_3 + 4FeI_2 + \textbf{x}\ HCl \rightarrow \textbf{y}\ FeCl_3 + \textbf{z}\ ICl + 15H_2O$$

A   4
B   5

C   9
D   15

E   22
F   25

END OF SECTION

Section 1D: Biology

The following information applies to questions 55 and 56:

Question 55
Which of the following numbers indicate where amylase functions?

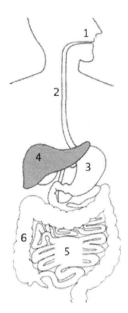

A 1 only	**E** 2 and 4
B 3 only	**F** 3 and 4
C 1 and 3	**G** 5 and 6
D 1 and 5	

Question 56
In which of the following does the majority of chemical digestion occur?

A 1	**D** 4
B 2	**E** 5
C 3	**F** 6

The following information applies to questions 57 and 58:

The diagram below shows the genetic inheritance of colour-blindness, which is inherited in a sex-linked recessive manner [transmitted on the X chromosome and requires the absence of normal X chromosomes to result in disease]. X^B is the normal allele and X^b is the colour-blind allele.

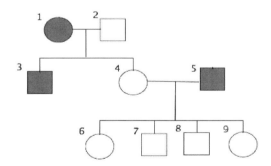

Question 57
What is the genotype of the individual marked 4?

A $X^B X^b$	**C** $X^b X^b$	**E** $X^b Y$
B $X^B X^B$	**D** $X^B Y$	**F** None of the above.

Question 58
If 8 were to reproduce with 6, what is the probability of producing a colour-blind boy?

A 100%	**C** 50%	**E** 12.5%
B 75%	**D** 25%	**F** 0%

Question 59
Which row of the table is correct regarding the cell shown?

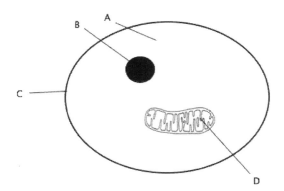

	Most chemical reactions occur here	Involved in energy release	Cell type
A	A	B	Animal
B	A	B	Bacterial
C	A	D	Animal
D	B	D	Bacterial
E	B	B	Animal
F	B	A	Bacterial
G	D	D	Animal
H	D	B	Bacterial

The following information applies to questions 60 & 61:

Professor Huang accidentally touches a hot pan and her hand moves away in a reflex action. The diagram below shows a schematic of the reflex arc involved.

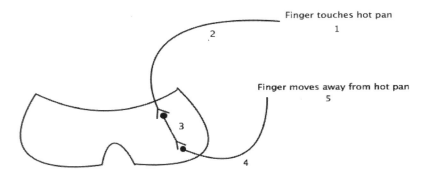

Question 60
Which option correctly identifies the labels in the pathway?

	Muscle	Sensory Neurone	Receptor	Motor Neurone
A	1	2	3	4
B	2	3	4	5
C	5	2	1	4
D	1	4	5	2
E	3	4	5	2

Question 61
Which one of the following statements is correct?

1. Information passes between 1 and 2 chemically.
2. Information passes between 2 and 3 electrically.
3. Information passes between 3 and 4 chemically.

A 1 only	**D** 1 and 2	**G** All of the above.
B 2 only	**E** 2 and 3	**H** None of the above.
C 3 only	**F** 1 and 3	

Question 62

Why do cells undergo mitosis?

1. Asexual Reproduction
2. Sexual Reproduction
3. Growth of the human embryo
4. Replacement of dead cells

A 1 only	**C** 3 only	**E** 2 and 3	**G** 1, 3, and 4
B 2 only	**D** 4 only	**F** 1, 2, and 3	**H** 2, 3, and 4

Question 63

Which of the following is **NOT** present in the Bowman's capsule?

A Urea	**C** Sodium	**E** Haemoglobin
B Glucose	**D** Water	

Question 64

The primary ions responsible for an action potential on a muscle cell membrane are Sodium and Potassium. Sodium concentration is higher than that of potassium outside the cell. Potassium concentration is higher than that of sodium inside the cell.

A muscle cell membrane depolarises. Which of the following **must** be true?

A More potassium moves into the muscle cell than sodium.

B More sodium moves into the muscle cell than potassium.

C There is no net flow of sodium or potassium ions.

D The membrane potential becomes more negative

E None of the above

Question 65

Which of the following best describes the events that occur during expiration?

A The ribs move up and in; the diaphragm moves down.

B The ribs move down and in; the diaphragm moves up.

C The ribs move up and in; the diaphragm moves up.

D The ribs move down and out; the diaphragm moves down.

E The ribs move up and out; the diaphragm moves down.

F The ribs move up and out; the diaphragm moves up.

Question 66

Antibiotics can have serious side effects such as liver failure and renal failure. Therefore, scientists are always trying to develop antibiotics to minimise these effects by targeting specific cellular components. Which of these cellular components offers the best way to treat infections and minimise side effects?

A Mitochondrion	**C** Nucleic acid	**E** Flagellum
B Cell membrane	**D** Cytoskeleton	

Question 67

Which of the following statements about white blood cells is correct?

1. They act by engulfing pathogens such as bacteria.
2. They are able to kill pathogens.
3. They transport carbon dioxide away from dying cells.

A Only 1	**C** Only 3	**E** 2 and 3	**G** All of the
B Only 2	**D** 1 and 2	**F** 1 and 3	above.
			H None.

Question 68

A person responds to the starting gun of a race and begins to run. Place the following order of events in the most likely chronological sequence. Which option is a correct sequence?

1	**Blood CO$_2$ increases**	**5**	**Impulses travel along relay neurones**
2	The eardrum vibrates to the sound	**6**	Quadriceps muscles contract
3	Impulses travel along motor neurones	**7**	Glycogen is converted into glucose
4	Impulses travel along sensory neurones	**8**	Creatine phosphate rapidly re-phosphorylates ADP

A $\to 5 \to 4 \to 3 \to 6 \to 7$ **C** $\to 3 \to 4 \to 6 \to 7 \to 1$ **E** $\to 4 \to 3 \to 6 \to 8 \to 7$
B $\to 4 \to 3 \to 8 \to 6 \to 1$ **D** $\to 4 \to 3 \to 1 \to 6 \to 7$

Question 69

A newly discovered species of beetle is found to have 29.6% Adenine (A) bases in its genome. What is the percentage of Cytosine (C) bases in the beetle's DNA?

A 20.4%   **C** 40.8%   **E** 70.6%
B 29.6%   **D** 59.2%   **F** More information is required

Question 70

In carbon monoxide poisoning, carbon monoxide binds irreversibly to the oxygen binding site of haemoglobin. Regarding carbon monoxide poisoning, which of the following statements is true?

A Carbon monoxide poisoning has no serious consequences
B Haemoglobin is heavier, as both oxygen and carbon monoxide bind to it
C Affected individuals have a raised heart rate
D The CO$_2$ carrying capacity of the blood is decreased
E The oxygen carrying capacity of the blood is unchanged as it dissolves in the plasma instead

Question 71

In a healthy person, which one of the following has the highest blood pressure?

A The vena cava   **C** The pulmonary artery   **E** The aorta
B The systemic capillaries   **D** The pulmonary vein   **F** The coronary arteries

Question 72

Study the following diagram of the human heart. What is true about structure **A**?

A It is closed during systole
B It prevents blood flowing into the left ventricle during systole
C It prevents blood flowing into the right ventricle during systole
D It prevents blood flowing into the left ventricle during diastole
E It opens due to left ventricular pressure being greater than aortic pressure.
F It is open when the right ventricle is emptying

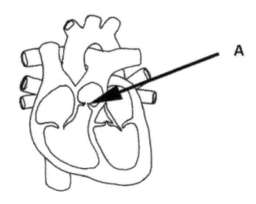

END OF SECTION

Section 1E: Advanced Maths & Physics

Question 73

Two bodies of mass m_1 and m_2 that are traveling rightward at V ms^{-1} and leftward at -3V ms^{-1} respectively. Suppose that a collision takes place, and the bodies begin to move together to the left.

What is a suitable expression for the combined velocity of the new body, $v_{combined}$?

A $\dfrac{2V}{m_1+m_2}$

C $\dfrac{V(m_1-3m_2)}{(m_1+m_2)}$

E $\dfrac{(3m_1+m_2)}{V(m_1-m_2)}$

B $-\dfrac{2V}{m_1+m_2}$

D $\dfrac{V(m_1+3m_2)}{(m_1-m_2)}$

F $\dfrac{(m_1+m_2)}{V(m_1-3m_2)}$

Question 74

Suppose that a scientist travels to the planet Va-Voom, a planet lacking in an atmosphere. Suppose further that he wishes to discover the magnitude of gravitational acceleration on this planet, and only has the aid of a ruler and a stopwatch, with which he is able to measure a fixed height, h, and to measure the time taken for an object to fall through that height on the planet, t.

Which of these is a suitable expression for the magnitude of gravitational acceleration, g, on planet Va-Voom?

A $\dfrac{h}{\sqrt{2t}}$

C $\dfrac{2h}{t^2}$

E $\dfrac{t^2}{2h}$

B $\dfrac{2h}{\sqrt{2t}}$

D $\dfrac{h}{2t^2}$

F $\dfrac{\sqrt{2t}}{h}$

Question 75

Driver A, has a reaction time of t = 1s and is travelling at velocity u ms^{-1}. A second driver, B, is travelling alongside A at velocity 3u ms^{-1}.

A deer suddenly appears on the road. Both drivers react by braking and thus come to a stop with constant deceleration a = -5 ms^{-2}.

If driver B's reaction time is 3 times slower than driver A's, how much further will driver B travel before their car comes to a stop?

A $\dfrac{(3u+8u^2)}{15}$

C $\dfrac{(20u+8u^2)}{10}$

E $\dfrac{(10u+4u^2)}{10}$

B 2u

D $\dfrac{(10u+8u^2)}{20}$

F $5u$

Question 76

A physics lecture theatre is located 3m due east and 4m above the building lobby. What is the minimum energy that a 60kg student would have to expend in order to reach the lecture theatre?

A 1800J   C 3000J   E 2000J
B 2400J   D 4200J   F 3600J

Question 77

Suppose that two children are playing a game on a seesaw, and they decide to make a sport of it. One of the children, of mass m_1, climbs on top of a 2m tall ladder and jumps down onto the seesaw, propelling the other child, of mass m_2, up into the air with an initial starting velocity of v. Which of the following is a suitable expression for the velocity v in terms of m_1, m_2, and g?

A $4\sqrt{\dfrac{m_1 g}{m_2}}$ C $4\sqrt{\dfrac{m_1}{m_2 g}}$ E $\sqrt{\dfrac{4m_1 g}{m_2}}$

B $2\sqrt{\dfrac{m_1 g}{m_2}}$ D $2\sqrt{\dfrac{m_1}{m_2 g}}$ F $\sqrt{\dfrac{m_2}{m_1 g}}$

Question 78

Suppose you are using either a coin or a spoon as a pivot to open the lid of a container, and it takes x Nm of torque to open the lid. Supposing that the diameter of the spoon is twice that of the coin, how many times stronger does the force on the spoon need to be relative to that on the coin in order to cause the bottle to open?

A 2   C $\frac{1}{2}$ E 4
B 5   D $\frac{1}{5}$ F 10

Question 79

Consider a block m_1, of mass 5kg, on a plane with an incline of angle $\theta = 60°$ and a frictional coefficient of $\mu = 0.4$, as shown to the right:

I want to push the block upward along the incline, as shown by the directional arrow shown above. What is the minimal amount of force that I must exert in order to begin accelerating the block at 2 ms^{-2}? Assume that g = 10 ms^{-2}.

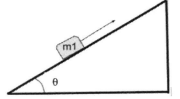

A 15N   C 25N   E 30N
B 10N   D 20N   F 35N

Question 80

A car of mass 1500kg travels along a straight horizontal road. When its speed is v ms^{-1}, the car experiences a resistive force of magnitude 25v Newtons.

Find the acceleration of the car when it is travelling at 15 ms^{-1} on this road with a power of 44100W.

A $1.7ms^{-2}$ C $0.8ms^{-2}$ E $1.2ms^{-2}$
B $2.5ms^{-2}$ D $1.6ms^{-2}$ F $2.2ms^{-2}$

Question 81

Which of the graphs below best describes the vertical motion of a plane as it lands on a runway, where 'h' is the plane's height above the ground and 't' is time?

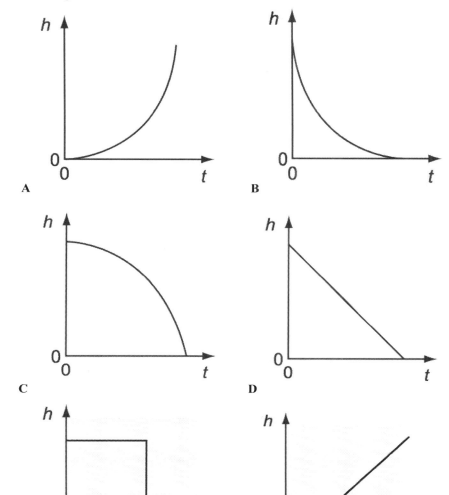

A   B

C   D

E   F

Question 82

A car accelerates steadily from 0 m/s to 20 m/s in a distance **d** and a time **t**. Another car takes a time **2t** to accelerate steadily from stationary to the same final velocity. What distance does the second car cover during the new acceleration?

A 0.25d	**C** d	**E** 3d
B 0.5d	**D** 2d	**F** 3.5d

Question 83

If the lines $y_1 = (n + 1)x + 10$ and $y_2 = (n + 3)x + 2$ are perpendicular then n must equal which of the following?

A 2	**C** 3	**E** 0
B -2	**D** -3	**F** 1

Question 84

The curve $y = x^2 + 3$ is reflected about the line $y = x$ and subsequently translated by the vector $\binom{4}{2}$. Which of the following is the x-intercept of the resulting curve?

A -2   C 7   E 8

B 11   D -11   F -8

Question 85

Given that $a^{3x}b^x c^{4x}= 2$, where a > 0, b > 0, and c > 0, then x =

A $\dfrac{2}{3a+b+4c}$ C $\dfrac{\log_{10} 2}{\log_{10}(a^3 bc^4)}$ E $\dfrac{\log_2 10}{\log_2(a^3 bc^4)}$

B $\dfrac{2}{(\log_{10} a^3 bc^4)}$ D $\log_{10} \dfrac{2}{(ab^2 c^3)}$ F $\log_{10} \dfrac{2}{(a^3 bc^4)}$

Question 86

The sum of the roots of the equation $2^{2x} - 8 \times 2^x + 15 = 0$ is

A 4   C $\log_{10}\left(\dfrac{15}{2}\right)$ E 8

B 16   D $\dfrac{\log_{10} 15}{\log_{10} 2}$ F $\log_2(\tfrac{2}{3})$

Question 87

For what values of the non-zero real number a does the equation $ax^2 + (a - 2)x = 2$ have real and distinct roots?

A $a \neq -2$ C $a > -2$ E $a \neq 0$

B $a > 2$ D No values of a.   F $a > 5$

Question 88

A bag only contains 2n blue balls and n red balls. All the balls are identical apart from colour. One ball is randomly selected and not replaced. A second ball is then randomly selected. What is the probability that at least one of the selected balls is red?

A $\dfrac{4n}{3(3n-1)}$ C $\dfrac{5n-5}{3(3n-1)}$ E $\dfrac{n-5}{9(n-1)}$

B $\dfrac{5n-1}{3(3n-1)}$ D $\dfrac{4n-2}{3(3n-1)}$ F $\dfrac{4n-1}{3(3n-1)}$

Question 89

Which of the following equations is a correct simplification of the equation $\dfrac{x^2-16}{x^2-4x}$?

A $1 - \dfrac{4}{x}$ C $\dfrac{x-4}{x}$ E $\dfrac{x(x-4)}{x}$

B $\dfrac{x+4}{x}$ D $\dfrac{4}{x}$ F $\dfrac{x+4}{4x}$

Question 90

What is the equation of the quadratic function that passes through the x-coordinates of the stationary points of $y = x^2 e^x$?

A This quadratic function does not exist.   C x^2 E $x^2 + 4x$

B $x^2 + 2x$ D $x^2 - 2x$ F $2x^2 - 1$

END OF SECTION

Section 2

Physics: Question 1

a) The graph below describes the velocity of a ball B of mass 1.2kg as it collides head on with   a stationary ball C of mass 3.6kg.

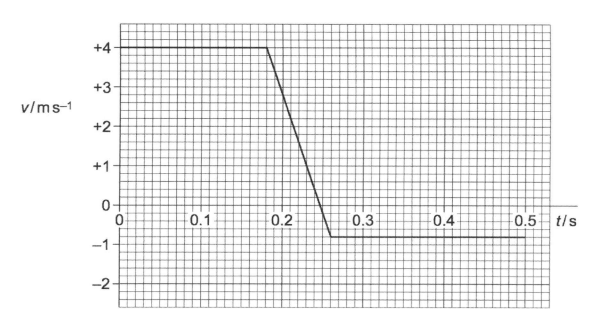

i) What is happening to the velocity of the ball B between 0.18s and 0.26s?

[2 marks]

ii) What does a negative velocity mean in this context?

[2 marks]

iii) How should we describe the motion of the ball from the evidence in the graph?

[2 marks]

b) Based on the figure above:

i) What was the change in momentum of Ball B during the collision?

[2 marks]

ii) What was the total force acting on Ball B throughout the course of the collision?

[2 marks]

c) What was the speed of ball C right after the collision?

[3 marks]

d) Deduce quantitatively whether the collision was elastic, or inelastic.

[3 marks]

e) Now, consider this graph showing the variation with time t of the distance d moved of a ball falling vertically in the air from rest.

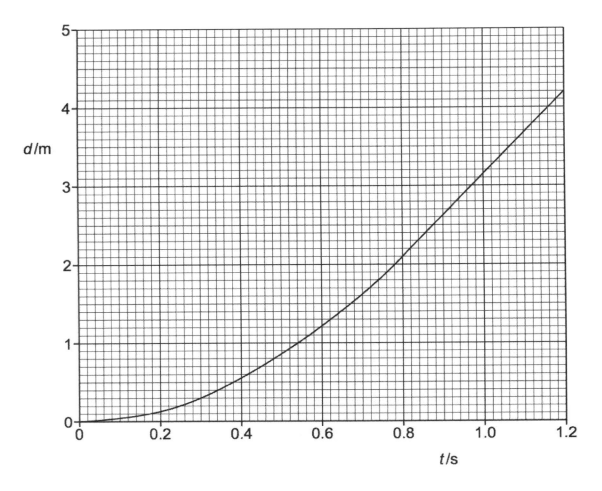

i) By referring to the figure, how can you infer that air resistance is not negligible?

[3 marks]

ii) How can you infer that the ball was initially at rest?

[3 marks]

iii) What was the speed of the ball at t = 0.4s?

[3 marks]

[Total 25 marks]

Physics: Question 2

Jack is a 65kg man who is in the desert. He is sitting on a carpet attached to a rope, which is in turn tied to his donkey, named Jill. You may assume that Jill has zero mass.

Jill pulls Jack at a constant velocity of $20\ ms^{-1}$, such that the rope is directed at 30° to the horizontal.

a)   Suppose that the coefficient of kinetic friction on the ground is initially $\mu_k = 0.8$. How much horsepower is being generated by Jill?

[3 marks]

b)   What is the tension in the rope at this point?

[2 marks]

c)   Suppose that Jack whips Jill at t =10, and Jill's acceleration goes up to $2ms^{-2}$ for 2.5 seconds. Subsequently, the angle of the rope changes to 25 degrees.

i) What is the new tension in the rope from t=10 to t=12.5?

[3 marks]

ii) What is Jill's new "horsepower"?

[3 marks]

d)   Suppose now that Jill hits a slippery slide, where the coefficient of kinetic friction is 0.3 instead, but she continues to go forward, generating the same amount of force as before. What is Jack's new acceleration?

[4 marks]

Suppose the acceleration due to hitting the slippery slide continues for 2 seconds, then Jack tells Jill to stop, right as they both hit a patch of ground that has a frictional coefficient of 0.9. At this point, Jill begins to exert a constant 200N force on the ground.

i) How long will Jill take to stop?

[4 marks]

ii) How far will she travel throughout the stopping process?

[2 marks]

e)   Provide a velocity-time graph describing Jack and Jill's motion throughout the entire journey. Your graph doesn't need to be exact, but should to mark key features on the graph.

[4 marks]

[Total 25 marks]

Chemistry: Question 3

Large quantities of ammonia are manufactured through the Haber process. This is an exothermic reaction with an enthalpy of formation of $\Delta H = -92$kJ/mol.

a) Briefly describe the Haber Process.

[4 marks]

b) Under conditions of equilibrium in the Haber process, what happens if the temperature of the reaction vessel is lowered?

[4 marks]

c) Suggest two possible usages for ammonia.

[4 marks]

d) Ammonium nitrate fertilizer is manufactured from ammonia. The first reaction that takes place in this process is the catalytic oxidation of ammonia to form nitrogen monoxide, NO. This is a reversible reaction that is carried out at 10 atmospheres of pressure (1000kPa) and a temperature of about 800 Celsius. $\Delta H = -906 kJ\ mol^{-1}$.

Write out a balanced chemical equation that describes this process.

[3 marks]

e)
i) Write out the expression for the equilibrium constant, K_p.

[3 marks]

ii) What units are the equilibrium constant in?

[2 marks]

f) The reaction for the formation of nitrogen monoxide, NO(g) from ammonia and oxygen, is shown below:

$4NH_3(g) + 5O_2(g) \leftrightarrow 4NO(g) + 6H_2O$

$\Delta H^\theta = -906\ kJ\ mol^{-1}$

The standard enthalpy changes of formation of ammonia, NH_3 and water, H_2O are as follows:

$NH_3(g), \Delta H_f^\theta = -46.0kJ\ mol^{-1}$
$H_2O(g), \Delta H_f^\theta = -242\ kJ\ mol^{-1}$

Calculate the standard enthalpy change of formation of NO(g), including a sign in your answer.

[5 marks]

[Total 25 marks]

Chemistry: Question 4

Internal combustion engines are materially different in terms of how they facilitate combustion, as compared to combustion in the open air. When combinations of alkenes and alkanes combust in the open air, they produce carbon dioxide and water: this is what we see when we combust a sample of hydrocarbons in the lab. On the other hand, when there is insufficient oxygen, they often produce gases other than carbon dioxide.

a) Suppose that the hydrocarbon under consideration is only composed of methane. Write out a balanced chemical reaction to showcase:

i) Complete combustion in the presence of excess oxygen.

[2 marks]

ii) Incomplete combustion in the absence of sufficient oxygen.

[2 marks]

b) Correspondingly, when combinations of hydrocarbons combust in the confines of a closed engine, they often also produce a variety of other gases, including nitrogen monoxide. Taking aside the question of how much oxygen is present in the confines of the engine at the time of combustion, nitrogen is an inert gas and typically does not react.

i) What is a possible explanation for how NO is formed in a combustion engine but not when petrol is burnt in an evaporating basin?

[3 marks]

ii) Suggest a possible catalyst that may be used so as to reduce the atmospheric pollution that would result from the presence of nitrogen monoxide.

[2 marks]

iii) Write two balanced chemical reactions, firstly between nitrogen monoxide and carbon monoxide, and secondly between nitrogen monoxide and carbon, that illustrate how nitrogen monoxide can be processed in a catalytic converter.

[2 marks]

c) Consider the combustion of magnesium in nitrogen. Magnesium burns in nitrogen to give magnesium nitride, a yellow solid with the chemical formula Mg_3N_2, which reacts with water, H_2O, to form ammonia and magnesium hydroxide.

i) Why is the formula of magnesium nitride Mg_3N_2?

[2 marks]

ii) Construct a formula for the reaction of magnesium nitride with water.

[2 marks]

iii) Did a redox reaction take place? If so, why? If not, why not?

[2 marks]

d) Sulphur dioxide is an atmospheric pollutant that arises from such internal combustion engines, which causes acid rain.

i) What are two sources of atmospheric sulphur dioxide, SO_2?

[2 marks]

ii) Describe a possible chemical pathway through which sulphur dioxide turns into acid rain.

[2 marks]

e) Some people claim that incomplete combustion of hydrocarbons on a large scale may actually lead to less global warming. Why might they make this case?

[4 marks]

[Total 25 marks]

Biology: Question 5

a) The diagram below shows an electron micrograph of a cell:

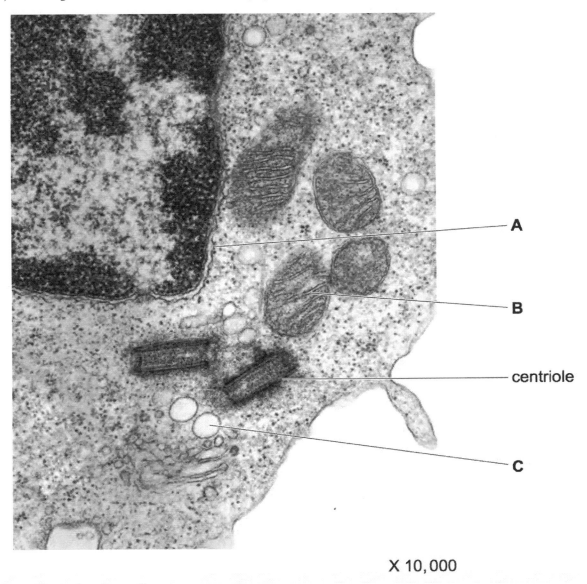

X 10,000

Fill in the names of the structures labelled A-C.
i) A:

[2 marks]

ii) B:

[2 marks]

iii) C:

[2 marks]

b) Describe the role of the centriole in the animal cell.

[3 marks]

c)   Why do we say that the mitochondrion is the powerhouse of the cell?

[3 marks]

d)   Name a feature in the image that indicates this cell is an animal, not a plant cell. Explain the reason for this difference in structure between the two cell types.

[3 marks]

e)   Describe the changes that occur within the cell between the beginning of prophase and the end of metaphase.

[5 marks]

f)   In many multicellular organisms, such as mammals, the time taken for the mitotic cell cycle varies considerably between different tissues, but is very carefully controlled in each cell.

Why is this control a matter of importance to mammals and what happens if the control mechanisms fail?

[5 marks]

[Total 25 marks]

Biology: Question 6

Malaria and tuberculosis (TB) are two prominent infectious diseases. Malaria is caused by the protist *Plasmodium* and is transmitted to humans by the female *Anopheles* mosquito, or by the exchange of blood with an infected individual. *Plasmodium* are single-celled organisms with a complex life-cycle comprising several distinct life stages, including dormant, and sexually-reproducing stages. *Anopheles* thrives in warm, humid conditions, and around 90% of cases of Malaria occur in sub-Saharan Africa.

TB is caused by the bacterium *Mycobaterium tuberculosis*, and is transmitted via droplets expelled during coughing. Patients can transmit TB when they have active TB, but the disease can exist in the body as latent TB for long periods of time. Around 25% of the world's population is estimated to have latent TB.

a) Define the term *infectious disease*.

[3 marks]

b) Give 4 examples of how malaria could be transmitted.

[4 marks]

c) Why is Malaria is largely limited to the Southern Hemisphere, while TB is found worldwide?

[4 marks]

d) Explain how vaccination works and why it is difficult to eradicate some diseases completely even if they only occur very rarely in humans.

[4 marks]

e) Explain how the human response to antigens works and how this has made it difficult to develop a vaccine against malaria in the past, evaluating some considerations about the nature of the disease. How else might malaria be prevented, besides vaccines?

[6 marks]

f) Explain why certain vaccinations (say, for measles) are not appropriate during the first few months of a child's life, or for individuals who have compromised immune system.

[4 marks]

[Total 25 marks]

END OF PAPER

Mock Paper B

Section 1A: Maths

Question 1

Solve $y = 2x - 1$ and $y = x^2 - 1$ for x and y.

A   (0, -1) and (2, 3)   C   (1, 4) and (3, 2)   E   (3, -1) and (3, 1)
B   (1, -1) and (2, 2)   D   (2, -3) and (4, 5)

Question 2

Tim stands at the waterfront and holds a 30 cm ruler horizontally at eye level one metre in front of him. It lines up so it appears to be exactly the same length as a cruise ship 1 km out to sea. How long is the cruise ship?

A   299.7 m   C   333 m   E   30,000 m
B   300 m   D   29,970 m

Question 3

Bob is twice as old as Kerry, and Kerry is three times as old as Bob's son. Their ages combined make 50 years. How old was Bob when his son was born?

A   15   C   25   E   35
B   20   D   30

Question 4

A crocodile's tail weighs 30kg. Its head weighs as much as the tail and one half of the body and legs. The body and legs together weigh as much as the tail and head combined.

What is the total weight of the crocodile?

1. 220kg   3. 260kg   5. 300kg
2. 240kg   4. 280kg

Question 5

A formula: $\sqrt[3]{\dfrac{z(x+y)(l+m-n)}{3}}$ is given. Would you expect this formula to calculate:

A   A length   C   A volume   E   A geometric average
B   An area   D   A volume of rotation

Question 6

Evaluate the following: $\dfrac{4.2 \times 10^{10} - 4.2 \times 10^{6}}{2 \times 10^{3}}$

A 2.09979×10^{6} C 2.09979×10^{8} E 2.09979×10^{10}
B 2.09979×10^{7} D 2.09979×10^{9}

Question 7
Calculate a − b

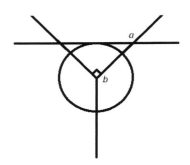

A   0°
B   5°
C   10°
D   15°
E   20°

Question 8
Jack has a bag with a complete set of snooker balls (15 red, 1 yellow, 1 green, 1 brown, 1 blue, 1 pink and 1 black ball) within it. Blindfolded Jack draws two balls from the bag.

What is the probability that he draws a blue and a black ball in any order?

A $\frac{2}{41}$

B $\frac{2}{210}$

C $\frac{1}{210}$

D $\frac{1}{105}$

Question 9
Rearrange the following equation in terms of t: $x = \frac{\sqrt{b^3 - 9st}}{13j} + \int_{-z}^{z} 9a - 7$

A $t = \frac{(13jx - \int_{-z}^{z} 9a - 7)^2 - b^3}{9s}$

B $t = \frac{13jx^2}{b^3 - 9s} - \int_{-z}^{z} 9a - 7$

C $t = x - \frac{\sqrt{b^3 - 9s}}{13j} - \int_{-z}^{z} 9a - 7$

D $t = \frac{x^2}{\frac{b^3 - 9s}{13j} + \int_{-z}^{z} 9a - 7}$

E $t = \frac{[13j(x - \int_{-z}^{z} 9a - 7)]^2 - b^3}{-9s}$

Question 10
An investment of £500 is made in a compound interest account. At the end of 3 years the balance reads £1687.50. What is the interest rate?

A   20%   B   35%   C   50%   D   65%   E   80%

Question 11

What is the equation of the line of best fit for the scatter graph below?

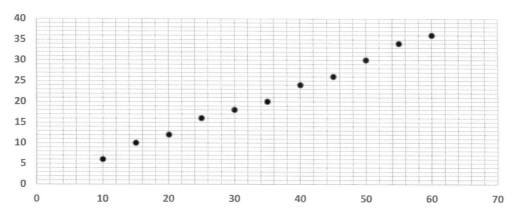

i. $y = 0.2x + 0.35$
ii. $y = 0.2x - 0.35$
iii. $y = 0.4x + 0.35$

iv. $y = 0.4x - 0.35$
v. $y = 0.6x + 0.35$

Question 12

Simplify : $m = \sqrt{\dfrac{9xy^3z^5}{3x^9yz^4}} - m$

i. $m = \sqrt{\dfrac{3y^2z}{x^8}} - m$

ii. $m^2 = \dfrac{3y^2z}{x^8} - m$

iii. $2m = \sqrt{\dfrac{3y^2z}{x^8}}$

iv. $2m^2 = 3x^{-8}y^2z$

v. $4m^2 = 3x^{-8}y^2z$

Question 13

A rotating disc has two wells, in which bacteria are cultured. The first well is 10 cm from the centre whereas the second well is 20 cm from the centre. If the inner well completes a revolution in 1 second, how much faster is the outer well travelling?

    A 0.314 m/s   **B** 0.628 m/s   **C** 0.942 m/s   **D** 1.256 m/s   **E** 1.590 m/s

Question 14

Which is the equivalent function to: $y = 9x^{-\frac{1}{3}}$?

A $y = \dfrac{1}{x}$

B $y = \sqrt[3]{9x}$

C $y = \dfrac{1}{\sqrt[3]{9x}}$

D $y = \dfrac{9}{\sqrt[3]{x}}$

E $y = \dfrac{3}{\sqrt[3]{x}}$

Question 15

Make y the subject of the formula: $\dfrac{y+x}{x} = \dfrac{x}{a} + \dfrac{a}{x}$

A $y = \dfrac{x^2}{a} + a$

B $y = \dfrac{x^2 + a^2 - ax}{a}$

C $y = \dfrac{-ax}{x^2 + a^2}$

D $y = \dfrac{x^2}{ax} + a - x$

E $y = a^2 - ax$

Question 16

Consider the equations: A: $y = 3x$ and B: $y = \frac{6}{x} - 7$. At what values of x do the two equations intersect?

A   x=2 and x=9

B   x=3 and x=6

C   x=6 and x=27

D   x=6

E   x=18

Question 17

What is the median of the following numbers: $\frac{7}{36}$; $0.\dot{3}$; $\frac{11}{18}$; 0.25; 0.75; $\frac{62}{72}$; $\frac{7}{7}$

A $\frac{7}{36}$

B $0.\dot{3}$

C $\frac{11}{18}$

D $\frac{62}{72}$

E   0.75

Question 18

Simplify fully: $\frac{(3x^{½})^3}{3x^2}$

A $\frac{3x}{\sqrt{x}}$

B $\frac{9}{x}$

C $3x^{½}$

D $3x\sqrt{x}$

E $\frac{9}{\sqrt{x}}$

END OF SECTION

Section 1B: Physics

Question 19

Which of the following Energy-Temperature graphs best represents the melting of ice to water?

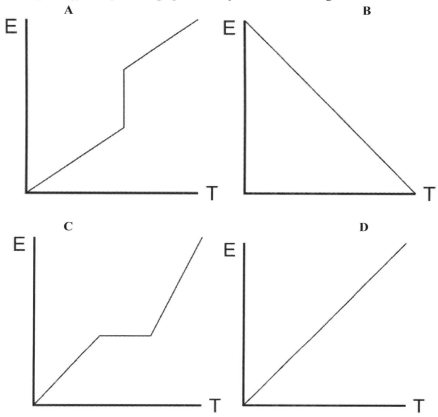

Question 20

Which of the following units is **NOT** a measure of power?

A	W	C	Nms^{-1}	E	V$^2\Omega^{-1}$
B	Js^{-1}	D	VA	F	None of the above

Question 21

The buoyancy force of an object is the produce of its volume, density and the gravitational constant, *g*. A boat weighing 600 kg with a density of 1000kgm^{-3} and hull volume of 950 litres is placed in a lake. What is the minimum mass that, if added to the boat, will cause it to sink? Use g = 10ms^{-1}.

A	3.55 kg	D	355 kg	F	None, the boat has already
B	35 kg	E	3,550 kg		sunk
C	350 kg				

Question 22

Which of the following statements is **FALSE**?

A   Energy cannot be created or destroyed.
B   Energy can be turned into matter.
C   Efficiency is the ratio of useful energy to wasted energy.
D   Energy can be dispersed through a vacuum.
E   There are always losses when energy is transformed from one type to another.

Question 23
Which of the following statements is **FALSE**?

A   A beam of light exits a pane of glass at a different angle than it entered.
B   A beam of light reflects at an angle dependent on the angle of incidence.
C   Light travels a shorter distance to reach the bottom of a pool filled with water than a pool without water.
D   Any neutrally charged atom has the potential to emit light.
E   Photons are particles without a mass.

Question 24
The diagram shown below depicts an electrical circuit with multiple resistors, each with equal resistance, **Z**. The total resistance between A and B 22 MΩ. Calculate the value of **Z**.

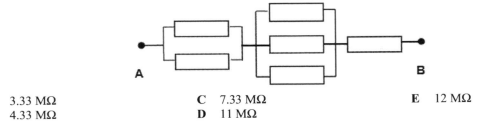

A   3.33 MΩ
B   4.33 MΩ
C   7.33 MΩ
D   11 MΩ
E   12 MΩ

Question 25
A tourist at Victoria Falls accidentally drops her 400g camera. It falls 125 metres into the water below. Assuming resistive forces to be zero and $g = 10 ms^{-1}$, what is the momentum of the camera the instant before it strikes the water? [Momentum = mass x velocity]

A $4 kgms^{-1}$
B $13 kgms^{-1}$
C $16 kgms^{-1}$
D $20 kgms^{-1}$
E $50 kgms^{-1}$

Question 26
Mr Khan fires a bullet at a speed of 310 ms⁻¹ from a height of 1.93m parallel to the floor. Mr Weeks drops an identical bullet from the same height. What is the time difference between the bullets first making contact with the floor?[Assume that there is negligible air resistance; $g= 10 ms^{-2}$]

A   0 s
B   0.2 s
C   1.93 s
D   2.1 s
E   More information is
needed

Question 27
A 1.4kg fish swims through water at a constant speed of 2ms⁻¹. Resistive forces against the fish are 2N. Assuming $g = 10 ms^{-2}$, how much work does the fish do in one hour?

A   7,200 J
B   10,080 J
C   14,400 J
D   19,880 J
E   22,500 J
F   More information is
needed

Question 28
When electricity flows through a metal, which of the following are true?

1.   Ions move through the metal to create a current.
2.   The lattice in the metal is broken.
3.   Only electrons which were already free of their atoms will flow.

A   1 only
B   2 only
C   3 only
D   1 and 2
E   1 and 3
F   2 and 3

Question 29
Which of the following statements is false?

A   A nuclear power plant may have an accident if free neutrons in a fuel rod aren't captured.
B   Humans cannot currently harness the energy from nuclear fusion.
C   Uncontrolled nuclear fission leads to a large explosion.
D   Mass is conserved during nuclear explosions caused by nuclear bombs.
E   Nuclear fusion produces much more energy than nuclear fission.

Question 30
A candle is used to heat a bucket for 45 minutes. It releases 250 kJ of energy as heat. It is used to heat a 2 litre bucket of water at 25°C. Assuming the bucket is completely insulated, what is the water temperature after 45 minutes? (For reference: One calorie heats one cm^3 of water by one degree Celsius, 1 kCal = 4,200J).

A   34°C   C   55°C   E   72°C
B   47°C   D   62°C   F   The water boils

Question 31
The figure below shows a schematic of a wiring system. All the bulbs have equal resistance. The power supply is 24V.

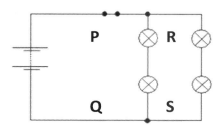

If headlight Q is replaced by a new one with twice the resistance, with the switch closed, which of these combinations of voltage drop across the four bulbs is possible?

	P	Q	R	S
A	8V	16V	12V	12V
B	8V	16V	16V	8V
C	8V	16V	8V	16V
D	12V	24V	24V	24V
E	12V	12V	12V	12V
F	16V	8V	12V	12V
G	16V	8V	8V	16V
H	24V	24V	24V	24V

Question 32

A man drives along a road as shown in the figure to the right.

Which of the following statements is true?

A   He drives a total of 30 m.
B   He has an average velocity of 30 m/s.
C   He has a final velocity of 30 m/s.
D   He has an average acceleration of 30 m/s^2.
E   His velocity decreases between 5 and 9 seconds.

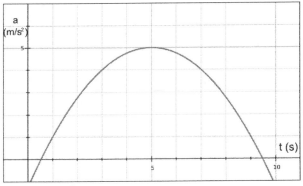

Question 33

Which of the following points regarding electromagnetic waves are correct?

1.   Radio waves have the longest wavelength and the lowest frequency
2.   Infrared has a shorter wavelength than visible light and is used in optical fibre communication, heater and night vision equipment
3.   All of the waves from gamma to radio waves travel at the speed of light (about 300,000,000 m/s)
4.   Infrared radiation is used to sterilize food and to kill cancer cells
5.   Darker skins absorb more UV light, so less ultraviolet radiation reaches the deeper tissues

   A   1 and 2   B   1 and 3   C   1, 3 and 5   D   2 and 3   E   2 and 4

Question 34

Two carriages of a train collide and then start moving together in the same direction. Carriage 1 has mass 12,000 kg and moves at 5ms^{-1} before the collision. Carriage 2 has mass 8,000 kg and is stationary before the collision. What is the velocity of the two carriages after the collision?

A   2 ms^{-1} B   3 ms^{-1} C   4 ms^{-1} D   4.5 ms^{-1} E   5 ms^{-1}

Question 35

Which of the following statements are true?

1.   Control rods are used to absorb electrons in a nuclear reactor to control the chain reaction
2.   Nuclear fusion is commonly used as an energy source
3.   An alpha particle is comprised of two protons and two neutrons and is the same as a helium nucleus
4.   When $^{14}_{6}C$ undergoes beta decay, an electron and $^{14}_{7}N$ are produced
5.   Beta particles are less ionising than gamma rays and more ionising than alpha particles

   A   1 and 2   C   1 and 3   E   3 and 4
   B   2 and 3   D   1 and 4   F   1,2,3 and 4

Question 36

A ball is projected vertically upwards with an initial speed of 40 ms^{-1}. What is the maximum height reached? (Take gravity to be 10 ms^{-2} and assume negligible air resistance).

   A   25m   C   60m   E   80m
   B   45m   D   75m

END OF SECTION

Section 1C: Chemistry

Question 37

The concentration of chloride in the blood is 100mM. The concentration of thyroxine is 1×10^{-10}kM. Calculate the ratio of thyroxine to chloride ions in the blood.

A   Chloride is 100,000,000 times more concentrated than thyroxine
B   Chloride is 1,000,000 times more concentrated than thyroxine
C   Chloride is 1000 times more concentrated than thyroxine
D   Concentrations of chloride and thyroxine are equal
E   Thyroxine is 1000 times more concentrated than chloride
F   Thyroxine is 1,000,000 times more concentrated than chloride

Question 38

Which of the following below is **NOT** an example of an oxidation reaction?

A $Li^+ + H_2O \rightarrow Li^+ + OH^- + \frac{1}{2}H_2$ C $2CH_4 + 2O_2 \rightarrow 2CH_2O + 2H_2O$ E $I_2 + 2e^- \rightarrow 2I^-$
B $N_2 \rightarrow 2N^+ + 2e^-$ D $2N_2 + O_2 \rightarrow 2N_2O$ F   All of the above are oxidation reactions

Question 39

Which of the following statements are true about the electrolysis of brine?

1.   It describes the reduction of 2 chloride ions to Cl_2.
2.   The amount of NaOH produced increases in proportion with the amount of NaCl present in solution, provided there is enough H_2 present to dissolve the NaCl.
3.   The redox reaction of the electrolysis of brine results in the production of dissolved NaOH, which is a strong acid.

A   Only 1   C   Only 3   E   1 and 3   G   All of the above.
B   Only 2   D   1 and 2   F   2 and 3   H   None of the above.

Question 40

For the following reaction, which of the statements below is true?

$$6CO_{2\ (g)} + 6H_2O \rightarrow C_6H_{12}O_6 + 6O_{2\ (g)}$$

A   Increasing the concentration of the products will increase the reaction rate.
B   Whether this reaction will proceed at room temperature does not depend on the entropy.
C   The reaction rate can be monitored by measuring the volume of gas released.
D   This reaction represents aerobic respiration.
E   This reaction represents anaerobic respiration.

Question 41

When comparing different isotopes of the same element, which of the following may change?
1.   Atomic number   3.   Number of electrons
2.   Mass number   4.   Chemical reactivity

i.   1 only   iii.   3 only   v.   All of the above
ii.   1 and 2 only   iv.   2 and 3 only

Question 42

From which of the following elemental groups are you most likely to find a catalyst?

A   Alkali Metals   C   Alkaline Earth Metals   E   Halogen
B   d-block elements   D   Noble Gases

Question 43
1.338kg of francium are mixed in a reaction vessel with an excess of distilled water. What volume will the hydrogen produced occupy at room temperature and pressure?

A $20.4dm^3$ C $40.8dm^3$ E $72dm^3$
B $36dm^3$ D $60.12dm^3$

Question 44
The composition of a compound is Carbon 30%, Hydrogen 40%, Fluorine 20%, and Chlorine 10%.
What is the empirical formula of this compound?

a. CH_2FCl c. C_3H_4FCl e. $C_4H_4F_2Cl$
b. $C_3H_2F_2Cl$ d. $C_3H_4F_2Cl$

Question 45
1.2×10^{10} kg of sugar is dissolved in 4×10^{12}L of distilled water. What is the concentration?

A 3×10^{-2} g/dL   C 3×10^1 g/dL   E 3×10^3 g/dL
B 3×10^{-1} g/dL   D 3×10^2 g/dL

Question 46
Which of the following is not essential for the progression of an exothermic chemical reaction?

A   Presence of a catalyst
B   Increase in entropy
C   Achieving activation energy
D   Attaining an electron configuration more closely resembling that of a noble gas
E   None of the above

Question 47
What is a common use of cationic surfactants?

A   Shampoo   C   Cosmetics   E   All of the above
B   Lubricant   D   Detergents

Question 48
A warehouse receives 15 tonnes of arsenic in bulk. Assuming that the sample is at least 80% pure, what is the minimum amount, in moles, of arsenic that they have obtained?

A 1.6×10^5 B 2×10^5 C 1.6×10^6 D 2×10^6 E 1.6×10

Question 49
A sample of silicon is run in a mass spectrometer. The resultant trace shows m/z peaks at 26 and 30 with relative abundance 60% and 30% respectively. What other isotope of silicon must have been in the sample to give an average atomic mass of 28?

A   28   B   30   C   32   D   34   E   36

Question 50
72.9g of pure magnesium ribbon is mixed in a reaction vessel with the equivalent of 54g of steam. The ensuing reaction produces $72dm^3$ of hydrogen. Which of the following statements is true?

A   This is a complete reaction   D   There is an excess of magnesium
B   This is a partial reaction   E   Magnesium hydroxide is a product
C   There is an excess of steam

Question 51

Which species is the reducing agent in: $3Cu^{2+} + 3S^{2-} + 8H^+ + 8NO_3^- \rightarrow 3Cu^{2+} + 3SO_4^{2-} + 8NO + 4H_2O$

i. Cu^{2+} ii. S^{2-} iii. H^+ iv. NO_3^- v. H_2O

Question 52

Which of the following is not true of alkanes?

A   CnH2n+2   C   Reactive   E   None of the above
B   Saturated   D   Produce only CO_2 and water
                                       when burnt in an excess of
                                       oxygen

Question 53

What is the value of C when the equation is balanced?

_5_ PhCH$_3$ + _A_ KMnO$_4$ + _9_ H$_2$SO$_4$ = _5_ PhCOOH + _B_ K$_2$SO$_4$ + _C_ MnSO$_4$ + _14_ H$_2$O

A   3   B   4   C   5   D   7   E   9

Question 54

Which of the following statements are false?
1.   Simple molecules do not conduct electricity because there are no free electrons and there is no overall charge
2.   The carbon and silicon atoms in silica are arranged in a giant lattice structure and it has a very high melting point
3.   Ionic compounds do not conduct electricity when dissolved in water or when melted because the ions are too far apart
4.   Alloys are harder than pure metals

A   1 and 2   C   1, 2, 3 and 4   E   3 only
B   1, 2 and 4   D   2 and 4

END OF SECTION

Section 1D: Biology

The following information applies to questions 55 and 56:
In pea plants, colour and stem length are inherited in an autosomal manner. The allele for yellow colour, Y, is dominant to the allele for green colour, y. Furthermore, the allele for tall stem length, T, is dominant to short stem length, t.

When a pea plant of unknown genotype is crossed with a green short-stemmed pea plant, the progeny are 25% yellow + tall-stemmed plants, 25% yellow + short-stemmed plants, 25% green + tall-stemmed plants and 25% green + short-stemmed plants.

Question 55
What is the genotype of the unknown pea plant?

A Yytt	**C** YyTT	**E** yyTT	**G** More information
B YyTt	**D** yyTt	**F** yytt	needed.

Question 56
Taking both colour and height into account, how many different combinations of genotypes and phenotypes are possible?

A 6 genotypes and 3 phenotypes	**C** 8 genotypes and 4 phenotypes	**E** 9 genotypes and 3 phenotypes
B 8 genotypes and 3 phenotypes	**D** 9 genotypes and 4 phenotypes	**F** 10 genotypes and 3 phenotypes

Question 57
Which of the following statements are true?

1. Natural selection always favours organisms that are faster or stronger.
2. Genetic variation leads to different adaptations to the environment.
3. Variation is purely due to genetics.

A Only 1	**C** Only 3	**E** 2 and 3	**G** All of the above.
B Only 2	**D** 1 and 2	**F** 1 and 3	**H** None of the above.

Question 58
What is the **MOST** important reason for each cell in the human body to have an adequate blood supply?

A To allow protein synthesis.
B To receive essential minerals and vitamins for life.
C To kill invading bacteria.
D To allow aerobic respiration to take place.
E To maintain an optimum cellular temperature.
F To maintain an optimum cellular pH.

The following information applies to questions 59 & 60:
Duchenne muscular dystrophy (DMD) is inherited in an X-linked recessive pattern [transmitted on the X chromosome and requires the absence of normal X chromosomes to result in disease]. A man with DMD has two boys with a woman carrier.

Question 59
What is the probability that both boys have DMD?

A	100%	C	50%	E	12.5%
B	75%	D	25%	F	0%

Question 60
If the same couple had two more children, what is the probability that they are both girls with DMD?

A	100%	C	50%	E	12.5%
B	75%	D	25%	F	0%

Question 61
The normal cardiac cycle has two phases, systole and diastole. During diastole, which of the following is **NOT** true?

A   The aortic valve is closed
B   The ventricles are relaxing
C   The volume of blood in the ventricles is increasing
D   The pressure in the aorta increases
E   There is blood in the ventricles

Question 62
Below is a graph showing the concentration of product over time as substrate concentration is increased. Some enzyme inhibitors are introduced.

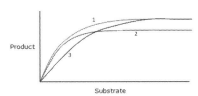

Which, if any, line represents the effect of competitive inhibition?
A   Line 1   C   Line 3
B   Line 2   D   None of these lines

Question 63
Which of the following is **NOT** present in the plasma membrane?

A	Extrinsic proteins	C	Phospholipids	E	Nucleic Acids
B	Intrinsic proteins	D	Glycoproteins	F	They are all present

Question 64

A pulmonary embolism occurs when a main artery supplying the lungs becomes blocked by a clot that has travelled from somewhere else in the body.

Which option best describes the path of a blood clot that originated in the leg and has caused a pulmonary embolism?

A) Inferior Vena cava   F) Left ventricle
B) Superior Vena cava   G) Pulmonary artery
C) Right atrium   H) Pulmonary vein
D) Right ventricle   I) Aorta
E) Left atrium   J) Coronary artery

A C, D, H, G	**C** I, E, F, G	**E** A, C, D, J, G
B B, C, D, H, G	**D** A, C, D, G	**F** A, C, D, J, E, F, G

Question 65

Which of the following is **NOT** a hormone?

A Insulin   **C** Noradrenaline   **E** Thyroxine   **G** None of the above
B Glycogen   **D** Cortisol   **F** Progesterone

Question 66

Which of the following statements regarding neural reflexes is **false**?

A Reflexes are usually faster than conscious decisions

B Reflexes can involve the brain

C The heat-withdrawal reflex is a type of spinal reflex

D Reflexes are completely unaffected by conscious acts

E Reflexes are present in many types of simple animals

F Reflexes have both a sensory and motor component

Question 67

Which of the following statements, regarding normal human digestion, is **FALSE**?

A Amylase is an enzyme which breaks down starch

B Amylase is produced by the pancreas

C Bile is stored in the gallbladder

D The small intestine is the longest part of the gut

E Insulin is released in response to feeding

F None of the above

Question 68

Jane is one mile into a marathon. Which of the following statements is **NOT** true, relative to before she started?

A Blood flow to the skin is increased

B Blood flow to the muscles is increased

C Blood flow to the lungs is increased

D Blood flow to the gut is decreased

E Blood flow to the kidneys is decreased

F None of the above

Question 69

SIADH is a metabolic disorder caused by an excess of Anti-Diuretic Hormone (ADH) release by the posterior pituitary gland. Which row best describes the urine produced by a patient with SIADH?

	Volume	Salt Concentration	Glucose
A	High	Low	Low
B	High	High	Low
C	High	High	High
D	Low	Low	Low
E	Low	High	Low
F	Low	High	High

Question 70

Which of the following cannot be classified as an organ?

1. Blood
2. Bone
3. Larynx
4. Pituitary Gland
5. Prostate
6. Skeletal Muscle
7. Skin

A   1 and 6
B   2 and 3
C   5 and 7
D   1 and 5
E   1,4, 5 and 6

Question 71
An increase in aerobic respiratory rate could be associated with which of the following physiological changes?
A) A larger percentage of water vapour in expired air
B) Increased expired CO_2
C) Increased inspired O_2
D) Perspiration
E) Vasodilatation

A 3 only
B 1 and 2 only
C 1, 2 and 3 only
D 2, 3 and 5
E All of the above

Question 72
The nephron is to the kidney, as the _____ is to striated muscle:

A   Actin filament
B   Artery
C   Myofibril
D   Sarcomere
E   Vein

END OF SECTION

Section 1E: Advanced Maths & Physics

Question 73

Consider the infinite series, $x - \left(\frac{1}{2}\right)x^2 + \left(\frac{1}{4}\right)x^3 - \left(\frac{1}{8}\right)x^4 \ldots$

Given that we know that the fifth term of the series is $\left(\frac{1}{32}\right)$, what is summation of the series given that the series converges as it heads toward infinity?

A $\dfrac{16^{\frac{1}{5}}}{2+\frac{(16^{\frac{1}{5}})}{2}}$

C $\dfrac{8^{\frac{1}{5}}}{1+8^{\frac{1}{5}}}$

E $\dfrac{-2}{2+(16)^{\frac{1}{4}}}$

B $\dfrac{1}{1-(32)^{\frac{1}{4}}}$

D $\dfrac{2}{2-(16)^{\frac{1}{4}}}$

F $\dfrac{1}{64-8^{\frac{1}{5}}}$

Question 74

If $\log_2 3 . \log_3 4 . \log_4 5 \ldots \log_n(n+1) \le 10$, what is the largest value of n that satisfies this equation?

A   1022

C   842

E   1020

B   824

D   1023

F   890

Question 75

a,b,c is a geometric progression where a,b,c are real numbers. If $a+b+c = 26$ and $a^2 + b^2 + c^2 = 364$, find b.

A $3\sqrt{2}$

C $2\sqrt{6}$

E   4

B   6

D   9

F $2\sqrt{3}$

Question 76

Given that a>0, find the value of a for which the minimal value of the function $f(x) = (a^2+1)x^2 - 2ax + 10$ in the interval $x \in [0; 12]$ is $\frac{451}{50}$.

A   7

C   5

E   8

B   12

D $\frac{50}{125}$

F   10

Question 77

If the probability that it will rain tomorrow is $\frac{2}{3}$ and the probability that it will rain and snow the following day is $\frac{1}{5}$, given that the probability of rain and snow occurring on any given day are independent from one another, what is the probability that it will snow the day after tomorrow?

A $\frac{10}{3}$

C $\frac{2}{15}$

E $\frac{4}{9}$

B $\frac{3}{10}$

D $\frac{15}{2}$

F $\frac{1}{5}$

Question 78

If $\cos 2\theta = \frac{3}{4}$, then $\frac{1}{\cos^2\theta - \sin^2\theta} =$

A $\frac{4}{3}$

C -1

E   2

B   4

D $\frac{3}{4}$

F   1

Question 79
Describe the geometrical transformation that maps the graph of $y = 0.2^x$ onto the graph of $y = 5^x$.

A   Reflection in the x-axis
B   Reflection in the y-axis

C   Multiplication by a scale factor of 25
D   Addition of the constant term 4.8

E   Multiplication by scale factor of 5
F   Multiplication by scale factor 1/25

Question 80
Find the solution to the equation $\log_4(2x + 3) + \log_4(2x + 15) - 1 = \log_4(14x + 5)$

A   There is no solution.
B $\frac{2}{5}$

C $\frac{5}{2}$
D -1

E   1
F   0

Question 81
The normal to the curve $y = e^{2x-5}$ at the point $P(2, e^{-1})$ intersects the x-axis at the point A and the y-axis at the point B. Which of the following is an appropriate formula for the area of the triangle that is formed in terms of e, m, and n, where m and n are integers?

A $\frac{(e^2+1)^m}{e^n}$

B $\frac{(e^3+1)^{\frac{1}{n}}}{m}$

C $\frac{e^n}{(e^2+1)^m}$

D $\frac{m^{\frac{1}{n}}}{e^3+1}$

E $\frac{e^{2m}}{e^n+1}$

F $\frac{(e^2-1)^m}{e^{2n}}$

Question 82
In the diagram, a stationary body explodes into two pieces, as shown to the right. In the process, the heavier piece, of mass 3kg, gains a kinetic energy X and begins to move leftward. Correspondingly, the lighter body, of mass 1kg, gains a kinetic energy Y and begins to move rightward.

What is the value of the kinetic energy ratio, X/Y?

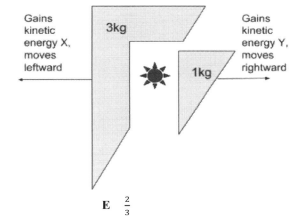

A $\frac{3}{1}$

B $\frac{1}{3}$

C $\frac{1}{4}$

D $\frac{4}{1}$

E $\frac{2}{3}$

F $\frac{3}{2}$

Question 83
Particles of masses 8kg, 4kg, 7kg, and 11kg are attached to vertices A, B, C, D respectively of a rectangular frame ABCD.

In the frame, CD = 90cm and BC = 60cm, as shown in the diagram to the right.
Find the distance of the centre of mass of the particles from the line AD.

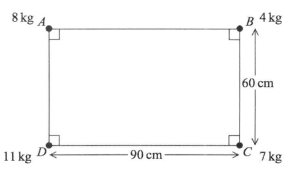

A   35cm
B   33cm

C   78cm
D   89cm

E   65cm
F   72cm

Question 84
Three particles are attached to a frame OABC, which is fixed in a horizontal plane. Take OA and OC as the x and y axes respectively.
➢ Particle P has mass 1kg and is attached at (25,10)
➢ Particle Q has mass 4kg and is attached at (12,7)
➢ Particle R has mass 5kg and is attached at (4,18)
Find the centre of mass of these three particles.

A	(12.8, 9.3)	C	(10.2, 9.8)	E	(12.6, 9.8)
B	(9.3, 12.8)	D	(9.8, 10.2)	F	(10.2, 9.3)

Question 85
A child of mass 35kg slides down a 20-metre-long slide in a water park. The child starts from rest, slides from Point A to Point B, which is 10 meters vertically below the level of A, and reaches point B while travelling at a speed of $12 \ m \ s^{-1}$.
Given that the sum of resistive forces has a magnitude of F newtons, what is the value of F? (Gravitational acceleration, g, is $9.8 \ ms^{-1}$)

A	53N	C	47.5N	E	49.5N
B	45.5N	D	55N	F	51N

Question 86
A 0.4kg package lies on a horizontal surface, and is attached to a horizontal string passing over a smooth pulley. When a mass of 0.2kg is attached to the other end of the string (hanging vertically), the package almost begins to move. Find the coefficient of static friction, μ_s.

A	0.5	B	0.6	C	0.7	D	0.8	E	0.9

Question 87
A small ball is projected from a point O, which is height h above horizontal ground. The ball has an initial speed of $20 \ ms^{-1}$ and is projected at an angle of 30° above the horizontal. If the ball strikes the ground 3 seconds after reaching its maximum height, what was its starting height, h? Assume $g = 10ms^{-2}$ and that there are no resistive forces acting on the ball.

A	15m	B	20m	C	25m	D	35m	E	10m	F	40m

Question 88
Given that $\sec x - \tan x = -5$, find the value of cos x.

A	-0.2	C	$-\frac{13}{5}$	E	0.5
B	0.2	D	$\frac{-5}{13}$	F	-0.5

Question 89
Consider the line with equation $y = 2x + k$ where k is a constant, and the curve $y = x^2 + (3k - 4)x + 13$. Given that the line and the curve do not intersect, what are the possible values of k?

A	$-\frac{1}{3} < k < 3$	C	$\frac{1}{2} < k < \frac{5}{3}$	E	$\frac{1}{3} < k < 3$
B	$-\frac{4}{9} < k < 4$	D	$\frac{3}{2} < k \leq \frac{8}{3}$	F	$-3 < k < \frac{1}{3}$

Question 90
A circle with centre C(5,-3) passes through A(-2,1), and the point T lies on the tangent to the circle such that AT = 4. What is the length of the line CT?

A	9	C	$\sqrt{95}$	E	$\sqrt{69}$
B	18	D	$8\sqrt{2}$	

END OF SECTION

Section 2

Physics: Question 1

a)   A positron is a particle with the same mass as an electron with a charge of $+1.6 \times 10^{-19}C$. It interacts with an electron to form two γ ray photons, in accordance with the following equation:

$$_{+1}^{0}e + {}_{-1}^{0}e \rightarrow 2\gamma$$

Assume that the kinetic energy of the positron and the electron are negligible when they interact.

i) Suggest why the photons produced will move off in opposite directions with equal energy.

[2 marks]

ii) Calculate the energy of the photons produced.

[2 marks]

b)   Consider the variation with nucleon number A of binding energy per nucleon B_E of nuclei, as shown in the figure below.

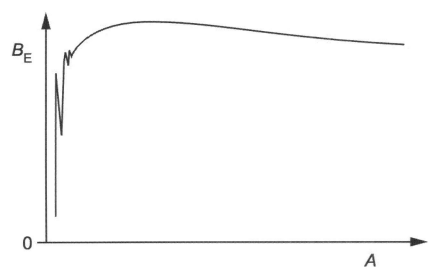

On this figure, mark the positions of:
i) iron-56
ii) zirconium-97
iii) hydrogen-2

[4 marks]

c)   i) Describe the process of nuclear fission.

[3 marks]

ii) Describe the process of nuclear fusion.

[3 marks]

iii) Does the graph that you used to respond to part b) explain anything about nuclear fusion or fission?

[2 marks]

d)   What is meant by:

i) α particle:

[1 mark]

ii) β particle:

[1 mark]

iii) γ radiation:

[1 mark]

e)   Describe what happens to the proton number and nucleon number of a nucleus when emission occurs of:

i) An *α particle*

[2 marks]

ii) A *β particle*

[2 marks]

iii) *γ* radiation

[2 marks]

[Total 25 marks]

Physics: Question 2

a)

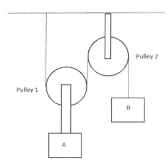

Joe is experimenting with 2 pulleys with 2 blocks attached. Pulley 1 is free to move whereas pulley 2 is fixed. Block A is fixed to pulley 1 whereas block B is free to move. Ignore the masses of the pulleys and the strings, and assume the system is frictionless. The string is also inextensible. Block A has mass m_1, Block B has mass m_2. The system is initially at rest and then block B accelerates downwards and Block A accelerates upwards.

i)   Find the acceleration of Block A in terms of g, m_1 and m_2.

[5 marks]

ii)   Find the acceleration of Block B in terms of g, m_1 and m_2.

[1 mark]

iii) Find the tension in the string in terms of g, m_1 and m_2.

[3 mark]

iv) What is the condition on m_1 and m_2 such that the system never moves?

v)

[2 marks]

vi) After time t what is the overall kinetic energy of the system in terms of g, m_1, m_2 and t. Does your answer to d) make sense in this expression?

[3 marks]

b)

Joe has a rubber band around his finger, the rubber band has a radius **r** when placed around his finger. Joe stretches the rubber band in such a way that it is 1mm above his finger all the way around the circumference of his finger at that point.

i)   Find the extension of the rubber band in terms of overall length after being stretched

[2 marks]

ii)   How does the extension of the rubber band Δ**r** relate to **r**?

[1 mark]

iii) If one of the rings around Saturn increased in radius by 1km how much greater would the circumference of the ring become?

[1 mark]

iv) If a disc expands by 1%, what is the percentage increase in the surface area of the disc assuming it is flat?

[3 marks]

v)   If a sphere's radius expands by 1% what is the percentage increase in the volume of the sphere?

[4 marks]

[Total 25 marks]

Chemistry: Question 3

a) Account for the following observations in terms of atomic structure, intermolecular forces, or intramolecular forces.

i. The stable form of nitrogen is a diatomic molecule with a low boiling point while the most stable form of phosphorus is a network solid at room temperature.

[2 marks]

ii. The melting point of the Group I elements decrease with increasing atomic number, while the melting points of the Group 17 elements (Halogens) increase with increasing atomic number.

[2 marks]

iii. The first ionization energies of the Group II elements decrease with increasing atomic number, and the first three elements (Be, Mg, Ca) show a greater change (899 to 590kJ/mol)

[2 marks]

iv. The Group 14 elements exhibit a gradual progression from non-metallic to metallic behaviour with increasing atomic number

[2 marks]

v) Diamonds and graphite are both composed of carbon. What explains their difference in hardness?

[2 marks]

b) Xenon forms several compounds, including XeF_2, XeF_4, and XeO_3.

i) Draw a Lewis structure for each of these compounds.

[3 marks]

ii) Describe the geometry of each compound including bond angles.

[2 marks]

iii) State and explain whether each compound is polar or nonpolar.

[2 marks]

iv) Account for the observation that these compounds are highly reactive.

[2 marks]

c) Consider the following section of the polymer polypropylene.

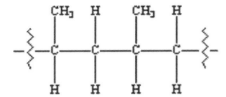

i)   Explain whether this is an addition or condensation polymer.

[2 marks]

ii) Compare the melting points for the following polymers. Give reasons for your answers.

1. Polypropylene containing 1000 monomer units vs. polypropylene containing 10,000 monomer units

2. Polypropylene vs. a polymer in which the CH3 group is replaced with a CH2CH2CH2CH3 group

3. Isotactic polypropylene (all the CH3 groups on the same side of the carbon backbone) vs. atactic polypropylene (CH3 groups arranged at random)

[4 marks]

[Total 25 marks]

Chemistry: Question 4

A compound only contains C, H, O, and Cu. It is analyzed for its carbon and hydrogen content by combustion. The copper content is obtained by reacting it with I^- according to the following equation:

$$2Cu^{2+}(aq) + 5I^-(aq) \rightarrow 2CuI(s) + I_3^-(aq)$$

and reacting the I_3^- formed with standard thiosulfate, $S_2O_3^{2-}$ according to the following equation:

$$I_3^-(aq) + 2S_2O_3^{2-}(aq) \rightarrow 3I^-(aq) + S_4O_6^{2-}(aq)$$

a) The combustion of a 0.25g sample of the compound produces 0.504g of CO_2 and 0.0743g of H_2O. What are the mass percentages of carbon and hydrogen in the compound?

[4 marks]

b) In the analysis for the first equation, a 0.115g sample of the compound is reacted with concentrated nitric acid, evaporated, and the residue is dissolved in H_2O. The Cu^{2+} in the resulting solution is reacted with excess with I^- and the resulting I_3^- is titrated with 11.75mL of 0.0320 M $S_2O_3^{2-}$.

i. What was the indicator used for the titration of I_3^- with 11.75mL of 0.0320 M $S_2O_3^{2-}$?

[2 marks]

ii. Determine the moles of Cu^{2+} and calculate the mass percentage of Cu in the compound.

[2 marks]

c) Find the mass percentage of oxygen in the compound, and write the empirical formula.

[3 marks]

d) A sample of copper metal is dissolved in 6 M nitric acid contained in a round bottom flask. This reaction yields a blue solution and emits a colourless gas which is found to be nitric oxide. Write a balanced equation for this reaction.

[2 marks]

e) The water is evaporated from the blue solution to leave a blue solid. When the blue solid is heated further, a second reaction occurs. This reaction produces a mixture of nitrogen dioxide gas, oxygen gas and a black oxide of copper.

i. A sample of the dried gas, collected in a 125 mL flask at 35 °C and 725 mm Hg, weighed 0.205 g. Find the average molar mass of the gas and the molar NO2/O2 ratio in it.

[4 marks]

ii. These data were obtained for the black solid;

Mass of empty flask: 39.49 g Mass of flask + copper metal: 40.86 g Mass of flask + oxide of copper: 41.21 g

Determine the formula of the oxide of copper.

[2 marks]

f)

i. If some of the blue solution from d) and e) were lost due to splattering during the evaporation, what would be the effect on the calculated percentage of copper in the black oxide? Explain.

[3 marks]

ii. If all of the blue solid were not decomposed into the black oxide during the final heating, what would be the effect on the calculated percentage of copper in the oxide? Explain.

[3 marks]

[Total 25 marks]

Biology: Question 5

The enzyme that is responsible for carbon assimilation in plants is called RuBisCO. This enzyme catalyses the reaction of CO_2 with RuBP in photosynthesis, but also the reaction of O_2 with RuBP, in a process known as photorespiration. The products of photorespiration require energy to turn back into compounds the plant can use, which is one reason that RuBisCO can be thought of as an inefficient enzyme.

Stomata are small pores, generally present on the lower surfaces of leaves. They open and close in response to environmental stimuli to enable gas exchange across the surface of the leaf. They are key in regulating the internal environment of a leaf such that photosynthesis and respiration can occur.

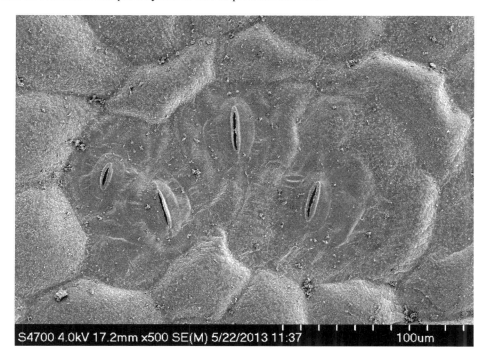

Figure 1: SEM micrograph of stomatal cluster on Begonia leaf.

a) Name 3 factors that might influence the rate of reaction of RuBisCO

[3 marks]

b) Where in the cell does photorespiration occur, and why is it less useful to plants than photosynthesis?

[3 marks]

c) Draw a graph illustrating the rates of photosynthesis and respiration in a leaf as light increases from darkness to very high light intensity

[3 marks]

d) In the graph drawn in part c), at what point would the plant start to decrease the CO_2 concentration in the air immediately around it, and why?

[3 marks]

e) Some plants have evolved specialised photosynthetic mechanisms. Crassulacean Acid Metabolism (CAM) photosynthesis is one such mechanism, and is found in plants that live in hot, dry environments like deserts. In CAM photosynthesis, CO_2 is taken in at night and stored as an acid, and then used in photosynthesis during the day. How might the behaviour of the stomata differ between CAM-photosynthesising plants and normal plants, and what are the advantages to desert plants of CAM photosynthesis?

[5 marks]

f) Discuss how the balance between photosynthesis and respiration is important in carbon cycles, both within plants and in the wider environment.

[8 marks]

[Total 25 marks]

Biology: Question 6

Cow's milk comprises around 80% water, and around 3.4% protein. The most abundant protein is Casein, which forms micelles in the milk. In the formation of micelles, kappa-casein plays a vital role, in a manner similar to phospholipids in a cell membrane.

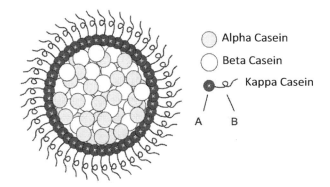

a) In the production of cheese, milk is mixed with an enzyme known as chymosin which cleaves the part marked B off the Kappa Casein molecule. This results in the casein floating to the surface of the milk, allowing it to be removed.

    Explain how the process happens.

    [6 marks]

b) A cheese producer is looking for alternatives to the enzyme chymosin. There are two particular proteases that are being investigated for their suitability. Enzyme A originates from an algae and enzyme B is from a fungus. For the experiment they were both used in the same quantities and it can be assumed that the proteases have the same action as chymosin.

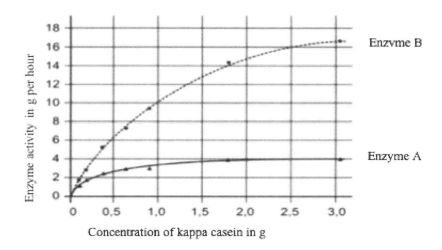

Compare the enzyme activity of the two enzymes at a casein concentration of 2.0g. Explain the consequences of an increase of casein concentration by 0.5g. What does this mean for the overall activity of the enzymes?

[7 marks]

c) The digestion of protein in the human body varies depending on the source. The following graph shows the digestion speed of whey protein compared to casein protein. The different speed of digestion is often used by strength athletes to ensure amino acid delivery over specific time frames. Under conditions of long term fasting, i.e. overnight a slow digesting protein might be chosen to ensure a steady supply of amino acids to support muscle protein synthesis.

Using the graph, which type of protein is the most appropriate to maintain amino acid delivery over night and why?

[4 marks]

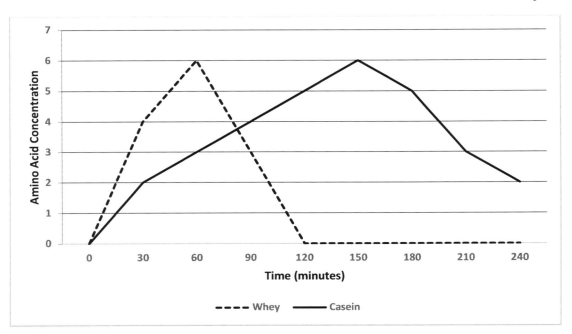

d) Milk contains many valuable nutrients designed to feed the babies of mammals. Milk from different species contains different levels of nutrients. The below graph shows the concentration of different nutrients in different types of milk. Considering the relative brain size in relation to body size, how might this explain the composition of human breast milk?

[3 marks]

Species	Fat %	Protein %	Sugar %
Cat	10.9	11.1	3.4
Bear	31	10.2	0.5
Cow	4.1	3.6	4.7
Dolphin	14.1	10.4	5.9
Dog	8.3	9.5	3.7
Human	4.5	1.1	6.8
Elephant	15.1	4.9	3.4

e) Lactose intolerance seems to be more prevalent in the Mediterranean areas than in northern European countries. Use your understanding of how climate influences agriculture and how agricultural products influence expression of operons to propose an answer to the question.

[2 marks]

f) Milk components are being used for many products, including cosmetics. One of the components is lecithin which is produced by the cleavage via Phospholipase A which also occurs in the digestive tract of calves. Like all other enzymes, activity of this enzyme is temperature dependent. Investigating the enzyme reveals that its activity is highest at about 50°C and lowest at 70°C. Its activity at 40°C (bovine core temperature) is approximately 90% compared to its optimal temperature. The enzyme activity also shows pH dependence; its activity increases as pH increases from 2.5 to 4.5 and then drops as pH increases from 5 upwards. Provide an explanation for the behaviour of the enzyme.

[3 marks]

[Total 25 marks]

END OF PAPER

	Paper A				Paper B		
1	F	46	A	1	A	46	A
2	B	47	C	2	B	47	E
3	C	48	B	3	C	48	A
4	D	49	F	4	B	49	D
5	E	50	C	5	C	50	A
6	C	51	E	6	B	51	B
7	D	52	F	7	A	52	C
8	B	53	H	8	C	53	E
9	E	54	F	9	E	54	E
10	C	55	D	10	C	55	B
11	C	56	E	11	E	56	D
12	A	57	A	12	E	57	B
13	D	58	D	13	B	58	D
14	B	59	C	14	D	59	D
15	C	60	C	15	B	60	E
16	C	61	C	16	C	61	D
17	B	62	G	17	C	62	C
18	B	63	E	18	E	63	E
19	B	64	B	19	A	64	D
20	A	65	B	20	F	65	B
21	D	66	E	21	D	66	D
22	F	67	D	22	E	67	F
23	B	68	E	23	A	68	E
24	C	69	A	24	E	69	E
25	B	70	C	25	D	70	A
26	B	71	E	26	A	71	E
27	D	72	F	27	C	72	D
28	B	73	C	28	C	73	A
29	A	74	C	29	D	74	D
30	E	75	C	30	C	75	B
31	D	76	B	31	A	76	A
32	B	77	B	32	C	77	B
33	D	78	C	33	C	78	A
34	D	79	D	34	B	79	B
35	E	80	A	35	C	80	C
36	C	81	B	36	E	81	A
37	E	82	D	37	B	82	B
38	A	83	B	38	E	83	B
39	A	84	B	39	H	84	B
40	B	85	C	40	C	85	B
41	F	86	D	41	D	86	A
42	E	87	A	42	B	87	F
43	B	88	B	43	E	88	D
44	F	89	B	44	D	89	B
45	B	90	B	45	B	90	A

Mock Paper A Answers

Section 1A: Maths

Question 1: F
$1 + (3\sqrt{2} - 1)^2 + (3 + \sqrt{2})^2 = 1 + (18 - 2(3\sqrt{2}) + 1) + (9 + 2(3\sqrt{2}) + 2)$
$= 31 - 6\sqrt{2} + 6\sqrt{2} = \underline{31}$

Question 2: B
Equate the volume with the surface area in the proportion. $3(^4/_3\pi r^3) = 4\pi r^2$, simplifies to r = 1.

Question 3: C
Number of annual flights = Flights per hour x Number of hours in one year x Number of airports
$= 4 \times (24 \times 365) \times 1000$
$= 96 \times 365 \times (1000) \approx 100 \times 365 \times 10 \times 100$
$= 365 \times 10^5 = 36.5\ Million$
However, this is an overestimate since we have multiplied by 100 instead of 96. Hence, the actual answer will be slightly lower. 35 Million is the only other viable option available.
365x24=8760 is the number of hours in a year, then 8760 x number of flights per hour (4) = 35040 flights per year per airport. Multiply by the number of airports – 42 million to the nearest million.

Question 4: D
Add the first and last equations together to give: 2F = 4, thus F = 2.
Then add the second and third equations to give 2F – 2H= 5. Thus, H = -0.5
Finally, substitute back in to the first equation to give 2 + G – 0.5 = 1. Thus, G = -0.5
Therefore, FGH = 2 x -0.5 x -0.5 = 0.5.

Question 5: E
The way to solve this is to break the calculation down into parts, almost working backwards. The number of seconds in 66 weeks is given by: 60 x 60 x 24 x 7 x 66:
$= (10 \times 6) \times (12 \times 5) \times (4 \times 6) \times 7 \times (11 \times 6)$
$= 1 \times 4 \times 5 \times 6 \times 6 \times 6 \times 7 \times 10 \times 11 \times 12$
$= 1 \times 4 \times 5 \times 6 \times (6) \times 7 \times 10 \times 11 \times (12 \times 6)$
$= 1 \times 4 \times 5 \times 6 \times (3 \times 2) \times 7 \times 10 \times 11 \times (72)$
$= 1 \times 2 \times 3 \times 4 \times 5 \times 6 \times 7 \times 10 \times 11 \times (9 \times 8)$
$= 1 \times 2 \times 3 \times 4 \times 5 \times 6 \times 7 \times 8 \times 9 \times 10\ x11$

Question 6: C
Remember the interior angles of a pentagon add up to 540° (three internal triangles), so each interior angle is 540/5 = 108°. Therefore angle **a** is 108°. Recalling that angles within a quadrilateral sum to 360°, we can calculate **b**. The larger angle in the central quadrilateral is 360° – 2 x 108° (angles at a point) = 144°. Therefore the remaining angle, **b** = (360 – 2(144)]/2 = 36°. The product of 36 and 108 is 3,888°.

Question 7: D
The key here is to note that the answers are several orders of magnitude apart so you can round the numbers to make your calculations easier:
Probability of bacteria being resistant to every antibiotic =
P (Res to Antibiotic 1)x P (Res to Antibiotic 2)x P (Res to Antibiotic 3) x P (Res to Antibiotic 4)
$= \frac{100}{10^{11}} x \frac{1000}{10^9} x \frac{100}{10^8} x \frac{1}{10^5}$
$= \frac{10^8}{10^{33}} = \frac{1}{10^{25}}$

Question 8: B

Let $y = 3.4 \times 10^{10}$; this is not necessary, but helpful, as the question can then be expressed as:

$$\frac{10y + y}{200y} = \frac{11y}{200y} = \frac{11}{200} = \frac{5.5}{100} = 5.5 \times 10^{-2}$$

Question 9: E

From the rules of angles made by intersections with parallel lines, all of the angles marked with the same letter are equal. There is no way to find if $d = 90°$, only that $b + d = c = 180° - a = 135°$, so b is unknown.

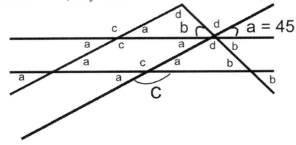

Question 10: C

The formula for the sum of internal angles in a regular polygon is given by: $180(n - 2)$, where n is the number of sides of the polygon Thus: $180n - 360 = 150n$

$3n = 36$ → n = 12

Each side is 15cm so the perimeter is 12 x 15cm = 180cm

Question 11: C

The radius and tangent to a circle always form a right angle, so using Pythagoras:

$3^2 \text{ m}^2 + 4^2 \text{ m}^2 = X^2 \text{ m}^2$

$X = 5$ m

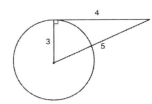

Question 12: A

Don't be afraid of how difficult this initially looks. If you follow the pattern, you get (e-e) which = 0. Anything multiplied by 0 gives zero.

Question 13: D

It is extremely helpful to draw diagrams to simplify this.

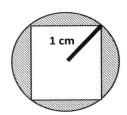

Shaded area = area of circle – area of square

The area of the circle is $\pi r^2 = 3 \times 1^2 = 3\text{cm}^2$.

We don't know the side length of the square, but we do know the length of the diagonal is 2cm, splitting the shape into two triangles.

The hypotenuse is therefore = radius x 2 = 2
Using Pythagoras' theorem, $2^2 = x^2 + x^2$ (where x = length and width of square)

Hence $2x^2 = 4$
$x^2 = 2$ = the area of the square
Therefore, the shaded area = $3 - 2 = 1\text{cm}^2$

Question 14: B

The shortest distance between points A and B is a direct line. Using Pythagoras:

The diagonal of a sports field = $\sqrt{40^2 + 30^2} = \sqrt{1,600 + 900} = \sqrt{2,500} = 50$.

The diagonal between the sports fields = $\sqrt{4^2 + 3^2} = \sqrt{16 + 9} = \sqrt{25} = 5$.

Thus, the shortest distance between A and B = $50 + 5 + 50 = 105\ m$.

Question 15: C

Let $y = 1.25 \times 10^8$; this is not necessary, but helpful, as the question can then be expressed as:

$$\frac{100y + 10y}{2y} = \frac{110y}{2y} = 55$$

Question 16: C

Transform all numbers into fractions then follow the order of operations to simplify. Move the surds next to each other and evaluate systematically:

$$= \left(\frac{6}{8} x \frac{7}{3} \div \frac{7}{5} x \frac{2}{6}\right) x \frac{4}{10} x \frac{15}{100} x \frac{5}{100} x \frac{5}{25} x \pi x \left(\sqrt{e^2}\right) x e\pi^{-1}$$

$$= \left(\frac{42}{24} \div \frac{14}{30}\right) x \frac{4 \times 3 \times 25}{10 \times 20 \times 100 \times 25} x \pi x \pi^{-1} x e^{-1} x e$$

$$= \left(\frac{21}{12} \div \frac{7}{15}\right) x \frac{12}{200 \times 100} x \frac{\pi}{\pi} x \frac{e}{e}$$

$$= \left(\frac{21}{12} x \frac{15}{7}\right) x \frac{3}{50 \times 100}$$

$$= \frac{45}{12} x \frac{3}{5000}$$

$$= \frac{9}{4} x \frac{1}{1000}$$

$$= \frac{9}{4000}$$

Question 17: B

$$\left(\frac{T}{4\pi}\right)^2 = \frac{l(M + 3m)}{3g(M + 2m)}$$

$$\frac{T^2}{16\pi^2} x \frac{3g}{l} = \frac{M + 3m}{M + 2m}$$

$$3gT^2 (M + 2m) = 16l\pi^2(M + 3m)$$

$$3gT^2M + 6gT^2m = 16l\pi^2M + 48l\pi^2m$$

$$6gT^2m - 48l\pi^2m = 16l\pi^2M - 3gT^2M$$

$$m(6gT^2 - 48l\pi^2) = 16l\pi^2M - 3gT^2M$$

$$m = \frac{16l\pi^2M - 3gT^2M}{6gT^2 - 48l\pi^2}$$

Question 18: B

The mean is the sum of all the numbers in the set divided by the number of members in the set. The sum of all the numbers in the original set must be: 11 numbers x mean of 6 = 66. The sum of all the numbers once two are removed must then be: 9 numbers x mean of 5 = 45. Thus any two numbers which sum to 66 − 45 = 21 could have been removed from the set.

END OF SECTION

Section 1B: Physics

Question 19: B

An alpha particle is a helium nucleus consisting of 2 protons and 2 neutrons. An alpha decay therefore reduces the atomic (proton) number by 2 and the mass number by 4. After a single alpha decay, the resulting proton number is 88 and the resulting mass number is 184. As this then splits in to two, the resulting element has a proton number of 44 and a mass number of 92. Gamma radiation does not alter the subatomic particle make-up of an atom.

Question 20: A

If the two isotopes were in equal abundance, the A_r would be 77, half-way between the two isotope masses (the average). The A_r is 76.5 (a weighted average), one quarter of the way between the isotopes, so there must be three times as much of the lighter isotope to move the A_r closer to its mass of 76 ($0.75 \times 76 + 0.25 \times 78 = 76.5$).

Though there is more of ^{76}X than ^{78}X, this does not necessarily imply that ^{78}X is lost through decay, as opposed to naturally less abundant from the beginning, so there is no way to know the relative stability of the isotopes.

Question 21: D

A Moment of force = Force x Perpendicular distance to pivot

If the lifting arm is a uniform 5m long, the weight exerts $2000 \, x \, 10 \, x \, 5 \, = \, 100,000 \, Nm$ of torque. In addition, there is a $250 \, x \, 10 \, x \, 2.5 \, = \, 6,250 \, Nm$ contribution from the weight of the beam ($\frac{5}{7}$ the mass, acting through the centre of mass of the beam).

On the other side, the remaining $\frac{2}{7}$ of the beam makes a $100 \, x \, 10 \, x \, 1 \, = \, 1,000 \, Nm$ contribution.

Therefore, the counterbalance must make a $(100,000 \, + \, 6,250) - 1,000 \, = \, 105,250 \, Nm$ contribution. As the counterbalance arm is 2 m long, this requires a weight of $\frac{105,250}{2} \, = \, 52,625 \, N$ weight, or a mass of 5,263 kg.

The crane's height is a distracter and not needed for this question

Question 22: F

Using the principle of conservation of energy, all the potential energy, mgh, at the top of the ramp will be converted to kinetic energy, ½mv², at the bottom.

Rearranging the formula, it is clear that mass cancels and there is no need to use the density and volume information:

mgh = ½mv², so gh = ½v²

v = √(2gh) = √400 = 20 ms⁻¹

Question 23: B

The Doppler Effect applies to all waves including members of the electromagnetic spectrum. A wave emitted from a moving object, like the sound from a siren, will be compressed as it moves toward you, causing sounds or light of higher frequency (pitch, energy). When an ambulance drives toward you, the siren will become higher in pitch, as it drives past it will move neither towards or away from you, so there will be no Doppler Effect, then the Doppler Effect will cause a lower pitch as it drives away and the waves are stretched to longer wavelengths.

Question 24: C

Power= Current x Voltage

Thus, one battery generates: 1.2 V x 2500 mAh

= 1.2 V x 2.5 Ah = 3 Watt hours

The light uses: 30 W x 1 h = 30 Wh

Therefore, it will take 30 Wh / 3 Wh = 10 batteries to power the light for one hour.

Question 25: B
The energy stored on descent is equal to the change in gravitational potential energy. The same energy is required to increase the height again, with an excess of the energy needed to lift the passengers. The energy needed to lift the passengers is therefore $= mg\Delta h = 72 \times 10 \times 10 \times 80 = 576kJ$. If the carriage moves at $4ms^{-1}$ for 200m, it takes 50 seconds to ascend. Therefore the rate of energy transfer is $576/50 = 11.52 \text{ kJs}^{-2} = 11.52W$.

Question 26: B
Work out the total energy transferred - $20 \times 50W = 1,000W$ of overall power by the 20 strings of lights when on. As $W = Js^{-1}$, can use the time the lights are on to find the energy used over this time period. 8pm – 6am is 10 hours, so in seconds is $10 \times 60 \times 60 = 36,000s$. When multiplying this by the power of all sets of lights, gives the energy used as:

$1000W \times 36,000s = 36,000,000J$ of energy, or 36,000 kJ. Multiply this by 20 to account for the lights being on for 20 days = gives 720,000kJ

As 100kJ of energy costs 2p, need to do $720,000/100 = 7,200$. Multiply this by 2p = 14,400p. Convert to pounds by dividing by $100 = £144$.

Question 27: D
Waves do not transfer mass, but their net neutral motions can interfere with each other to cause standing waves or other interference patterns. The energy of a wave depends on frequency, so waves have many different energies. Gamma rays have the highest energy for light, while visible light is lower in energy.

Question 28: B
Gravitational potential energy increases as the grain is lifted further from floor; this is equal to the work done against gravity to attain the higher position. The potential energy equal to $mg\Delta h$, so it is dependent upon the mass of the grain that is lifted.

Question 29: A
Multiply by the denominator to give: $(7x + 10) = (3z^2 + 2)(9x + 5)$

Partially expand brackets on right side: $(7x + 10) = 9x(3z^2 + 2) + 5(3z^2 + 2)$

Take x terms across to left side: $7x - 9x(3z^2 + 2) = 5(3z^2 + 2) - 10$

Take x outside the brackets: $x[7 - 9(3z^2 + 2)] = 5(3z^2 + 2) - 10$

Thus: $x = \frac{5(3z^2 + 2) - 10}{7 - 9(3z^2 + 2)}$

Simplify to give: $x = \frac{(15z^2)}{[7 - 9(3z^2 + 2)]}$

Question 30: E
This is a tricky question that requires a conceptual leap. Only the top candidates will get this correct.

Surface Area of Earth $= 4\pi r^2$
$= 4 \times 3 \times (0.6 \times 10^7)^2$
$= 12 \times (6 \times 10^6)^2$
$= 12 \times 36 \times 10^{12}$
$= 3.6 \times 10^{14}$

Since $= \frac{Force}{Area}$, $Atmospheric\ Pressure = \frac{Force\ exerted\ by atmosphere}{Surface\ Area\ of\ Earth}$

Therefore: $Force = 10^5 \times 3.6 \times 10^{14} = 3.6 \times 10^{19}\ N$

The force exerted by the atmosphere is equal to its weight therefore:
$Force = Weight = mass \times g$

Hence, $Atmospheric\ Mass = \frac{3.6 \times 10^{19}}{10} = 3.6 \times 10^{18}\ Kg$

Question 31: D

$F = ma$; therefore the difference in force is equal to $m_1a_1 - m_2a_2$.

This equals $(6 \times 6) - (2 \times 8) = 20N$

Question 32: B

R of series circuit $= R + R = 2R$

R parallel $= \frac{1}{\frac{1}{R}+\frac{1}{R}} = \frac{1}{\frac{2}{R}} = \frac{R}{2}$

Thus, the parallel circuit has a smaller resistance than the series circuit.
Since $I = V/R$, the parallel circuit will have a greater current than the series.

Question 33: D

Firstly, convert 36km/h to m/s to conserve units:

$$\frac{36,000\ m}{3600\ seconds} = \frac{360\ m}{36s} = 10\frac{m}{s}$$

Before the driver can react the car travels at 36 km/hour for 0.5 seconds. Thus, it covers a distance of $0.5 \times 10 = 5$ metres.

There are 100 m left to the deer and the car must slow from 10 m/s to 0 m/s.

Using: $v^2 = u^2 + 2as$ gives: $0 = 10^2 + 2\ x\ a\ x\ 100$
Thus, $-200a = 100$
Thus, $-200a = 100$
Thus, $a = -0.5\ ms^{-2}$
Finally, using $F = ma$: $2000\ x\ 0.5 = 1,000\ N$

Question 34: D

The distance travelled is the area under the curve ($v \times t = d$ at every v and t, sum for each t to find the total d, which also is the area; think of the case for constant v if confused).

Each square corresponds to 1 m (1 m/s x 1 s = 1 m), so counting squares gives an approximate distance of 30 m travelled: 31 m in a positive direction and 1 m in the negative direction (negative velocity).

Question 35: E

Remember to order by wavelength from low to high, i.e. from high energy to low energy. After that it's simply a case of knowledge.

Question 36: C

Work this out by $\Delta GPE = mg\Delta h$, and solve to find Δh. Since one Watt $= 1Js^{-1}$, we know the energy input to each litre of water (1kg) is 100J. Then solve $\Delta h = \Delta GPE/mg = 100/1 x10 = 10m$.

END OF SECTION

Section 1C: Chemistry

Question 37: E
Group 6 elements are non-metals whilst group 3 elements are metals. Thus, the group 3 element must lose electrons when it reacts with the group 6 element. The donation of electrons from its outer shell will decrease atomic size.

Question 38: A
The polymerisation reaction opens the double bond between the two C atoms to allow the formation of a long chain of monomers.

Question 39: A
The hydrogen halide binds to the alkene's unsaturated double bond. This results in a fully saturated product that consists purely of covalent bonds.

Question 40: B
This is an example of an addition reaction, the fluorine and hydrogen atoms are added at the unsaturated bond. If you're unsure about this type of question draw it out and the answer will be obvious.

Question 41: F
All of the above are true. Every mole of gas occupies the same volume. The left side therefore occupies 4 volumes, and the right side occupies 2 volumes. Increasing pressure will favour the lower volume side, and the equilibrium will shift right to produce ammonia and decrease the overall volume that the products and reactants occupy. If more N_2 gas is added, equilibrium will shift to react away this gas and lower the concentration again, with the result that more ammonia will be formed.

Question 42: E
Sodium is element 11 on the periodic table, a group 1 element, so has electron configuration: 2, 8, 1. It forms a metallic bond with other sodium atoms. Chlorine is element 17 in group 7, so has 17 electrons and 7 valence electrons, giving configuration: 2, 8, 7. Chlorine forms the covalent gas Cl_2, sharing one electron for a full valence shell.

Salt (NaCl) is an ionic compound, where sodium gives its single valence electron to chlorine so both atoms have full outer electron shells (8 electrons, so 2, 8:2, 8, 8).

Question 43: B
The volume of candle burned in 0.5 hour $= 0.5 \, x \, (\pi \, x \, 2^2) \; = \; 6cm^{-3}$
$6cm^{-3} = 6 \, x \, 10^{-3} \, m^3$
Since $Density = \frac{mass}{volume}$, in this case $900 \, kgm^{-3} = \frac{mass}{6 \, x \, 10^{-3} \, m^3}$
Thus, Mass burned $= \; 900 \, x \, 6 \, x \, 10^{-3} \; = 5400 \, x \, 10^{-3}kg = 5.4 \, g$
The Mr of $C_{24}H_{52} = 12 \, x \, 24 \, + \, 52 \, x \, 1 \; = \; 340$.
Thus the number of moles burned $= \frac{5.4}{340} \; = \; 0.016 \, moles$.
Total Energy transferred $= \; 0.016 \, x \, 11,000$
$= \; 16 \, x \, 10^{-3} \, x \, 11 \, x \, 10^3 = 11 \, x \, 16$
$= \; 176 \, kJ \; = \; 175,000 \, J$

Question 44: F
The information given can only be used to work out the empirical formula. You would need to know the molar mass in order to calculate the chemical formula.

Question 45: B
The trick in this question is to conserve your units to prevent silly mistakes from creeping in.
$200 \, cm^{-3} \; = \; 0.2 \, dm^{-3}. \; Number \; of \; moles \; = \; concentration \; x \; volume$ so: $0.2 \, x \, 1.8 \; = \; 0.36 \, mol$

Question 46: A

This is an example of an addition reaction: the chloride and hydrogen atoms are added at the unsaturated bond of the but-2-ene, which is between the 2nd and the 3rd C-atom. If you're unsure about this type of question draw it out and the answer will be obvious.

Question 47: C

The electrolysis reaction for brine is: $2\,NaCl\ +\ 2\,H_2O\ =\ 2\,NaOH\ +\ H_2\ +\ Cl_2$

Thus, keeping in mind the stoichiometry of the given equation, the solution must be C.

Question 48: B

During electrolysis a current is used to draw charged ions to electrodes. The anode is positively charged and draws anions like sulphate, and the cathode is negatively charged and attracts positively charged cations like copper. For electrolysis to work well, the electrodes need to keep their positive or negative charge. If an alternating AC-current was used, the anode and cathode would repeatedly switch places, and the ions would make no net movement toward either electrode.

Question 49: F

A polymer consists of repeating monomeric subunits. Polythene consists of multiple ethenes; glycogen of glucose; collagen of amino acids, starch of glucose; DNA of nucleotide bases, but triglycerides are not composed of monomeric subunits.

Question 50: C

Potassium is more reactive than sodium, as it has a greater number of electron shells, with the outermost single electron being more loosely attracted to the nucleus because of this, and hence more likely to be lost. Following this pattern, sodium is the next most reactive and copper the least.

Question 51: E

144ml of water is 144g, which is the equivalent of 8 moles. 8 times Avogadro's constant gives the number of molecules present, which is 4.8×10^{24}. There are 10 protons and 10 electrons in each water molecule, hence there are 4.8×10^{25} electrons.

Question 52: F

Write the equation to calculate molar ratios:

$C_8H_{18} + 12.5\,O_2 \rightarrow 8CO_2 + 9H_2O$

Travelling 10 miles uses: 228 x 10 = 2,280g of Octane.

M$_r$ of Octane = 12 x 8 + 18 x 1 = 114

Number of moles of octane used = 2,280/114 = 20 moles.

Thus, 160 moles of CO$_2$ must be produced.

M$_r$ of CO$_2$ = 12 + 16 x 2= 44

Mass of CO$_2$ produced = 44 x 160

= 7,040 g = <u>7.04 kg</u>

Question 53: H

Most polymers are made up of alkenes, which are unsaturated molecules. Polymerisation does not release water, as it is an addition reaction. Depending on the monomer, polymers can several different shapes.

Question 54: F

To balance the equation, start working from what you're given – the oxygen. Since you know there is 15 oxygen on the right, there must be the same on the left. Therefore **w** = 3. Now you know the iodine on the left is 13, so on the right, **z** = 13 to balance. You also know the iron on the left is 4, so **y** = 4 to balance. No you can deduce there are 12 + 13 = 25 chlorine on the right, therefore **x** = 25 to balance. Finally, check the whole equation to ensure it fits.

END OF SECTION

Section 1D: Biology

Question 55: D
The enzyme amylase catalyses the breakdown of starch into sugars in the mouth (1) and the small intestine (5).

Question 56: E
Whilst there is some enzymatic digestion in 1 and 3, the vast majority occurs in the small intestine (5). The liver facilitates digestion via the production of bile, and the large intestine is primarily responsible for the absorption of water.

Question 57: A
Re-plotting the genetic diagram with genotype information produces the diagram:

If squares were female, all of 5's circular male offspring would be affected. Circles must be females, so 1 must be homozygous recessive.

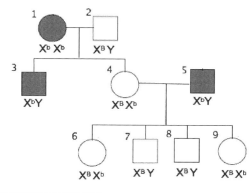

Question 58: D
The genotype of individual 6 must be $X^B X^b$, and 8 $X^B Y$. Plotting the information in a Punnett square:

		Individual 6 (Female carrier)	
		X^B	X^b
Individual 8 (Unaffected male)	X^B	$X^B X^B$	$X^B X^b$
	Y	$X^B Y$	$X^b Y$

The progeny produced are 25% $X^B X^B$ (homozygous normal female), 25% $X^B X^b$ (heterozygous carrier female), 25% $X^B Y$ (normal male) and 25% $X^b Y$ (affected male). So the chance of producing a colour blind boy is 25%.

Question 59: C
Chemical reactions take place in the cytoplasm, and the mitochondrion is the site for aerobic respiration releasing energy. The lack of a cell wall means that this is an animal cell.

Question 60: C
A sensory receptor (1) senses the heat of the pan. This information is passed down the sensory neurone (2) through a relay neurone to the motor neurone (4), which then causes the muscle (5) to contract, pulling the finger away.

Question 61: C
The receptor is directly coupled to the sensory neurone, so the communication here is electrical. All information between neurones passes via synapses, which use neurotransmitters to convey the information chemically. This occurs between the sensory neurone and the relay neurone, and between the relay neurone and the motor neurone. Therefore, the answer is C).

Question 62: G
The replacement of dying, damaged, and lost cells, the growth of the embryonic cell to a multi-cellular organism, and asexual reproduction are the three main reasons why cells divide through mitosis.
Question 63: E

Haemoglobin is contained within red blood cells and is not free in the blood. Additionally, as a protein it is too large to normally pass through the glomerular filtration barrier. All the other substances are freely filtered.

Question 64: B
More sodium than potassium must move inwards in order to depolarise the membrane. This results in a net movement of positive charge into the cell, causing a depolarisation.

Question 65: B
Intra-thoracic volume must decrease during expiration. Thus, the intercostal muscles relax causing the ribs must move down and in. The diaphragm moves up as well.

Question 66: E
The most effective method in minimising side effects would be to only target bacteria. Only bacteria have a flagellum.

Question 67: D
White blood cells can engulf/phagocytose pathogens in order to kill them. CO_2 is transported in the plasma, not in blood cells.

Question 68: E
E is the correct sequence. Remember sensory neurone take sensory information to the brain, and motor neurones take information away.

Question 69: A
Since A-T and C-G are the DNA base pairings, 29.6% Adenine implies 29.6% Thymine as well. Therefore the remaining $100 - 59.2 = 40.8\%$ is shared between Guanine and Cytosine equally, so there is 20.4% cytosine.

Question 70: C
Since CO binds to the oxygen binding site of haemoglobin, it reduces oxygen binding and therefore oxygen carrying capacity of blood. Hence, the blood becomes less oxygenated. Since more blood needs to flow to deliver the same amount of oxygen, this must be accomplished by an increased in heart rate. Haemoglobin does not become heavier as the CO binds **instead** of oxygen rather than in **addition** to. Carbon Dioxide is carried in plasma so is unaffected by carbon monoxide poisoning which affects haemoglobin.

Question 71: E
Blood pressure in the aorta is the highest of any vessel in the body, as blood has just been ejected from the left ventricle to go to the body. The pressure in the left ventricle (and hence the Aorta) is higher than that in the right ventricle (and hence the Pulmonary Artery) because the pressure must be sufficient to pump to the entire body, rather than just the lungs.

Question 72: F
Structure A is the right semi-lunar valve, the pulmonary valve. It opens in systole to allow flow of blood from the right ventricle into the pulmonary artery and to the lungs. It closes in diastole to ensure the right ventricle fills only from the right atrium, maintaining a one-way flow of blood. Therefore F is true, it opens when the right atrium is emptying. None of the other statements are true.

END OF SECTION

Section 1E: Advanced Maths & Physics

Question 73: C

Due to conservation of momentum, $m_1 v_1 + m_2 v_2 = (m_1 + m_2)v_3$

Substituting in the values of velocity and mass for m2, we get:

$$m_1 V - 3m_2 V = (m_1 + m_2)v_3$$

$$\frac{V(m_1 - 3m_2)}{(m_1 + m_2)} = v_3$$

Question 74: C

Applying the formula $s = ut + \frac{1}{2}at^2$, where u=0, a=g, and s=h,

$$h = 0(t) + \frac{1}{2}gt^2$$

$$h = \frac{1}{2}gt^2$$

$$g = \frac{2h}{t^2}$$

Question 75: C

The stopping distance for each driver is the sum of the distance that they would travel in the course of their reaction time, and the distance that they would travel while braking.

Stopping Distance = Distance travelled during reaction time + distance travelled during braking

Thinking Distance = Speed of Vehicle × Reaction Time

Braking distance = distance travelled between brakes being applied and car stopping.

For a car that is constantly decelerating, $v^2 = u^2 + 2as$, which yields: $braking\ distance = -\frac{u^2}{2a}$.

The stopping distance for Driver A (reaction time = 1s, initial velocity u) is:

$$Stopping\ distance\ A = u - \frac{u^2}{-10} = u + \frac{u^2}{10} = \frac{(10u + u^2)}{10}$$

The stopping distance for Driver B (reaction time = 3s, initial velocity 3u) is:

$$Stopping\ distance\ B = 3u - \frac{((3u))^2}{-10} = 3u + \frac{9u^2}{10} = \frac{30u + 9u^2}{10}$$

The difference between their stopping distances is: $\frac{30u + 9u^2 - (10u + u^2)}{10} = \frac{(20u + 8u^2)}{10}$

Question 76: B

A trick question! Gravitational potential energy = mgh = $60 * 10 * 4 = 2400J$

Question 77: B

The first child has climbed up on the ladder to a height of 2m, and immediately jumps onto the seesaw. At this point, his gravitational potential energy is $2m_1g$ J. When he jumps down, this potential energy is converted into the kinetic energy of his friend, who promptly flies into the air.

Equating potential energy with kinetic energy, we get: $2m_1g = \frac{1}{2}m_2v^2$

Solving for the velocity, we get: $v = \sqrt{\frac{4m_1g}{m_2}}$ which gives $v = 2\sqrt{\frac{m_1g}{m_2}}$

Question 78: C

The torque required to open the bottle with a spoon is:

$$x = F_{spoon} \times d_{spoon}$$

Consequently, the force required is:

$$F_{spoon} = \frac{x}{d_{spoon}}$$

The torque required to open the bottle with a coin is:

$$x = F_{coin} \times d_{coin}$$

Consequently, the force required is:

$$F_{coin} = \frac{x}{d_{coin}}$$

Since $d_{spoon} = 2d_{coin}$

$$F_{coin} = \frac{x}{\frac{d_{spoon}}{2}}$$

$$F_{coin} = 2\frac{x}{d_{spoon}}$$

$$F_{coin} = 2F_{spoon}$$

$$F_{spoon} = \frac{1}{2}F_{coin}$$

Question 79: D

Let us first find the opposing frictional force along the inclined plane. To do so, we must first find the normal force, which is equivalent to $mg\cos\theta$ *by Newton's Second Law*. Thus, the frictional force is F = $\frac{2}{5}(5)(10)\left(\frac{1}{2}\right) = 10N$. To accelerate the block to $2\ ms^{-2}$ in the absence of friction, I would have to push it with a force of $F = 5(2) = 10N$.

To overcome friction, I would have to add an additional 10N of force to accelerate the block, and hence the minimal amount of force I must exert is 20N in total.

Question 80: A

Power = Force $\times$ Velocity, therefore when the speed of the car is $15\ ms^{-1}$, the maximum force exerted is $\frac{44100}{15} = 2940N$.

Consequently, the resistance force is $25 \times 15 = 375N$

The force that accelerates the car, as a result, is $2940 - 375 = 2565N$

Therefore, the acceleration of the car along the road can be found using the formula $F = ma$. i.e.,

$$2565 = 1500a$$

$$a = 1.7ms^{-1}$$

Question 81: B

The plane's height from the ground decreases smoothly up until the point where it hits the runway. The vertical component of the plane's velocity decreases as it nears the runway, becoming effectively zero once it is travelling along the runway.

Question 82: D

Using the formula for displacement, $s = ut + \frac{1}{2}at^2$, we let d_1 and a_1 represent the distance travelled by the first car and its acceleration respectively. We know that $d_1 = (0)t + \left(\frac{1}{2}\right)a_1 t_1^2$. Subsequently, we let d_2 and a_2 represent the distance travelled by the first car and its acceleration respectively. We know that $d_2 = (0)t + \left(\frac{1}{2}\right)a_2 t_2^2$.

We know that the cars are subjected to a constant acceleration. The first car reaches a final speed of 20m/s in time t, which means that its acceleration is $\frac{20}{t} \, ms^{-2}$, whereas the second car reaches a speed of 20m/s in time $t_2 = 2t_1$, which means that its acceleration is $a_2 = \frac{10}{t} \, ms^{-2} = \frac{1}{2}a_1$.

Therefore, by substitution, we know that $d_2 = (0)t + \left(\frac{1}{2}\right)\left(\frac{1}{2}\right)a_1(2t_1)^2 = a_1 t_1^2 = 2d_1$. The answer is D.

Question 83: B

We know that the product of slopes of perpendicular lines equals -1. Therefore: $(n+1)(n+3) = -1$.
$n^2 + 4n + 3 = -1$
$n^2 + 4n + 4 = 0$
Factorising gives (n+2)(n+2), therefore n = -2 for the lines to be perpendicular.

Question 84: B

Algebraically, we can find the result of reflecting the curve $y = x^2 + 3$ across the line y=x by replacing y with x in the equation, and solving for the value of y in order to find the relevant equation, which is:

$x = f(y) = \sqrt{y-3}$

Replacing y with x gives:

$y = \sqrt{x-3}$

Translating the resulting equation by $\binom{4}{2}$ corresponds to introducing (-4) to the x term and (+2) to the y:

$y + 2 = \sqrt{x-4-3}$
$y = \sqrt{x-7} + 2$

The x-intercept is found by setting f(x) = 0.

$\sqrt{x-7} + 2 = 0$
$\sqrt{x-7} = -2$
$x - 7 = 4$
$x = 11$

Question 85: C

Take logs of each side and separate out the LHS:
$3x \log_{10} a + x \log_{10} b + 4x \log_{10} c = \log_{10} 2$
$x(3\log_{10} a + \log_{10} b + 4\log_{10} c) = \log_{10} 2$
$x \log_{10}(a^3 b c^4) = \log_{10} 2$
$x = \frac{\log_{10} 2}{\log_{10}(a^3 b c^4)}$

Question 86: D

Let $y = 2^x$. Then, $y^2 - 8y + 15 = 0$.

Solving this either using the quadratic equation or otherwise, we obtain y = 3 or y = 5.

If $3 = 2^x \rightarrow x = log_2 3 = \frac{log_{10} 3}{log_{10} 2}$

If $5 = 2^x \rightarrow x = \frac{log_{10} 5}{log_{10} 2}$.

The sum of the roots is $\frac{log_{10} 3}{log_{10} 2} + \frac{log_{10} 5}{log_{10} 2} = \frac{log_{10}(3*5)}{log_{10} 2} = \frac{log_{10} 15}{log_{10} 2}$

Question 87: A

Recall   the   discriminant   condition   for   the   existence   of   real   and   distinct   roots, $b^2 - 4ac > 0$

Using the coefficients in our question, this is: $(a - 2)^2 > 4a(-2)$

$a^2 + 4a + 4 > 0$

$(a + 2)^2 > 0$

Since this is a squared number, all values but a = -2 will satisfy this equation.

Question 88: B

We can use the inclusion-exclusion principle to find the probability that none of the balls are red.

Since there are 2n blue balls, n red balls, and 3n balls altogether, the probability of drawing no red balls within the

two draws is: $\frac{2n}{3n} \times \frac{(2n-1)}{(3n-1)} = \frac{4n-2}{3(3n-1)}$

Therefore, the probability of drawing at least one red ball is equal to:

$1 - \frac{4n-2}{3(3n-1)} = \frac{3(3n-1)-(4n-2)}{3(3n-1)} = \frac{9n-3-4n+2}{3(3n-1)} = \frac{5n-1}{3(3n-1)}$

Question 89: B

The numerator of $\frac{x^2-16}{x^2-4x}$ is in the form $a^2 - b^2$, which means that it can be expressed as the quantity

$(a + b)(a - b) = (x + 4)(x - 4)$

In turn, the numerator can be simplified into: $x(x - 4)$.

$\frac{x^2-16}{x^2-4x}$ can therefore be expressed as: $\frac{(x+4)(x-4)}{x(x-4)}$

Which simplifies to: $\frac{(x+4)}{x}$

Question 90: B

At the stationary point, $\frac{dy}{dx} = 0$. Using the product rule: $\frac{dy}{dx} = x^2 e^x + e^x \times 2x$

When $\frac{dy}{dx} = 0$, $x^2 e^x + e^x \times 2x = 0$

Hence, $xe^x(x + 2) = 0$

Which shows that the x-coordinates passing through the stationary points of $y = x^2 e^x$ are x=0 and x= -2

respectively. Therefore, the equation of the quadratic function is: $x(x + 2) = x^2 + 2x$.

END OF SECTION

Section 2

Question 1

a)

    i.   There is a negative change in velocity over this period of time - An acceleration of magnitude $-\frac{4.8}{0.08} = -60ms^{-2}$.

    ii.   ii) It means that the ball is moving in the opposite direction to its original motion (away from ball C).

    iii.   Ball B collided with Ball C at t = 0.18s, began decelerating at $60ms^{-2}$ for 0.08s and then bounced back in the opposite direction with speed $0.8ms^{-1}$.

b)

    i.   Change in momentum for ball B = 1.2(4.0 + 0.8) = 5.76 N s

    ii.   ii) Force $= \frac{\Delta p}{\Delta t} = \frac{5.76}{0.08} = 72N$

c)   By conservation of momentum, the change in momentum for the two bodies as a result of the collision is equal. In other words, change in momentum for ball B = Change in momentum for ball C.

$$5.76 = m_{ballC} v_{ballC}$$
$$5.76 = 3.6(v_{ballC})$$
$$v_{ballC} = \frac{5.76}{3.6} = 1.6 \ m \ s^{-1}$$

d)   Kinetic energy prior to collision $= \frac{1}{2} \times 1.2 \times 4^2 = 9.6J$

Kinetic energy after collision $= \frac{1}{2} \times 1.2 \times 0.8^2 + \frac{1}{2} \times 3.6 \times 1.6^2 = 4.99J$

Since kinetic energy after collision is less than kinetic energy prior to collision, it is an inelastic collision.

e)

    i.   The gradient of the graph becomes constant. Meaning the ball is no longer accelerating, so must be experiencing a force to counteract its weight at this point

    ii.   At t = 0s, the gradient of the graph was zero.

    iii.   We draw a tangent to the curve at the point corresponding to t = 0.4s, and obtain the gradient. The speed is $2.8 \ m \ s^{-1}$.

Question 2

a) First, we must find the frictional force that Jack is subjected to as he is on the ground.

We know that frictional force, F_f, is the product of the normal force from the ground, N, and the coefficient of kinetic friction, μ_k. The normal force is equal to the gravitational force that Jack exerts on the ground, mg minus the component of the tension, T, in the vertical direction. As Jack is traveling at a constant velocity, the frictional force must equal the component of the tension in the horizontal direction.

$$F_g = 9.8 \times 65 = 637$$

$$N = F_g - \sin(30)\,T$$
$$0.8 \times N = \cos(30) \times T$$

Solving these simultaneous equations for N we get $N = \frac{9.8 \times 65}{1 + \tan(30) \times 0.8} = 435.7N$

Therefore $F_f = 348.6N$

Subsequently, since Jill is travelling at $20ms^{-1}$, the power that is generated is
$Power = Fv$
$Power = 348.6N * 20ms^{-1} = 6972W.$

b) Using trigonometry: $348.6 = T\cos 30$

$$T = \frac{348.6}{\cos(30)}$$

$$T = 402.5N$$

c)

i. In order to accelerate Jack at $2ms^{-2}$, Jill must overcome the force of friction and also cause his mass to accelerate.

Therefore, the force that she must generate in the horizontal direction is equivalent to:

$$F = 348.6 + 65(2) = 478.6N$$

The tension in the rope, which has now adjusted to being 25 degrees to the horizontal, is now:

$$T = \frac{478.6}{\cos 25} = 528.1N$$

ii. $Final\ velocity = u + at = 20 + (2)(2.5) = 25ms^{-1}$

The new horsepower is therefore: $Power = Fv = 478.6 \times 25 = 12,000W$

d) $New\ force\ of\ friction = 0.3 * 435.7N = 130.7N$

$Net\ force = 478.6 - 130.7 = 347.9N$

$New\ acceleration = \frac{347.9}{65} = 5.4ms^{-2}$

e)

    i.   *Velocity after slippery slide acceleration* $= 25 + (3.4 \times 2) = 35.7\ m\ s^{-1}$

             Frictional force, F_f *after Jill puts hoof down* $= 0.9 * (435.7 + 200) = 572.2N$

             Net force $= 478,6 - 572.2 = -93,6N$

             Acceleration $= -\dfrac{113.7}{65} = -1.440m\ s^{-2}$

             Time taken to stop: Using $v = u + at, 0 = 35.7 + (-1.440)t$

             Time taken to stop $= 24.80s$

    ii.   *Using* $s = ut + \frac{1}{2}at^2$

             $s = (35.7)(24.80) + \frac{1}{2}(-1.440)(24.80^2)$

             $s = 443m$ as

f)

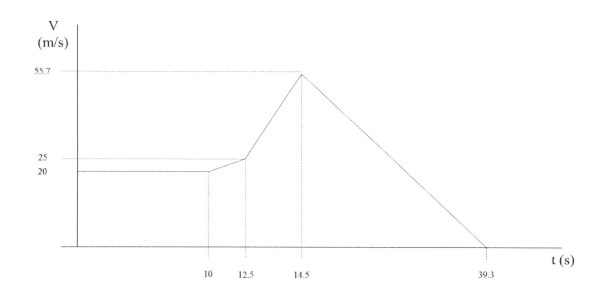

Question 3

a) The Haber Process combines nitrogen from the air with hydrogen mainly from natural gas in a 1:3 ratio by volume, subjecting this gas to temperatures of 400-500°C under 200 atmospheres of pressure in the presence of an iron catalyst.

b) More ammonia is produced as a result of Le Chatelier's Principle. When temperature is lowered, the system responds so as to restore a new equilibrium state by producing more ammonia so as to release more heat to restore the temperature.

c) a) Nitrogenous fertilizers

b) Manufacture of refrigerants, nylon, cleaning agents, explosives

d) $4NH_3 + 5O_2 \leftrightarrow 4NO + 6H_2O$

e)

i. $K_p = \dfrac{p(NO)^4 p(H_2O)^6}{p(NH_3)^4 p(O_2)^5}$

ii. Atmospheres, or Pa, or kPa.

f) Let $y = \Delta H_f^\theta$ for NO.

$4NH_3(g) + 5O_2(g) \leftrightarrow 4NO(g) + 6H_2O$

$\Delta H^\theta = -906 \; kJ \; mol^{-1}$

Therefore, $\Delta H^\theta = -906 = 4y + 6*(-242) - (4*-46)$

$\Delta H^\theta = -906 = 4y - 1452 + 184$

Hence, $4y = -906 + 1452 - 184 = 362$

$y = +90.5 \; kJ \; mol^{-1}$

Question 4

a)

    i. $2CH_4 + 4O_2 \rightarrow 2CO_2 + 4H_2O$

    ii. $2CH_4 + 3O_2 \rightarrow 2CO + 4H_2O$

b)

    i.   The high temperature and pressure within the system provides the energy to break the Nitrogen-Nitrogen triple bond, and provides the activation energy for the reaction between nitrogen gas and oxygen gas.

    ii. Possible catalysts include Pt or Pd, Pt/Rh, or Pt/Pd/Rh.

    iii. $2NO + 2CO \rightarrow 2CO_2 + N_2$

        $2NO + C \rightarrow CO_2 + N_2$

c)

    i.   Mg forms Mg^{2+} ions, and N has five valence electrons. In the situation in which they react, 3 Mg^{2+} ions will have a shortfall of 6 valence electrons, and 2 N atoms have 3 valence electrons on their outer orbitals respectively, which allows the compound Mg_3N_2 to form stably.

    ii. $MgN_2 + 6H_2O \rightarrow 3Mg(OH)_2 + 2NH_3$

    iii. No.

        In Mg_3N_2 the oxidation number of N is -3

        In NH_3 N remains -3.

        Since there is no change in the oxidation number of N or in any other one of the ions, no redox has taken place.

d)

    i.   Coal-fired power stations, automobiles, contact process, cement manufacture, etc. are acceptable solutions.

    ii. $2SO_2 + O_2 \rightarrow 2SO_3$

        $SO_3 + H_2O \rightarrow H_2SO_4$

e) Incomplete combustion of hydrocarbons on a large scale produces carbon monoxide as opposed to carbon dioxide, which is a worse greenhouse gas. By producing carbon monoxide instead, there may be less negative consequences as the result of the global warming that is caused by the presence of excess carbon dioxide.

Question 5

a)

      i.   Nuclear membrane/envelope/nucleus

     ii.   Mitochondrion

   iii.   Golgi vesicle/vacuole

b)   Centrioles help in the formation of spindle fibres that separate chromosomes during anaphase, in which chromosomes move towards different poles of the cell.

c)   Mitochondria serve the purpose of releasing the majority of the cell's energy through the process of cellular respiration, by taking in nutrients, breaking them down, and creating energy rich molecules known as adenosine triphosphate (ATP) for the cell's usage.

That is why the mitochondrion is the powerhouse of the cell.

d)   The main structural difference between animal and plant cells is the lack of a cell wall in animal cells. This can be seen in the image as there is a thin lipid bilayer membrane, and the outline of the cell is too irregular for a cell wall. In plants, the cell wall exists to maintain structural integrity and to enable the plant to withstand influences of the outside world. Plants must be able to compensate for and protect the cell against changes in temperature and hydration due to their stationary habit. Having a cell wall allows the plants cells to resist changes in osmotic pressure associated with changes in hydration. Most plant cells do not have centrioles, which is another reason the cell in the image is an animal cell.

e)   The parent cell chromosomes condense and become thousands of times more compact than they were during interphase. Each duplicated chromosome, which consists of two identical sister chromatids, become visible as a result. Subsequently, the centrioles move to the opposite poles of the cell, and the nucleolus disappears. Then, spindle fibres begin to form, creating the network that will eventually pull the chromosomes apart. Subsequently, the nuclear envelope disintegrates, and the chromosomes move to the equatorial plate (otherwise known as the metaphase plate). When this has happened, the centromeres attach themselves to the spindle fibers, completing the spindle in such a way that the microtubules extend from the spindle pole to the cell membrane.

f)   Control of mitosis means control of tissue growth. Tissue growth is essential to compensate for loss due to cell death, degeneration and injury and therefore holds an essential role in the survival of an organism. Energy is needed, however, to build and then maintain tissue. . If tissue growth occurs in a controlled manner, the benefits outweigh the costs. Uncontrolled growth consumes uncontrollable amounts of resources and the costs outweigh the benefits for the organism.

If growth control fails and cells replicate uncontrollably, this can lead to cancer.

Question 6

a) An infectious disease is a disorder that is caused by a pathogen that is transmissible, communicable, contagious, and can be passed from one person or organism to another.

b) Malaria is primarily transmitted when a female *Anopheles* mosquito spreads the *Plasmodium* parasite through her saliva, although it can also be transmitted through blood transfusions, needle sharing, through the placenta of the mother, and during childbirth.

c) Malaria requires a living vector, i.e. the female *Anopheles* mosquito, to be able to spread. The primary habitat of the *Anopheles* mosquito is within hot and humid regions. Additionally, the plasmodium parasite that is contained in the *Anopheles* mosquito's saliva must be able to reproduce within the mosquito, and it only manages to do so at temperatures that are above 20 degrees Celsius, which rules out the possibility of it doing so within colder and drier climates. TB, on the other hand, is an airborne disease that may be transmitted by the droplets from a person's cough or the mucus from their sneeze.

d) Vaccination is the process of injecting inactive antigens into the human body so that the body will facilitate a primary immune response, during which the immune system comes into contact with the antigen for the first time, and begins to produce B lymphocytes and B cells that synthesize and release antibodies in response to the antigen through the humoral response, eventually producing memory cells that will grant the vaccinated person immunity to the disease in the future, and thereby ensure that they will not be able to pass on the disease after they have been vaccinated.

Vaccination programs result in herd immunity across communities, which allows unimmunized people to stay safe. Moreover, vaccination programs allow for surveillance of the population for signs of disease when there is an outbreak.

Vaccination programs alone however can only eradicate diseases if they have few hosts that can all be vaccinated. Any disease that has multiple potential hosts and therefore has a large natural reservoir is very difficult to eradicate.

e) The human immune system recognizes foreign surface proteins known as antigens. These surface proteins are picked up by antibodies which mark the cells expressing these proteins on their surface as a threat and therefore allow their destruction through phagocytosis. Antibodies that function against specific antigens are replicated whilst those that do not bind, fail to be produced. Some antibody expressing cells migrate to lymph nodes where they continue to exist and produce small quantities of antibodies even after the diseases has been fought off. They basically form an antibody memory. This is the basis for vaccinations conveying immunity.

In the case of malaria, the antigen is a protein that is produced by the *Plasmodium* parasite. Due to the genetic complexity of *Plasmodium*, it has the potential to produce many different antigens, each of which requires a tailored immune system response. Additionally, antigenic variation ensures that the antigen can evolve or change throughout the course of the *Plasmodium*'s life.

Malaria can also be prevented by preventing mosquito bites; this can be achieved by using mosquito nets for sleeping, wearing protective clothing, preventing transmission via blood, or preventing mosquitoes from breeding, either through genetic modification or reducing their potential breeding sites.

f) This is because antibodies from the mother passed across the placenta and through the colostrum interact with measles antigens and so prevents an active immune response in the first few months of a child's life. It is too early for an immune response to occur, particularly because the T and B cells are too immature at this point of the child's life. Individuals with compromised immune systems may not be able to produce antibodies against the vaccines, leading either to symptoms or the vaccine being ineffective.

END OF PAPER

Mock Paper B Answers

Section 1A: Maths

Question 1: A

Equate y to give:

$2x - 1 = x^2 - 1$

$\rightarrow x^2 - 2x = 0$

$\rightarrow x(x - 2) = 0$

Thus, x = 2 and x = 0

There is no need to substitute back to get the y values as only option A satisfies the x values.

Question 2: B

The ruler and the cruise ship look to be the same size because their edges are in line with Tim's line of sight. His eyes form the apex of two similar triangles. All the sides of two similar triangles are in the same ratio since the angles are the same, therefore:

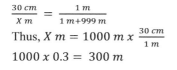

Thus, $X\,m = 1000\,m\,x\,\frac{30\,cm}{1\,m}$

$1000\ x\ 0.3\ =\ 300\ m$

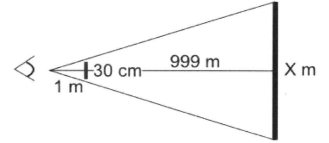

Question 3: C

Bob = B, Kerry = K, Son = S.

B = 2K

K = 3S

B + K + S = 50

50 = 2K + K + K/3 = 6K/3 + 3K/3 + K/3 = 10K/3

K = 15

B = 30

S = 5

So: B – S = 30 – 5 = 25.

Question 4: B

Let tail = T, body and legs = B and head = H.

As described in the question H = T + 0.5B and B = T + H.

We have already been told that T = 30Kg.

Therefore substitute the second equation into the first as H = 30 + 0.5(30 + H).

Re-arranging reveals that -0.5H = 45Kg and therefore the weight of the head is 90Kg, the body and legs 120Kg and as we were told the tail weighs 30Kg.

Thus giving a total weight of 240Kg

Question 5: C

The numerator of the fraction consists of 3 distinct terms or 3 distinct dimensions. As all other functions within the equation are constants one would consider this the volume of a complex 3D shape.

Question 6: B

Expand the larger scientific number so that it reads 10 to the power 6 like so: 4.2 x 1010 = 42000 x 106. Now that the powers are the same across the numerators, a simple subtraction can be performed (42000 – 4.2) x 106 = 41995.8 x 106 which can be simplified to 4.19958 x 1010. Next consider the division which can be competed in a two-step process, first divide the numerator by 2 like so (4.19958/2) x 1010 = 2.09979 x 1010 and then subtract the powers like so 2.09979 x 10(10-3) = 2.09979 x 107.

Question 7: A
Note the triangle formed by the right angle lines and the tangent. Recall that as this is a right angle triangle then the other two angles must be 45o. As angles along a straight line add up to 180o a must equal $180 - 45 = 135$o. Angles around the origin must add up to 360o and therefore $b = (360 - 90)/2 = 135$o. Therefore the correct answer is A.

Question 8: C
The probability of drawing a blue ball (1/21) and then a black ball (1/20) is $1/21 \times 1/20 = 1/420$. However note that it is also possible that these balls could also be drawn out in the opposite order. Therefore the probability must be multiplied by two like so $1/420 \times 2 = 2/420 = 1/210$.

Question 9: E
Begin by subtracting the integral from both sides producing $x - \int_{-z}^{z} 9a - 7 = \frac{\sqrt{b^3-9st}}{13j}$. Next multiply both sides by 13j and square, rendering $[13j(x - \int_{-z}^{z} 9a - 7)]^2 = b^3 - 9st$. Finally subtract b^3 from both sides and divide by -9s leaving the correct answer: $\frac{[13j(x-\int_{-z}^{z}9a-7)]^2 - b^3}{-9s} = t$.

Question 10: C
The formula for calculating compound interest can be given as investment x interest rate [years] or in short hand for this situation: $1687.5 = 500x^3$. Therefore, in order to calculate the interest rate (x) the above formula must be rearranged to $\sqrt[3]{1687.5/500} = 1.5$ revealing an interest rate of 50%.

Question 11: E
Begin by drawing your line of best fit, remembering not to force it through the origin. Begin fitting the general equation $y = mx + c$ to your line. Calculate the gradient as $\Delta y/\Delta x$ and read the y intercept off your annotated graph.

Question 12: E
In order to start rearranging the fraction begin by adding m to both sides and squaring to yield $4m^2 = \frac{9xy^3z^5}{3x^9yz^4}$. Now it is clear to see that this can be most simply displayed in terms of powers. Therefore E is the correct answer.

Question 13: B
Begin by calculating the speed of the innermost well as the circumference of travel over time $= 20 \times 3.14 = 62.8$m/s. Calculate the outermost well speed in the same manner $= 40 \times 3.14 = 125.6$m/s. $125.6 - 62.8 = 62.8$m/s faster.

Question 14: D
This question is testing your knowledge of indices. Since this is a negative power, $9x^{-\frac{1}{3}}$ can first be written as $\frac{9}{x^{\frac{1}{3}}}$. Recall that with a fractional power apply the rule $x^{\frac{a}{b}} = \sqrt[b]{x^a}$ and thus the term $x^{\frac{1}{3}}$ can be simplified to $\sqrt[3]{x}$ given the final answer $= \frac{9}{\sqrt[3]{x}}$ or D.

Question 15: B
Start by multiplying each term by ax to give: $a(y+x)=x^2+a^2$
Expand the brackets: $ay+ax=x^2+a^2$
Subtract ax from both sides: $ay=x^2+a^2-ax$
Lastly, divide the both sides by a to get: $y = \frac{x^2+a^2-ax}{a}$

Question 16: C
Solve as simultaneous equations
Start by substituting $x = \frac{y}{3}$ into equation B.
This gives $y = \frac{18}{y} - 7$
Multiply every term by y to give:
$0 = y^2 + 7y - 18$
Factorise this quadratic to give:
$0 = (y+9)(y-2)$
Where the graphs meet, y is equal to 2 and 9
$y = 3x$ so the graphs meet when $x = 6$ and $x = 27$

Question 17: C
The numbers can all be written as a fraction over 36:
$0.\dot{3}$ is the same as $\frac{12}{36}$
$\frac{11}{18}$ is the same as $\frac{22}{36}$
0.25 is the same as $\frac{9}{36}$
0.75 is the same as $\frac{27}{36}$
$\frac{62}{72}$ is the same as $\frac{31}{36}$
$\frac{7}{7}$ is the same as $\frac{36}{36}$

Ordering them from lowest to highest gives: $\frac{7}{36}$; 0.25 ; $0.\dot{3}$; $\frac{11}{18}$; 0.75 ; $\frac{62}{72}$; $\frac{7}{7}$
Therefore the median value is $\frac{11}{18}$

Question 18: E
Firstly, deal with the term in the brackets: $3^3 = 27$
$(x^{1/2})^3 = x^{1.5}$
$(3x^{1/2})^3 = 27x^{1.5}$
Next, divide by $3x^2$: $\frac{27}{3} = 9$
$\frac{x^{1.5}}{x^2} = x^{-0.5} = \frac{1}{\sqrt{x}}$
Answer $= \frac{9}{\sqrt{x}}$

END OF SECTION

Section 1B: Physics

Question 19: A

As energy is added to ice, the molecules increase their vibrations and the temperature increases. As the ice begins to melt, all energy goes into breaking the bonds to form water, and none goes to increasing the temperature. Once all bonds are broken, the energy again goes to increasing the temperature of the water.

Question 20: F

All the above units are measures of power, the amount of work done per unit time.

Question 21: D

Firstly, convert Litres → m³: 950 Litres = 0.95 m³

Buoyancy Force = Volume x Density x g.

= 0.95 x 1000 x 10 = 9,500 N

Weight of the boat = mg= 600 x 10 = 6,000 N

Since buoyancy force > Weight, the boat will float.

The difference between Buoyancy Force + weight = 9500 – 6000 = 3,500N

Hence adding mass of 350kg (=3,500N as g is 10) will balance both forces.

Adding further mass will cause the boat to sink. Hence, the answer is 355kg

(350kg won't cause sinking – merely balance the force).

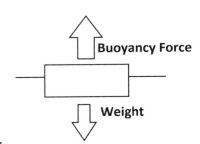

Question 22: E

Although energy is usually wasted when transformed, e.g. in power plants and engines, there are times when energy can be transformed without any losses to extraneous energy forms, e.g. a ball free-falling through a vacuum loses potential energy and gains kinetic energy without losses to other energy forms. Energy can be dispersed through vacuums e.g. solar heat energy through space.

Question 23: A

A beam of light is refracted toward the normal to the glass-air interface when it enters the glass, but refracted away by the same amount when it exists, for overall no net change. The angle of reflection of a beam is equal to (and thus dependent on) the angle of incidence. Beams of light entering a denser medium are refracted toward the normal to the interface, so light entering a pool of water would descend more steeply. Excited electrons in any atom can emit a mass less photon to reduce their energy.

Question 24: E

For Resistors in parallel, $\frac{1}{R_T} = \frac{R_1 \, x \, R_2 \cdots}{R_1 + R_2 \cdots}$

For the first segment: $\frac{1}{R} = \frac{1}{Z} + \frac{1}{Z} = \frac{2}{Z}$

For the second segment: $\frac{1}{R} = \frac{1}{Z} + \frac{1}{Z} + \frac{1}{Z} = \frac{3}{Z}$

For the third segment: R = Z

Thus the total resistance is: $Z + \frac{Z}{2} + \frac{Z}{3} = 22$.

$\frac{6Z + 3Z + 2Z}{6} = 22$

$11Z = 22 \, x \, 6$

$Z = \frac{132}{11} = 12M\Omega$

Question 25: D

Using s = ut + 0.5at².

125 = 0.5x10x t²

125 = 5 t²

t = 5 seconds

Therefore the final speed is 50ms⁻¹, and the momentum is about 50ms⁻¹ x 0.4 kg = 20kgms⁻¹

Question 26: A
Remember that you can separate the vertical and horizontal components of both bullets. Both bullets actually have zero vertical velocity at t=0. Thus, only gravity affects them- and it does so equally. Therefore, rather counter-intuitively, they hit the floor at the same time.

Question 27: C
You don't need to know the mass of the fish for this one, since there is no acceleration or deceleration taking place. The resistive forces are equivalent to the force of thrust of the fish. Recall that work done = force x distance. Travelling at 2ms⁻¹, the fish travels 60 seconds x 60 minutes x 2 ms⁻¹ = 7200 m in one hour. Therefore the work done against resistive forces is f x d = 2N x 7200 = <u>14,400J</u>

Question 28: C
Electric conduction is a consequence of metallic bonding: metal atoms lose their valence electrons to obtain their optimum energy state, with the cations forming a lattice held together by electromagnetic attraction to the cloud of free electrons. These free electrons can then conduct electricity, as they are not bound to any particular atom. This does not require the movement of ions or the breaking of the cation lattice.

Question 29: D
The energy in a nuclear bomb comes from $E = mc^2$. When two nuclei fuse, the combined mass is slightly smaller than the two individual nuclei, and the mass lost is converted to energy according to Einstein's equation. Fusion releases much more energy than fission, as in the sun, and humans cannot harness this energy yet.
Uncontrolled fission causes the explosion in an atom bomb and is created by a neutron-induced chain reaction. In power plants these neutrons are tightly controlled, so as not to overload the reactors and cause an explosion.

Question 30: C
$$250 \, kJ = 25 \times 10^4 \, J$$
$$25 \times 10^4 \, J = \frac{25 \times 10^4}{4.2 \times 10^3} \, kCal$$
$$= \frac{250}{4.2} \approx 60 \, kCal$$
$$2 \, Litres = 2000 \, cm^3$$
Thus, each cm³ of water is heated by $\frac{60 \, kCal}{2000} = -30°C$
$$Final \, Temperature = initial \, temperature + change \, in \, temperature$$
$$= 25 + 30 = 55°C$$

Question 31: A
Because the two sides of the circuit are in parallel, both sets of lights experience a 24v voltage drop across them. In lights R and S this is shared equally between them, but in lights P and Q, the new light with twice the resistance takes twice the voltage.

Question 32: C
Although the magnitude of acceleration decreases after 5 seconds he is still increasing his velocity. In this case, the velocity is given by the area under the curve. Summing the velocity gained over each second gives the final velocity, with squares here corresponding to 1 m/s² x 1 s = 1 m/s. He only ever loses velocity between 0-0.5 s and 9.5-10 s.

Question 33: C
Statements 1 and 3 are true. Statement 2 is false because infrared has a longer wavelength than visible light Statement 4 is false because gamma radiation and not infrared radiation is used to sterilise food and to kill cancer cells. Statement 5 is true because darker skins contain a higher amount of melanin pigment, which absorbs UV light.

Question 34: B
This question requires the use of the equation:
$P=mv$ where p=momentum, m=mass and v=velocity

The total momentum before the collision is equal to the sum of the momentum of carriage 1 (12000 x 5) and carriage 2 (8000 x 0), which is 60,000 kg ms-1. Momentum is conserved before and after the collision so the total momentum after the event also equal 60,000 kg ms-1. The carriages now move together so the combined mass is 20,000kg. Using the equation again, the total momentum (60,000 kg ms-1) divided by the total mass (20,000 kg) gives the velocity of the train carriages after the crash, which is equal to 3 ms-1.

Question 35: C
Statement 1 is false. In a nuclear reactor, every uranium nuclei split to release energy and three neutrons. An explosion could occur if all of the neutrons are absorbed by further uranium nuclei as the reaction would escalate out of control. Control rods that are made of boron absorb some of the neutrons and control the chain reaction.

Statement 2 is false. Nuclear fusion occurs when a deuterium and tritium nucleus are forced together. The nuclei both carry a positive charge and consequently, very high temperatures and pressures are required to overcome the electrostatic repulsion. These temperatures and pressures are expensive and hard to repeat and so fusion is not currently suitable as a source of energy.

Statement 4 is true. During beta decay, a neutron transforms into a proton and an electron. The proton remains in the nucleus, whereas the electron is emitted and is referred to as a beta particle. The carbon-14 nucleus now has one more proton and one less neutron so the atomic number increases by 1 and the atomic mass number remains the same. Statement 5 is false. Beta particles are more ionising than gamma rays and less ionising than alpha particles.

Question 36: E
This question requires the use of the equation: $v^2=u^2+2as$ (where s = height)
From the information provided in the question, we know that v=0ms-1, u=40ms-1 and a=-10ms-2. Inserting these values into the equation gives: 0=1600 + 2(-10h). The maximum height reached is therefore 80m.

END OF SECTION

Section 1C: Chemistry

Question 37: B

Note that the units are the same ($M = moldm^{-3}$), only the orders of magnitude are different. Convert the orders of magnitude to discover a 10^6 difference with more chloride than thyroxine

Question 38: E

Recall that reduction is the gain of electrons whilst oxidation is a loss. Also remember that oxidation the gain of oxygen, while reduction is loss. Only Iodine is gaining electrons.

Question 39: H

Chloride is oxidised during this process to form Cl_2. Although the first part of 2) is correct, H_2O is required to dissolve the NaCl (not H_2 which is a product of the reaction). NaOH is a strong base.

Question 40: C

Increasing the concentration of the reactants (not products) would affect reaction rate, which can be monitored by measuring the gas volume released (proportional to molar concentration). This is the reaction for photosynthesis, which does not occur spontaneously and is endothermic.

Question 41: D

Isotopes of an element all contain the same number of protons but a different number of neutrons. As atomic number refers solely to the number of protons it will not change. However as mass number is the sum of atomic number and neutron number – it would be expected to change. If an isotope contains one extra proton, then assuming that the charge of that isotope is 0, then it must also contain one extra electron. Chemical properties are the same for all isotopes. Therefore the correct answer is D.

Question 42: B

The transition metals are the most abundant catalysts – presumably due to their ability to achieve a variable number of stable states. Therefore the correct answer is the d-block elements.

Question 43: E

Begin by writing down the balanced equation that describes the reaction of francium with water: $2Fr + 2H2O \rightarrow 2FrOH + H2$. Next calculate the moles of francium entering the reaction as $1338/223 = 6$. We therefore know from the stoichiometry of the equation that this reaction will produce 3 moles of hydrogen. Recall that 1 mole of gas at room temperature and pressure occupies 24dm3. Therefore the hydrogen produced in this reaction will occupy 3 x 24 = 72dm3.

Question 44: D

The simplest way to approach this type of question is to assume that there are 10 atoms within the compound. In this case that produces the following result: $C_3H_4F_2Cl$. Next look to see if any of the subscript numbers are divisible by a common factor. Also if there are any decimals, multiply up by a common factor until only integers are present. In this case the correct answer is achieved straight away.

Question 45: B

The calculation in this question is simple: concentration = mass/volume, what this question is really testing is the manipulation of unorthodox units. Begin by noting the use of g/dL in the final answers and therefore begin by converting the quantities in the question into these units. 1.2 x 1010 kg = 1.2 x 1013 grams and with 10 decilitres in a litre, 4 x 1012 L = 4 x 1013 dL. $\frac{(1.2 \times 10^{13})}{(4 \times 10^{13})} = 3 \times 10^{-1}$ g/dL.

Question 46: A

A catalyst is not essential for the progression of a chemical reaction, it only acts to lower the activation energy and therefore increase the likelihood and rate of reaction.

Question 47: E
Cationic surfactants represent a class of molecule that demonstrates both hydrophilic and hydrophobic domains. This allows it to act as an emulsifying agent which is particularly useful in the disruption of grease or lipid deposits. Therefore cationic surfactants have applications in all of the products listed.

Question 48: A
Begin by converting the total weight of arsenic into grams like so 15 x 106 = 1.5 x 107. Then divide by the Mr of arsenic which is 75 (2sf) giving 2 x 105. Don't forget that the sample is at worst 80% pure. Therefore there will be a minimum of (2 x 105) x 0.8 = 1.4 x 105 moles of pure arsenic.

Question 49: D
Recall that average atomic mass is calculated as the sum of (isotope mass x relative abundance). Therefore 28 = (26 x 0.6) + (30 x 0.3) + 0.1x. Rearranging this equation reveals that 0.1x = 3.4 and that the mystery isotope therefore has an atomic mass of 34.

Question 50: A
First recall that when a group 2 metal is reacted with steam a metal oxide is formed and therefore the following chemical equation can be drawn: $Mg + H_2O(g) \rightarrow MgO + H_2$. Note the stoichiometric ratio which is simply 1. Next calculate that there is 72/24 = 3 mol of hydrogen produced. Therefore assuming that there is 3 mol of all other reactants and the reaction is complete one would expect 3 x 24.3 = 72.9g of magnesium and 3 x 18 = 54g of steam. This is indeed the case and therefore the reaction is complete.

Question 51: B
The reducing agent is the species which is itself reduced in this instance from looking at the oxidation states we can see that that species is S2-. As after the reaction has taken place it has an oxidation state of +6 which would require a loss of negative charge i.e. electrons.

Question 52: C
The highly stable bonds between carbon atoms, and between carbon and hydrogen atoms renders alkanes relatively unreactive. This is important to note as it highlights the major difference between alkanes and alkenes.

Question 53: E
There are 9 Sulphur atoms on the left so there must be 9 on the right. Therefore, the values of B and C must add to make 9. This can be written as an equation: B+C=9
It is now useful to try to balance the Oxygen atoms: 4A+36 = 10+4B+4C+14
Simplify to give: 12 = 4B+4C-4A
Equation 1 can now be substituted into equation 2 to give: 12 = (4x9)-4A
24 = 4A. Hence, A = 6
There are 6 Potassium atoms on the left. This means that there must also be 6 potassium atoms on the right so B must by 3. As shown in equation 1, B and C add to make 9 so C must be 6.
5 $PhCH_3$ + 6 $KMnO_4$ + 9 H_2SO_4 = 5 $PhCOOH$ + 3 K_2SO_4 + 6 $MnSO_4$ + 14 H_2O.

Question 54: E
The question is asking for which of the statements are false
Statement 1 is true
Statement 2 is true
Statement 3 is false. Ionic compounds do conduct electricity when dissolved in water or when melted because the ions can move and carry current. On the other hand, solid ionic compounds do not conduct electricity.
Statement 4 is true. Alloys contain different sized atoms, making it harder for the layers of atoms to slide over each other.

END OF SECTION

Section 1D: Biology

Question 55: B

As the known parent has both recessive genotypes, it can only have the gametes, y and t. The next generation has a phenotypic ratio of 1:1:1:1. As both recessive and dominant traits are present in the progeny, the unknown parent's genotype must contain both the recessive and dominant alleles. Hence the unknown parent's genotype must be YyTt as this would produce the gamete combinations of YT, Yt, yT and yt, which when combined with the known yt gametes would result in YyTt, Yytt, yyTt and yytt in equal ratios.

Question 56: D

The possible genotypes are: YYTT (yellow, tall), YyTT (yellow, tall), yyTT (green, tall), YYTt (yellow, tall), YYtt (yellow, short), YyTt (yellow, tall) Yytt (yellow, short), yyTt (green, tall), yytt (green, short). Thus, 9 different genotypes and 4 different phenotypes are possible.

Question 57: B

Natural selection favours those who are best suited for survival – this can mean faster and stronger organisms, but not always. For example, snails are pervasive, despite being weak and slow. Variation can arise due to both genetic and environmental components.

Question 58: D

Whilst getting vitamins, killing bacteria, protein synthesis, and maintaining cellular pH and temperature are all important processes that require a blood supply, the MOST important reason for having a blood supply is the delivery of oxygen and removal of CO_2. This allows aerobic respiration to take place, which produces energy for all of the cell's metabolic processes.

Question 59: D

Taking the diseased allele to be X^D and X as the normal allele, we can model the scenario in the Punnett square below:

		Carrier Mother	
		X^D	X
Diseased Father	X^D	$X^D X^D$	$X^D X$
	Y	$X^D Y$	XY

Boys are XY and girls are XX. 50% of the boys produced would have DMD. So the probability that both boys would have the disease is 0.5 x 0.5 = 0.25

Question 60: E

We can see from the Punnett square that the probability of having a girl with DMD is 25% ($X^D X^D$). The probability that both are girls with DMD is 0.25 x 0.25 = 0.125.

Question 61: D

Diastole is the relaxation phase of the cardiac cycle. In diastole the pressure in the aorta decreases as the contractile force from the ventricles is reduced. All of the other statements are true; the aortic valve closes after ventricular systole. All four chambers of the heart have blood in them throughout the cardiac cycle.

Question 62: C

Competitive inhibition occurs when the inhibitor prevents a reaction by binding to the enzyme active site. Hence, a higher concentration of the substrate can result in the same overall rate of reaction. i.e. the substrate outcompetes the competitor.

Non competitive inhibition is where the inhibitor binds to the enzyme (not at the active site) and prevents the reaction from taking place. Increasing the substrate concentration therefore does not increase the reaction rate i.e. the substrate cannot outcompete the competitor as the enzymes are disabled and the competitor is not binding to the active site. In this graph, line 1 shows the normal reaction without inhibition, line 2 shows competitive inhibitor and line 3 shows non-competitive inhibition.

Question 63: E

Nucleic acids are only found in the nucleus (DNA & RNA) and cytoplasm (RNA). They are not a component of the plasma membrane, whereas the other molecules are.

Question 64: D

The main artery to the lungs is the pulmonary artery, which gets blocked. The clot must therefore travel through the inferior vena cave and right side of the heart. It does not enter the superior vena cava or left (systemic) circulation.

Question 65: B

Glycogen is not a hormone, it is a polysaccharide storage product primarily found in muscle and the liver.

Question 66: D

Reflexes can be influenced consciously. If you willingly pick up a hot plate, you will be able to withstand much greater heat than if you touch it by accident and discover it is hot.

Question 67: F

None of the above, they are all true facts about digestion.

Question 68: E

Blood flow to the kidneys is not exercise dependant. It is constant. Overall cardiac output increases, there is more blood flow to the muscles to fuel them and to the skin to help lose excess heat. Blood flow to the gut decreases to increase availability to muscles. Blood flow to vital organs such as the kidney and brain is constant.

Question 69: E

Increased ADH causes more water re-absorption. This concentrates the sodium in the urine by reducing urine volume. In the healthy kidney, all glucose is reabsorbed and none is excreted into the urine.

Question 70: A

An organ is defined as comprising multiple tissue types. As blood and skeletal muscle are themselves tissues they cannot be classified as organs.

Question 71: E

This question is best considered in terms of the aerobic respiration equation. With that in mind it becomes apparent that increased forward drive through the reaction will produce large amounts of water and CO2 whilst demanding an increased supply of O2. Further from this equation we realise that aerobic respiration produces large amounts of heat, and as such it is expected – in the interest of thermoregulation – that the body will both perspire and vasodilate in attempt to increase heat loss. Therefore E is the correct answer.

Question 72: D

Recall that the nephron is the smallest functional unit of the kidney. The question therefore is asking you what is the smallest basic functional unit of striated muscle? To which the answer is the sarcomere. Note that a myofibril is a collection of many sarcomeres and is therefore not the correct answer.

END OF SECTION

Section 1E: Advanced Maths & Physics

Question 73: A

We can find the common ratio of the series by dividing the second term of the series by the first, yielding the common ratio $r = \left(-\frac{1}{2}\right)x$

Since we know that the fifth coefficient is equivalent to $\frac{1}{32}$, we can solve for the value of x, the first term in the series, by equating 1/32 to the formula for the fifth term of a geometric series:

$$\frac{1}{32} = ar^4$$

$$\frac{1}{32} = x\left(\left(-\frac{1}{2}\right)x\right)^4$$

$$\frac{1}{32} = \left(\frac{1}{16}\right)x^5$$

$$x^5 = \left(\frac{16}{32}\right)$$

$$x = \frac{(16)^{\left(\frac{1}{5}\right)}}{2}$$

This is an infinite geometric series with a first term of $a = x = \frac{(16)^{\left(\frac{1}{5}\right)}}{2}$. We can simply find the common ratio by

substituting $r = \left(-\frac{1}{2}\right)x = \left(-\frac{1}{2}\right)\frac{(16)^{\left(\frac{1}{5}\right)}}{2}$.

The sum to infinity of a geometric series is given by $S_\infty = \frac{a}{1-r}$. Therefore, the sum of the series is given by:

$$S_\infty = \frac{\left(\frac{16^{\frac{1}{5}}}{2}\right)}{1-\left(-\frac{1}{2}\right)\left(\frac{(16)^{\left(\frac{1}{5}\right)}}{2}\right)}$$

$$S_\infty = \frac{16^{\frac{1}{5}}}{2+\frac{(16^{\frac{1}{5}})}{2}}$$

Question 74: D

$$\log_2 3 \times \frac{\log_2 4}{\log_2 3} \times \frac{\log_2 5}{\log_2 4} \cdots \frac{\log_2 (n+1)}{\log_2 n} \le 10$$

Solving the above equation, we have that $\log_2 (n+1) \le 10$. Consequently, $n+1 \le 1024$. The largest value of n that satisfies this equation is 1023.

Question 75: B

We have:
$(a+b+c)^2 = a^2 + b^2 + c^2 + 2(ab+bc+ca) = 364 + 2(ab+bc+ca) = 26^2 = 676$
so $ab + bc + ca = 156$.

Since b and c are the second and third terms of a geometric progression respectively, let us denote $b = ar,$ and $c = ar^2$

We have $a + b + c = a + ar + ar^2 = 26$ and $ab + bc + ca = a^2r + a^2r^3 + a^2r^2 = 156$
$a(1 + r + r^2) = 26$ and $a^2 r(1 + r + r^2) = 156 = 6 \cdot 26$.

We can divide both equations to get
$a^2 r(1 + r + r2)/a(1 + r + r^2) = 6$, or $ar = b = 6$.

Question 76: A

$f(x)$ is a parabola, which is opened up (since its leading coefficient is $a^2 + 1 > 0$), so it has only one extremum and it is a global minimum. $f'(x) = 0 <=> 2(a^2 + 1)x - 2a = 0, or \ x = \frac{a}{a^2+1}$. Luckily for us, $\frac{a}{a^2+1} = \frac{1}{2} \times \frac{2a}{a^2+1} \leq 1/2$

(since $0 \leq \frac{2a}{a^2+1} \leq 1$ for any positive a).

As a result, the minimum in the interval is reached for $x = \frac{a}{a^2+1}$.

We substitute into $f(x)$ to reach

$$fmin(x) = f\left(\frac{a}{a^2+1}\right) = (a^2 + 1).\left(\frac{a}{a^2+1}\right)^2 - 2a \times \frac{a}{a^2+1} + 10$$

$$= \frac{a^2}{a^2+1} - \frac{2a^2}{a^2+1} + 10 = 10 - \frac{a^2}{a^2+1} = \frac{9a^2+10}{a^2+1}$$

We want this value to be equal to $\frac{451}{50}$.

$\frac{9a^2+10}{a^2+1} = \frac{451}{50}$, so we cross multiply: $450a^2 + 500 = 451a^2 + 451, or \ a^2 = 49$.

Which means that a=7, since *a*>0.

Question 77: B

We know that rain and snow are independent events. If the probability that it will rain is $\frac{2}{3}$ and the probability that it will both rain and snow the following day is $\frac{1}{5}$, we can find the probability that it will snow the day after tomorrow by simply solving the equation: $\frac{2}{3}x = \frac{1}{5}$

Which yields: $x = \frac{3}{10}$

Question 78: A

Let us use the double angle formula, $\cos 2\theta = cos^2\theta - sin^2\theta$.

Given we know that $\cos 2\theta = \frac{3}{4} = cos^2\theta - sin^2\theta$, we know that $\frac{1}{cos^2\theta - sin^2\theta} = \frac{1}{\frac{3}{4}} = \frac{4}{3}$.

Question 79: B

If you draw the graphs, you will notice that the two graphs are the reflections of one another in the y-axis.

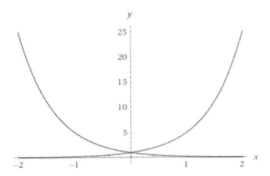

Question 80: C

Note that $1 = \log_4(4)$.
$\log_4(2x + 3) + \log_4(2x + 15) - \log_4(4) =$
$\log_4(14x + 5)$
$\log_4(2x + 3)(2x + 15) = \log_4 4(14x + 5)$
$(2x + 3)(2x + 15) = 56x + 20$
$4x^2 + 36x + 45 = 56x + 20$
$4x^2 - 20x + 25 = 0$
By factoring,
$4x^2 - 20x + 25 = 0$
$(2x - 5)^2 = 0$

Hence, $x = \frac{5}{2}$

Question 81: A

The gradient of the curve is $\frac{dy}{dx} = 2e^{2x-5}$. We know that the gradient of the normal to the curve is $-\frac{1}{\frac{dy}{dx}}$.

Consequently, the equation of the normal is $y - e^{-1} = -\frac{e}{2}(x-2)$.

At the point A, where y=0, $x = 2 + \left(\frac{2}{e^2}\right)$

At point B, where x = 0, $y = e + \frac{1}{e} = \frac{e^2+1}{e}$

Since the area of a triangle is $\frac{1}{2} \times Base \times Height$, the area of the triangle OAB is:

$$Area = \frac{1}{2} \times \frac{e^2+1}{e} \times 2 \times \frac{1+e^2}{e^2} = \frac{(e^2+1)^2}{e^3}$$

Question 82: B

Due to conservation of momentum, both bodies will end up with the same momentum, but end up moving at different speeds.

Specifically, let m_1 and m_2 be the mass of the heavier body and the mass of the lighter body respectively, and let v_1 and v_2 be the velocity of the heavier and the lighter bodies respectively.

$m_1 v_1 = m_2 v_2$

We know that $m_1 = 3m_2$, and correspondingly, to maintain conservation of momentum, the velocity v_2 will adjust such that $v_1 = \frac{1}{3}v_2$ to maintain conservation of momentum. As such, the kinetic energy X of the heavier body is:

$X = \frac{1}{2} \times m_1 \times v_1^2$

The kinetic energy Y of the lighter body is:

$Y = \frac{1}{2} \times m_2 \times v_2^2$

$Y = \frac{1}{2} \times \left(\frac{1}{3}\right) m_1 \times (3v_1)^2$

$Y = 3 \times \frac{1}{2} \times m_1 \times v_1^2$

$Y = 3X$

The ratio of kinetic energies $\frac{X}{Y}$, therefore, is $\frac{1}{3}$.

Question 83: B

We find the centre of mass as follows:

$\bar{x} = \frac{(4 \times 90)+(7 \times 90)}{4+7+8+11}$

$= \frac{990}{30} = 33cm$

Question 84: B

$\bar{X} = \frac{(25 \times 1)+(12 \times 4)+(4 \times 5)}{1+4+5} = \frac{93}{10} = 9.3$

$\bar{Y} = \frac{(10 \times 1)+(7 \times 4)+(18 \times 5)}{10} = \frac{128}{10} = 12.8$

Therefore, the centre of mass is located at (9.3,12.8).

Question 85: B

The child's initial gravitational potential energy is mgh.

The kinetic energy of the child is equal to $\frac{1}{2}mv^2$.

The total energy lost by the child by the time they reach the end of the slide is $mgh - \frac{1}{2}mv^2 = (35 \times 9.8 \times 10) -$

$(\frac{1}{2} \times 35 \times 12^2) = 910J$

The work done to cause the energy loss is $F \times 20 = 910$.

$20F = 910J$

$F = 45.5N$

Question 86: A

Draw a free body diagram of the forces, as shown.

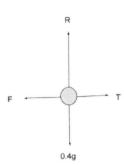

Since the vertical forces are in equilibrium, R = 0.4g

On the point of moving, $F = \mu_s R = \mu_s(0.4g)$ and F = T

Since the pulley is smooth, the tension in the string, T = 0.2g

Hence, $\mu_s(0.4g) = 0.2g$. Thus, $\mu_s = \frac{0.2g}{0.4g} = 0.5$

Question 87: F

First step is to find the height the ball travels upwards to the top of its arc (let this equal h_2):

Initial vertical component of velocity: $u_1 = 20\sin 30$

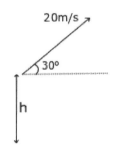

Vertical velocity component at highest point: $v_1 = 0$

Acceleration: $a = -g$

Using formula: $v^2 = u^2 + 2as$

$0^2 = (20\sin 30)^2 + (2 \times -g \times h_2)$

$\sin 30 = 0.5$ and $g = 10ms^{-2}$

$0 = 100 - 20h_2$

$h_2 = 5m$

We know that it takes 3s for the ball to travel from its highest point down to the ground. At the highest point, the initial vertical velocity is 0 and it is accelerating towards the ground at g.

By calculating the total height the ball falls, s, we can calculate h using: $h = s - h_2$

$s = ut + \frac{1}{2}at^2$

Therefore: $s = 0 + (0.5 \times 10 \times (3^2))$

$s = 45m$. Thus, $h = 45 - 5 \rightarrow h = 40m$

Question 88: D

We know that (sec x + tan x)(sec x – tan x) = $\sec^2 x - \tan^2 x$.

Using the trigonometric identity $\sec^2 x - \tan^2 x = 1$, as well as the information provided in the question, we know that:

$-5(\sec x + \tan x) = 1$

Therefore,

$(\sec x + \tan x) = -\frac{1}{5}$

By substitution, we know that $\sec x - \tan x + (\sec x + \tan x) = -5 + \left(-\frac{1}{5}\right)$

$2 \sec x = -5.2$

$\sec x = -\frac{5.2}{2} = -2.6 = -\frac{13}{5}$

Since sec x $= \frac{1}{\cos x}$,

$\cos x = \frac{1}{\sec x} = -\frac{5}{13}$

Question 89: B

First, let us find the points along which any potential intersection between the line and the curve would take place, by setting the two equations equal to one another.

$x^2 + (3k - 4)x + 13 = 2x + k$

$x^2 + 3kx - 6x + 13 - k = 0$

$x^2 + 3(k - 2)x + 13 - k = 0$

Since the line and the curve do not intersect, we know that there must not be any real roots.

As such, by the discriminant condition, we know that $b^2 - 4ac < 0$.

Therefore:

$$\left(3(k-2)\right)^2 - 4(13 - k) < 0$$
$$9(k^2 - 4k + 4) - 52 + 4k < 0$$
$$9k^2 - 32k - 16 < 0$$
$$(9k + 4)(k - 4)$$

We know that the critical values therefore extend from $-\frac{4}{9} < k < 4$.

Question 90: A

The distance AC (equivalent to the radius of the circle) can be determined given the coordinates of A and C:

A =(-2,1) C = (5,-3)

Therefore $AC = \sqrt{(5 + 2)^2 + (1 + 3)^2} = \sqrt{65}$

To find the length of the line CT, we use Pythagoras' Theorem:

$CT^2 = AT^2 + AC^2$

$CT^2 = 4^2 + 65$

$CT^2 = 81$

$CT = 9$

END OF SECTION

Section 2

Question 1

a)

    i.   Due to conservation of momentum and the assumption of negligibility of kinetic energy, the two photons will have gained equal amounts of energy to that contained within the electron and the positron.

    ii.   Using the formula $E = mc^2$, taking into consideration the mass of the electron and the positron together, we get:

$$E = (2 \times 9.1 \times 10^{-31} \times (3.0 \times 10^8)^2)$$
$$= 1.64 \times 10^{-13} J$$
$$= \frac{1.64 \times 10^{-13} J}{1.6 \times 10^{-13}} MeV$$
$$= 1\ MeV$$

b)   Iron-56 should be near the peak of the curve, zirconium-97 should be toward the right and on the plateau of the curve, and H should be at about half of the maximum height of the curve.

c)

    i.   Nuclear fission is a process that takes place when a heavy or large nucleus breaks off into smaller nuclei or fragments of approximately equal mass that are more energetically stable relative to the parent atom.

    ii.   Nuclear fusion involves two smaller atomic nuclei joining together to make a larger nucleus, which causes a large release of energy.

    iii. The graph allows us to predict what possible elements may be released from nuclear fission based on their respective binding energies. Generally, we can see that the binding energy of parent nuclei in fission is less than the sum of finding energies of their fragments. Also, the biding energy of the daughter nucleus in fusion is greater than the combined binding energy of the parent nuclei.

d)

    i.   A helium nucleus

    ii.   An electron.

    iii. A gamma photon.

e)

    i.   Proton number: Decreases by 2. Nucleon number: Decreases by 4.

    ii.   Proton number: Increases by 1. Nucleon number: No change.

    iii. Proton number: No change. Nucleon number: No change.

Question 2

a)

    i.   Force equations for the blocks

        ① $m_1 - 2T = m_1 a_1$

        ② $T - m_2 g = m_2 a_2$

        ① + 2 × ②

        ③ $m_1 g - 2 m_2 g = m_1 a_1 + 2 m_2 a_2$

        By geometry block B goes down by **s** as block A goes up by **s/2**

        Using equations of motion

        ④ $s = \dfrac{a_2 t^2}{2}$

        ⑤ $\dfrac{s}{2} = \dfrac{a_1 t^2}{2}$

        Divide ④ by ⑤

        $2 = \dfrac{a_2}{a_1}$

        $2a_1 = a_2$

        Substitute into ③ $g(m_1 - 2m_2) = a_1(4m_2 + m_1)$

        $a_1 = \dfrac{g(m_1 - 2m_2)}{4m_2 + m_1}$

    ii.   By $2a_1 = a_2$

        $a_2 = \dfrac{2g(m_1 - 2m_2)}{4m_2 + m_1}$

    iii.   From ②

        $T = m_2 g + m_2 a_2$

        Substitute values in for **a_2**

        $T = \dfrac{3gm_1 m_2}{4m_2 + m_1}$

    iv.   System won't move if **a_1** and **a_2** are zero, therefore $m_1 = 2m_2$

    v.   Gain in kinetic energy = loss in gravitational potential energy

        Loss in gravitational potential energy = $gs \left| m_2 - \dfrac{m_1}{2} \right|$

        $= \dfrac{g|2m_2 - m_1|\left(\frac{1}{2}a_2 t^2\right)}{2}$

        $= \dfrac{g^2 t^2 (m_1 - 2m_2)^2}{2(4m_2 + m_1)}$

b)

    i.   Extra length given by $2\pi(r+\Delta r)-2\pi r=2\pi\Delta r=6.3$mm

    ii.   It doesn't Δr is independent of r

    iii.   **6.3**km

    iv.   Surface area given by $A = 2\pi r^2$

$$A + \Delta A = 2\pi(r + \Delta r)^2 = 2\pi(r^2 + 2r\Delta r + (\Delta r)^2)$$

$\Delta A \approx 4\pi r\Delta r$ as terms with order $(\Delta r)^2$ or above are neglible

So: $\frac{\Delta A}{A} = 2\frac{\Delta r}{r}$

Therefore, the surface area increases by **2%**

    v. $V = \frac{4}{3}\pi r^3$

$$V + \Delta V = \frac{4}{3}\pi(r + \Delta r)^3 = \frac{4}{3}\pi(r^3 + 3r^2\Delta r + 3r(\Delta r)^2 + (\Delta r)^3) \approx \frac{4}{3}\boldsymbol{\pi(r^3 + 3r^2\Delta r)}$$

as terms with order $\boldsymbol{(\Delta r)^2}$ or above are neglible

Therefore: $\Delta V = 4\pi r^2\Delta r$

So: $\frac{\Delta V}{V} = 3\frac{\Delta r}{r}$

Therefore, the surface are increases by 3%

Question 3

a)

    i.   p orbitals in the small nitrogen atom overlap to form strong π bonds, leading to triple bonded N_2 molecules with weak intermolecular forces. The phosphorus atom is larger and forms weaker *π bonds but stronger σ bonds*. This results in a network solid held together with single bonds.

    ii.   The Group I elements exhibit metallic bonding, whereby the cations are held together with free electrons. The attraction between cation and electron becomes weaker as cations increase in size, causing a decrease in melting point as we move through the family. The Group 17 elements consist of diatomic molecules. These molecules are bonded to one another with London forces which become stronger with the number of electrons in the molecule, so melting points increase in that direction.

    iii.   Ionization energies decrease with increasing size of atoms because the removed electron is farther from the nucleus and shielded by more inner electrons. The first three elements show greater change because the electrons added are in s and p orbitals and screen the outermost electron more efficiently while some of the core electrons added in the last three elements are in d orbitals which do not shield as well as s and p.

    iv.   Ionization energies decrease down the family, making it easier for the atoms to lose electrons and form cations. The s and p orbitals combine to form bonding and antibonding orbitals. In carbon, there is a large energy gap between these, which makes diamond an insulator. The gap is smaller in Si and Ge which behave as semiconductors with a few electrons jumping the gap. In Sn and Pb the gap is zero, and electrons flow readily from the valence band to the conduction bond, which explains the metallic behaviour.

    v.   Diamonds and graphite are both different allotropes, giant covalent structures of carbon. In the case of graphite, the carbon atoms form layers that slide over one another, whereas in the case of diamond, each individual carbon atom forms a lattice with four other carbon atoms that gives rise to extremely strong intramolecular forces that give rise to the hardness of each diamond.

b)

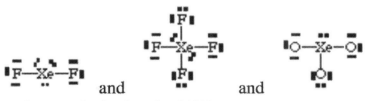

    i.

    ii.   *XeF_2 is linear with a bond angle of $180°$*
           XeF_4 is square planar with a bond angle of $90°$

    iii.   *XeO_3 is trigonal pyramidal with a bond angle of $107° XeF_2$ is nonpolar because both $Xe - F$ bond dipoles are the same size, but offset each other due to the linear geometry.*

    XeF_4 is nonpolar, because all Xe
$- F$ dipoles are the same size, but due to square planar geometry, they offset each other.
           XeO_3 is polar, because the $Xe - O$ bond dipoles are the same size, and the non-planar geometry leads to a net dipole.

    iv.   Xe has a formal positive charge in all of these compounds. Hence, they are good oxidizing agents and hence are reactive.

c)

    i.   It is an addition polymer. The double bond in a monomer breaks to give a lone electron that forms bonds to other monomers. No other products are formed, so it cannot be condensation.

           1.   Polypropylene with 10,000 units melts at a higher temperature than that with 1000 units. The larger molecule has stronger dispersion forces due to the higher molar mass.

           2.   Replacing CH_3 with $CH_2CH_2CH_2CH_3$ will lower melting temperature, since the larger group will impede the packing of the polymer chains and decrease the strength of the intermolecular forces.

           3.   Isotactic polypropylene melts at a higher temperature, because the more regular structure of the isotactic form allows for better packing and stronger intermolecular forces.

Question 4

a)

$$0.504g \text{ of } CO_2 \times \frac{1}{44.01} mol = 0.1145\ mol\ C \times 12.01 = 0.1375g\ C$$

$$0.073\ g\ H_2O \times \frac{1}{18.01} mol \times 2\ mol\ H \div 1\ mol\ H_2O = 8.25 \times 10^{-3} mol\ H$$

$$8.25 \times 10^{-3} mol\ H \times 1.008g = 8.317 \times 10^{-3} g\ H$$

$$Percentage\ mass\ of\ C = \frac{0.1375}{0.25} \times 100 = 55\%\ C$$

$$Percentage\ mass\ of\ H = \frac{8.317 \times 10^{-3} g\ H}{0.25g} \times 100 = 3.327\%\ H$$

b)

  i. Starch is used for the titration, and the blue solution turns colourless with excess I_3^-.

  ii. $$0.0320\frac{mol}{L} \times 0.1175\ L = 3.76 \times 10^{-4} mol\ S_2O_3^{2-} = 3.76 \times 10^{-4} mol\ Cu^{2+}$$

$$3.76 \times 10^{-4} mol\ Cu^{2+} \times \left(63.54\frac{g}{mol}\right) = 0.02389g\ Cu$$

$$\%\ Cu = \left(\frac{0.02389}{0.115}\right) \times 100 = 20.77\%$$

c) $55\ \%\ C + 3.33\%\ H + 20.77\ \%\ Cu = 79.1\%$.
Consequently, the proportion of O is 20.9%.
$55.0\ C \div 12.01 = 4.58 \div 0.327 = 14$
$3.33\ H \div 1.008 = 3.30 \div 0.327 = 10$
$20.9\ O \div 16.0 = 1.31 \div 0.327 = 4.0$
$20.77\ Cu \div 63.54 = 0.327$
The empirical formula is $C_{14}H_{10}O_4Cu$

d) $$3Cu + 8H^+ + 2NO_3^- \rightarrow 3Cu^{2+} + 2NO + 4H_2O$$

e)

  i. Average molecular mass =
$$\frac{mRT}{PV} = \frac{(0.205g)(0.0821\ L*atm*mol^{-1}*K^{-1})(308K)}{(0.125L)\left(725\ mm\ Hg*\frac{1atm}{760mm\ Hg}\right)} = 43.5g\ mol^{-1}$$

To solve for the ratio, let x be the fraction of NO_2.

$$xMM_{NO_2} + (1-x)MM_{O_2} = 43.5$$

$$46x + 32(1-x) = 43.5$$

$$x = 0.821$$

$$\frac{NO_2}{O_2} = \frac{0.821}{0.189} = 4.59$$

  ii. 40.86 g - 39.49 g = 1.37 g Cu
41.21 g - 40.86 g = 0.35 g O
1.36 g Cu × 1 mol Cu 63.55 g Cu = 0.0216 mole Cu
0.35 g O × 1 mol O 16.0 g O = 0.0219 mole O
Therefore, the ratio is 1:1, and the formula is CuO.

f)

  i. The lost solution will cause the mass of CuO to be lower relative to the mass of Cu. Therefore, percentage determination for copper would be higher.

  ii. The mass of CuO will be too high. Therefore, the percentage determination for copper will be too low.

Question 5

a) Temperature, pH, concentration of CO_2/O_2, light intensity [other reasonable suggestions of factors influencing rate of reactions].

b) Answer: Photorespiration occurs in chloroplasts (1 mark). Photosynthesis generates glucose that can be used in respiration, hence providing energy for the plant (1 mark). Photorespiration, however, uses up energy to return its products to usable compounds, and is therefore inefficient (1 mark).

c) 1 mark for respiration as flat horizontal line (or just flat rate depending on how axes drawn). 1 mark for photosynthetic rate increasing with light intensity. 1 mark for rate of photosynthesis levelling off at high light intensity.

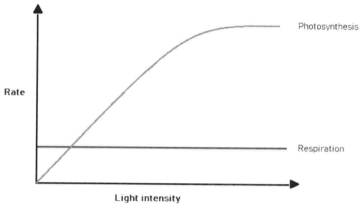

d) The point at which the graphs for photosynthesis and respiration intersect (1 mark), because at this point the plant is fixing more CO_2 in photosynthesis than it is releasing in respiration (1 mark) hence reducing the CO_2 concentration in the air immediately surrounding it (1 mark).

e) Normal plants are likely to have their stomata open in the day to allow gas exchange (1 mark), but may close at night in response to darkness (1 mark), to prevent water loss, and a lack of need to take up CO_2 (1 mark). CAM photosynthesis allows stomata to remain closed during the day (1 mark) which therefore prevents water loss but allows plants to continue to generate food via photosynthesis in hot, dry environments (1 mark).

f) Up to 3 marks for:
The idea that photosynthesis and respiration require CO_2, H_2O and O_2, and that stomata help to maintain the internal concentrations of these gasses, balancing water loss through open stomata with CO_2 uptake from the environment.

Up to 5 marks for:

Photosynthesis and respiration on a wider scale; the idea of a growing plant as a net absorber of CO_2, as carbon is assimilated into tissues. If environmental conditions change such that water is not available, photosynthesis may cease to be possible. This is why stomata close to reduce water loss, at the risk of lower internal CO_2 concentrations.

If the plant cannot photosynthesise, it cannot survive. If plants die, their tissues will be broken down via respiration and decomposition, and the CO_2 stored in them will be released into the atmosphere, contributing to the global CO_2 cycle.

Marks also awarded for references to fossil fuel combustion releasing ancient CO_2 that was fixed via photosynthesis but not respired, and other valid arguments linking CO_2 cycling with plant metabolism.

Question 6

a) The chymosin enzyme cleaves the hydrophilic tail off the Kappa casein molecule, leaving only the hydrophobic part. This in turn causes the rejection of the micelle from the water as it now is exposed to the hydrophobic part of the casein molecule. This causes the casein micelles to separate from the water and float to the surface where they can be removed.

b) At 2 g of casein, enzyme A is cleaving roughly 4g of casein per hour. In comparison to that, Enzyme B is cleaving roughly 15g of casein per hour. An increase of concentration to 2.5g means that enzyme A is still only producing 4g of casein per hour, whereas enzyme B is now producing 16 g of casein per hour. In terms of enzyme activity this means that enzyme A is significantly less responsive to changes in concentration of casein, but also works significantly slower.

c) Whey protein is digested into amino acids much faster than casein protein. For this reason, the amino acids contained in the whey protein will be delivered to the blood stream much faster causing an earlier peak in concentration followed by a subsequent sharp drop. In comparison to that, the casein protein is digested slower and over much longer times, therefore amino acids will remain in the blood stream for longer and allowing for muscle protein synthesis. For this reason, casein protein is better suited for maintenance of amino acid levels during periods of prolonged starvation.

d) Human breast milk has by far the lowest concentration of protein out of all the species mentioned. Fat content is also fairly low, but on similar levels as cow's milk. With regards to lactose, human breast milk has a rather high concentration compared to the other species in this graph. This is in line with relative muscle bulk at birth where human babies score comparatively low, especially since human babies are born before reaching full maturity due to intra-uterine size constraints. The high sugar content in human breast milk can be explained by relative brain size as the human brain primarily is fuelled by glucose. Direct introduction via breast milk provides the easiest supply of sugars to the new-born to supply the large brain with adequate sugars as development continues.

e) Climate influences the range of products that can be grown in colder climates, agriculture becomes more difficult which is why historically cattle raising is more prevalent in northern European countries. In keeping with that, milk products become more commonly used in food. This in turn maintains activation of lactase expressing genes. In Mediterranean areas reliance on cattle and therefore milk is less, which is why lactase expression is more limited.

f) The enzyme is likely to be found in the stomach as it is most active around a pH of 4.5. With regards to the temperature, animal body temperature is slightly higher than that of humans with normal ranges of roughly 40°C. As the text states, at this temperature the enzyme functions with nearly optimal efficiency therefore resulting in an effective balance between high product output and function within physiological range. Despite the fact that function would be ideal at 50°C, this is not feasible due to the constrains of protein denaturation of other enzymes

END OF PAPER

~ 424 ~

Final Advice

Arrive well rested, well fed and well hydrated

The NSAA is an intensive test, so make sure you're ready for it. Unlike the UKCAT, you'll have to sit this at a fixed time (normally at 9AM). Thus, ensure you get a good night's sleep before the exam (there is little point cramming) and don't miss breakfast. If you're taking water into the exam then make sure you've been to the toilet before so you don't have to leave during the exam. Make sure you're well rested and fed in order to be at your best!

Move on

If you're struggling, move on. Every question has equal weighting and there is no negative marking. In the time it takes to answer on hard question, you could gain three times the marks by answering the easier ones. Be smart to score points- especially in section 2 where some questions are far easier than others.

Afterword

Remember that the route to a high score is your approach and practice. Don't fall into the trap that *"you can't prepare for the NSAA"*– this could not be further from the truth. With knowledge of the test, some useful time-saving techniques and plenty of practice you can dramatically boost your score.

Work hard, never give up and do yourself justice.

Good luck!

About Us

Infinity Books is the publishing division of *Infinity Education*. We currently publish over 85 titles across a range of subject areas – covering specialised admissions tests, examination techniques, personal statement guides, plus everything else you need to improve your chances of getting on to competitive courses such as medicine and law, as well as into universities such as Oxford and Cambridge.

Outside of publishing we also operate a highly successful tuition division, called UniAdmissions. This company was founded in 2013 by Dr Rohan Agarwal and Dr David Salt, both Cambridge Medical graduates with several years of tutoring experience. Since then, every year, hundreds of applicants and schools work with us on our programmes. Through the programmes we offer, we deliver expert tuition, exclusive course places, online courses, best-selling textbooks and much more.

With a team of over 1,000 Oxbridge tutors and a proven track record, UniAdmissions have quickly become the UK's number one admissions company.

Visit and engage with us at:
Website (Infinity Books): www.infinitybooks.co.uk
Website (UniAdmissions): www.uniadmissions.co.uk
Facebook: www.facebook.com/uniadmissionsuk
Twitter: @infinitybooks7

YOUR FREE BOOK

Thanks for purchasing this Ultimate Book. Readers like you have the power to make or break a book –hopefully you found this one useful and informative. *UniAdmissions* would love to hear about your experiences with this book. As thanks for your time we'll send you another ebook from our Ultimate Guide series absolutely <u>FREE</u>!

How to Redeem Your Free Ebook

1) Either scan the QR code or find the book you have on your Amazon purchase history or your email receipt to help find the book on Amazon.

2) On the product page at the Customer Reviews area, click 'Write a customer review'. Write your review and post it! Copy the review page or take a screen shot of the review you have left.

3) Head over to www.uniadmissions.co.uk/free-book and select your chosen free ebook!

Your ebook will then be emailed to you – it's as simple as that!
Alternatively, you can buy all the titles at

www.uniadmissions.co.uk/our-books